D1289876

Android Programming for Beginners

Second Edition

Build in-depth, full-featured Android 9 Pie apps starting
from zero programming experience

John Horton

BIRMINGHAM - MUMBAI

Android Programming for Beginners
Second Edition

Copyright © 2018 Packt Publishing

All rights reserved. No part of this book may be reproduced, stored in a retrieval system, or transmitted in any form or by any means, without the prior written permission of the publisher, except in the case of brief quotations embedded in critical articles or reviews.

Every effort has been made in the preparation of this book to ensure the accuracy of the information presented. However, the information contained in this book is sold without warranty, either express or implied. Neither the author, nor Packt Publishing or its dealers and distributors, will be held liable for any damages caused or alleged to have been caused directly or indirectly by this book.

Packt Publishing has endeavored to provide trademark information about all of the companies and products mentioned in this book by the appropriate use of capitals. However, Packt Publishing cannot guarantee the accuracy of this information.

Commissioning Editor: Amarabha Banerjee
Acquisition Editor: Larissa Pinto
Content Development Editor: Onkar Wani
Technical Editor: Akhil Nair
Copy Editor: Safis Editing
Project Coordinator: Sheejal Shah
Proofreader: Safis Editing
Indexer: Pratik Shirodkar
Graphics: Alishon Mendonsa
Production Coordinator: Arvindkumar Gupta

First published: December 2015

Second Edition: October 2018

Production reference: 1301018

Published by Packt Publishing Ltd.
Livery Place
35 Livery Street
Birmingham B3 2PB, UK.

ISBN 978-1-78953-850-2

www.packtpub.com

`mapt.io`

Mapt is an online digital library that gives you full access to over 5,000 books and videos, as well as industry leading tools to help you plan your personal development and advance your career. For more information, please visit our website.

Why subscribe?

- Spend less time learning and more time coding with practical eBooks and videos from over 4,000 industry professionals

- Learn better with skill plans designed especially for you

- Get a free eBook or video every month

- Mapt is fully searchable

- Copy and paste, print, and bookmark content

Packt.com

Did you know that Packt offers eBook versions of every book published, with PDF and ePub files available? You can upgrade to the eBook version at www.Packt.com and, as a print book customer, you are entitled to a discount on the eBook copy. Get in touch with us at customercare@packtpub.com for more details.

At www.Packt.com, you can also read a collection of free technical articles, sign up for a range of free newsletters, and receive exclusive discounts and offers on Packt books and eBooks.

Contributors

About the author

John Horton is a programming and gaming enthusiast based in the UK. He has a passion for writing apps, games, books, and blog articles. He is the founder of Game Code School.

About the reviewers

Natarajan Raman has close to 15 years' experience in software design and development. He is a Google-certified Nano degree holder on Android development and was invited by Google as a guest for the I/O 2017. His Android App Idea for special children got selected as one of the top SIX ideas out of roughly 80, and was also featured by Google on its "Code it possible" program. He works for Patterns as Principal Architect and is also the managing trustee of Dream India — dreamindia.org

Natarajan is co-author of the book entitled "Learning Kotlin by building Android Applications". He holds a B.Tech degree from NIT, Jaipur. He is a design coach and public speaker. Dream India is a part-time NGO run by his team of friends since 2003.

> I want to thank my wife, Ms. Krupa, my parents, Mr. Raman and Mrs. Alamu, my child Siddhu, my in-laws, my guru, Mr. Suresh Kamath, my colleagues at Patterns, my children of Vasantham — vasantham.org, and the rest of my family who supported and encouraged me in spite of all the time it took me away from them. Without their support, my review of this book wouldn't have been possible.
>
> Thanks to the Packt team for giving me an opportunity to review this book.

Ashok Kumar S has been working in the mobile development domain for about six years. He is a Google-certified engineer, a speaker at global scale conferences, and he also runs a YouTube channel called AndroidABCD for Android developers. He is a computer science and engineering graduate who is passionate about innovation in technology. He contributes to open source heavily to improve his e-karma. He has also written books on *Wear OS programming* and *Mastering Firebase Toolchain*.

> I would like to thank my family, mostly my mother, for her infinite support in every possible way, and family members Shylaja, Sumitra, Krishna, Vinisha, and my fiancé, Geetha Shree.

Packt is Searching for Authors Like You

If you're interested in becoming an author for Packt, please visit `authors.packtpub.com` and apply today. We have worked with thousands of developers and tech professionals, just like you, to help them share their insights with the global tech community. You can make a general application, apply for a specific hot topic that we are recruiting an author for, or submit your own idea.

Table of Contents

Preface   **xvii**

Chapter 1: Beginning Android and Java   **1**

What's new in the second edition?   **2**

Why Java and Android?   **2**

The beginner's first stumbling block   **3**

How Java and Android work together   **4**

   The Android API   5

   Java is object-oriented   6

   Run that by me again – What exactly is Android?   8

   Android Studio   9

Setting up Android Studio   **10**

   Final step – for now   16

What makes an Android app?   **17**

   Android resources   17

The structure of Android's Java code   **18**

   Packages   18

   Classes   19

   Methods   19

Our first Android app   **20**

   Extra step 1   27

   Extra step 2   28

Deploying the app so far   **28**

   Running and debugging the app on an Android emulator   30

   Running the app on a real device   33

Frequently asked questions   **34**

Summary   **34**

Chapter 2: First Contact – Java, XML, and the UI Designer   **35**

Examining the log output   **35**
    Filtering the logcat output   36
A note for early adopters of this book   **37**
Exploring the project's Java code and the main layout's XML code   **38**
    Examining the HelloWorldActivity.java file   38
      Code folding (hiding) in Android Studio   40
      The package declaration   40
      Importing classes   40
      The class   41
      Methods inside the class   41
      Summary of the Java code so far   42
    Examining the main layout file   42
      UI layout elements   44
      UI text elements   45
Adding buttons to the main layout file   **46**
    Adding a button via the visual designer   46
      Editing the button's attributes   48
    Examining the XML code for the new button   51
    Adding a button by editing the XML code   52
    Giving the buttons unique id attributes   54
    Positioning the two buttons in the layout   55
    Making the buttons call different methods   57
Leaving comments in our Java code   **58**
Coding messages to the user and the developer   **59**
Writing our first Java code   **59**
    Adding message code to the onCreate method   60
      Examining the output   61
    Writing our own Java methods   62
      Examining the output   64
Frequently asked questions   **65**
Summary   **66**

Chapter 3: Exploring Android Studio and the Project Structure   **67**

A quick guided tour of Android Studio   **68**
Project Explorer and project anatomy   **70**
    The Empty Activity project   70
    Exploring the Empty Activity project   73
      The manifests folder   74
      The java folder   77
      The res folder   79
      The res/drawable folder   80
      The res/layout folder   80
      The res/mipmap   81
      res/values   83

The Basic Activity project   87
Exploring the Basic Activity project   89
   The MainActivity.java file   89
   The activity_main.xml file   90
   The extra methods in MainActivity.java   92
   The content_main.xml file   93
Exploring the Android emulator   **93**
Emulator control panel   94
Using the emulator as a real device   96
   Accessing the app drawer   97
   Viewing active apps and switching between apps   98
Summary   **99**

Chapter 4: Getting Started with Layouts and Material Design   **101**
Material design   **102**
Exploring Android UI design   **102**
Layouts   **103**
Creating the Exploring Layouts project   **103**
Building a menu with LinearLayout   **105**
Adding a LinearLayout to the project   105
Preparing your workspace   106
Examining the generated XML   107
Adding a TextView to the UI   108
Adding a multi-line TextView to the UI   111
Wiring up the UI with the Java code (part 1)   **112**
Adding layouts within layouts   **115**
Making the layout look pretty   **118**
Wiring up the UI with the Java code (part 2)   **120**
Building a precise UI with ConstraintLayout   **120**
Adding a CalenderView   120
Resizing a view in a ConstraintLayout   121
Using the Component Tree window   122
Adding constraints manually   124
Adding and constraining more UI elements   125
Making the text clickable   129
Laying out data with TableLayout   **130**
Adding a TableRow to TableLayout   130
Using the Component Tree when the visual designer won't do   131
Organizing the table columns   132
Linking back to the main menu   133
Summary   **134**

Chapter 5: Beautiful Layouts with CardView and ScrollView   **135**

Attributes quick summary   **135**
   Sizing using dp   136
   Sizing fonts using sp   136
   Determining size with wrap or match   137
   Using padding and margin   139
   Using the layout_weight property   140
   Using Gravity   141
Building a UI with CardView and ScrollView   **143**
   Setting the view with Java code   145
   Adding image resources   145
   Creating the content for the cards   146
   Defining dimensions for CardViews   150
   Adding CardViews to our layout   151
   Including layout files inside another layout   152
Themes and material design   **155**
   Using the Android Studio theme designer   156
Creating a tablet emulator   **159**
Frequently asked questions   **162**
Summary   **162**

Chapter 6: The Android Lifecycle   **163**

The life and times of an Android app   **164**
   How Android interacts with our apps   164
A simplified explanation of the Android lifecycle   **165**
   The lifecycle phases demystified   166
How we handle the lifecycle phases   **167**
Lifecycle demo app   **170**
   Coding the lifecycle demo app   170
   Running the lifecycle demo app   173
   Examining the Lifecycle Demo app output   174
Some other overridden methods   **176**
The structure of Java code – revisited   **177**
Summary   **179**

Chapter 7: Java Variables, Operators, and Expressions   **181**

Java is everywhere   **181**
Syntax and jargon   **182**
More code comments   **183**
Storing and using data with variables   **185**
   Types of variables   186
     Primitive types   187

Reference types 189

Using variables **190**

Variable declaration 191

Variable initialization 191

Changing values in variables with operators 192

The assignment operator 193

The addition operator 193

The subtraction operator 193

The division operator 194

The multiplication operator 194

The increment operator 194

The decrement operator 195

Expressions **195**

Expressing yourself demo app 196

Summary **199**

Chapter 8: Java Decisions and Loops **201**

Making decisions in Java **202**

Indenting code for clarity 202

More operators 203

The comparison operator 203

The logical NOT operator 204

The NOT equal operator 204

The greater than operator 204

The less than operator 204

The greater than or equal to operator 205

The less than or equal to operator 205

The logical AND operator 205

The logical OR operator 205

How to use all of these operators to test variables 206

Using the Java if keyword 206

Switching to make decisions 210

Switch Demo app 211

Repeating code with loops **212**

While loops 213

Breaking out of a loop 215

The continue keyword 216

Do while loops 216

For loops 217

Loops demo app 218

Summary **222**

Chapter 9: Java Methods **223**

Methods revisited **223**

What exactly are Java methods? **224**

Method structure **224**

Modifier 226
Return type 227
Name of a method 229
Parameters 229
The body 230
Using methods demo apps **231**
Real world methods 231
Discovering variable scope 233
Exploring method overloading 233
Scope and variables revisited **236**
Frequently asked questions **237**
Further reading **238**
Summary **239**

Chapter 10: Object-Oriented programming **241**
Important memory management warning **241**
Object-oriented programming **242**
What is OOP exactly 242
Encapsulation 242
Polymorphism 243
Inheritance 243
Why do it like this? 244
Class recap 244
Looking at the code for a class **245**
Class implementation 245
Declaring, initializing, and using an object of the class 246
Basic classes app **249**
More things that we can do with our first class 253
Frequently asked questions **254**

Chapter 11: More Object-Oriented Programming **257**
Remember that encapsulation thing? **257**
Controlling class use with access modifiers 259
Class access modifiers 259
Class access in summary 259
Controlling variable use with access modifiers 260
Variable access modifiers 260
Variable access summary 261
Methods have access modifiers too 261
Method access modifiers 261
Method access summary 263
Accessing private variables with getters and setters 263
Setting up our objects with constructors 266
Static methods 268

Encapsulation and static methods mini-app   271
OOP and inheritance   275
Inheritance example app   278
Polymorphism   282
  Abstract classes   283
  Interfaces   285
Frequently asked questions   286
Summary   287

Chapter 12: The Stack, the Heap, and the Garbage Collector   289
All the Android UI elements are classes too   290
  Re-introducing references   290
    A quick break to throw out the trash   291
    Seven facts about the Stack and the Heap   291
  So how does this Heap thing help me?   292
  Using Buttons and TextView widgets from our layout   293
  The Inner and Anonymous classes   303
Frequently asked questions   304
Summary   304

**Chapter 13: Anonymous Classes – Bringing Android
Widgets to Life**   305
Declaring and initializing the objects   306
Creating UI widgets from pure Java without XML   307
Exploring the palette – part 1   308
  The EditText widget   308
  The ImageView widget   309
  Radio button and group   310
Anonymous classes   311
Exploring the palette – Part 2, and more anonymous classes   315
  Switch   315
  CheckBox   316
  TextClock   317
Widget exploration app   317
  Setting up the widget exploration project and UI   318
  Coding the widget exploration app   327
    Getting a reference to the parts of the UI   328
    Coding the checkboxes   329
    Coding the RadioButtons   332
    Using an anonymous class for a regular button 334
    Coding the Switch   335
  Running the Widget Exploration app   336
Converting layouts to ConstraintLayout   338

Summary	**338**
Chapter 14: Android Dialog Windows	**339**
Dialog windows	**339**
Creating the Dialog Demo project	340
Coding a DialogFragment class	340
Using chaining to configure the DialogFragment	342
Using the DialogFragment class	344
The Note to self app	**346**
Using naming conventions and String resources	346
How to get the code files for the Note to self app	347
The completed app	348
Building the project	352
Preparing the String resources	352
Coding the Note class	353
Implementing the Dialog designs	356
Coding the dialog boxes	361
Coding the DialogNewNote class	361
Coding the DialogShowNote class	365
Showing our new dialogs	369
Coding the floating action button	372
Summary	**375**
Chapter 15: Arrays, ArrayList, Map and Random Numbers	**377**
A random diversion	**378**
Handling large amounts of data with arrays	**378**
Arrays are objects	380
Simple array example mini-app	**381**
Getting dynamic with arrays	**383**
Dynamic array example	383
Entering the nth dimension with Arrays	**385**
Multidimensional Array mini app	385
Array out of bounds exceptions	389
ArrayLists	**389**
The enhanced for loop	391
Arrays and ArrayLists are polymorphic	**391**
More Java Collections – Meet Java Hashmap	**393**
The Note to Self app	**395**
Frequently asked questions	**395**
Summary	**395**
Chapter 16: Adapters and Recyclers	**397**
RecyclerView and RecyclerAdapter	**397**
The problem with displaying lots of widgets	398

The solution to the problem with displaying lots of widgets   398
How to use RecyclerView and RecyclerAdapter   398
What we will do to set up RecyclerView with RecyclerAdapter
and an ArrayList of notes   400
**Adding RecyclerView, RecyclerAdapter, and ArrayList to
the Note to Self project**   **401**
Removing the temporary Show Note button and adding the
RecyclerView   401
Creating a list item for the RecyclerView   402
Coding the RecyclerAdapter class   404
Coding the NoteAdapter constructor   407
Coding the onCreateViewHolder method   408
Coding the onBindViewHolder method   408
Coding getItemCount   409
Coding the ListItemHolder inner class   410
Coding MainActivity to use the RecyclerView and
RecyclerAdapter classes   411
Adding code to onCreate   411
Modifying the addNote method   412
Coding the showNote method   413
Running the app   **414**
Frequently asked questions   **417**
Summary   **417**
Chapter 17: Data Persistence and Sharing   **419**
Android Intents   **419**
Switching Activity   420
Passing data between Activities   421
Adding a settings page to Note to Self   **422**
Creating the SettingsActivity   422
Designing the Settings screen layout   423
Enabling the user to switch to the settings screen   425
Persisting data with SharedPreferences   **427**
Reloading data with SharedPreferences   **428**
Making the Note to Self settings persist   **429**
Coding the SettingsActivity class   429
Coding the MainActivity class   431
More advanced persistence   **433**
What is JSON?   434
Java exceptions – try, catch, and finally   434
Backing up user data in Note to Self   **435**
Frequently asked questions   **442**
Summary   **442**

Chapter 18: Localization   **445**

Making the Note to Self app for Spanish, English, and German speakers   **445**

Adding Spanish support   446

Adding German support   446

Adding the string resources   447

Running Note to Self in German or Spanish   **450**

Making the translations work in Java code   452

Summary   **454**

Chapter 19: Animations and Interpolations   **455**

Animations in Android   **455**

Designing cool animations in XML   456

Fading in and out   456

Move it, move it   456

Scaling or stretching   457

Controlling the duration   457

Rotate animations   457

Repeating animations   457

Combining animation's properties with Set   458

Instantiating animations and controlling them with Java code   458

More animation features   459

Listeners   459

Animation interpolators   460

Animations Demo App – introducing SeekBar   **460**

Laying out the animation demo   461

Coding the XML Animations   466

Wiring up the Animation Demo app in Java   470

Frequently asked questions   **480**

Summary   **481**

Chapter 20: Drawing Graphics   **483**

Understanding the Canvas class   **483**

Getting started drawing with Bitmap, Canvas, and ImageView   484

Canvas and Bitmap   484

Paint   484

ImageView and Activity   485

Canvas, Bitmap, Paint, and ImageView – quick summary   485

Using the Canvas class   **486**

Preparing the instances of the required classes   486

Initializing the objects   487

Setting the Activity content   487

The Canvas Demo app   **488**

Creating a new project   488

Coding the Canvas demo app   488

Drawing on the screen   490
Android coordinate system   **493**
Plotting and drawing   493
Creating Bitmaps   **494**
Manipulating Bitmaps   **495**
What is a Bitmap exactly?   496
The Matrix class   496
Inverting a bitmap to face the opposite direction   497
Rotating the bitmap to face up and down   498
Bitmap manipulation demo app   **499**
Add the graphic to the project   499
Frequently asked question   **503**
Summary   **504**

Chapter 21: Threads, and Starting the Live Drawing App   505
Creating the Live Drawing project   **505**
Looking ahead at the Live Drawing app   **506**
Coding the LiveDrawingActivity class   **506**
Coding the LiveDrawingView class   **509**
Coding the LiveDrawingView class   **512**
Adding the member variables   513
Coding the LiveDrawingView constructor   516
Coding the draw method   517
Adding the printDebuggingText method   518
Understanding the draw method and the SurfaceView class   519
The game loop   **521**
Threads   **523**
Problems with threads   524
Implementing the game loop with a thread   **527**
Implementing Runnable and providing the run method   528
Coding the thread   528
Starting and stopping the thread   529
Using the Activity lifecycle to start and stop the thread   530
Coding the run method   531
Running the app   **534**
Summary   **534**

Chapter 22: Particle Systems and Handling Screen Touches   537
Adding custom buttons to the screen   **537**
Implementing a particle system effect   **538**
Coding the Particle class   540
Coding the ParticleSystem class   542
Spawning particle systems in the LiveDrawingView class   547

Handling touches	**549**
Coding the onTouchEvent method	551
Finishing the HUD	552
Running the app	**552**
Summary	**555**
Chapter 23: Supporting Different Versions of Android, Sound Effects, and the Spinner Widget	**557**
Handling different versions of Android	**557**
Detecting the current Android version	558
The Soundpool class	**558**
Initializing SoundPool the new way	559
Initializing SoundPool the old way	560
Loading sound files into memory	561
Playing a sound	562
Stopping a sound	563
Sound demo app introducing Spinner widget	**563**
Making sound FX	563
Laying out the sound demo	566
Coding the Sound demo	569
Summary	**575**
Chapter 24: Design Patterns, Multiple Layouts, and Fragments	**577**
Introducing the model-view-controller pattern	**578**
Model	578
View	578
Controller	578
Android design guidelines	**579**
Real-world apps	**580**
Device detection mini-app	**582**
Coding the MainActivity class	586
Unlocking the screen orientation	587
Running the app	588
Configuration qualifiers	**590**
The limitation of configuration qualifiers	592
Fragments	**593**
Fragments have a lifecycle too	593
onCreate	593
onCreateView	593
onAttach and onDetach	593
onStart, onPause, and onStop	593
Managing Fragments with FragmentManager	594
Our first Fragment app	**595**
Fragment reality check	**602**

Frequently asked question	**603**
Summary	**603**
Chapter 25: Advanced UI with Paging and Swiping	**605**
Angry birds classic swipe menu	**606**
Building an image gallery/slider app	**606**
Implementing the layout	607
Coding the PagerAdapter class	608
Coding the MainActivity class	611
Running the gallery app	613
Building a Fragment Pager/slider app	**615**
Coding the SimpleFragment class	615
The fragment_layout	618
Coding the MainActivity class	618
The activity_main layout	620
Running the fragment slider app	621
Summary	**622**
Chapter 26: Advanced UI with Navigation Drawer and Fragment	**623**
Introducing the NavigationView	**624**
Examining the Simple Database app	**625**
Insert	627
Delete	628
Search	629
Results	630
Starting the Simple Database project	**631**
Exploring the auto-generated code and assets	**633**
Coding the Fragment classes and their layouts	**636**
Creating the empty files for the classes and layouts	636
Coding the classes	637
Designing the layouts	640
Designing content_insert.xml	640
Designing content_delete.xml	641
Designing content_search.xml	642
Designing content_results.xml	642
Using the Fragment classes and their layouts	**643**
Editing the Navigation Drawer menu	643
Adding a holder to the main layout	644
Coding the MainActivity.java	644
Summary	**646**

Chapter 27: Android Databases	**647**
Database 101	**648**
What is a database	648
What is SQL	648
What is SQLite	648
SQL syntax primer	**649**
SQLite example code	649
Creating a table	650
Inserting data into the database	650
Retrieving data from the database	651
Updating the database structure	651
Android SQLite API	**651**
SQLiteOpenHelper and SQLiteDatabase	652
Building and executing queries	652
Database cursors	654
Coding the database class	**655**
Coding the Fragment classes to use the DataManager	**660**
Running the Age Database app	**663**
Summary	**665**
Chapter 28: Coding a Snake Game Using Everything We Have Learned So Far	**667**
How to play	**668**
Getting started with the Snake game	**669**
Make the app full screen and landscape	670
Adding some empty classes	670
Coding SnakeActivity	670
Adding the sound effects	672
Coding the game engine	**672**
Coding the members	672
Coding the constructor	674
Coding the newGame method	676
Coding the run method	677
Coding the updateRequired method	678
Coding the update method	679
Coding the draw method	679
Coding onTouchEvent	681
Coding pause and resume	681
Running the game	**682**
Adding the graphics	**683**
Coding the apple	**683**
The Apple constructor	684

Using the apple	**686**
Running the game	688
Summary	**688**
Chapter 29: Enumerations and Finishing the Snake Game	**689**
Enumerations	**690**
Add the sound to the project	**692**
Coding the Snake class	**692**
Coding the constructor	694
Coding the reset method	696
Coding the move method	697
Coding the detectDeath method	699
Coding the checkDinner method	700
Coding the draw method	701
Coding the switchHeading method	703
Using the snake class and finishing the game	704
Running the completed game	**707**
Summary	**708**
Chapter 30: A Quick Chat Before You Go	**709**
Publishing	**709**
Making an app!	**710**
Carrying on learning	**711**
Carrying on reading	711
GitHub	711
StackOverflow	712
Android user forums	714
Higher-level study	714
My other channels	**715**
Goodbye and thank you	**715**
Other Books You May Enjoy	**717**
Index	**721**

Preface

Are you trying to start a career in programming, but haven't found the right way in? Do you have a great idea for an app, but don't know how to make it a reality? Or maybe you're just frustrated that to learn Android, you must know Java. If so, then this book is for you.

This new and expanded second edition of Android Programming for Beginners will be your companion to create Android Pie applications from scratch. We will introduce you to all the fundamental concepts of programming in an Android context, from the basics of Java to working with the Android API. All examples use the up-to-date API classes and are created from within Android Studio, the official Android development environment that helps supercharge your application development process.

After this crash-course, we'll dive deeper into Android programming and you'll learn how to create applications with a professional-standard UI through fragments and store your user's data with SQLite. In addition, you'll see how to make your apps multilingual, draw to the screen with a finger, and work with graphics, sound, and animations too.

By the end of this book, you'll be ready to start building your own custom applications in Android and Java.

Who this book is for

This book is for you if you are completely new to Java, Android, or programming, and want to make Android applications. This book will also act as a refresher for those of you who already have experience of using Java on Android to enable you advance your knowledge and make rapid progress through the early projects.

What this book covers

Chapter 1, Beginning Android and Java, Welcome to Android Programming for Beginners, Second Edition: In this first chapter, we won't waste any time in getting started developing Android apps. We will look at what is so great about Android, what exactly Android and Java are, how they work and complement each other, and what that means to us as future developers. Moving quickly on, we will set up the required software so that we can build and deploy a simple first app.

Chapter 2, First Contact – Java, XML, and the UI Designer: By this stage, we have a working Android development environment and we have built and deployed our first app. It is obvious, however, that auto-generated code by Android Studio is not going to make the next top selling app on Google Play. We need to explore this auto-generated code so that we can begin to understand Android and then learn how to build on this useful template

Chapter 3, Exploring Android Studio and the Project Structure: In this chapter, we will create and run two more Android projects. The purpose of these exercises is to explore more deeply Android Studio and the structure of Android projects.

When we build our apps ready for deployment, the code and the resource files need to be packed away in the APK file just so. Therefore, all the layout files and other resources that we will soon discover need to be in the correct structures.

Fortunately, Android Studio handles this for us when we create a project from a template. However, we still need to know how to find and amend these files, how to add our own, and sometimes remove the files created by Android Studio, and how the resource files are interlinked, sometimes with each other, and sometimes with the Java code (auto-generated and our own).

Along with understanding the composition of our projects, it will also be beneficial to make sure we get the most from the emulator.

Chapter 4, Getting Started with Layouts and Material Design: We have already seen the Android Studio UI designer, as well as a little bit of Java, in action. In this hands-on chapter, we will build three more layouts—still quite simple, yet a step up from what we have done so far.

Before we get to the hands-on part, we will have a quick introduction to the concept of **Material Design**.

We will see another type of layout called `LinearLayout`, and step through it, using it to create a usable UI. We will then take things a step further, using `ConstraintLayout`, both with understanding constraints, and with designing more complex and precise UI designs. Finally, we will meet the `TableLayout`, for laying out data in an easily readable table.

We will also write some Java code to switch between our different layouts within a single app/project. This is the first major app that links together multiple topics into one neat parcel.

Chapter 5, Beautiful Layouts with CardView and ScrollView: This is the final chapter on layouts before we spend some time focusing on Java and object-oriented programming. We will formalize our learning on some of the different attributes we have already met, and we will also introduce two more cool layouts: `ScrollView` and `CardView`. To conclude this chapter, we will run the `CardView` project on a tablet emulator.

Chapter 6, The Android Lifecycle: In this chapter, we will get familiar with the lifecycle of an Android app. At first, this might sound a bit strange, that a computer program has a lifecycle, but it will soon make sense.

The lifecycle is the way that all Android apps interact with the Android OS. Just as the lifecycle of humans interacts with the world around them, we have no choice but to interact with it, and must be prepared to handle different events without notice if we want our apps to survive.

We will see the phases of the lifecycle that an app goes through, from creation to destruction, and how this helps us know *where* to put out Java code, depending on what we are trying to achieve.

Chapter 7, Java Variables, Operators, and Expressions: In this chapter and the one that follows it, we are going to learn and practice the core fundamentals of Java; the code that goes into the classes and the methods that we create, along with the data that the code acts upon. In this chapter, we will focus on the data.

We will also quickly recap on what we learned in the earlier chapters about Java and then immediately dive into learning how to write our very own Java code. The principles we are about to learn are not limited to Java, but are also applicable to other programming languages as well.

By the end of the chapter, you will be comfortable writing Java code that creates and uses data within Android.

Chapter 8, Java Decisions and Loops: We have just learned about variables and we know how we can change the values that they hold with expressions, but how can we take a course of action dependent upon the value of a variable?

We can certainly add the number of new messages to the number of previously unread messages, but how might we, for example, trigger an action within our app when the user has read all their messages?

The first problem is that we need a way to test the value of a variable and then respond when that value falls within a range of values or is a specific value.

Another problem that is common to all sorts of programming is that we need sections of our code to be executed a certain number of times (more than once or sometimes not at all), depending on the value of variables.

To solve the first problem, we will look at making decisions in Java with `if`, `else`, and `switch`. To solve the latter, we will look at loops in Java with `while`, `do - while`, `for`, and `break`.

Chapter 9, Java Methods: As we are starting to get comfortable with Java programming, in this chapter, we will take a closer look at methods, because although we know that you can **call** them to make them execute their code, there is more to them than we have discussed so far.

Chapter 10, Object-Oriented Programming: In this chapter, we will discover that in Java, classes are fundamental to just about everything. We will begin to understand why the software engineers at Sun Microsystems back in the early 1990s made Java the way they did.

We have already talked about reusing other people's code, specifically the Android API, but in this chapter, we will really get to grips with how this works and learn about object-oriented programming and how to use it.

Chapter 11, More Object-Oriented Programming: This chapter is the second part of our whirlwind tour (theoretical and practical) into OOP. We have already briefly discussed the concepts of encapsulation, inheritance, and polymorphism, but in this chapter, we will get to see them in action in some demo apps. While the working examples will show these concepts in their simplest forms, it will still be a significant stepping stone toward taking control of our XML layouts via our Java code.

Chapter 12, The Stack, the Heap and the Garbage Collector: By the end of this chapter, the missing link between Java and our XML layouts will be fully revealed, leaving us with the power to add all kinds of widgets to our apps, as we have done before, but this time we will be able to control them through our Java code.

In this chapter, we will get to take control of some fairly simple UI elements, such as Button and TextView, and, in the next chapter, we will take things further and manipulate a whole range of UI elements.

To enable us to understand what is happening, we need to find out a bit more about the memory in an Android device and two areas of it—the **Stack** and the **Heap**.

Chapter 13, Anonymous Classes – Bringing Android Widgets to Life: This chapter could have been called "Even More OOP", as anonymous classes are very much still part of that subject, but, as we will see, anonymous classes offer us so much flexibility, especially when it comes to interacting with the UI, that I thought they deserved a chapter title dedicated to them and one of their key uses in Android.

Now that we have a good overview of both the layout and coding of an Android app, as well as our newly acquired insight into object-oriented programming and how we can manipulate the UI from our Java code, we are ready to experiment with more widgets from the palette alongside anonymous classes.

OOP is a tricky thing at times, and anonymous classes are known to sometimes be a bit awkward for beginners, but, by gradually learning these new concepts and then practicing them repeatedly, over time they will become our friend.

In this chapter, we will diversify a lot by going back to the Android Studio palette and looking around at half a dozen widgets that we have either not seen at all or have not used fully yet.

Once we have done so, we will put them all into a layout and practice manipulating them with Java code.

Chapter 14, Android Dialog Windows: In this chapter, we will see how to present the user with a pop-up dialog window. We can then put all that we know into the first phase of our first major app, *Note to self*. We will also then learn about new Android and Java features in this chapter and the four following (up to chapter 18), and then use our newly acquired knowledge to enhance the Note to self app each time.

In each chapter, we will also build a selection of smaller apps that are separate from this main app.

Chapter 15, Arrays, ArrayList, Map and Random Numbers, In this chapter, we will learn about Java arrays, which allow us to manipulate a potentially huge amount of data in an organized and efficient manner. We will also use a close Java relation to arrays, the ArrayList, and see the differences between them.

Once we are comfortable handling substantial amounts of data, we will see what the Android API has in order to help us easily connect our new-found data handling skills to the user interface without breaking a sweat.

Chapter 16, Adapters and Recyclers: In this brief chapter, we will achieve much. We will first go through the theory of adapters and lists. How we can extend `RecyclerAdapter` in Java code and add a `RecyclerView`, which acts as a list to our UI, and then, through the apparent magic of the Android API, bind them together so that the `RecyclerView` displays the contents of the `RecyclerAdapter` and allows the user to scroll through the contents. You have probably guessed that we will be using this technique to display our list of notes in the Note to Self app.

Chapter 17, Data Persistence and Sharing: In this chapter, we will look at a couple of different ways to save data to the Android device's permanent storage. Also, for the first time we will add a second `Activity` to our app. It often makes sense when implementing a separate "screen", like a settings screen in our app, to do so in a new `Activity`. We could go to the trouble of hiding the original UI and then showing the new UI, but this would quickly lead to confusing and error-prone code. So, we will see how to add an `Activity` and navigate the user between them.

Chapter 18, Localization: This chapter is quick and simple, but what we will learn to do here can make your app accessible to millions of more potential users. We will see how to add additional languages. We will see how adding text the correct way via String resources benefits us when it comes to adding multiple languages.

Chapter 19, Animations and Interpolations: Here we will see how we can use the `Animation` class to make our UI a little less static and a bit more interesting. As we have come to expect, the Android API will allow us to do some quite advanced things with relatively straightforward code, and the `Animation` class is no different,

Chapter 20, Drawing Graphics: This entire chapter will be about the Android `Canvas` class and a number of related classes, such as `Paint`, `Color`, and Bitmap. These classes combined bring great power when it comes to drawing to the screen. Sometimes, the default UI provided by the Android API isn't what we need. If we want to make a drawing app, draw graphs, or perhaps a game, we need to take control of every pixel that the Android device has to offer.

Chapter 21, Threads, and Starting the Live Drawing App: In this chapter, we will get started on our next app. This app will be a kid's style drawing app where the user can draw on the screen with their finger. This drawing app will be slightly different, however. The lines that the user draws will be comprised of particle systems that explode into thousands of pieces. We will call the project Live Drawing.

Chapter 22, Particle Systems and Handling Screen Touches: We already have our real-time system that we implemented in the previous chapter using a thread. In this chapter, we will create the entities that will exist and evolve in this real-time system as if they have a mind of their own and form the appearance of the drawings that the user can achieve.

We will also see how the user draws these entities by learning how to respond to interaction with the screen. This is different to interacting with a widget in a UI layout.

Chapter 23, Supporting Different Versions of Android, Sound Effects, and Spinner Widget: In this chapter, we will learn about how we can detect and handle different versions of Android. We will then be able to study the SoundPool class and the different ways we use it, depending on the Android version the app is running on. At this point, we can then put everything we have learned into producing cool sound demo app that will also introduce us to a new UI widget; the **Spinner**.

Chapter 24, Design Patterns, Multiple Layouts, and Fragments: We have come a long way since the start when we were just setting up Android Studio. Back then, we went through everything step by step, but, as we have proceeded, we have tried to show not just how to add x to y, or feature a to app b, but to enable you to use what you have learned in your own ways to bring your own ideas to life.

This chapter is more about your future apps than anything in the book so far. We will look at a few aspects of Java and Android that you can use as a framework or template for making ever more exciting and complex apps at the same time as keeping the code manageable. Furthermore, I will suggest areas of further study which there is simply not enough room to even scratch the surface of in this book.

Chapter 25, Advanced UI with Paging and Swiping: **Paging** is the act of moving from page to page and, on Android, we do this by swiping a finger across the screen. The current page transitions in a direction and speed to match the finger movement. It is a useful and practical way to navigate around an app, but perhaps even more than this, it is an extremely satisfying visual effect for the user. Also, as with RecyclerView, we can selectively load just the data required for the current page and perhaps the data for the previous and following pages.

The Android API, as you would have come to expect, has some solutions for achieving paging in a quite simple manner.

Chapter 26, Advanced UI with Navigation Drawer and Fragment: In this chapter, we will see what is (arguably) the most advanced UI on. The NavigationView, or navigation drawer because of the way it slides out its contents, can be created simply by choosing it as a template when you create a new project. We will do just that and then we will examine the auto-generated code and learn how to interact with it. Then, we will use all we know about Fragment to populate each of the "drawers" with different behaviors and views. Then, in the next chapter, we will learn about databases to add some new functionality to each Fragment.

Chapter 27, Android Databases: If we are going to make apps that offer our users significant features, then almost certainly we are going to need a way to manage, store, and filter significant amounts of data.

It is possible to store efficiently very large amounts of data with JSON, but when we need to use that data selectively, rather than simply restricting ourselves to the options of "save everything" and "load everything", we need to think about which other options are available.

A good computer science course would probably teach the algorithms necessary to handle sorting and filtering our data, but the effort involved would be quite extensive, and what are the chances of us coming up with a solution that is as good as the people who provide us with the Android API?

As is so often the case, it makes sense to use the solutions provided in the Android API. As we have seen, JSON and SharedPreferences classes have their place but, at some point, we need to move on to using real databases for real-world solutions. Android uses the SQLite database management system and, as you would expect, there is an API to make it as easy as possible.

Chapter 28, Coding a Snake Game Using Everything We Have Learned So Far: In this bonus and final project, we will use a bit of everything we have leaned throughout the book: interfaces, creating classes, graphics, sound, threads, screen touches, and more.

The history of the Snake game goes back to the 1970s. However, it was the 1980s when the game took on the look that we will be using in this chapter. It was sold under numerous names and many platforms, but probably gained widespread recognition when it was shipped as standard on Nokia mobile phones in the late 1990s.

Chapter 29, Enumerations and Finishing the Snake Game: Welcome to the final practical chapter of the book and the last Java topic. We will first learn about Java enumerations, and then we will put them straight to work in helping us finish the Snake game.

Chapter 30, A Quick Chat Before You Go: We are just about done with our journey. This chapter is just a few ideas and pointers that you might like to look at before rushing off and making your own apps.

To get the most out of this book

- To succeed with this book, you don't need any experience whatsoever. If you are confident with your operating system of choice (Windows, macOS or Linux), you can learn to make Android apps while learning the Java programming language. Learning to develop professional quality apps is a journey that anybody can embark upon and stay on for as long as they want.

- If you do have previous programming (Java or any other language), Android, or other development experience, then you will make faster progress with the earlier chapters.

Download the example code files

You can download the example code files for this book from your account at http://www.packt.com. If you purchased this book elsewhere, you can visit http://www.packt.com/support and register to have the files emailed directly to you.

You can download the code files by following these steps:

1. Log in or register at http://www.packt.com.
2. Select the **SUPPORT** tab.
3. Click on **Code Downloads & Errata**.
4. Enter the name of the book in the **Search** box and follow the onscreen instructions.

Once the file is downloaded, please make sure that you unzip or extract the folder using the latest version of:

- WinRAR/7-Zip for Windows
- Zipeg/iZip/UnRarX for Mac
- 7-Zip/PeaZip for Linux

The code bundle for the book is also hosted on GitHub at https://github.com/PacktPublishing/Android-Programming-for-Beginners. In case there's an update to the code, it will be updated on the existing GitHub repository.

We also have other code bundles from our rich catalog of books and videos available at https://github.com/PacktPublishing/. Check them out!

Conventions used

There are a number of text conventions used throughout this book.

`CodeInText`: Indicates code words in text, database table names, folder names, filenames, file extensions, pathnames, dummy URLs, user input, and Twitter handles. For example: "Now we can turn our attention to the inner class, `ListItemHolder`."

A block of code is set as follows:

```
public void showNote(int noteToShow){
    DialogShowNote dialog = new DialogShowNote();
    dialog.sendNoteSelected(noteList.get(noteToShow));
    dialog.show(getSupportFragmentManager(), "");
}
```

When we wish to draw your attention to a particular part of a code block, the relevant lines or items are set in bold:

```
public void createNewNote(Note n){
    // Temporary code
    //mTempNote = n;
    noteList.add(n);
    mAdapter.notifyDataSetChanged();
}
```

Bold: Indicates a new term, an important word, or words that you see on screen. For example, words in menus or dialog boxes, appear in the text like this. Here is an example: "When you are ready, click the **Next >** button."

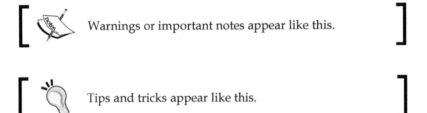

Warnings or important notes appear like this.

Tips and tricks appear like this.

Get in touch

Feedback from our readers is always welcome.

General feedback: If you have questions about any aspect of this book, mention the book title in the subject of your message and email us at customercare@packtpub.com.

Errata: Although we have taken every care to ensure the accuracy of our content, mistakes do happen. If you have found a mistake in this book, we would be grateful if you would report this to us. Please visit, http://www.packt.com/submit-errata, selecting your book, clicking on the Errata Submission Form link, and entering the details.

Piracy: If you come across any illegal copies of our works in any form on the internet, we would be grateful if you would provide us with the location address or website name. Please contact us at copyright@packt.com with a link to the material.

If you are interested in becoming an author: If there is a topic that you have expertise in, and you are interested in either writing or contributing to a book, please visit http://authors.packtpub.com.

Reviews

Please leave a review. Once you have read and used this book, why not leave a review on the site that you purchased it from? Potential readers can then see and use your unbiased opinion to make purchase decisions, we at Packt can understand what you think about our products, and our authors can see your feedback on their book. Thank you!

For more information about Packt, please visit packt.com.

1

Beginning Android and Java

Welcome to Android Programming for Beginners, Second Edition. In this first chapter, we won't waste any time in getting started developing Android apps.

We will look at what is so great about Android, what exactly Android and Java are, how they work and complement each other, and what that means to us as future developers.

Moving quickly on, we will set up the required software so we can build and deploy a simple first app.

By the end of this chapter, we will have have achieved the following:

- Discovered what is new in this second edition
- Learned how Java and Android work together
- Set up our development environment, Android Studio, which takes care of all the components involved in building Android apps that we will learn about next
- Learned about the Java Development Kit (JDK), the Android Application Programming Interface (API), and how we use them through Android Studio
- Built our very first Android app
- Deployed the app on an Android emulator
- Run our app on an Android emulator and a real device

That's a lot to get through, so let's get started.

What's new in the second edition?

All the major apps have been changed. The three big apps from the earlier edition have been replaced by four new apps. In this edition, we will build a Memo app, a drawing app, a database app, and a fully playable clone of the classic Snake game. In addition, many of the mini-apps have been scrapped, updated or improved, and over the course of this book, you will get to build over a dozen functioning mini-apps to put into practice what you learn.

Furthermore, I have added more images, tips, and information boxes to help emphasize and clarify important points, as well as adding to and improving virtually every page. Even if you have already read the first edition, there is still plenty in this book for you.

Why Java and Android?

When Android first arrived in 2008, it was a bit drab compared to the much more stylish iOS on the Apple iPhone. But quite quickly, through a variety of handset offers that struck a chord with both the practical and price-conscious and the fashion-conscious and tech-savvy, Android user numbers exploded.

For many, myself included, developing for Android is the most rewarding pastime and business bar none.

Quickly putting together a prototype of an idea, refining it, and then deciding to run with it and wire it up into a fully-fledged app is such an exciting and rewarding process. Any programming can be fun, and I have been programming all my life, but creating for Android is somehow extraordinarily rewarding.

Defining exactly why this is the case is quite difficult. Perhaps it is the fact that the platform is free and open. You can distribute your apps without needing the permission of a big controlling corporation—nobody can stop you. And, at the same time, you have the well-established, corporate controlled mass markets, such as Amazon App Store and Google Play Store.

More likely, the reason developing for Android gives such a good feeling is the nature of the devices themselves. They are deeply personal. You can develop apps that interact with people's lives to educate, entertain, tell a story, and so on, but it is there in their pocket ready to go—in the home, in the workplace, or on holiday.

You can certainly build something bigger for the desktop, but knowing that thousands (or millions) of people are carrying your work in their pockets and sharing it with friends is more than just a buzz.

No longer is developing apps considered geeky, nerdy, or reclusive. In fact, developing for Android is considered highly skillful and the most successful developers are hugely admired, or even revered.

If all this fluffy and spiritual stuff doesn't mean anything to you, then that's fine too; developing for Android can make you a living, or even make you wealthy. With the continued growth of device ownership, the ongoing increase in CPU and GPU power, and the non-stop evolution of the Android operating system itself, the need for professional app developers is only going to grow.

In short, the best Android developers—and, more importantly, the Android developers with the best ideas and most determination—are in greater demand than ever. Nobody knows who these future Android app developers are, and they might not even have written their first line of Java yet.

So why isn't everybody an Android developer? Obviously, not everybody will share my enthusiasm for the thrill of creating software that can help people make their lives better, but I am guessing that because you are reading this, you might do?

The beginner's first stumbling block

Unfortunately, for those that do share my enthusiasm, there is a kind of glass wall on the path of progress that frustrates many aspiring Android developers.

Android uses Java to make apps. Every Android book, even those aimed at so-called beginners, assumes readers to have at least an intermediate level of Java, and most need an advanced level. So, good-to-excellent Java knowledge was a prerequisite for learning Android.

Unfortunately, learning Java in a completely different context to Android can sometimes be a little dull, and much of what you learn is not directly transferable into the world of Android anyway. You can see why beginners to Android and Java are often put off from starting.

But it doesn't need to be like this. In this book, I have carefully placed all the Java topics you would learn in a thick and weighty Java-only beginner's tomb and reworked them into four multi-chapter apps and more than a dozen quick mini-apps, starting from a simple memo app and progressing to a cool drawing app, a database app, and a playable game.

If you want to become a professional Android developer or just want to have more fun when learning Java and Android, this book will help.

How Java and Android work together

Before we start our Android quest, we need to understand how Android and Java work together. After we write a program in Java for Android, we click a button and our code is transformed into another form, the form that is understood by Android. This other form is called **Dalvik Executable,** or **DEX** code, and the transformation process is called **compiling**.

[We will see this process in action right after we set up our development environment later in the chapter.]

Android is a complex system, but you do not need to understand it in depth to be able to make amazing apps.

[Full understanding will come after using and interacting with it over time.]

To get started, we only need to understand the basics. The part of the Android system that **executes** (runs) the compiled DEX code is called the **Dalvik Virtual Machine (DVM)**.

The DVM itself is a piece of software written in another language that runs on a specially adapted version of the Linux operating system. So, what the user sees of Android is itself just an app running on yet another operating system.

Android is a system within a system. The typical Android user doesn't see the Linux operating system and most probably doesn't even know it is there.

The purpose of the DVM is to hide the complexity and diversity of hardware and software that Android runs on, but, at the same time, exposing all its useful features. This exposing of features works in two ways:

1. First, the DVM itself must have access to the hardware, which it does.
2. Second, this access must be programmer friendly and easy to use, and it is because of the Android **Application Programming Interface** or **API**.

Let's continue by talking more about the Android API.

The Android API

The Android API is code that makes it easy to do exceptional things. A simple analogy could be drawn with a machine, perhaps a car. When you press on the accelerator, a whole bunch of things happen under the hood. We don't need to understand about combustion or fuel pumps because some smart engineer has made an **interface** for us; in this case a mechanical interface—the accelerator pedal.

For example, the following line of Java code probably looks a little intimidating at this stage in the book, but it serves as a good example of how the Android API helps us:

```
locationManager.getLastKnownLocation(LocationManager.GPS_PROVIDER)
```

Once you learn that this single line of code searches for available satellites in space, then communicates with them in their orbits around the Earth, and then retrieves your precise latitude and longitude on the surface of the planet, it becomes easy to begin to glimpse the power and depth of the Android API in conjunction with the DVM.

For sure, that code does look a little challenging, even mind boggling at this stage of the book, but imagine trying to talk to a satellite some other way!

The Android API has a whole bunch of Java code that has already been written for us to use as we like.

There are many different estimates to the number of lines of code that has gone into Android. Some estimates are as low as 1 million, some as high as 20 million. What might seem surprising is that despite this vast amount of code, Android is known in programming circles for being.

The question we must ask, and the one this book tries to answer, is as follows:

How do we use all this code to do cool stuff? Or, to frame the question to fit the earlier analogy: How do we find and manipulate the pedals, steering wheel, and sunroof of the Android API?

The answer to this question is the Java programming language and the fact that Java was designed to help programmers handle complexity. Let's talk a bit about Java and **object-oriented programming (OOP)**.

Java is object-oriented

Java is a programming language that has been around a lot longer than Android. It is an **object-oriented** language. This means it uses the concept of reusable programming objects. If this sounds like technical jargon, another analogy will help. Java enables us and others (like the Android development team) to write Java code that can be structured based on real-world things, and here is the important part: it can be **reused**.

So, using the car analogy, we could ask the following question: if a manufacturer makes more than one car in a day, do they redesign every part for each and every car?

The answer, of course, is no. They get highly skilled engineers to develop exactly the right components, honed, refined, and improved over years. Then that same component is reused again and again, as well as being occasionally improved.

If you are going to be fussy about my analogy, then you can point out that each of the car's components still has to be built from the raw materials using real-life engineers or robots.

This is true. What the software engineers do when they write their code is build a blueprint for an object. We then create an object from their blueprint using Java code, and once we have that object we can configure it, use it, combine it with other objects, and more besides.

Furthermore, as well as this, we can design blueprints ourselves and make objects from them as well. The compiler then transforms (manufactures) our bespoke creation into DEX code. Hey presto! We have an Android app.

In Java, a blueprint is called a **class.** When a class is transformed into a real working "thing", we call it an **object** or an **instance** of the class.

Objects in short

We could go on making analogies all day long. As far as we care at this point:

Java is a language that allows us to write code once that can then be used repeatedly.

This is very useful because it saves us time and allows us to use other people's code to perform tasks we might otherwise not have the time or knowledge to write for ourselves.

Most of the time, we do not even need to see this code or even know how it does its work!

One last analogy: We just need to know how to use that code just as we need to learn to drive a car.

So, some smart software engineer up at Android HQ writes a desperately complex Java program that can talk to satellites. He then considers how he can make this code useful to all the Android programmers who want to make amazing apps that use users' locations to do cool things. One of the things he will do is make features such as getting the device's location in the world into a simple one-line task.

So, the single line of code we saw previously sets in action many more lines of code that we don't see and don't need to see. This is an example of using somebody else's code to make our code infinitely simpler.

If the fact you don't have to see all the code is a disappointment to you, then I understand how you feel. Some of us, when we learn about something, want to learn every intricate detail. If this is you, then be reassured that the best place to start learning how the Android API works internally is to use it as the API programmers intended. And, throughout the book, I will regularly point out further learning opportunities in which you can find out the inner workings of the Android API. Also, we will be writing classes that are themselves reusable, kind of like our own API, except that our classes will focus on what we want our app to do.

Welcome to the world of **object-oriented programming (OOP)**. I will constantly refer to OOP in every chapter and there is the big reveal in *Chapter 10, Object Oriented Programming*.

Run that by me again – What exactly is Android?

To get things done on Android, we write Java code of our own, which also uses the Java code of the Android API. This is then compiled into DEX code and run by the DVM, which in turn has connections to an underlying operating system called Linux that handles the complex and extremely diverse range of hardware that are the different Android devices.

The manufacturers of the Android devices and of the individual hardware components obviously know this too, and they write advanced software called **drivers** that ensure that their hardware (for example, CPU, GPU, GPS receivers, memory chips, and hardware interfaces) can run on the underlying Linux operating system.

The DEX code (along with some other resources) is placed in a bundle of files called an **Android application PacKage** (APK), and this is what the DVM needs to run our app:

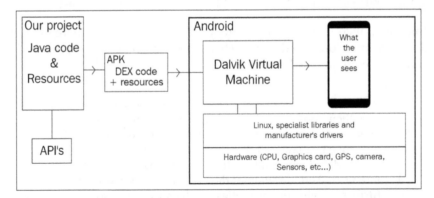

 It is not necessary to remember the details of the steps that our code goes through when it interacts with the hardware. It is enough just to understand that our Java code goes through some automated processes to become the apps that we will publish to the Google Play Store.

The next question is where exactly does all this Java coding and compiling into DEX code, along with APK packaging, take place? Let's look at the development environment we will be using.

Android Studio

A **development environment** is a term that refers to having everything you need to develop, set up, and be ready to go in one place. We need two things to get started.

1. We talked a fair bit about compiling our Java code, as well as other people's Java code, into DEX code that will run on the DVM on the user's Android device. To use Java code, we need some free software called the **Java Development Kit (JDK)**. The JDK also includes even more code from other people that is separate from the Android API.

2. There is an entire range of tools needed to develop for Android, and we also need the Android API, of course. This whole suite of requirements is collectively known as the **Android Software Development Kit (SDK)**. Fortunately, downloading and installing a single application will give us these things all bundled together. The application is called **Android Studio**.

Android Studio is an **integrated development environment (IDE)** that will take care of all the complexities of compiling our code and linking with the JDK and the Android API. Once we have installed Android Studio, we can do everything we need inside this single application and put to the back of our minds many of the complexities we have been discussing.

 Over time, these complexities will become like second nature. It is not necessary to master them to make further progress.

So we had better get our hands on Android Studio.

Setting up Android Studio

Setting up Android Studio is quite straightforward, if a little time-consuming. Grab some refreshment and get started with the following steps:

1. Visit `developer.android.com/studio/index.html`. Click the big green **DOWNLOAD ANDROID STUDIO** button to proceed:

2. Accept the terms and conditions by checking the checkbox, and then click the big blue button **DOWNLOAD ANDROID STUDIO FOR WINDOWS**:

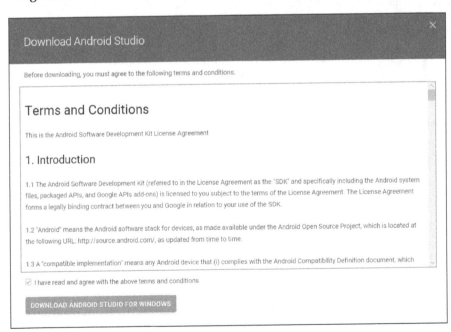

3. When the download is complete, run the file you just downloaded. It has a name that starts `android-studio-ide…`, while the end of the name of the file will vary based on the current version at the time of reading.

4. Click the **Next >** button to proceed:

5. Leave the default options selected, as shown in the following screenshot, and click the **Next >** button:

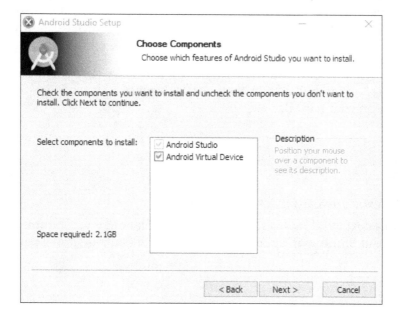

6. Next, we need to choose where to install Android Studio, as shown in the following screenshot:

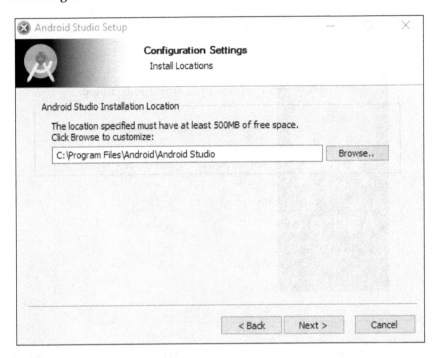

The install wizard recommends **500 MB** of free space, but you probably noticed from the previous screen that 2.1 GB was suggested. However, there are even more requirements later in the install process. Furthermore, it is much easier if you have all your Android Studio parts, as well as your project files, on the same hard drive.

For these reasons, I recommend having at least 4 GB of free space. If you need to switch drives to accommodate this, then use the **Browse...** button to browse to a suitable place on your hard drive.

 Note down the location you choose.

1. When you are ready, click the **Next >** button.
2. In this next window, you are choosing the folder in your start menu in which **Android Studio** will appear. Leave it at the default, as shown next:

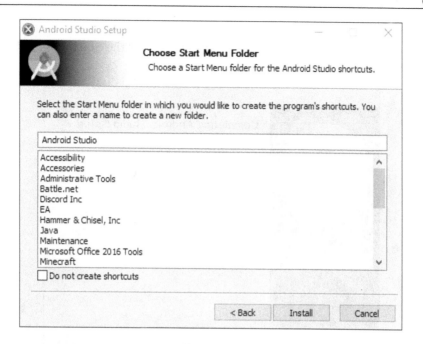

3. Click **Install**. This step might take some time, especially on older machines or if you have a slow internet connection. When this stage is done, you will see the following screen:

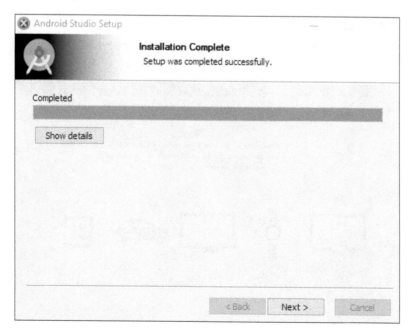

4. Click **Next >**.

5. Android Studio is now installed — kind of. Check the **Start Android Studio** checkbox and click the **Finish** button:

6. You will be greeted with the **Welcome** screen, as shown in the following screenshot:

7. Click the **Next** button.

8. Choose **Standard** install type, as shown in the following screenshot:

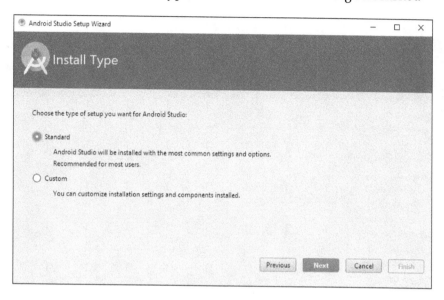

9. Click the **Next** button.

10. Choose whichever color scheme looks nice to you. I chose **IntelliJ,** as shown in the following screenshot:

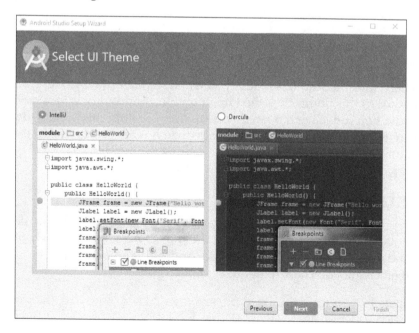

11. Click **Next**.

12. Now you will see the **Verify Settings** screen:

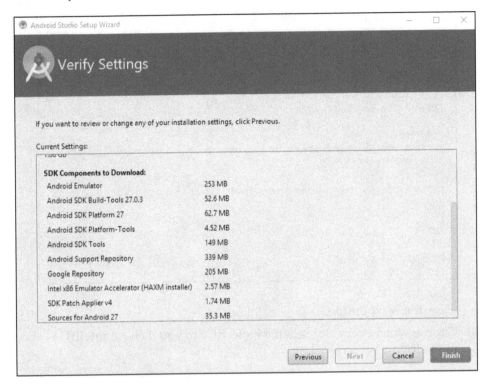

13. Click the **Finish** button. Android Studio will now commence some more downloads, which could take some time.

14. When Android Studio is ready, you will have the option to run Android Studio. At this point, click the **Finish** button. Android Studio is most likely ready. You can leave it open if you are carrying straight on with the next section, or you can close it and then reopen it when instructed in the next section.

Final step – for now

Using your preferred file manager software, perhaps Windows Explorer, create a folder called AndroidProjects. Make it at the root of the same drive where you installed Android Studio. So, if you installed Android Studio at C:/Program Files/ Android, then create your new folder at C:/AndroidProjects.

Or, if you installed Android Studio at D:/Program Files/Android, then create your new folder at D:/AndroidProjects.

Note that the screenshots in the next section show the AndroidProjects folder on the D: drive. This is because my C: drive is a bit full up. Either is fine. I did the install tutorial screen captures on a borrowed PC with plenty of space on the C: drive because that is the default for Android Studio. Keeping it on the same drive as the Android installation is neater and could avoid future problems, so do so if you can.

Notice that there is no space between the words Android and Projects, and that the first letter of both words is capitalized. The capitalization is for clarity and the lack of a space is required by Android Studio.

Android Studio and the supporting tools that we need are installed and ready to go. We are really close now to building our first app.

Now, let's look a little bit at the composition of an Android app.

What makes an Android app?

We already know that we will write Java code that will itself use other people's Java code and will be compiled into DEX code that runs on the DVM on our users' Android devices. In addition to this, we will also be adding and editing other files that get included in the final APK. These files are known as **Android resources**.

Android resources

Our app will include resources such as images, sound, and user interface layouts that are kept in separate files from the Java code. We will slowly introduce ourselves to them over the course of the book.

They will also include files that have the textual content of our app. It is convention to refer to the text in our app through separate files because it makes them easy to change, and makes it easy to create apps that work for multiple different languages and geographical regions.

Furthermore, the actual **User Interface (UI)** layout of our apps, despite the option to implement them with a visual designer, are actually read from text-based files by Android.

Android (or any computer) of course cannot read and recognize text in the same way that a human can. Therefore, we must present our resources in a highly organized and predefined manner. To do so, we will use Extensible Markup Language (**XML**). XML is a huge topic, but fortunately, its whole purpose is to be both human-and machine-readable. We do not need to learn this language; we just need to note (and then conform to) a few rules. Furthermore, most of the time we interact with XML, we will do so through a neat visual editor provided by Android Studio. We can tell when we are dealing with an XML resource because the filename will end with the extension .xml.

You do not need to memorize this as we will constantly be returning to this concept throughout the book.

The structure of Android's Java code

In addition to these resources, it is worth noting that Java as used in Android has a structure to its code. There are many millions of lines of code that we can take advantage of. This code will obviously need to be organized in a way that makes it easy to find and refer to. It is organized into **packages** that are specific to Android.

Packages

Whenever we create a new Android app, we will choose a unique name known as a **package**. We will see how we do this in the section "**Our first Android app**". Packages are often separated into **sub-packages,** so they can be grouped together with other similar packages. We can simply think of these as folders and sub-folders, which is almost exactly what they are.

We can think of all the packages that the Android API makes available to us as code from a code library. Some common Android packages that we will use include the following:

- android.graphics
- android.database
- android.view.animation

As you can see, they are arranged and named to make what is in them as obvious as possible.

 If you want to get an idea of the sheer depth and breadth of the Android API, then look at the Android package index: https://developer.android.com/reference/packages

Classes

Earlier, we learned that the reusable code blueprints that we can transform into objects are called **classes**. Classes are contained in these packages. We will see in our very first app how we can easily **import** other people's packages, along with specific classes from those packages for use in our projects. A class will almost always be contained in its own file with the same name as the class, and it will also have the .java file extension.

Methods

In Java (and therefore Android), we further break up our classes into sections that perform the different actions of our class. We call these action-oriented sections **methods**. It is most often the methods of the class that we will use to access the functionality provided within all those millions of lines of code.

We do not need to read the code. We just need to know which class has what we need, which package it is in, and which methods from within the class give us precisely the result we are after.

The following diagram shows a representation of the Android API. We can think of the structure of the code we will write ourselves in the same way, although we will usually have just one package per app.

Of course, because of the object-oriented nature of Java, we will only be using selected parts from this API. Notice also that each class has its own distinct **data**. Typically, if you want access to the data in that class, you need to have an object of that class:

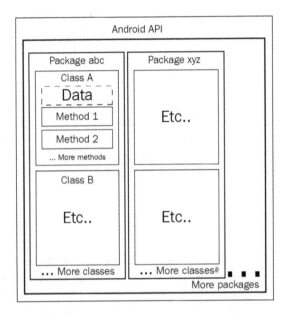

You do not need to memorize this as we will constantly be returning to this concept throughout the book.

By the end of this chapter, we will have imported multiple packages, as well as dozens of classes from them, and we will have used many of their methods as well. By the end of *Chapter 2, First Contact: Java, XML and the UI Designer* we will have even written our very own methods.

Our first Android app

Now we can get started on the first app. In programming, it is tradition for the first app of a new student to use whatever language/OS they are using to say hello to the world. We will quickly build an app that does just that, and in *Chapter 2, First Contact: Java, XML and the UI Designer*, we will go beyond that and add some buttons that respond to the user when they are pressed.

The complete code as it stands at the end of this chapter is in the download bundle in the Chapter 1 folder for your reference. You can't simply copy and paste this code, however! You still need to go through the project creation phase explained in this chapter (and at the beginning of all projects), as Android Studio does lots of work behind the scenes. Once you become familiar with these steps and understand which code is typed by you, the programmer, and which code/files are generated by Android Studio, you will then be able to save time and typing by copying and pasting the files I supply in the download bundle.

Follow these steps to start the project.

1. Run Android Studio in the same way you run any other app. On Windows 10, for example, the launch icon appears in the start menu.

    If you are prompted to **Import Studio settings from...:**, choose **Do not import settings**.

2. You will be greeted with the Android Studio welcome screen, as shown in the following screenshot. Locate the **Start a new Android Studio project** option and left-click it:

3. After this, Android Studio will bring up the **New Project** window. This is where we will perform the following:

   ◦ Name the new project

   ◦ Choose where on our computer the project files should go

   ◦ Provide a **Company domain** to distinguish our project from any others in case we should ever decide to publish it on the Play Store

4. The name of our project is going to be `Hello World`, and the location for the files will be your `AndroidProjects` folder that we created in the *Setting up Android Studio* section.

5. The company domain can be almost anything you like. If you have a website, you could use the format `Yourdomain.com`. If not, feel free to use `gamecodeschool.com`, or something that you just make up yourself. It is only important when you come to publish.

6. To be clear, in case you can't see the details in the following screenshot clearly, here are the values I used. Remember that yours might vary depending upon your choices of company domain and project location:

Option	Value entered
Application name:	`Hello World`
Company domain:	`gamecodeschool.com`
Include C++ support	Leave this option unchecked (see the next information box if you want to know more)
Project location:	`D:\AndroidProjects\HelloWorld`

 Note that the application name has a space between "Hello" and "World," but the project location does not and will not work if it does.

The following screenshot shows the **New Project** screen once you have entered all the information:

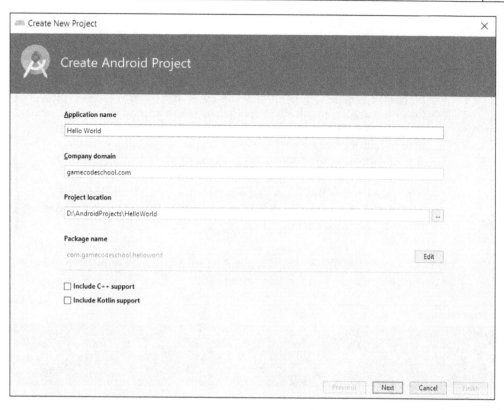

7. In the previous screenshot, you can see that Android Studio has auto-generated a **Package name** based on the information entered. Mine is **com. gamecodeschool.helloworld**. Yours might be the same or it may differ; it doesn't matter.

> You can write Android apps in a few different languages, including C++ and Kotlin. There are various advantages and disadvantages to each compared to using Java. Learning Java will be a great introduction to other languages, and Java is also the official language of Android. Most top apps and games on the Play Store are written in Java.

8. Click the **Next** button, and then we will continue to configure the Hello World project. The following set of options is the **Target Android Devices** window. We can leave the default options selected as we are only making apps for **Phone and Tablet**. The **Minimum SDK** option can be left as it is because it means our game will run on most (nearly all) Android devices, from Android 4.0 to the latest version.

We already know that the Android SDK is the collection of packages of code that we will be using to develop our apps. Like any good SDK, the Android SDK is regularly updated, and each time it gets a significant update the version number is increased. Simply put, the higher the version number, the newer the features you get to use; the lower the version number, the more devices our app will work on. For now, the default **API 15, Android 4.0.3 (Ice Cream Sandwich)**, will give us lots of great features and near 100% compatibility with the Android devices currently in use. If, at the time of reading, Android Studio is suggesting a newer API, then go with that.

If you are reading this some years in the future, then the **Minimum SDK** option will probably default to something different, but the code in this book will still work.

9. This next screenshot shows the **Target Android Devices** window we have just discussed, mainly just for your reference:

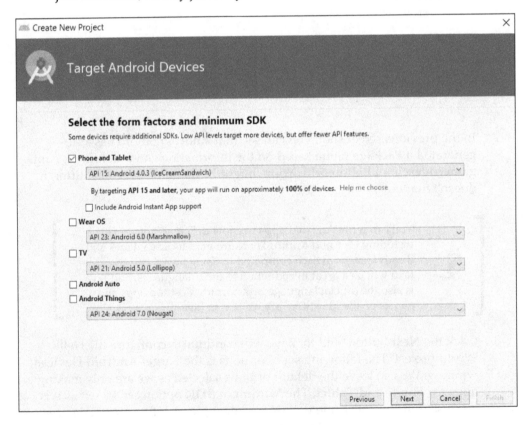

10. Click the **Next** button, and then we will move on.

11. The window that follows has the slightly obscure-sounding title **Add an Activity to Mobile**. These are some useful project templates that Android Studio can generate for you depending on the type of app you are going to develop. We will learn all about Android Activity as the book progresses.

> As a brief introduction, an Activity is a special class from the API and every Android app must have at least one. It is the part of the code in which our app will begin when it is launched by the user and handles interaction with the user. The options on this screen provide different ready-made templates of Activity class code to give programmers a fast start when creating various types of app. As we are starting from scratch, the most appropriate option for us is **Basic Activity**.

12. We will use the **Basic Activity** option. Android Studio will auto-generate a small amount of code and a selection of resources to get our project started. We will discuss the code and the resources in detail in the next chapter.

13. Select **Basic Activity**. Here is a screenshot of the **Add an Activity to Mobile** tab with the **Basic Activity** option selected:

14. Make sure **Basic Activity** is selected and click **Next**.

15. On the **Customize Activity** screen, which you should now be looking at, we have a few changes to make. We could leave the defaults as they are, but then Android would generate more files than we need. In addition, we want to change the **Activity Name** to something more appropriate than **MainActivity**. Follow this short list of changes to configure the **Customize Activity** screen:

    ○ Change **Activity Name** to `HelloWorldActivity`

    ○ Notice that **Layout Name** changes automatically to **activity_hello_world**. Leave this as it is. We will explore the significance of this in the next chapter.

    ○ Notice that **Title** changes automatically to **HelloWorldActivity**. Change it to **My First Activity**.

    ○ Leave the **Use a Fragment** option unchecked. We will explore Android Fragments later in the book.

16. Check that this is what the **Customize Activity** screen looks like when you're done with the previous step:

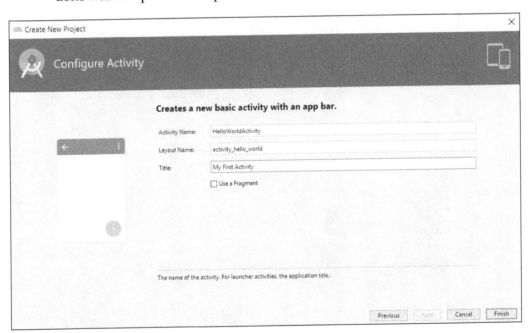

17. Finally for this section, you can click the **Finish** button and we will explore a little of what we (and Android Studio) have just achieved.

Android Studio will prepare our new project for us. This might take a few seconds or a few minutes, depending upon how powerful your PC is.

At this stage, you might be ready to proceed, but depending on the install process, you might need to click a couple of extra buttons.

 This is why I mentioned that we are "probably" finished installing and setting up.

Look in the bottom window of Android Studio to see if you have the following message:

 Note that if you do not see a horizontal window at the bottom of Android Studio like the one shown below, you can skip these two extra steps.

Extra step 1

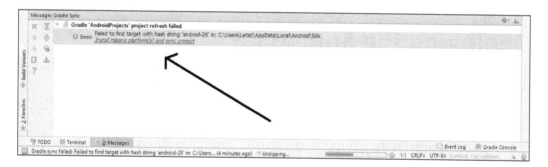

If you do, click **Install missing platform(s) and sync project**, accept the license agreement, and then click **Next**, followed by **Finish**.

Extra step 2

If you get another message like this:

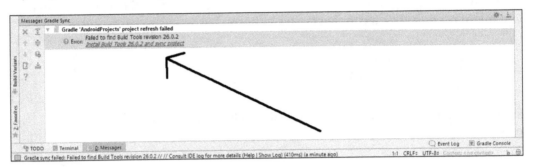

Click **Install Build tools....** and then click **Finish**.

[

You can tidy up the screen a bit and close this bottom horizontal window by clicking the **Messages** tab on the very bottom of Android Studio, but this isn't compulsory.
]

Deploying the app so far

Before we explore any of the code and learn our first bit of Java, you might be surprised to learn that we can already run our project. It will just be a fairly featureless screen, but as we will be running the app as often as possible to check our progress, let's see how to do that now. You have three options:

- Run the app on the emulator on your PC (part of Android Studio) in debug mode
- Run the app on a real Android device in USB debugging mode
- Export the app as a full Android project that can be uploaded to the Play store

The first option (debug mode) is the easiest to set up because we did it as part of setting up Android Studio. If you have a powerful PC, you will hardly see the difference between the emulator and a real device. However, screen touches are emulated by mouse clicks and proper testing of the user's experience is not possible in some of the later apps, such as the drawing app and the Snake game. Furthermore, you might just prefer to test out your creations on a real device; I know I do.

The second option of using a real device has a couple of additional steps, but once set up it is as good as option one and the screen touches are for real.

The final option takes about five minutes (at least) to prepare, and then you need to manually put the created package onto a real device and install it (every time you make a change to the code).

Probably the best way is to use the emulator to quickly test and debug minor increments in your code, and then fairly regularly use USB debugging mode on a real device to make sure things are still as expected. Only occasionally will you want to export an actual, deployable package.

> If you have an especially slow PC or a particularly aging Android device, you will be fine running the projects in this book using just one option or the other. Note that a slow Android phone will probably be OK and will cope, but a very slow PC will probably not handle the emulator running some of the later apps and you will benefit from running them on your phone/tablet.

For these reasons, I will now go through how to run the app using the emulator and USB debugging on a real device.

Beginning Android and Java

Running and debugging the app on an Android emulator

Follow these simple steps to run the game on the default Android emulator:

1. On the Android Studio main menu bar, select **Tools | Android AVD Manager**. AVD stands for Android Virtual Device (an emulator). You will see the following window:

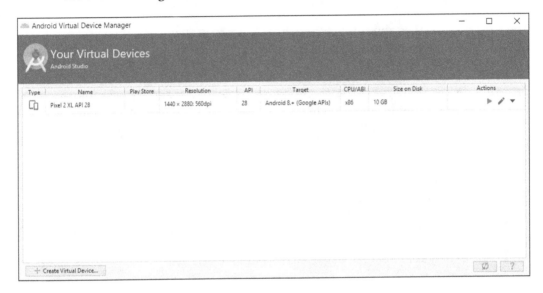

2. Notice that there is an emulator in the list. In my case, it is **Pixel 2 XL API 28**. If you are following this sometime in the future, it will be a different emulator that was installed by default. It won't matter. Click the green play icon (to the right) shown in the following screenshot and wait while the emulator boots up:

3. Now you can click the play icon on the Android Studio quick-launch bar as shown in the following screenshot, and when prompted, choose **Pixel 2 XL API 28** (or whatever your emulator is called) and the app will launch on the emulator:

You're done. Here is what the app looks like so far in the emulator. Remember that you might (and probably do) have a different emulator — that's fine:

Clearly, we have more work to do before we move to Silicon Valley and look for financial backing, but it is a good start.

We need to test and debug our apps often throughout development to check for any errors, crashes, or anything else unintended.

[We will see how we get errors and other feedback for debugging from our apps in the next chapter.]

It is also important to make sure it looks good and runs correctly on every device type/size that you want to target. Obviously, we do not own one of each of the many thousands of Android devices. This is where emulators come in.

Emulators, however, are sometimes a bit slow and cumbersome, although they have improved a lot recently. If we want to get a genuine feel for the experience our user will get then you can't beat deploying to a real device. So, we will want to use both real devices and emulators while developing our apps.

[If you are planning on using the emulator again soon, leave it running to avoid having to wait for it to start again.]

If you want to try out your app on a tablet, you're going to need a different emulator.

[

Creating a new emulator

If you want to create an emulator for a different Android device, this is simple. From the main menu, select **Tools | AVD Manager**. In the AVD Manager window, left-click **Create New Virtual Device**. Now left-click on the type of device you want to create—**TV**, **Phone**, **Wear OS**, or **Tablet**. Now simply left-click **Next** and follow the instructions to create your new AVD. Next time you run your app, the new AVD will appear as an option to run the app on. We will create a new tablet emulator step by step in the next chapter.

]

Now we can look at how to get our app onto a real device.

Running the app on a real device

The first thing to do is to visit your device manufacturer's website and obtain and install any drivers that are needed for your device and operating system.

 Most newer devices won't need a driver, so you may want to just try the following steps first.

The next few steps will set up the Android device for debugging. Note that different manufacturers structure the menu options slightly differently to others. But the following sequence is probably very close, if not exact, for enabling debugging on most devices:

1. Tap the **Settings** menu option or the **Settings** app on your phone/tablet.

2. This next step will vary slightly for different versions of Android. The **Developer options** menu is hidden away so as not to trouble regular users. You must perform a slightly odd task to unlock the menu option. Tap the **About device** or **About Phone** option. Find the **Build Number** option and repeatedly tap it until you get a message informing you that **You are now a developer!**

 Some manufacturers have different and obscure methods for achieving this step. If this step doesn't work, do a web search for your device and "unlocking developer options."

3. Go back to the **Settings** menu.

4. Tap **Developer options.**

5. Tap the checkbox for **USB Debugging.**

6. Connect your Android device to the USB port of your computer.

7. Click the play icon from the Android Studio toolbar, as shown in the following screenshot:

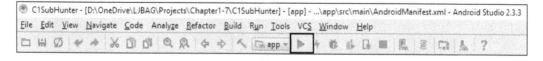

8. When prompted, click **OK** to run the game on your chosen device.

We are now ready to learn some Java and add our own Java code to the Hello World project.

Frequently asked questions

Q1) So, Android isn't really an operating system. Is it just a virtual machine and all the phones and tablets are really Linux machines?

A) No, all the different subsystems of an Android device, which include Linux, the DVM, and the libraries and drivers together, are what makes up the Android operating system.

Q2) I still don't understand all these technical terms, such as DVM, object-oriented and APK. Should I re-read this chapter?

A) No, this isn't necessary, as we just need to introduce this jargon and will be revisiting it all, as well as clarifying it as the book progresses. If you understand the following two points, you are ready to proceed to *Chapter 2, First Contact: Java, XML and the UI Designer*:

- We will be writing Java code and creating other resources
- Android Studio with the help of the JDK and will turn this code and resources into real Android apps.

Summary

So far, we have set up an Android development environment and created and deployed an app on both an emulator and a real device. If you still have unanswered questions (and you probably have more than at the start of the chapter) don't worry, because as we dig deeper into the world of Android and Java things will become clearer.

As the chapters progress, you will build a very rounded understanding of how everything fits together, and then success will just be a matter of practice and digging even deeper into the Android API.

In the next chapter, we will edit the UI using the visual designer and raw XML code, as well as write our first Java methods and get to use some of the methods provided for us by the Android API.

2
First Contact – Java, XML, and the UI Designer

At this stage, we have a working Android development environment and we have built and deployed our first app. It is obvious, however, that code auto-generated by Android Studio is not going to make the next top-selling app on the Google Play Store. We need to explore this auto-generated code so that we can begin to understand Android and then learn how to build on this useful template. With this aim in mind, in this chapter, we will do the following:

- See how to get technical feedback from our apps
- Examine the Java code and UI XML code from our first app
- Get our first taste of using the Android **User Interface** (**UI**) designer
- Write our first Java code
- Learn some core Java fundamentals and how they relate to Android

First, let's see how to get feedback from our apps.

Examining the log output

In the previous chapter, we mentioned that our app was running in debug mode on the emulator or real device so that we can monitor it and get feedback when things go wrong. So where is all this feedback then?

You might have noticed a whole load of scrolling text at the bottom of the Android Studio window. If not, click on the **logcat** tab, as shown by the highlighted area labelled as 1 in the following screenshot:

Note that the emulator must be running, or a real device must be attached in debugging mode, for you to see the following window. Furthermore, if you restarted Android Studio for some reason and have not yet executed the app, then the **logcat** window will be empty. Refer to the first chapter to get the app running on an emulator or a real device:

You can drag the window to make it taller, just like you can in most other Windows applications, if you want to see more.

This window is called the **logcat,** or sometimes it is referred to as the **console**. It is our app's way of telling us what is going on underneath what the user sees. If the app crashes or has errors, the reason or clues to the reason will appear here. If we need to output debugging information, we can do so here as well.

If you just cannot work out why your app is crashing, copy and pasting a bit of text from logcat into Google will often reveal the reason.

Filtering the logcat output

You might have noticed that most, if not all, of the content of logcat is almost unintelligible. That's OK. Now we are only interested in errors that will be highlighted red and the debugging information, about which we will learn next. So that we see less of the superfluous text in our **logcat** window, we can turn on a number of filters that will make things clearer.

In the previous screenshot, I highlighted two more areas as 2 and 3. Area 2 is the drop-down list that controls the first filter. Left-click it now and change it from **Verbose** to **Info**. We have cut down the text output significantly. We will see how this is useful when we have made some changes to our app and redeployed it. We will do this after we have explored the code and the assets that make up our project. Also, double check in the area that is labelled as 3 that it says **Show only the selected application**. If it doesn't, left-click on it and change it to **Show only the selected application** now.

Now we can look at what Android Studio automatically generated for us and then we can set about changing and adding to the code to personalize it beyond what we got from the project creation phase.

A note for early adopters of this book

At time of completing this book, Android 9 and Android Studio 3.2 had just been released. This book was written to accommodate these latest versions. One of the changes in the new releases is the way that Android supports devices running older versions of Android. It has just been significantly improved. Android uses a support library, which means that old devices (within reason) can make use of newer features.

The good news is that this book uses the new, improved version!

However, if you are a very early adopter (late 2018 and maybe into early 2019) of this book and you look very closely at the code generated by Android Studio, you will notice some slight differences with the code presented in the book. The differences occur in the import... statements at the top of the Java code files. The book presents code that looks a bit like this:

```
import androidx.appcompat.app.AppCompatActivity;
```

Whereas you might notice code in Android Studio 3.2 or earlier that looks a little more like this:

```
Import android.support.v7.app.AppCompatActivity;
```

Perhaps surprisingly, Android Studio version 3.2 auto-generates code that uses the old-style support library despite already fully supporting the new style (used in this book).

For the purposes of learning to make Android apps and code in Java, you can safely ignore these slight differences. All the code that this book uses remains the same, regardless of whether you are using the old style or the new style.

If Android Studio is auto-generating the old style and you want to bring your code up to date and have the exact same code as shown in this book, you can simply select **Refactor | Migrate to AndroidX...** immediately after you have started each new project and Android Studio has auto-generated the code from your chosen project template. This is optional and not required.

Note that for this refactoring option to be available you need Android Studio 3.2. So, if you had previously been learning Android programming with an older version of Android Studio then you will need to update it (when prompted at application startup). Again, this is optional; you could just ignore the slight differences.

If you keep Android Studio up to date when prompted to do so occasionally when you start the application, then soon you will notice that the new-style code is auto-generated for you.

Exploring the project's Java code and the main layout's XML code

We are going to look at the resource files that have the code that defines our simple UI layout and the file that has our Java code. At this stage, we will not try to understand it all as we need to learn some more basics before it makes sense to do so. What we will see, however, is the basic content and structure of both files so we can reconcile their content with what we already know about Android resources and Java.

Examining the HelloWorldActivity.java file

Let's look at the Java code first. You can see this code by left-clicking on the `HelloWorldActivity.java` tab, as shown in the following screenshot:

As we are not looking at the intricate details of the code, an annotated screenshot is more useful than reproducing the actual code in text form. Regularly refer to the following screenshot while reading on with this section:

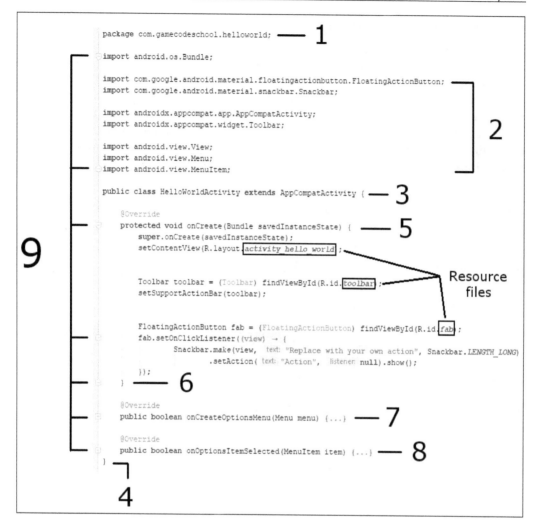

```
package com.gamecodeschool.helloworld;  —— 1

import android.os.Bundle;

import com.google.android.material.floatingactionbutton.FloatingActionButton;
import com.google.android.material.snackbar.Snackbar;

import androidx.appcompat.app.AppCompatActivity;
import androidx.appcompat.widget.Toolbar;                         2

import android.view.View;
import android.view.Menu;
import android.view.MenuItem;

public class HelloWorldActivity extends AppCompatActivity {  —— 3

    @Override
    protected void onCreate(Bundle savedInstanceState) {  —— 5
        super.onCreate(savedInstanceState);
        setContentView(R.layout.activity_hello_world);

        Toolbar toolbar = (Toolbar) findViewById(R.id.toolbar);
        setSupportActionBar(toolbar);

        FloatingActionButton fab = (FloatingActionButton) findViewById(R.id.fab);
        fab.setOnClickListener((view) -> {
            Snackbar.make(view, text: "Replace with your own action", Snackbar.LENGTH_LONG)
                    .setAction( text: "Action", listener: null).show();
        });
    }  —— 6

    @Override
    public boolean onCreateOptionsMenu(Menu menu) {...}  —— 7

    @Override
    public boolean onOptionsItemSelected(MenuItem item) {...}  —— 8
}
```

Resource files

9

4

The first thing to note is that I have added a few empty lines amongst the code to space things out a little bit and present a clearer image.

Code folding (hiding) in Android Studio

Now look at the left-hand side of the screenshot where multiple parts are labelled as **9**. This points to all the little **+** and **-** buttons in the editor that can collapse and expand parts of the code. I have indeed collapsed some parts of the code, and other parts I have left visible. So, what you can see on your screen is slightly different to what you will see if you look at the screenshot. In Android Studio, play with the **+** and **–** buttons for a while to practice hiding and unhiding sections of the code. You might like to get your screen to look like the screenshot, but this is not a requirement for continuing. The technical term for hiding code like this is **folding**.

The package declaration

Part **1** is called the **package declaration** and, as you can see, it is the package name we chose when we created the project preceded by the word `package`. Every Java file will have a package declaration at the top.

Importing classes

Part **2** is eight lines of code that all begin with the word `import`. After the word `import`, we can see there are various dot-separated words. The last word of each line is the name of the class that line imports into our project, and all the earlier words in each line are the packages and sub-packages that contain these classes.

For example, this next line imports the `AppCompatActivity` class from the `androidx.appcompat.app` package and sub-packages:

```
import androidx.appcompat.app.AppCompatActivity;
```

 The semi-colon at the end of the lines indicates to the compiler that it is the end of that line of code.

This means that in our project, we will have access to these classes. In fact, it is these classes that the auto-generated code uses to make our simple app that we saw in action in the previous chapter.

We will not discuss all these classes in this chapter. It is just the concept that we can do this `importing` that is significant right now. Note that we can add extra classes from any package at any time, and we will do so when we improve upon our app shortly.

The class

Part **3** of our code is called the **class declaration**. Here is that line in full and I have highlighted one part of it:

```
public class HelloWorldActivity extends AppCompatActivity {
```

The class declaration is the start of a class. Notice that the highlighted part, HelloWorldActivity, is the name we chose when we created the project, and it is also the same as the filename HelloWorldActivity.java, as we would expect having discussed Java classes previously. The extends keyword means that our class called HelloWorldActivity will be of the type AppCompatActivity. We can, and will, use some classes without this extends part.

We use extends here because we want to use all the code that went into the AppCompatActivity class, as well as adding our own code to it as well. So we **extend** it. All this and more will become clear in *Chapter 10, Object-Oriented Programming*.

Finally, for part **3,** look at the opening curly brace at the end of the line: {. Now look at the bottom of the screenshot at part **4** of our code. This closing curly brace } denotes the end of the class. Everything between the opening and closing curly braces, { . . . }, is part of the class.

Methods inside the class

Now look at part **5** of the code. Here is that line of code in full, with the key part for our current discussion highlighted:

```
protected void onCreate(Bundle savedInstanceState) {
```

This is a method **signature**. The highlighted part, onCreate, is the method **name**. We make a method execute its code by using its name. We say we are **calling** a method when we do this.

Although we will not concern ourselves now with the parts of the code on either side of the method name, you might have noticed Bundle, one of the classes we imported at part **2** of our code. If we removed that related import line, Android Studio would not know what Bundle was and it would be unusable and indicated by a red underline as an error.

Our code would then not compile and run. Notice the very last thing in the line of code above is an opening curly brace, {. This denotes the start of the code contained within the onCreate method. Now jump to part **6** of our code and you will see a closing curly brace, }. You might have guessed that this is the end of the method. Everything between the opening and closing curly braces of the onCreate method is the code that executes when the method is called.

We do not need to go into what this code does yet but, as an overview, it sets up the appearance/layout of the app by referring to some resource files that were auto-generated by Android Studio when we created the project. I have highlighted these resource files with an outline in the previous screenshot.

Parts **7** and **8** are also methods that I have collapsed to make the screenshot and this discussion more straightforward. Their names are `onCreateOptionsMenu` and `onOptionsItemSelected`.

We know enough about our Java code to make some progress. We will see this code for real and change it later in this chapter.

Summary of the Java code so far

It is true that contained within the code we have just had an overview of there is some complex syntax. However, what we are doing is building up just enough knowledge about this code so we can work within it to begin to make fast progress learning Java and Android without having to learn hundreds of pages of Java theory first. By the end of the book, all the code will make sense, but in order to make quick progress now, we just need to accept that some of the details will remain a mystery for a little while longer.

Examining the main layout file

Now we will look at just one of the many `.xml` files. There are several different layout files and we will meet them all throughout the course of the book, but let's start with the most significant one that decides most of the appearance of our app.

Left-click on the `content_hello_world.xml` tab next to the `HelloWorldActivity.java` tab that we have been discussing.

In the main window on the right-hand side, you will see the **Design** view of our app, as shown in the following screenshot:

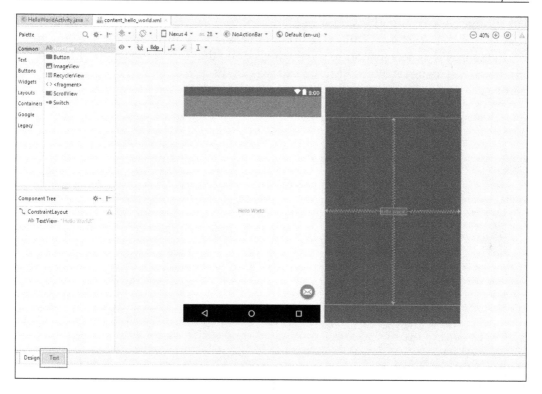

Most of the work that we do throughout the book when we design apps will be done in this design view. It is important, however, to know what is going on behind the scenes.

The design view is a graphical representation of the XML code contained in the `content_hello_world.xml` file. Click on the **Text** tab (as outlined near the bottom-left in the previous screenshot) to see the XML code that forms the layout. I have annotated a screenshot of the XML text so we can discuss it next:

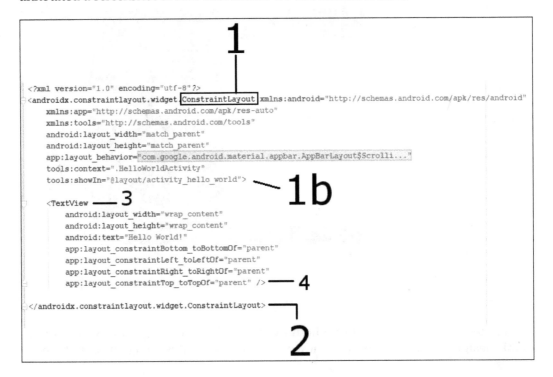

The first thing to note is that this file does not represent the entire layout. It does, however, represent most of the surface area and the **Hello World** message in the centre. Also, on the left-hand side, we can see the now- familiar **+** and **–** icons with which we can fold and unfold sections of the code.

UI layout elements

If we first look at the part of the code labeled **1**, we can see that the very first thing is ...`ConstraintLayout`.... A `ConstraintLayout` is a UI element that is used to wrap other parts of the UI.

When we add a new element to a UI in Android, we always start a line with a < followed by the element's name.

The code that follows that rather long and cumbersome looking line defines the **attributes** this element will have. This can include dozens of different things, depending on the type of UI element it is. Here, amongst a bit of other XML, we can see things such as `layout_width`, `layout_height` and `showIn`. All these attributes define how the `ConstraintLayout` will appear on the user's screen. The attributes for the `ConstraintLayout` end at the first `>` labelled **1b**.

If we look at the bottom of our XML screenshot, we will see the code labeled **2**. This code, `</...ConstraintLayout>`, marks the end of the `ConstraintLayout`. Anything between the closing `>` of the element's attributes, and the `</...ConstraintLayout>` that defines its end is considered a **child** of the element. So, we can see that our `ConstraintLayout` has/contains a child. Let's look at that child now.

UI text elements

Using what we just learned, we can devise that the UI element that starts at position **3** in the screenshot is called a `TextView`. Just like its parent, it starts with a `<` and its name: `<TextView....` If we look further into our `TextView`, we can see it has several attributes. It has a `text` attribute that is set to `"Hello world!"` This, of course, is the exact text that our app shows to the user. It also has `layout_width` and `layout_height` attributes that are both set to `"wrap_content."` This tells the `TextView` that it can take up as much space as the content it has needs. As we will see throughout the book, there are many more attributes available for this and other UI elements. The final attribute in the `TextView` is `id`, and we will see how we and Android use the `id` attribute in the next section when we improve this first app.

Notice that the code at the **4** position on our XML screenshot is `/>`. This marks the end of the `TextView` element. This is slightly different to how the end of the `ConstraintLayout` was written. When an element in XML has no children, we can just end it like this `/>`. When the element has children and its end comes further on in the code from where its attributes are defined, it is much clearer to end the element by repeating its name like this – `</...ConstraintLayout>`.

 You might be wondering why the element name for the `TextView` is clear and concise (simply `TextView`), yet the full name for the `ConstraintView` is preceded by complicated apparent clutter (`androidx.constraintlayout.widget.ConstraintLayout`). This `ConstraintLayout` is a special layout that is used to ensure our app's compatibility with older versions of Android. As we will see in a minute, when we add buttons to the app, most elements have simple and concise names.

We will edit this code in the next section and learn more about the attributes, as well as seeing another type of UI element—a `Button`.

Adding buttons to the main layout file

Here, we will add a couple of buttons to the screen, and we will then see a fast way to make them actually do something. We will add a button in two different ways: first, using the visual designer, and second, by adding to and editing XML code directly.

Adding a button via the visual designer

To get started adding our first button, switch back to the design view by clicking the **Design** tab underneath the XML code we have just been discussing, as shown next:

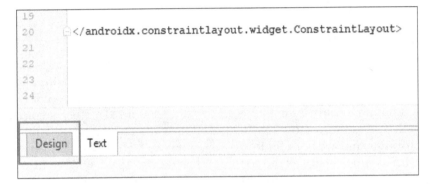

Notice that to the left-hand side of the layout, we have a window that is called the **Palette,** and this is shown next:

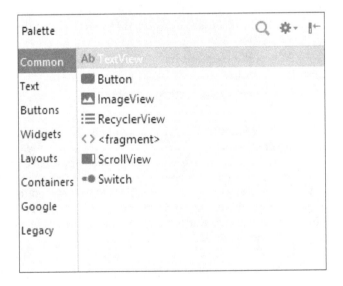

The palette is divided into two parts. The left-hand list has the categories of UI elements and allows you to select a category, while the right-hand side shows you all the available UI elements from the currently selected category.

Make sure that the **Common** category is selected as shown in the previous screenshot. Now, left-click and hold on the **Button** widget and then drag it onto the layout somewhere near the top and the center.

It doesn't matter if it is not exact. It is good to practice getting it right, however. So, if you are not happy with the position of your button, then you can left-click it to select it on the layout and then tap the *Delete* key on the keyboard to get rid of it. Now you can repeat the previous step until you have one neatly placed button that you are happy with, as demonstrated in the following diagram:

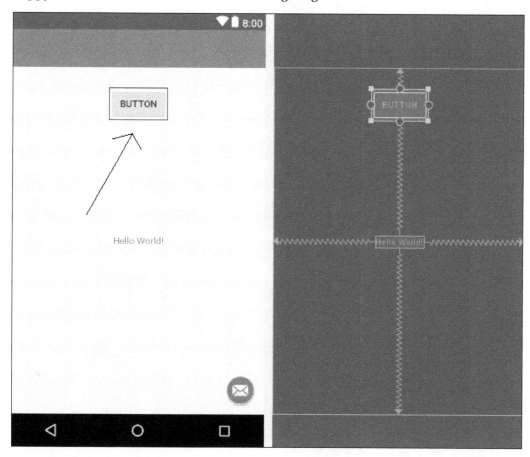

At this point, we could run the app on the emulator or on a real device and the button would be there. If we clicked it, there would even be a simple animation to represent the button being pressed and released. Feel free to try this now if you like.

However, the next best-selling app on the Google Play Store is going to need to do more than this. We are going to edit the attributes of our button using the **Attributes** window.

Editing the button's attributes

Make sure the button is selected by left-clicking it. Now find the **Attributes** window to the right of the editing window, as follows:

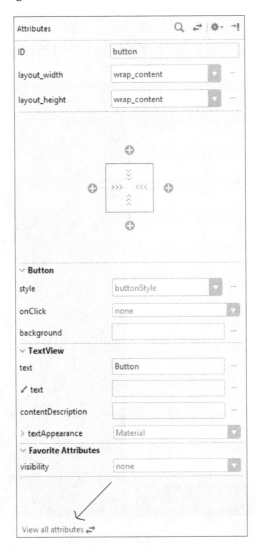

In the preceding screenshot, you can see that we have access to some, although not all, of the button's attributes. To reveal more of the attributes, click the **View all attributes** link (pointed to in the preceding screenshot).

Now you can see the full details of the button and we can set about editing it. It might seem surprising the substantial number of attributes something as apparently simple as a button has. This is a sign of the versatility and power that the Android API provides for UI manipulation. Look at the following screenshot showing the full attributes list for our recently added button:

Furthermore, notice that even the previous screenshot doesn't show everything, and you can use the scroll bar on the right of the **Attributes** window to reveal even more attributes.

As you can see, there is a large array of different attributes that we can edit right here in the UI designer. In *Chapter 11, More Object-Oriented Programming*, we will also edit and manipulate these attributes using our Java code. For now, we will edit just one attribute. Scroll through the **Attributes** window until you see the **onClick** attribute and then left-click it to select it for editing, as shown in the following screenshot:

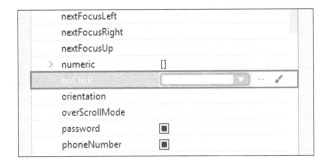

 The attributes are listed in alphabetical order, and **onClick** can be found about two-thirds of the way down the lengthy list.

Type `topClick` in the **onClick** attribute's edit box and press *Enter* on the keyboard. Be sure to use the same case, including the slightly counterintuitive lowercase `t` and upper-case `C`.

The **Attributes** window will look like this next screenshot when you are done:

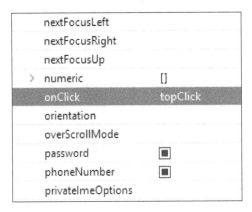

What we have done here is named the Java method in our code that we want to call when this button is clicked by the user. The name is arbitrary but, as this button is on the top part of the screen, the name seems meaningful and easy to remember. The odd casing that we used is a convention that will help us keep our code clear and easy to read. We will see the benefits of this as our code gets longer and more complicated.

Of course, the `topClick` method doesn't exist yet. Android Studio is very helpful, but there are some things we need to do for ourselves. We will write this method using Java code after we have added another button to our UI. You could run the app at this point and it would still work, but if you click the button it will crash and you will get an error because the method does not exist.

Examining the XML code for the new button

Before we add our final button for this project, click the **Text** tab below the editor to switch back to seeing the XML code that makes our UI.

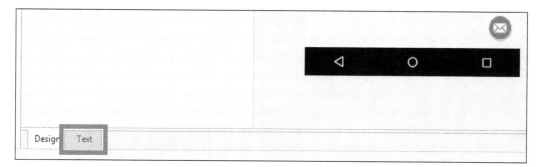

Notice that there is a new block of code amongst the XML that we examined earlier. Here is a screenshot of the new block of code:

```
<Button
    android:id="@+id/button"
    android:layout_width="wrap_content"
    android:layout_height="wrap_content"
    android:onClick="topClick"
    android:text="Button"
    tools:layout_editor_absoluteX="147dp"
    tools:layout_editor_absoluteY="30dp" />
```

Also notice the following details, which should correspond to what we know about XML and Android UI elements:

- The new code starts with the text `<Button` and ends with `/>`
- The code has a range of attributes that define the button, including `layoutWidth` and `layoutHeight`
- The code includes the `onClick` attribute that we added with a value of `"topClick"`
- The `topClick` value of the `onClick` attribute is underlined in red, showing an error
- The start and end of the code representing the button is enclosed within the `ConstraintLayout`.

Hover the mouse cursor over the red underlined `topClick` to reveal the details of the problem, as shown in this screenshot:

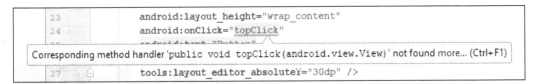

We can confirm that the issue is that Android Studio expects a method called `topClick` to be implemented within our code. We will do this as soon as we have added that second button.

Adding a button by editing the XML code

Just for variety, and to prove that we can, we will now add another button using only XML code, not the UI designer. Most of the time, we will use the UI designer, but this quick exercise should cement in your mind the relationship between the UI designer and the underlying XML code.

We will achieve this by copying and pasting the code for the existing button. We will then make some minor edits to the pasted code.

Left-click just before the button code that starts `<Button`. Notice that the beginning and end of the code now has a slight highlight:

```
<Button
    android:id="@+id/button"
    android:layout_width="wrap_content"
    android:layout_height="wrap_content"
    android:onClick="topClick"
    android:text="Button"
    tools:layout_editor_absoluteX="147dp"
    tools:layout_editor_absoluteY="30dp" />
```

This has identified the part of the code we want to copy. Now, left-click and drag to select all the button code, including the highlighted start and end, as shown in this next screenshot:

```
<Button
    android:id="@+id/button"
    android:layout_width="wrap_content"
    android:layout_height="wrap_content"
    android:onClick="topClick"
    android:text="Button"
    tools:layout_editor_absoluteX="147dp"
    tools:layout_editor_absoluteY="30dp" />
```

Press the *CTRL + C* keyboard combination to copy the highlighted text. Place the keyboard cursor below the existing button code and tap the *Enter* key a few times to leave some spare empty lines.

Press the *Ctrl + V* keyboard combination to paste the button code. At this point, we have two buttons. There are a couple of problems, however:

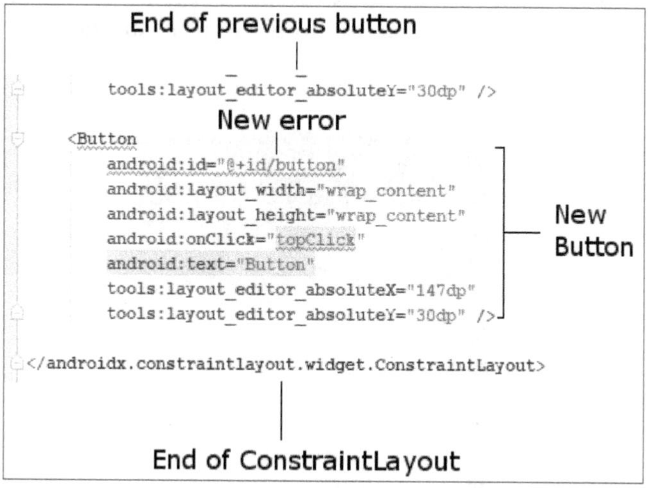

[53]

We have an additional error in both blocks of code that represent our buttons. The id attribute (in both blocks) is underlined in red. The reason for this error is that both buttons have an id attribute that is the same. The id attribute is supposed to distinguish a UI element from all other UI elements. Let's fix that.

Giving the buttons unique id attributes

We could solve the problem by calling the second button button2, but it would be more meaningful to change them both. Edit the code in the first button to give it an id of buttonTop. To do so, identify this following line of code (in the first button):

```
android:id="@+id/button"
```

And change it to this:

```
android:id="@+id/buttonTop"
```

 Notice the lowercase b in button and the uppercase T in Top.

Now identify this line of code in the second button:

```
android:id="@+id/button"
```

And change it to this:

```
android:id="@+id/buttonBottom"
```

The errors on the id attribute lines are gone. At this point, you might think we can move on to solve our missing method problem.

However, if you run the app and take a quick glance at it, you will see we only appear to have one button. Not only that, but the buttons are not in the place we expected them to be in either:

The reason for this is that we haven't explicitly positioned them, so they have defaulted to the top-left. The position we see on the **Design** tab is just a design-time position. Let's change that now.

Positioning the two buttons in the layout

The reason we can only see one button is that both buttons are in the same position. The second button is exactly covering the first button. And even in the **Design** tab (feel free to have a look), the buttons are still sat on top of each other, although they are in the middle of the screen:

 You might be wondering why the UI layout tool was designed in this apparently counterintuitive way. The reason is flexibility. As we will see in the next two chapters, not only is it possible to position UI elements differently at design time to when the app is running, but there is also a whole bunch of different layout schemes that the app designer (that's you) can choose from to suit their plans. This flexibility results in a little awkwardness while learning about Android and great design power once you have got past this awkwardness. Don't worry — we will move a step at a time until you have this thing beaten.

We will make Android Studio solve the problem for us automatically by first adding to our code and then using the UI designer. First, let's get the design time layout right. In the code for the second button, locate this line of code:

```
tools:layout_editor_absoluteY="30dp" />
```

Edit it to be the same as this:

```
tools:layout_editor_absoluteY="100dp" />
```

This subtle change will move the second button down a little, but only for design time. If you look in the **Design** tab, the button is positioned neatly underneath the first button, but if you run the app on the emulator, they are both still in the top-left corner and on top of one another.

Switch to the **Design** tab and find the **Infer Constraints** button shown in the following screenshot:

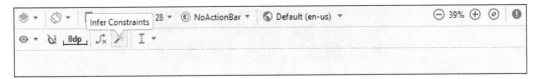

Click the **Infer Constraints** button. Android Studio will edit the XML. Let's take a brief look at what has happened behind the scenes. From the end of both of the buttons, the following lines of code were removed:

```
tools:layout_editor_absoluteX="147dp"
tools:layout_editor_absoluteY="30dp" />
```

These two lines of code were what positioned the buttons horizontally (...absoluteX) and vertically (...absoluteY).

Android Studio also added four lines of code to the first button and three to the second. Here is the code added near the start of the first button:

```
android:layout_marginTop="30dp"
```

This code causes the button to have a margin of 30 on the top. But on the top of what exactly? Look at these three lines of code that were added at the end of the first button:

```
app:layout_constraintEnd_toEndOf="parent"
app:layout_constraintStart_toStartOf="parent"
app:layout_constraintTop_toTopOf="parent" />
```

Notice the new attributes of `layout_constraintEnd_toEndOf`, `layout_constraintStart_toStartOf`, and `layout_constraintTop_toTopOf`. The value assigned to each of these attributes is `"parent"`. This causes the first button to be positioned relative to the *parent* UI element. The parent is the layout that contains everything else, the `ConstraintLayout`.

Now look at the three lines of code added to the second (bottom) button.

Near the start of the code we see the following:

```
android:layout_marginTop="22dp"
```

And at the end of the code for the second button, we see these two extra lines:

```
app:layout_constraintStart_toStartOf="@+id/buttonTop"
app:layout_constraintTop_toBottomOf="@+id/buttonTop" />
```

This means that the second button is positioned with a margin of 22 relative to `buttonTop`.

 The dp is a unit of measurement/distance and will be discussed in more depth in *Chapter 5, Beautiful Layouts with CardView and ScrollView*.

Now run the app and you will see that we have two distinct buttons. One has an id attribute of `buttonTop`, and it is above the other button, which has an id attribute of `buttonBottom`:

Clearly, there is more to layouts than I have alluded to so far, but you have had your first glance at one of the options provided by Android Studio to design the UI of our apps. We will be taking a closer look at `ConstraintLayout`, as well as exploring more layout options, in *Chapter 4, Getting Started with Layouts and Material Design*.

We want to make one more change to our XML code.

Making the buttons call different methods

Switch back to the **Text** tab and identify this next line of code in the second (`buttonBottom`) button:

```
android:onClick="topClick"
```

Edit the code to this:

```
android:onClick="bottomClick"
```

Now we have two buttons, one above the other. The top one has an `id` of `buttonTop` and an `onClick` attribute with a value of `topClick`. The other has an `id` of `buttonBottom` and an `onClick` attribute with a value of `bottomClick`.

These last XML code changes now mean we need to supply two methods (`topClick` and `bottomClick`) in our Java code.

 It is OK for two buttons to call the same method when they are clicked — it is not a syntax error. However, most buttons do have distinct purposes, so this exercise will be more meaningful if our buttons do different things.

We will do that soon, but before we do, let's learn a little bit more about Java comments and look at some Java code we can write to send messages to the user and to ourselves for debugging purposes.

Leaving comments in our Java code

In programming it is always a clever idea to write messages known as code comments and sprinkle them liberally amongst your code. This is to remind us of what we were thinking at the time we wrote the code. To do this, you simply append a double forward slash and then type your comment, as follows:

```
// This is a comment and it could be useful
```

In addition, we can use comments to comment out a line of code. Suppose we have a line of code that we temporarily want to disable. Then we can do so by adding two forward slashes, as follows:

```
// The code below used to send a message
// Log.i("info","our message here");
// But now it doesn't do anything
// And I am getting ahead of where I should be
```

 Using comments to comment out code should only be a temporary measure. Once you have found the correct code to use, commented-out code should be cut to keep the code file clean and organized.

Let's look at two separate ways to send messages in Android, and then we can write some methods that will send messages when our new UI buttons are pressed.

Coding messages to the user and the developer

In the introduction to this chapter and in the previous chapter, we talked a bit about using other people's code, specifically via the classes and their methods of the Android API. We saw that we could do some quite complex things with insignificant amounts of code (such as talking to satellites).

To get us started coding, we are going to use two different classes from the Android API that allow us to output messages. The first class, Log, allows us to output messages to the logcat window. The second class, Toast, is not a tasty breakfast treat, but it will produce a toast-shaped pop-up message for our app's user to see.

Here is the code we need to write to send a message to the logcat:

```
Log.i("info","our message here");
```

Exactly why this works will become clearer in *Chapter 10, Object-Oriented Programming*, but for now we just need to know that whatever we put between the two sets of quote marks will be output to the logcat window. We will see where to put this type of code shortly.

Here is the code we need to write in order to send a message to the user's screen:

```
Toast.makeText(this, "our message",
    Toast.LENGTH_SHORT).show();
```

This is a very convoluted-looking line of code, and exactly how it works will, again, not become clear until *Chapter 9, Java Methods*. The important thing here is that whatever we put between the quote marks will appear in a pop-up message to our users.

Let's put some code like we have just seen into our app for real.

Writing our first Java code

So, we now know the code that will output to logcat or the user's screen. But where do we put the code? To answer this question, we need to understand that the onCreate method in HelloWorldActivity.java executes as the app is preparing to be shown to the user. So, if we put our code at the end of this method, it will run just as the user sees it. Sounds good.

We know that to execute the code in a method, we need to **call** it. We have wired our buttons up to call a couple of methods, `topClick` and `bottomClick`. Soon, we will write these methods. But who or what is calling `onCreate`? The answer to this mystery is that Android itself calls `onCreate` in response to the user clicking the app icon to run the app. In *Chapter 6, The Android Lifecycle*, we will look deeper, and it will be clear exactly what code executes and when. You don't need to completely comprehend this now. I just wanted to give you an overview of what was going on.

Let's quickly try this out. Switch to the `HelloWorldActivity.java` tab in Android Studio.

We know that the `onCreate` method is called just before the app starts for real. Let's copy and paste some code into the `onCreate` method of our Hello World app and see what happens when we run it.

Adding message code to the onCreate method

Find the closing curly brace, }, of the `onCreate` method and add the highlighted code as shown next. In the code, I haven't shown the complete content of the `onCreate` method but have used ... to indicate a number of lines of code not being shown. The important thing is to place the new code (shown in full) right at the end, but before that closing curly brace, }:

```
@Override
protected void onCreate(Bundle savedInstanceState) {
...

...

...

    // Your code goes here
    Toast.makeText(this, "Can you see me?",
        Toast.LENGTH_SHORT).show();

    Log.i("info", "Done creating the app");
}
```

Notice that the two instances of the word `Toast` and the word `Log` are highlighted in red in Android Studio. They are errors. We know that `Toast` and `Log` are classes and that classes are containers for code.

The problem is that Android Studio doesn't know about them until we tell it about them. We must add an `import` for each class. Fortunately, this is semi-automatic.

Left-click anywhere in the `onCreate` method. Now hold the *Alt* key and then tap *Enter*. You need to do this step twice; once for `Toast` and once for `Log`. Android Studio adds the import directives at the top of the code with our other imports and the errors are gone.

Alt + Enter is just one of many useful keyboard shortcuts. The following is a keyboard shortcut reference for Android Studio. More specifically, it is for the IntelliJ Idea IDE, upon which Android Studio is based. Look at and bookmark this web page. It will be invaluable over the course of this book:

```
http://www.jetbrains.com/idea/docs/IntelliJIDEA_
ReferenceCard.pdf
```

Scroll to the top of `HelloWorldActivity.java` and look at the added `import` directives. Here they are for your convenience:

```
import android.util.Log;
import android.widget.Toast;
```

Run the app in the usual way and look at the output in the **logcat** window.

Examining the output

The following is a screenshot of the output in the logcat window:

```
com.gamecodeschool.helloworld  W/hool.helloworl: Accessing hidden
com.gamecodeschool.helloworld  W/hool.helloworl: Accessing hidden
com.gamecodeschool.helloworld  I/info: Done creating the app
com.gamecodeschool.helloworld  I/ConfigStore: android::hardware::
com.gamecodeschool.helloworld  I/ConfigStore: android::hardware::
```

Looking at the logcat, you can see that our message—**Done creating the app**—was output, although it is mixed up amongst other system messages that we are currently not interested in. If you watched the emulator when the app first starts, you will also see the neat pop-up message that the user will see:

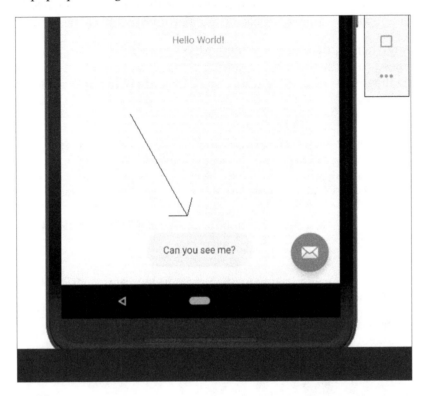

It is possible that you might be wondering why the messages were output at the time they were. The simple answer is that the onCreate method is called just before the app starts to respond to the user. It is common practice among Android developers to put code in this method to get their apps set up and ready for user input.

Now we will go a step further and write our own methods that are called by our UI buttons. We will place similar Log and Toast messages inside them.

Writing our own Java methods

Let's get straight on with writing our first Java methods with some more Log and Toast messages inside them. Open our Hello World project in Android Studio if it is not open already.

Now would be a good time, if you haven't done so already, to get the download bundle that contains all the code files. You can view the completed code for each chapter. For example, the completed code for this chapter can be found in the Chapter 2 folder. I have further subdivided the Chapter 2 folder into java and res folders (for Java and resource files). In chapters with more than one project, I will divide the folders further to include the project name. You should view these files in a text editor. My favourite is Notepad++, a free download from https://notepad-plus-plus.org/download/. The code viewed in a text editor is easier to read than from the book directly, especially the paperback version, and even more so where the lines of code are long. The text editor is also a great way to select sections of the code to copy and paste into Android Studio. You could open the code in Android Studio, but then you risk mixing up my code with the auto-generated code of Android Studio.

Identify the closing curly brace, }, of the HelloWorldActivity class.

Note that you are looking for the end of the entire class, not the end of the onCreate method, as in the previous section. Take your time to identify the new code and where it goes amongst the existing code.

Inside that curly brace, enter the following code that is highlighted:

```
@Override
protected void onCreate(Bundle savedInstanceState) {
    ...
    ...
    ...
    ...
}

    ...
    ...
    ...


public void topClick(View v){
        Toast.makeText(this, "Top button clicked",
            Toast.LENGTH_SHORT).show();

        Log.i("info","The user clicked the top button");
}

public void bottomClick(View v){
```

```
        Toast.makeText(this, "Bottom button clicked",
            Toast.LENGTH_SHORT).show();


        Log.i("info","The user clicked the bottom button");
    }

} // This is the end of the class
```

Notice that the two instances of the word View are red, indicating an error. Simply use the *Alt* | *Enter* keyboard combination to import the View class and remove the errors.

Deploy the app to a real device or emulator in the usual way and start tapping the buttons so we can observe the output.

Examining the output

At last, our app does something we told it to do when we told it to do it. We can see that the method names we defined in the button onClick attribute are indeed called when the buttons are clicked, and that the appropriate messages are added to the logcat window and the appropriate Toast messages shown to the user.

Admittedly, we still don't understand why Toast and Log really work, and neither do we fully comprehend the public void and (View v) parts of our method's syntax or much of the rest of the auto-generated code. This will become clear as we progress. As stated previously, in *Chapter 10, Object-Oriented programming,* we will take a deep dive into the world of classes, and in *Chapter 9, Java Methods,* we will master the rest of the syntax associated with methods.

Check the logcat output. You can see that a log entry was made from the onCreate method just as before, as well as from the two methods that we wrote ourselves, each time you clicked a button. In the following screenshot, you can see I clicked each button three times:

```
com.gamecodeschool.helloworld I/info: The user clicked the top button
com.gamecodeschool.helloworld I/info: The user clicked the top button
com.gamecodeschool.helloworld I/info: The user clicked the top button
com.gamecodeschool.helloworld I/info: The user clicked the bottom button
com.gamecodeschool.helloworld I/info: The user clicked the bottom button
com.gamecodeschool.helloworld I/info: The user clicked the bottom button
```

As you are now familiar with where to find the logcat window, in future, I will present logcat output as trimmed text as follows, as it is clearer to read:

```
The user clicked the top button
The user clicked the top button
The user clicked the top button
The user clicked the bottom button
The user clicked the bottom button
The user clicked the bottom button
```

And in the following screenshot, you can see that the top button has been clicked and that the `topClick` method was called, triggering the pop-up `Toast` message highlighted as follows:

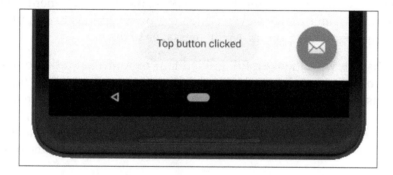

Throughout this book, we will regularly output to the logcat so we can see what is going on behind the UI of our apps. Toast messages are more for notifying the user that something has occurred. This might be that a download that has completed, that a new email has arrived, or some other occurrence that needs their attention.

Frequently asked questions

Q1) Can you remind me what methods are?

A) Methods are containers for our code that can be executed (called) from other parts of our code. Methods are contained within a class.

Q2) Like the first, I found this chapter tough going. Do I need to re-read it?

A) No. If you managed to build the app, you have made enough progress to handle all of the next chapter. All the blanks in our knowledge will be steadily filled in and replaced with glorious moments of realization as the book progresses.

Summary

We have achieved a lot in this chapter. It is true that much of the XML code is still generally incomprehensible. That's OK, because in the next two chapters, we will be really getting to grips with the visual designer and learning more about the XML code, although, ultimately, our aim is to use the XML as little as possible.

We have seen how, when we drag a button onto our design, the XML code is generated for us. Also, if we change an attribute in the **Attributes** window then, again, the XML code is edited for us. Furthermore, we can type (or, in our case, copy and paste) the XML code directly to create new buttons on our UI or edit existing ones.

We have seen as well as written our first Java code, including comments that help us document our code, and we have even added our own methods to output debugging messages to the logcat and pop-up `Toast` messages to the user.

In the next chapter, we will take a full guided tour of Android Studio to see exactly where different things get done, while at the same time understanding how our project's assets, such as files and folders, are structured and how we can manage them. This will prepare us for a more in-depth look at UI design in *Chapter 4, Getting started with layouts and Material Design,* and *Chapter 5, Beautiful Layouts with CardView and ScrollView,* when we will build some significant real-world layouts for our apps.

3
Exploring Android Studio and the Project Structure

In this chapter, we will create and run two more Android projects. The purpose of these exercises is to explore more deeply Android Studio and the structure of Android projects.

When we build our apps ready for deployment, the code and the resource files need to be packed away in the APK file—just so. Therefore, all the layout files and other resources, which we will be looking at soon, need to be in the correct structures.

Fortunately, Android Studio handles this for us when we create a project from a template. However, we still need to know how to find and amend these files, how to add our own and sometimes remove the files created by Android Studio, and how the resource files are interlinked—sometimes with each other and sometimes with the Java code (auto-generated Java code as well as our own).

Along with understanding the composition of our projects, it will also be beneficial to make sure we get the most from the emulator.

 Emulators are particularly useful when you want to make sure that your app will work on hardware that you don't own. Also, learning about some of the latest features (as we will in this book) often needs the latest handset, and an emulator is the cost-effective way of following along with all the mini-apps without buying the latest phone.

In this chapter, we will do the following:

- Explore the file and folder structure of the **Empty Activity** project template
- See the difference between the Empty Activity and the **Basic Activity** templates
- Find out how to get the most from the emulator

This chapter will leave us in a good position to build and deploy multiple different layouts in the next chapter.

A quick guided tour of Android Studio

To get started, look at this annotated diagram of Android Studio, and then we will reacquaint ourselves with the parts we have already seen and look more deeply too, finding out about the parts that we have not discussed yet:

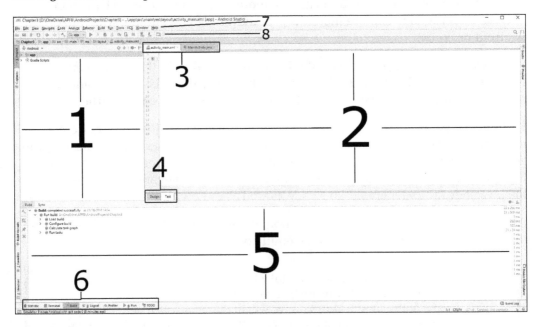

I thought it would be useful to formally point out and name the various parts of the Android Studio user interface so that I can refer to them by name rather than describing their location and showing images all the time. So, let's run through them from number 1:

1. This is the **Project** window and will be the focus of much of this chapter. It enables us to explore the folders, code, and resources of the project, and is also referred to as the Project Explorer. Double-click a file here to open the file and add a new tab to area 3 on the diagram. The structure of the files and folders here closely resembles the structure that will eventually end up in the finished APK.

> As we will see, while the structure of folders for an Android project remains the same, the files, the filenames, and the contents of the files vary considerably. Therefore, we will explore two projects in this chapter and then even more as we progress through the book.

2. This is the **Editor** window. As we have already seen, the editor window takes a few different forms depending on what it is we are editing. If we are editing Java, then we can see our code neatly formatted and ready for editing; if we are designing a UI, then it offers us either a visual editing view or a text/XML code view. You can also view and edit graphics and other files in this window.

3. These tabs let us switch between the different files in our project. The Editor window will display the file we select here. We can add another tab to this section by double-clicking on it in the **Project** window.

4. This allows us to switch between **Design** and **Text** (code) view on the file currently being edited.

5. This window varies depending upon the option selected in part 6 of the diagram. Typically, in this book, we will switch between the **Build** window, to see that our project has been compiled and launched without errors, and the **Logcat** window, to view the debugging output and any errors or crash reports from our apps.

6. This area of the UI is used to switch the different displays described in part 5.

> There are even more tabs in Android Studio, but we won't need them in the context of this book.

Now we know how to unambiguously refer to the various parts of the UI, let's turn our attention to the **Project/Project Explorer** window.

Project Explorer and project anatomy

When we create a new Android project, we most often do so using a project template, just as we did in *Chapter 1, Beginning Android and Java*. The template we use determines the exact selection and contents of files that Android Studio will generate. While there are big similarities across all projects that are worth noting, seeing the differences can also help. Let's build two template projects and examine the files, their contents, and how they are all linked together through the code (XML and Java).

The Empty Activity project

The simplest project type with an auto-generated UI is the Empty Activity project. The UI is empty, but it is there ready to be added to. It is possible to generate a project without a UI at all as well. When we create a project, even with an empty UI, Android Studio also auto-generates the Java code to display the UI. Therefore, when we add to it, it is ready to be displayed.

Let's create an **Empty Activity** project. This is almost the same process as we did in *Chapter 1, Beginning Android and Java*, but with one slight difference, which I will point out:

1. In Android Studio, select **File | New | New Project....**

2. In the **Create Android Project** screen, change the **Name** field to **Empty Activity App.**

3. The rest of the settings can be left at their defaults, so just click **Next.**

4. In the **Target Android Devices** window, leave all the default settings and click **Next.**

5. On the **Add an Activity to Mobile** window, select **Empty Activity,** as shown in the next screenshot. This is the bit that is different to what we did in *Chapter 1, Beginning Android and Java*:

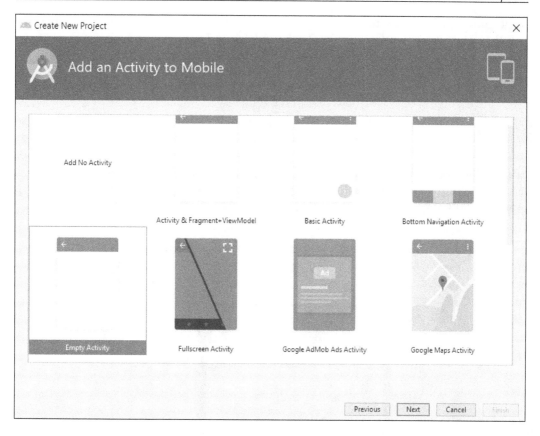

6. Click **Next.**

7. On the **Configure Activity** window, you can again leave the default settings, as we do want Android Studio to generate a layout file, as well as make the app backwards compatible for older versions of Android. So, just click the **Finish** button and wait for Android Studio to do its work.

Android Studio will generate all the code and the other project resources. Now we can see what has been generated and compare it to what we expected in the project explorer window.

If the emulator is not already running, launch it by selecting **Tools | AVD Manager** and then start your emulator in the **Android Virtual Devices** window if it's not already running. Run the app on the emulator by clicking the play button in the quick-launch bar:

Look at the app and notice how it is a little bit different to that of the first project. It is, well, empty. No menu at the top, no floating button at the bottom. It does, however, still have the **Hello World!** text:

 Don't worry about referring to the first project; we will build another one just like it soon.

Now that we have a brand new **Empty Activity App** project, let's explore the files and folders that Android Studio has generated for us.

Exploring the Empty Activity project

Now it is time to go on a deep-dive into the files and folders of our app. This will save us lots of time and head-scratching later in the book. Please note, however, that there is no need to memorize where all these files go, and there is even less need to understand the code within the files. In fact, parts of the XML will remain a mystery at the end of the book, but it will not stop you designing, coding, and releasing amazing apps.

Look at the project explorer window as it is just after the project is created:

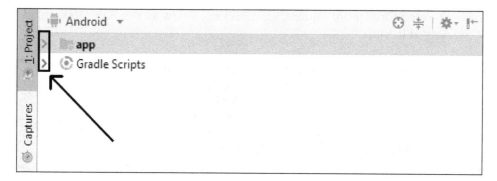

Notice the two arrows indicated in the previous screenshot. These, as you probably can guess, allow us to expand the app and Gradle Scripts folders.

We do not need to explore the Gradle Scripts folder in the context of this book. Gradle is a significant part of Android Studio, but its role is to hide from the user the quite complicated processes that Android Studio performs: things such as adding resource files and compiling and building projects. Therefore, we don't need to dig into this any further. If, however, you decide to take Android to the next level, then getting a good understanding of Gradle and its relationship with Android Studio is time well invested.

We will explore in detail the app folder. Click the arrow next to the app folder to expand its contents and we will begin exploring. The first level of contents is shown in the next screenshot:

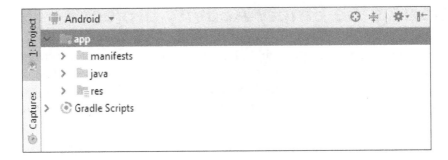

We have revealed three more folders: manifests, java, and res. Let's look in all three, starting at the top.

 The style guidelines that Packt uses for its books suggest **this font** for text that appears on the user's screen and this font for file and folder names. As the files and folders that we are discussing are both files and folders as well as appearing on the screen, I have opted for using just the latter font for consistency, and because it is more compact, and I will use this option whenever the choice is ambiguous throughout the book.

The manifests folder

The manifests folder has just one file inside it. Expand the manifests folder and double-click the AndroidManifest.xml file. Notice the file has been opened in the editor window and a tab has been added so we can easily switch back between this and other files. The next screenshot shows the new tab that has been added, as well as the XML code contained in the AndroidManifest.xml file within the manifests folder:

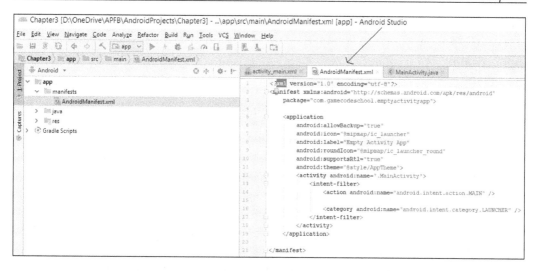

We don't need to understand everything in this file, but it is worth pointing out that we will make occasional amendments here; for example, when we need to ask the user for permission to access features of their device. We will also edit this file when we want to make a full-screen app for immersion, like, perhaps, for a game.

Notice that the structure of the file is very similar to the structure of the layout file that we saw in the previous chapter. For instance, there are clearly denoted sections which start with `<section name` and end with `</section name>`. Real examples of this are `<application` and `</application>` and `<activity` and `</activity>`.

Indeed, the entire file contents, apart from the first line, are wrapped in `<manifest` and `</manifest>`.

Just as though we were entering the brackets of a calculation into a calculator, these opening and closing parts must match or else the file will cause an error in our project. Android Studio indents (places tabs) in front of the lines to make the sections and their depth in this structure clearer.

A couple of specific parts of this code are worth noting, so I will point out some of the lines.

The line shown next tells Android that the icon we want to show the user in their app drawer/home screen to launch the app is contained in the `mipmap` folder and is called `ic_launcher`:

```
android:icon="@mipmap/ic_launcher"
```

We will verify this for ourselves as we continue our exploration.

The next line has two aspects worth discussing. First, it denotes the name that we gave our app; and second, that name is contained as a **String** with a label of `app_name`:

```
android:label="@string/app_name"
```

> In programming, including Java and XML, a String is any alphanumeric value. We will learn loads more about Strings throughout the book, starting in *Chapter 7, Java Variables, Operators, and Expressions*. We can therefore guess that the alphanumeric value of the label of `app_name` is `Empty Activity App`, because that is what we called the app when we created it.

This might sound slightly odd, but we will see this file soon, and its label. And, in later projects, we will add more labels and values to it. We will also come to understand the reasons why we add text to our apps in what might, at this stage, seem like a quite convoluted manner.

We could discuss every line in the `AndroidManifest.xml` file, but we don't need to. Let's look at just two more as they are related to each other. The line shown next indicates the name of our Activity, which we chose when we created the project. I have highlighted the Activity name just to make it stand out:

```
<activity android:name=".MainActivity">
```

And this next line, which appears within the `<activity` and `</activity>` tags, denotes that it is an attribute of the `activity`, showing that this Activity is the one which should run when the app is started. It is the LAUNCHER:

```
<category android:name="android.intent.category.LAUNCHER" />
```

This implies that our apps can have more than one Activity. Very often, if you have an app with multiple screens, such as a home screen or settings screen, those screens are built from multiple Activity class **instances**.

A note about `Activity` and `activity`. In XML, such as the `AndroidManifest` file, `activity` is in lowercase; but in Java, the `Activity` class has an uppercase `A`. This is just convention and nothing to be concerned about. As we have just seen, `activity` in XML has a `name` attribute with a value which refers to an instance of a Java `Activity`.

Let's dig into the `java` folder. I wonder what we will find in there.

The java folder

I apologize for the slightly sarcastic comment. We will, of course, find all the Java code. To begin with, this consists of just one file, but as our projects grow we will add more. Expand the `java` folder and you will find three more folders, as shown in this next screenshot:

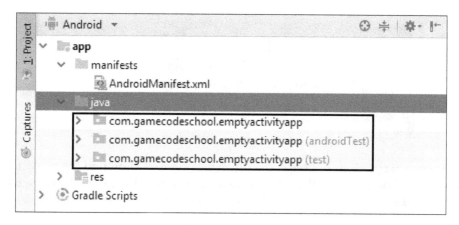

During this book, we will only need one of these three folders. The top one. The names of these folders are composed of the package name (chosen when we created the app) and the app name in all lowercase and no spaces (also chosen when we created the app).

 The reason there is more than one folder with the same name is for advanced reasons to do with automated testing, which is beyond the scope of this book. Therefore, you can safely ignore the folders that end with `(androidTest)` and `(test)`.

The only folder we are interested in during the course of this book is the top one, which for this app (on my screen) is com.gamecodeschool.emptyactivityapp. Depending upon your chosen package name and the name of the app we are currently working on, the folder name will change, but it will always be the top one that we need to access and add or edit the contents of.

Expand the com.gamecodeschool.emptyactivityapp (or whatever yours is called) folder now to view its contents. In the next screenshot, you can see that the folder has just one file:

It is MainActivity.java, although the file extension isn't shown in the project window even though it is in the tabs above the editor window. In fact, all the files in the java/packagename.appname folder will all be of the extension .java.

If you double-click the MainActivity.java file, it will open in the editor window, although we could have just clicked the MainActivity.java tab above the editor window. As we add more Java files, knowing where they are kept will be useful.

Examine the MainActivity.java file and you will see it is a simplified version of the Java file we worked with in the first project. It is mostly the same, except that there are fewer methods and less code in the onCreate method. The methods are missing because the UI is simpler and therefore they are not needed, and Android Studio didn't generate them.

For reference, look at the contents of the MainActivity.java file in this next screenshot. I have outlined one line from the code:

```
package com.gamecodeschool.emptyactivityapp;

import ...

public class MainActivity extends AppCompatActivity {

    @Override
    protected void onCreate(Bundle savedInstanceState) {
        super.onCreate(savedInstanceState);
        setContentView(R.layout.activity_main);
    }

}
```

It still has the onCreate method, which runs when the app is run, but there is much less code in it and onCreate is the only method. Look at the last line of code in the onCreate method, which we will discuss before moving on to explore the res folder. Here is the line of code under discussion:

```
setContentView(R.layout.activity_main);
```

The code is calling a method named setContentView, and it is passing some data into setContentView for the code in the setContentView method to make use of. The data being passed to setContentView is R.layout.activity.main.

For now, I will just mention that the setContentView method is provided by the Android API and it is the method that prepares and displays the UI to the user. So, what exactly is R.layout.activity_main

Let's find out by exploring the res folder.

The res folder

The res folder is where all the resources go. Left-click to expand the res folder and we will examine what's inside. Here is a screenshot of the top level of folders inside the res folder:

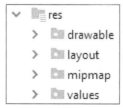

Let's begin with the top of the list. The drawable folder.

The res/drawable folder

The name gives things away a little bit, but the `drawable` folder holds much more than just graphics. As we progress through the book, we will indeed add graphics to this folder. However, now it holds just two files.

They are `ic_launcher_foreground` and `ic_launcher_background`. We will not examine these files because we will never need to alter them, but I will just mention what they are.

If you open the files, you will see they are quite long and technical. They include what appears to be lists of coordinates, colors, and more besides. They are what is known as a **graphical mask**.

They are used by Android to adapt/mask other graphics; in this case, the launcher icon of the app. The files are instructions to Android on how to adapt the app launcher icon.

This system is made available so that different device manufacturers can create their own masks to suit their own Android devices. The masks, which are in `drawable` by default (`ic_launcher_foreground` and `ic_launcher_background`), are default adaptive masks that add visually pleasing shadows and depth to the launcher icon.

If the concept of adaptive icons is interesting to you, then you can see a full and a very visual explanation at this link to the Android developer's website: `https://developer.android.com/guide/practices/ui_guidelines/icon_design_adaptive`.

We know enough about `drawable`; let's move on to `layout`.

The res/layout folder

Expand the `layout` folder and you will see our familiar layout file, which we edited in the previous chapter. There is less in it this time because we generated an Empty Activity project. It is not entirely empty, as it still holds a `ConstraintLayout` wrapping a `TextView` that says `Hello World!`.

Be sure to look at the contents—you should find it looks as you might expect, but it is not the contents that are most interesting here. Look closely at the name of the file (without the XML file extension): `activity_main`.

Now think back to the Java code in the `MainActivity.java` file. Here is the line of code that we said sets up the user interface. I have highlighted a portion of the code:

```
setContentView(R.layout.activity_main);
```

The `R.layout.activity_main` code is indeed a reference to the `activity_main` file within the `res/layout` folder. This is the connection between our Java code and our XML layout/design.

If you look closely at the name of the layout file in the last project, you will see it is quite different. It was `activity_hello_world`. And, as you would now expect, we had the following line of code that prepared the UI:

```
setContentView(R.layout.activity_hello_world);
```

The difference is because Android Studio interprets our chosen Activity name when it generates the layout file. In the previous project, we named the Activity `HelloWorldActivity`; in this project, we just left it at the default: `MainActivity`.

There is another difference in the first project. In the `layout` folder of the first project, there is an additional file. Later in this chapter, we will build another project using the same template we used in the first chapter (Basic Activity) to understand why.

Before that, let's explore the final two folders and all their sub-folders, starting with the next on the list, `mipmap`.

The res/mipmap

The `mipmap` folder is straightforward – that is, fairly straightforward. Expand the folder to see its contents, as shown in this next screenshot:

Here we can see two sub-folders. They are `ic_launcher` and `ic_launcher_round`. The contents of `ic_launcher` are the graphics for the regular launcher icon we see in the app drawer/home screen of the device, and `ic_launcher_round` holds the graphics for devices that use round icons. Double-click on one of the `.png` files from each folder to have a look. I have photoshopped one of each side by side in this next screenshot to aid our discussion:

You are probably also wondering why there are five `ic_launcher....png` files in each folder. The reason for this is that it is good practice to provide icons that are suitably scaled for different sizes and resolutions of screen. Providing an image with the qualifications `hdpi`, `mdpi`, `xhdpi`, `xxhdpi` and `xxxhdpi` allows different Android devices to choose the icon that will look best for the user.

> The letters `dpi` stand for **dots-per-inch,** and the h, m, xh, xxh, and xxxh prefixes stand for high, medium, extra high, extra extra high, and so on. These are known as **qualifiers**, and we will see as we progress that Android has lots of qualifiers, which help us build our apps to suit the wide range of different devices available for users to choose from.

The final conundrum from the `mipmap` folder is that there is also an XML file in each of the two sub folders. Open one of them up and you will see that they refer to the `ic_launcher_foreground` and `ic_launcher_background` files that we looked at in the `drawable` folder. This tells the Android device where to get the details for the adaptive icons. These files are not required, but they make the icons look better, as well as adding flexibility to the appearance.

We have one more folder and all its files to look at, and then we will understand the structure of an Android app well.

res/values

Open the `res/values` folder to reveal three files that we will talk about briefly in turn. All these files interlink/refer to each other and/or other files that we have seen already.

For the sake of completeness, here is a screenshot of the three files in the `res/values` folder:

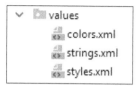

The key to understanding is not in memorizing the connections, and certainly not in trying to memorize or even understand the code in the files, but rather to get an appreciation of the interlinked nature of all the files and code we have seen so far.

Let's glance inside the files one at a time.

The colors.xml file

Look next at the contents of the `colors.xml` file:

```
<?xml version="1.0" encoding="utf-8"?>
<resources>
    <color name="colorPrimary">#008577</color>
    <color name="colorPrimaryDark">#00574B</color>
    <color name="colorAccent">#D81B60</color>
</resources>
```

Notice the starting and closing tags take the usual pattern we have come to expect from XML files. There is an opening `<resources>` tag and a closing `</resources>` tag. As children of `resources`, there are three pairs of `<color>` ... `</color>` tags.

Within each `color` tag is contained a `name` attribute and some curious-looking code consisting of numbers and letters. The `name` attribute is the name of a color. We will see, in another of the files that follow, that the various names are referred to.

The code is what defines an actual color itself. Therefore, when the name is referred to, the color defined by the related code is what is produced on the screen.

The code is called a hexadecimal code because in each position of the code, the values 0 through 9 and a through f can be used, giving 16 possible values. If you want to find out more and play around with hex colours, visit http://www.color-hex.com/color-wheel/. If you are intrigued about number bases, such as hexadecimal (base 16), binary (base 2), and others, then look at this article, which explains them and talks about why humans typically use base 10: https://betterexplained.com/articles/numbers-and-bases/.

We will see where these names are referred to in a moment.

The strings.xml file

Most modern apps are made for as wide an audience as possible. Furthermore, if the app is of a significant size or complexity, then the roles in the software company are often divided up into many different teams. For example, the person writing the Java code for an Android app very possibly had little to do with designing the layout of the user interface.

By separating the content of the app from the programming of the app, it is easier to make changes at any time, and it is also possible to create content for multiple different languages without altering the Java code for each.

Look at the contents of the strings.xml file:

```
<resources>
    <string name="app_name">Empty Activity App</string>
</resources>
```

We can see that, within the now-familiar <resources>...</resources> tags, we have a <string>...</string> tag. Within the string tag, there is an attribute called name with an app_name value and then a further value of Empty Activity App.

Let's look at one more line from the AndroidManifest.xml file we explored earlier in *The manifests folder* section. The line in question follows next, but refer to the file itself in Android Studio if you want to see the line in its full context:

```
android:label="@string/app_name"
```

The android:label attribute is being assigned a value of @string/app_name. In Android, @string refers to all the strings in the strings.xml file. In this specific app, the string attribute with the app_name label has the value Empty Activity App.

Therefore, the line of code in the `AndroidManifest.xml` file shown previously has the following effect on the screen when the app is running:

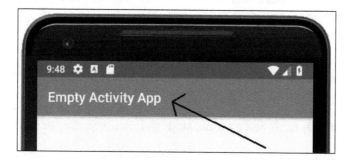

Although at first this system might seem convoluted, in practice it separates design and content from coding, which is very efficient to do. If the designers want to change the name of the app, they simply edit the `strings.xml` file. No need to interact with the Java programmers. And, if all text in an app is provided as a string resource, then all of it can be easily altered and adapted as the project proceeds.

Android takes the flexibility further by allowing developers to use different files for string resources for each language/locale. This means that a developer can cater to a planet full of happy users with exactly the same Java code. The Java programmer just needs to refer to the `name` attribute of a string resource instead of **hardcoding** the text itself, and then the other departments can design the text content and handle tasks such as translation. We will make an app multilingual in *Chapter 18, Localization*.

 It is possible to hardcode the actual text directly into the Java code instead of using string resources, and from time to time we will do so for the sake of easily showing some Java without getting bogged down with editing or adding to the `strings.xml` file.

We know enough now about `strings.xml` to move on to the final file that we will explore for the Empty Activity template.

The styles.xml file

Here we can see the pieces of the interconnectivity puzzle for this project template finally come together. Study the code in the `styles.xml` file, and we can then discuss it:

```
<resources>
<!-- Base application theme. -->
<style name="AppTheme"
parent="Theme.AppCompat.Light.DarkActionBar">
```

```
    <!-- Customize your theme here. -->
    <item name="colorPrimary">@color/colorPrimary</item>
    <item name="colorPrimaryDark">@color/colorPrimaryDark</item>
    <item name="colorAccent">@color/colorAccent</item>
</style>
</resources>
```

This is yet another resource file, but it is referring to the `colors.xml` file we saw earlier. Notice there is a `style` tag, which is enclosing multiple `item` tags. Each `item` tag has a name, such as `colorPrimary`, `colorPrimaryDark`, or `colorAccent`. Then each of these names is assigned a value, such as `@color/colorPrimary`.

You are rightly probably wondering what is going on. `@color` refers to the `colors.xml` file, and `colorPrimary`, `colorPrimaryDark`, and `colorAccent` refer to the actual colors defined with their hexadecimal values in that file. But why would you bother to create the colors and give them names and then in another file define `item` instances and assign those colors to `item` instances? Why not just assign hexadecimal color values directly to each `item`?

Look to the top of the code block to begin to understand the reason behind this apparently unnecessary convolutedness. I have shown the relevant lines of code again next so we can discuss them more easily:

```
<style name="AppTheme"
parent="Theme.AppCompat.Light.DarkActionBar">
```

What is going on is that items have been defined and the items are contained within a `style`. As we can see, the style is called `AppTheme`. Furthermore, the style has a parent called `Theme.AppCompat.Light.DarkActionBar`.

The system allows designers to choose a selection of colors and then define them in the `colors.xml` file. They can then further build up styles that use those colors in different combinations – there will often be more than one style per app. A style can further be associated with a theme (`parent = "..."`). This parent theme can be one completely designed by the styles and colors of the app designers, or it can be one of the default themes of Android, such as `Theme.AppCompat.Light.DarkActionBar`.

The UI designers can then simply refer to a style in the `AndroidManifest.xml` file, like in this line:

```
android:theme="@style/AppTheme"
```

UI designers can then happily tweak colors and where they are used (items) without interfering with the Java. It also allows for different styles to be created for different regions of the world without any changes to the actual layout file (in this case, `activity_main.xml`).

For example, in western culture, green can represent themes like nature and correctness, and in many middle-eastern countries green represents fertility and is the color associated with Islam. While you might just about get away with distributing green in both these regions, your app will be perceived very differently.

If you then roll your app out into Indonesia, green is culturally despised among many (although not all) Indonesians. Next, you launch in China and green has potential negative connotations to do with unfaithful spouses. It is a minefield that the typical Java programmer will never learn to navigate. And, fortunately, because of the way we can divide up responsibilities in Android Studio, they don't need to learn.

Colors, and therefore styles and themes, are very specialized topics. While we won't be exploring any more deeply than that quick foray into green, hopefully you see the benefit of a system that separates responsibility for programming, layout, color, and textual content.

 I thought it is also worth mentioning at this point that images can also be divided up into different locales so that users in different regions see different images within the same app. And, if you are wondering, yes, that would mean supplying different resolutions (hdpi, xhdpi, and so on) for each locale as well.

It is also worth mentioning that it is entirely possible to produce a fantastic app that is enjoyed by thousands or even millions of users without catering individually to every region. However, even if we are not going to employ teams of designers, translators, and cultural experts, we still must work within this system that was designed to enable them, and that is why we are going in to such depth.

At this stage, we have a good grasp of what goes into an Android project and how it all links together. Let's build one more app, not to go into it in the same detail, but to see the differences that different app templates make to the underlying files that Android Studio generates.

The Basic Activity project

The next simplest project type with an auto-generated UI is the Basic Activity project. This is the same type of project that we created in *Chapter 1*, *Beginning Android and Java*. Feel free to open that project up now, although it is just as quick to generate a new one, and we can then also examine it without any of our alterations and additions clouding the discussions.

Let's create a Basic Activity project:

1. In Android Studio, select **File | New | New Project...**

2. In the **Create Android Project** screen, change the **Name** field to **Basic Activity App**.

3. The rest of the settings can be left at their defaults (unless you want to change them), so just click **Next**.

4. In the **Target Android Devices** window, leave all the default settings and click **Next**.

5. On the **Add an Activity to Mobile** window, select **Basic Activity**, as shown in the next screenshot:

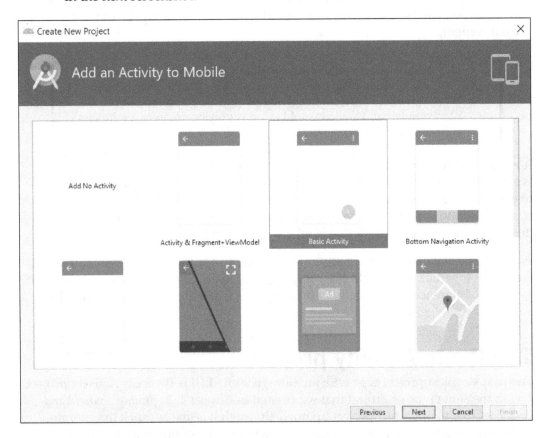

Now we can dig into the files. We won't look at everything in the same detail that we did for the Empty Activity project; we will just look at the differences and extra bits.

Exploring the Basic Activity project

Let's compare the Java code first. Look at the `MainActivity.java` tab in the code editor. They both contain a class called `MainActivity`. The difference is in the number of methods and the content of the `onCreate` method.

As already stated, the Basic Activity project has more to it than the Empty Activity project.

 You can open as many instances of Android Studio as you like. If you want to compare projects side by side, select **File | Open** and then choose the project. When prompted, select **New Window** to open the project without closing any that are already open.

The first difference is that there is some extra code in the `onCreate` method.

The MainActivity.java file

I mentioned very briefly back in *Chapter 2, First Contact: Java, XML and the UI Designer*, these interconnections in the Java code and the XML code. Let's look through the resources files and point out the XML files that this Java code points to.

Here is the Java code. I have slightly reformatted it to make it more readable in a book:

```java
Toolbar toolbar = (Toolbar) findViewById(R.id.toolbar);
setSupportActionBar(toolbar);

FloatingActionButton fab = (
                FloatingActionButton) findViewById(R.id.fab);
fab.setOnClickListener(new View.OnClickListener() {
    @Override
    public void onClick(View view) {
        Snackbar.make(view, "Replace with your own action",
                            Snackbar.LENGTH_LONG)
                    .setAction("Action", null).show();
    }
});
```

Understanding this code fully will take quite a few more chapters, but to point out where this code uses files in the resources will only take a moment and will then leave us even more aware of the components that make up our projects.

The code refers to two resources. The first is a `Toolbar` and is referred to via `R.id.toolbar`. The second is a `FloatingActionBar` and refers to the XML files we will see soon via `R.id.fab`.

If we open the `res/layout` folder in the project window, we can see that things look slightly differently to how they did in the Empty Activity project:

There are now two files that were auto-generated. We will explore the `content_main.xml` file and why it is required shortly.

The activity_main.xml file

For now, open up the `activity_main.xml` file and you will see there are some elements to represent both `toolbar` and `fab`. The Java code referring to these elements is setting up the tool bar and the floating action bar ready for use. The XML code, as we have come to expect, describes what they look like.

Here is the XML code for the toolbar:

```
<androidx.appcompat.widget.Toolbar
    android:id="@+id/toolbar"
    android:layout_width="match_parent"
    android:layout_height="?attr/actionBarSize"
    android:background="?attr/colorPrimary"
    app:popupTheme="@style/AppTheme.PopupOverlay" />
```

Notice it refers to a toolbar, a color, and a style, as well as some others.

For clarity, this is the toolbar in the actual working app:

Here is the XML code for the floating action button. I have slightly reformatted the first line of the code onto two lines so it looks better in the printed version of this book:

```
<com.google.android.material.floatingactionbutton.
FloatingActionButton

    android:id="@+id/fab"
    android:layout_width="wrap_content"
    android:layout_height="wrap_content"
    android:layout_gravity="bottom|end"
    android:layout_margin="@dimen/fab_margin"
    app:srcCompat="@android:drawable/ic_dialog_email" />
```

Notice it has an `id` of `fab`. It is through this `id` that we gain access to the floating action button in our Java code; specifically, this line in `MainActivity.java`:

```
FloatingActionButton fab = (
            FloatingActionButton) findViewById(R.id.fab);
```

After this line of code executes, `fab` in our Java code can now directly control the floating action button and all its attributes. In *Chapter 13, Anonymous Classes - Bringing Android Widgets to Life*, we will learn how to do this in detail.

Here is the floating action button in the actual app:

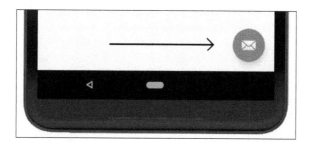

It is plain that I haven't explained the code in detail; there is no point at this stage. Just start to make a mental note of the interconnections:

- XML files can refer to other XML files

- Java can refer to XML files (and, as we will see soon, other Java files)

- Now we have seen that, in Java, we can grab control of a specific part of the UI in an XML file via its `id` attribute

We have seen enough from this file; let's move on and dip into the remaining files.

The extra methods in MainActivity.java

So, what do the methods do, when are they called, and by whom?

The next difference is this extra method (again, slightly reformatted for presentation):

```
@Override
public boolean onCreateOptionsMenu(Menu menu) {
    // Inflate the menu; this adds items to the
    // action bar if it is present.
    getMenuInflater().inflate(R.menu.menu_main, menu);
    return true;
}
```

This code prepares (inflates) the menu that is defined in the menu_main.xml file. And, just like onCreate, the method is an overridden method and it is called by the operating system directly.

Then there is yet another method, shown next:

```
@Override
public boolean onOptionsItemSelected(MenuItem item) {
    // Handle action bar item clicks here. The action bar will
    // automatically handle clicks on the Home/Up button, so long
    // as you specify a parent activity in AndroidManifest.xml.
    int id = item.getItemId();

    //noinspection SimplifiableIfStatement
    if (id == R.id.action_settings) {
        return true;
    }

    return super.onOptionsItemSelected(item);
}
```

This method is overridden as well. And it too is called directly by the operating system. It handles what happens when an item (option) from the menu is selected by the user. At the moment, it handles just one option, the settings option. And, currently, it takes no action:

```
if (id == R.id.action_settings) {
```

The preceding code determines whether the settings menu option was clicked, and if it was, the code return true executes and control is returned to whatever part of the app was executing before it was interrupted by the user clicking the **Settings** menu option.

We know nearly enough for now. Don't worry about memorizing all these connections. We will be coming back to each connection, investigating more deeply and cementing our understanding of each.

So, why that second file in the `res/layout` folder?

The content_main.xml file

The `MainActivity.java` file calls `setContentView` on `R.layout.activity_main`. Then, in turn, `activity_main` has this line of code highlighted next:

```
...
</com.google.android.material.appbar.AppBarLayout>

<include layout="@layout/content_main" />

<com.google.android.material.floatingactionbutton
.FloatingActionButton
...
```

The highlighted line of code `includes` the `content_main` file. So, just after the app bar is added to the layout, execution branches to `content_main`, where all its XML is turned into UI, and then execution goes back to `activity_main` and the floating action bar is added to the layout. We will use `include` in *Chapter 5, Beautiful Layouts with CardView and ScrollView*, wherein we build some neat scrolling `CardView` layouts, and separate the code which defines `CardView` from the actual contents of `CardView`.

Exploring the Android emulator

As we progress, it helps to be familiar with exactly how to use the Android emulator. If you haven't used the latest version of Android, some of the ways to achieve even simple tasks (such as viewing all the apps) can be different to how your current device works. In addition, we want to know how to use the extra controls that come with all emulators.

Emulator control panel

You probably noticed the mini control panel that appears beside the emulator when you run it. Let's go through some of the most useful controls. Look at this screenshot of the emulator control panel. I have annotated it to aid the discussion:

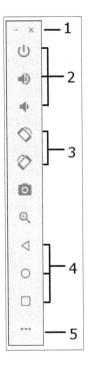

I will just mention the more obvious controls and go into a bit more depth when necessary:

1. These are the window controls. They minimize or close the emulator window.

2. From top to bottom, the first button is used to power off the emulator, simulating powering off the actual device. The next two icons raise and lower the volume.

3. These two buttons allow you to rotate the emulator left and right. This means you can test what your app looks like in all orientations, as well as how it handles orientation changes while the app is running. The icons immediately below these take a screenshot and zoom in, respectively. Here is the emulator after being rotated to horizontal:

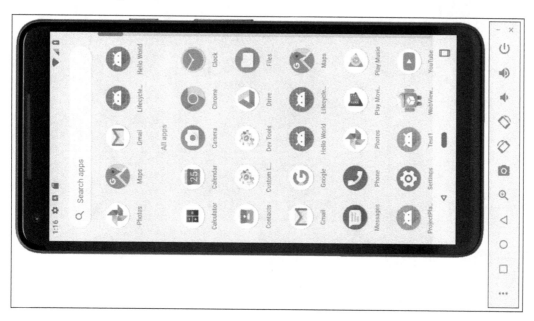

4. These icons simulate the back button, home button, and view running apps button. Have a play with these buttons — we will need to use them from time to time, including in *Chapter 6, The Android Life Cycle*.

5. Press this button to launch the Advanced Settings menu, wherein you can interact with things such as sensors, GPS, the battery, and the fingerprint reader. Have a play around with some of these settings if you are curious:

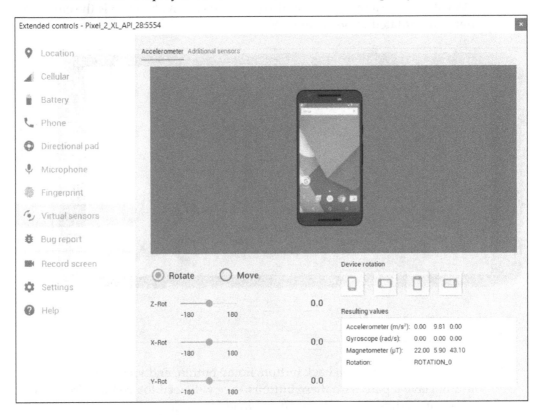

Let's have a play with the emulator itself.

Using the emulator as a real device

The emulator can emulate every feature of a real phone, so it would be possible to write a whole book on it alone. If you want to write apps that your users love, then understanding a whole range of Android devices is well worth taking the time to do. I just want to point out a few of the most basic features here, because without these basic interactions, it will be hard to follow along with the book. Furthermore, if you have an old Android device, then some essential basics (such as accessing the app drawer) have changed and you might be left a little baffled.

Accessing the app drawer

Hold the mouse cursor on the bottom of the home screen and drag upward to access the app drawer (all the apps). This screenshot shows this action halfway through:

Now you can run any app installed on the emulator. Note that when you run one of your apps through Android Studio, it remains installed on the emulator and, therefore, runnable from the app drawer. However, every change you make to the app in Android Studio will require you to run/install the app again by clicking the play button on the Android Studio quick-launch bar, as we have been doing.

Viewing active apps and switching between apps

To view active apps, you can use the emulator control panel, the square labelled as number 4 on the screenshot of the emulator control panel. To access the same option using the phone screen (as you would have to do on a real device), swipe up, just like accessing the app drawer, but do so only for about one quarter of the length of the screen, as shown in this next screenshot:

You can now swipe left and right through the recent apps, swipe an app up to close it, or tap the back button to return to what you were doing before you viewed this option. Do try this out as we will use these basic features quite often.

Summary

Remember that the goal of this chapter was familiarization with the system/ structure of Android/an Android project. Android projects are a sometimes-complex interweaving of Java and a multitude of resource files. Resource files can contain XML to describe our layouts, textual content, styles, and colors, as well as images. Resources can be produced to target different languages and regions of the world. Other resource types that we will see and use throughout the book include themes and sound effects.

It is not important to remember all the different ways in which the different resource files and the Java files are interconnected. It is only important to realize that they are interconnected, and to also be able to examine files of various types and realize when they are dependent on code in another file. Whenever we create connections from our Java code to the XML code, I will always point out the details of the connection again.

We do not need to learn XML as well as Java, but we will become a little bit familiar with it over the next 27 chapters. Java will be the focus of this book, but our Java code will frequently refer to the XML code, so understanding and having seen some examples of the interconnections will stand you in good stead to make faster progress.

We have also explored the emulator to get the most out of it when testing our apps.

In the next chapter, we will build two custom layouts using two different Android layout schemes. We will also write some Java code so that we can switch between them with the tap of a button.

4
Getting Started with Layouts and Material Design

We have already seen the Android Studio UI designer, as well as a little bit of Java in action. In this hands-on chapter, we will build three more layouts—still quite simple, yet a step up from what we have done so far.

Before we get to the hands-on part, we will have a quick introduction to the concept of **Material Design**.

We will see another type of layout called `LinearLayout` and step through, using it to create a usable UI. We will take things a step further by using `ConstraintLayout`, both with understanding constraints and with designing more complex and precise UI designs. Finally, we will meet the `TableLayout` for laying out data in an easily readable table.

We will also write some Java code to switch between our different layouts within one app/project. This is the first major app that links together multiple topics into one neat parcel. The app is called Exploring Layouts.

In this chapter, we will do the following:

- Find out about material design
- Build a `LinearLayout` and learn when it is best to use this type
- Build another, slightly more advanced `ConstraintLayout` and find out a bit more about using constraints
- Build a `TableLayout` and fill it with data to display
- Link everything together in a single app called Exploring Layouts.

First on the list is material design.

Material design

You might have heard of material design, but what exactly is it? The objective of material design is quite simply to achieve beautiful user interfaces. It is also, however, about making these user interfaces consistent across Android devices. Material design is not a new idea. It is taken straight from the design principles used in pen and paper design, like having visually pleasing embellishments such as shadows and depth.

Material design uses the concept of layers of materials that you can think of in the same way you would think of layers in a photo editing app. Consistency is achieved with a set of principles, rules, and guidelines. It must be stressed that material design is entirely optional, but it also must be stressed that material design works, and if you are not following it, there is a good chance your design will be disliked by the user. The user, after all, has become used to a certain type of UI and that UI was most likely created using material design principles.

So, material design is a sensible standard to strive for, but while we are learning the details of material design, we mustn't let it hold us back from learning how to get started with Android.

This book will focus on getting things done, while occasionally pointing out when material design is influencing how we do it, as well as pointing you to further resources for those who want to look at material design in more depth right away.

Exploring Android UI design

We will see with Android UI design that so much of what we learn is context sensitive. The way that a given widget's x attribute will influence its appearance might depend on a widget's y attribute or even on an attribute on another widget. It isn't easy to learn this verbatim. It is best to expect to gradually achieve better and faster results with practice.

For example, if you play with the designer by dragging and dropping widgets onto the design, the XML code that is generated will vary quite considerably depending upon which layout type you are using. We will see this as we proceed through this chapter.

This is because different layout types use different means to decide on the position of their children. For example, the LinearLayout we will explore next works very differently to the ConstraintLayout that was added by default to our project in *Chapter 1, Beginning Android and Java*.

This information might initially seem like a problem, or even a bad idea, and it certainly is a little awkward at first. What we will begin to learn, however, is that this clear abundance of layout options and their individual quirks are a good thing because they give us almost unlimited design potential. There are very few layouts you can imagine that are not possible to achieve.

This almost unlimited potential comes with a bit of complexity, however. The best way to start to get to grips with this is to build some working examples of several types. In this chapter, we will see three — a LinearLayout, a ConstraintLayout, and a TableLayout. We will see how to make things easier using the distinctive features of the visual designer, and we will also pay some attention to the XML that is auto-generated to make our understanding more rounded.

Layouts

We have already seen ConstraintLayout, but there are more. Layouts are the building blocks that group together the other UI elements. Layouts can, and often do, contain other layouts themselves.

Let's look at some commonly used layouts in Android because knowing the different layouts and their pros and cons will make us more aware of what can be achieved, and therefore expand the horizons of what is possible.

We have already seen that once we have designed a layout, we can put it into action using the setContentView method in our Java code.

Let's build three designs with different layout types, and then put setContentView to work and switch between them.

Creating the Exploring Layouts project

One of the toughest things in Android is not just finding out how to do something, but finding out how to do something in amongst other things. That is why throughout this book, as well as showing you how to do some neat stuff, we will link lots of topics together into apps that span multiple topics, and often chapters. The *Exploring Layouts* project is the first app of this type. We will learn how to build multiple types of layout while linking them all together in one handy app:

1. Create a new project in Android Studio. If you already have a project open, select **File | New Project**. When prompted, choose **Open in same window**, as we do not need to refer to our previous project.

If you are on the start screen of Android Studio, you can create a new project simply by clicking the **Start a new Android Studio project** option.

2. Enter `Exploring Layouts` for the **Application Name** and then click the **Next** button.

3. On the **Target Android Devices** screen, leave the default options and click the **Next** button.

4. Make sure to select the **Empty Activity** project template, as we will build most of the UI from scratch. Click the **Next** button.

5. On the **Configure Activity** screen, leave the default options as they are. We will let Android Studio generate a nearly empty `ConstraintLayout` that we will edit, and we will also create more layouts and then link them together.

6. Click the **Finish** button.

Look at the `MainActivity.java` file. Here is the entirety of the code, excluding `import...` statements:

```
public class MainActivity extends AppCompatActivity {

    @Override
    protected void onCreate(Bundle savedInstanceState) {
        super.onCreate(savedInstanceState);

        setContentView(R.layout.activity_main);
    }
}
```

Locate the call to `setContentView` and delete the entire line. The line is shown highlighted in the previous code.

This is just what we want because now we can build our very own layouts, explore the underlying XML, and write our own Java code to display these layouts. If you run the app now, you will just get a blank screen with a title, not even a Hello World! message.

The first type of layout we will explore is the `LinearLayout`.

Building a menu with LinearLayout

`LinearLayout` is probably the simplest layout that Android offers. As the name suggests, all the UI items within it are laid out linearly. You have just two choices — vertical and horizontal. By adding the following line of code (or editing via the Attribute window), you can configure a `LinearLayout` to lay things out vertically:

```
android:orientation="vertical"
```

You can then (as you could probably have guessed) change `"vertical"` to `"horizontal"` to lay things out horizontally.

Before we can do anything with `LinearLayout`, we need to add one to a layout file. And, as we are building three layouts in this project, we also need a new layout file.

Adding a LinearLayout to the project

In the project window, expand the `res` folder. Now right-click the `layout` folder and select **New**. Notice that there is an option for **Layout resource file,** as shown in the following screenshot:

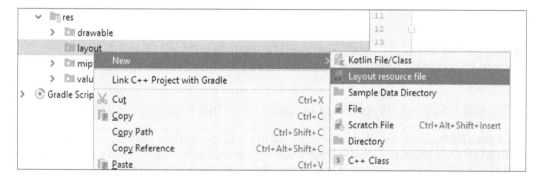

Select **Layout resource file** and you will see the **New Resource File** dialog window:

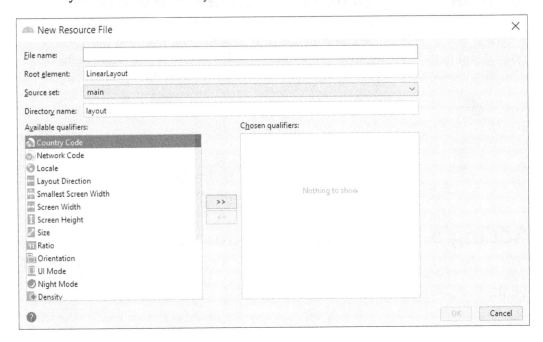

In the **File name** field, enter main_menu. The name is arbitrary, but this layout is going to be our main menu that is used to select the other layouts, so the name seems appropriate.

Notice that it has already selected **LinearLayout** as the **Root** element option.

Click the **OK** button, and then Android Studio will generate a new LinearLayout in an XML file called main_menu and place it in the layout folder ready for us to build our new main menu UI. Android Studio will also open the UI designer with the Palette on the left and the Attributes window on the right.

Preparing your workspace

Adjust the windows by dragging and resizing their borders (as you can in most windowed apps) to make the palette, design, and attributes as clear as possible but no bigger than necessary. This small screenshot shows the approximate window proportions I chose to make designing our UI and exploring the XML as clear as possible. The detail in the screenshot is not important:

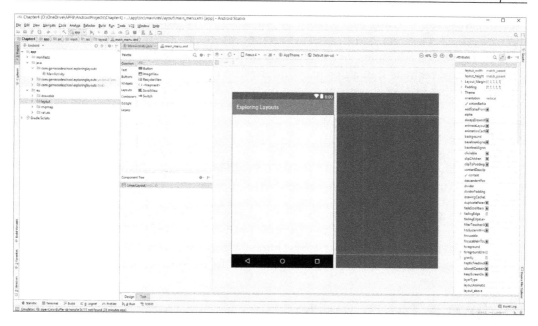

Observe that I have made the project, palette, and attribute windows as narrow as possible but without obscuring any content. I have also closed the Build/logcat window at the bottom of the screen, the result being that I have a nice clear canvas on which to build the UI.

Examining the generated XML

Click on the **Text** tab and we will have a look at the current state of the XML code that forms our design at this stage. Here is the code so we can talk about it. I have reformatted it slightly to make it appear more clearly on the page:

```xml
<?xml version="1.0" encoding="utf-8"?>
<LinearLayout
    xmlns:android="http://schemas.android.com/apk/res/android"

    android:orientation="vertical"
    android:layout_width="match_parent"
    android:layout_height="match_parent">

</LinearLayout>
```

We have the usual starting and closing tags and, as we could have predicted, they are `<LinearLayout` and `</LinearLayout>`. There is no child element yet, but there are three attributes. We know they are attributes and not children of the `LinearLayout` because they appear before the first closing `>`. The three attributes that define this `LinearLayout` have been highlighted in the previous code for clarity.

The first attribute is `android:orientation`, or, more succinctly, we will just refer to the attributes without the `android:` part. The `orientation` attribute has a value of `vertical`. This means that when we start to add items to this layout, it will arrange them vertically from top to bottom. We could change the value from `vertical` to `horizontal` and it would lay things out from left to right.

The next two attributes are `layout_width` and `layout_height`. These determine the size of the `LinearLayout`. The value given to both attributes is `match_parent`. The parent of a layout is the entire available space. By matching the parent horizontally and vertically, therefore, the layout will fill the entire space available.

Adding a TextView to the UI

Switch back to the **Design** tab, and we will add some elements to the UI.

First, find the **TextView** in the palette. This can be found in both the **Common** and **Text** categories. Left-click and drag the **TextView** onto the UI and notice that it sits neatly at the top of the `LinearLayout`.

Look at the XML on the **Text** tab to confirm that it is a child of the `LinearLayout` and that it is indented by one tab to make this clear. Here is the code for the `TextView` without the surrounding code for the `LinearLayout`:

```
<TextView
    android:id="@+id/textView"
    android:layout_width="match_parent"
    android:layout_height="wrap_content"
    android:text="TextView" />
```

Notice that it has four attributes: an `id` in case we need to refer to it from another UI element or from our Java code; it has a `layout_width` set to `match_parent`, which means the `TextView` stretches across the whole width of the `LinearLayout`; a `layout_height` set to `wrap_content`, which means the `TextView` is precisely tall enough to contain the text within it; and finally, for now, it has a `text` element, which determines the actual text it will display, and this is currently set to just `"TextView"`.

Switch back to the design tab and we will make some changes.

We want this text to be the heading text of this screen, which is the menu screen. In the Attributes window, click the search icon and type `text` into the search box and change the **text** attribute to `Menu`, as shown in the following screenshot:

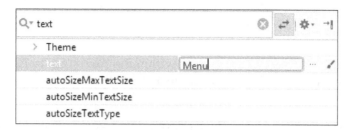

 You can find any attribute by searching or just by scrolling through the options. When you have found the attribute you want to edit, left-click it to select it and then press the *Enter* key on the keyboard to make it editable.

Next, find the `textSize` attribute using your preferred search technique and set `textSize` to `50sp`. When you have entered this new value, the text size will increase.

The `sp` stands for scalable pixels. This means that when the user changes the font size settings on their Android device, the font will dynamically rescale itself.

Now, search for the **gravity** attribute and expand the options by clicking the little arrow indicated in the following screenshot:

Set **gravity** to **center_horizontal,** as shown next:

fill_vertical	☐
center_horizontal	☑
fill_horizontal	☐

The gravity attribute refers to the gravity within the TextView itself, and our change has the effect of moving the actual text inside the TextView to the centre.

> Note that gravity is different to layout_gravity. The layout_ gravity sets the gravity within the layout; in this case, the parent LinearLayout. We will use layout_gravity later in this project.

At this point, we have changed the text of the TextView, increased its size, and centred it horizontally. The UI designer should now look like the following diagram:

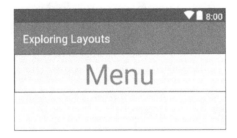

A quick glance at the **Text** tab to see the XML would reveal the following code:

```
<TextView
    android:id="@+id/textView"
    android:layout_width="match_parent"
    android:layout_height="wrap_content"
    android:gravity="center_horizontal"
    android:text="Menu"
    android:textSize="50sp" />
```

You can see the new attributes as follows: gravity, which is set to center_ horizontal, text, which has changed to Menu, and textSize, which is set to 50sp.

If you run the app, you might not see what you expected. This is because we haven't called setContentView in our Java code to load the UI. You will still see the blank UI. We will fix this once we have made a bit more progress with the UI.

Adding a multi-line TextView to the UI

Switch back to **Design** tab, find the **Multiline Text** in the **Text** category of the palette, and drag it onto the design just below the TextView we added a moment ago.

Using your preferred search technique, set text to Select a layout type to view an example. The onClick attribute of each button will call a method which executes setContentView to load the new layout.

Your layout will now look like the following diagram:

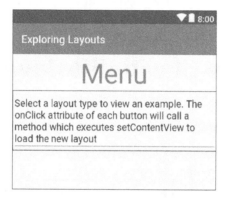

Your XML will be updated with another child in the LinearLayout, after the TextView, that looks like this code. I have reformatted it slightly for the purpose of presenting it on the page:

```
<EditText
    android:id="@+id/editText"
    android:layout_width="match_parent"
    android:layout_height="wrap_content"
    android:ems="10"
    android:inputType="textMultiLine"
    android:text="Select a layout type to view an example.
        The onClick attribute of each button will call a method
        which executes setContentView to load the new layout" />
```

You can see the details of the UI item and it turns out that the description on the palette of **Multiline Text** was not entirely obvious as to exactly what this would be. A look at the XML reveals we have an `inputType` attribute, indicating that this text is editable. There is also another attribute that we haven't seen before, and that is `ems`. The ems attribute controls how many characters can be entered per line, and the value of `10` was chosen automatically by Android Studio. However, another attribute, `layout_width="match_parent"` overrides this value because it causes the element to expand to fit its parent; in other words, the whole width of the screen.

When you run the app (in the next section), you will see that the text is indeed editable, although for the purposes of this demo app it serves no practical purpose.

Wiring up the UI with the Java code (part 1)

To achieve an interactive app, we will do three things:

1. We will call `setContentView` from the `onCreate` method to show the progress of our UI when we run the app

2. We will write two more methods of our own, and each one will call `setContentView` on a different layout (that we have yet to design)

3. Then, later in this chapter, when we design two more UI layouts, we will be able to load them at the click of a button

As we will be building a `ConstraintLayout` and a `TableLayout`, we will call our new methods `loadConstraintLayout` and `loadTableLayout`, respectively.

Let's do that now, and then we can see how we can add some buttons that call these methods alongside some neatly formatted text.

Inside the `onCreate` method, add the following highlighted code:

```
@Override
protected void onCreate(Bundle savedInstanceState) {
    super.onCreate(savedInstanceState);

    setContentView(R.layout.main_menu);
}
```

The code uses the `setContentView` method to load the UI we are currently working on. You can now run the app to see the following results:

Add these two new methods inside the `MainActivity` class after the `onCreate` method:

```
void loadConstraintLayout(View v){
    setContentView(R.layout.activity_main);
}

void loadTableLayout(View v){
    setContentView(R.layout.my_table_layout);
}
```

There is one error with the first method and two with the second. The first we can fix by adding an `import` statement so that Android Studio is aware of the `View` class. Left-click the word `View` to select the error. Hold down the *Alt* key and then tap the *Enter* key. You will see the following pop-up:

```
void loadConstraintLayout(View v){
    setContentView(R.layout.activity_main);
}

void loadTableLayout(View v){
    setContentView(R.layo    Import class
}                                Create class 'View'
}                                Create enum 'View'
                                 Create inner class 'View'
                                 Create interface 'View'

                                 Create field for parameter 'v'              ▸
                                 Generate overloaded method with default parameter values ▸
```

Chose **Import class**. The error is gone. If you scroll to the top of the code, you will see that a new line of code has been added by that shortcut we just performed. Here is the new code:

```
import android.view.View;
```

Android Studio no longer considers the `View` class an error.

The second method still has an error, however. The problem is that the method calls the `setContentView` method to load a new UI (`R.layout.my_table_layout`). As this UI layout does not exist yet, it produces an error. You can comment out this call to remove the error until we create the file and design the UI layout later this chapter. Add the double forward slash// as highlighted next:

```
void loadConstraintLayout(View v){
    setContentView(R.layout.activity_main);
}

void loadTableLayout(View v){
    // setContentView(R.layout.my_table_layout);
}
```

Now we want to add some buttons, that we can click to call our new methods and load the new layouts we will be building soon. But adding a couple of buttons with some text on is too easy—we have done that before. What we want to do is line up some text with a button to the right of it. The problem is that our `LinearLayout` has the `orientation` attribute set to `vertical` and, as we have seen, all the new parts we add to the layout will be lined up vertically.

Adding layouts within layouts

The solution to laying out some elements with a different orientation to others is to nest layouts within layouts. Here is how to do it.

From the **Layouts** category of the palette, drag a **LinearLayout (Horizontal)** onto our design, placing it just below the **Multiline Text**. Notice that there is a blue border occupying all the space below the **Multiline Text**:

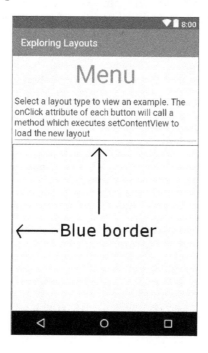

This indicates that our new **LinearLayout (Horizontal)** is filling the space. Keep this blue border area in mind as it is where we will put the next item on our UI.

Now go back to the **Text** category of the palette and drag a **TextView** onto the new LinearLayout we just added. Notice how the TextView sits snuggly in the top left-hand corner of the new LinearLayout:

This at first seems no different to what happened with the previous vertical LinearLayout, which was part of our UI from the start. But watch what happens when we add our next piece of the UI.

> The term used to refer to adding layouts within layouts is **nesting**. The Android term applied to any item that appears on the UI (buttons, text, for example) is **view**, and anything that contains views is a **view group**. As the terms view and view group do not always make their meanings clear in certain contexts, I will usually refer to parts of the UI either specifically (such as TextView, Button, and LinearLayout) or more broadly (UI element, item, or widget).

From the **Button** category, drag a **Button** onto the right-hand side of the previous TextView. Notice that the button sits to the right of the text, as shown in the following screenshot:

Next, select the LinearLayout (the horizontal one) by clicking on an empty part of it. Find the layout_height attribute and set it to wrap_content. Observe that the LinearLayout is now taking up only as much space as it needs:

Let's configure the text attribute of the TextView and the Button before we add the next part of the UI. Change the text attribute of the Button to LOAD. Change the text attribute of our new TextView to Load ConstraintLayout.

> Did that work? Yes, excellent. You are now familiar with editing attributes of Android Views. No? Left-click the item you want to edit (in this case, the TextView), search using the search icon or scroll to find the attribute you want to edit in the **Attributes** window (in this case, the text attribute), select the attribute, and press *Enter* to edit it. I can now give more succinct instructions on how to build future UI projects, and this makes your journey to becoming an Android ninja much quicker.

Now we can repeat ourselves and add another `TextView` and `Button` within another **LinearLayout (Horizontal)** just below the one we have just finished. To do so, follow these steps in order:

1. Add another **LinearLayout (Horizontal)** just below the previous one
2. Add a **TextView** to the new `LinearLayout`
3. Change the `text` attribute of the `TextView` to Load `TableLayout`
4. Add a `Button` on the right-hand side of the `TextView`
5. Change `text` attribute of the `Button` to LOAD
6. Resize the `LinearLayout` by changing the `layout_height` attribute to `wrap_content`

Now we have two neatly (and horizontally) aligned texts and buttons.

Just for fun, and for the sake of exploring the palette a bit more, find the **Widgets** category of the palette and drag a **RatingBar** onto the design just below the final `LinearLayout`. Now, your UI should look very similar to this next screenshot:

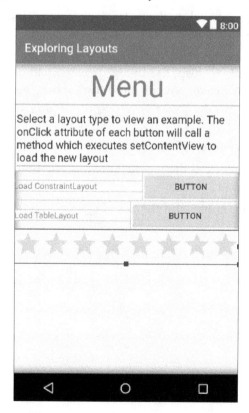

In the previous two screenshots, I hadn't yet changed the text attribute of the two Button elements. Everything else should be the same as yours.

Let's add some visual finishing touches to the layout.

Making the layout look pretty

In this section, we will explore some more attributes that control the finer details of our UI. You have probably noticed how the UI looks a bit squashed in some places and wonky and unsymmetrical in others. As we progress through the book, we will continually add to our repertoire to improve our layouts, but these short steps will introduce and take care of some of the basics:

1. Select the Multiline Text, and then expand the Padding attribute. Set the all option to 15sp. This has made a neat area of space around the outside of the text.

2. To make a nice space below the Multiline text, find and expand the Layout_Margin attribute and set bottom to 100sp.

3. On both TextView that are aligned/related to the buttons, set the textSize attribute to 20sp, the layout_gravity to center_vertical, the layout_width to match_parent, and the layout_weight to .7.

4. On both buttons, set the weight to .3. Notice how both buttons now take up exactly .3 of the width and the text .7 of the LinearLayout, making the whole appearance more pleasing.

5. On the RatingBar, find the Layout_Margin attribute and then set left and right to 15sp.

6. Still with the RatingBar and the Layout_Margin attribute, change top to 75sp.

You can now run the app and see our first full layout in all its glory:

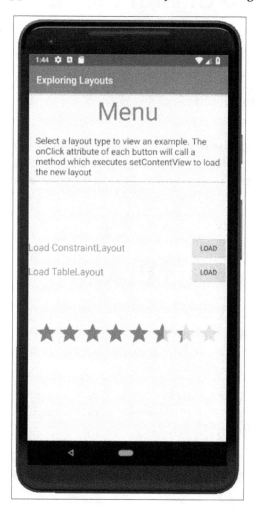

Notice that you can play with the RatingBar, although the rating won't persist when the app is turned off.

 By way of a reader challenge, find an attribute or two that could further improve the appearance of the LoadConstraintLayout and LoadTableLayout text. They look a little bit close to the edges of the screen. Refer to the section on attribute summary at the start of the next chapter for suggestions.

Unfortunately, the buttons don't do anything yet. Let's fix that.

Wiring up the UI with the Java code (part 2)

Select the button next to the text `Load ConstraintLayout`. Find the `onClick` attribute and set it to `loadConstraintLayout`.

Select the button next to the text `Load TableLayout`. Find the `onClick` attribute and set it to `loadTableLayout`.

Now the buttons will call the methods, but the code inside the `loadTableLayout` method is commented out to avoid errors. Feel free to run the app and see that you can switch to the `ConstraintLayout` by clicking the `loadConstraintLayout` button. But all it has is a **Hello World!** message.

We can now move on to building this `ConstraintLayout`.

Building a precise UI with ConstraintLayout

Open the `ConstraintLayout` that was auto-generated when we created the project. It probably is already in a tab at the top of the editor. If not, it will be in the `res/layout` folder. Its name is `activity_main.xml`.

Inspect the XML in the **Text** tab and note that it is empty apart from a `TextView` that says `Hello World`. Switch back to the **Design** tab, left-click the `TextView` to select it, and tap the *Delete* key to get rid of it.

Now we can build ourselves a simple, yet intricate, UI. `ConstraintView` is very useful when you want to position parts of your UI very precisely and/or relative to the other parts.

Adding a CalenderView

To get started, look in the **Widgets** category of the palette and find the `CalenderView`. Drag and drop the `CalenderView` near the top and horizontally central. As you drag the `CalenderView` around, notice that it jumps/snaps to certain locations.

Also notice the subtle visual cues that show when the view is aligned. I have highlighted the horizontally central visual cue in the following diagram:

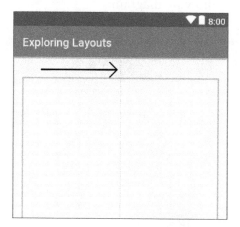

Let go when it is horizontally central, as it is in the diagram. Now we will resize it.

Resizing a view in a ConstraintLayout

Left-click and hold one of the corner squares that are revealed when you let go of the `CalenderView` and drag inwards to decrease the size of the `CalenderView`:

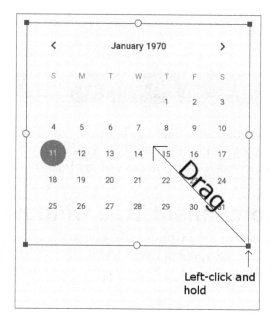

Reduce the size by about half and leave the CalenderView near the top and horizontally central. You might need to reposition it a little after you have resized it, a bit like in the following diagram:

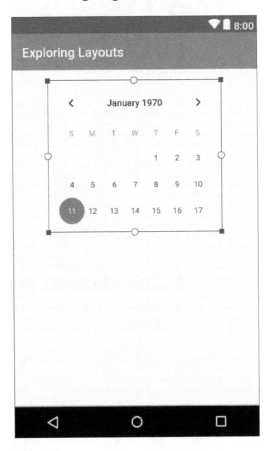

You do not need to place the CalenderView in exactly the same place as me. The purpose of the exercise is to get familiar with the visual cues that inform you where you have placed it, not to create a carbon copy of my layout.

Using the Component Tree window

Now look at the **Component Tree** window, the one to the left of the visual designer and below the palette. The component tree is a way of visualizing the layout of the XML, but without all the details.

In the following screenshot, we can see that the `CalenderView` is indented to the `ConstraintLayout` and is therefore a child. In the next UI we build, we will see that we sometimes need to take advantage of the **Component Tree** to build the UI.

For now, I just want you to observe that there is a warning sign by our `CalenderView`. I have highlighted it in the following screenshot:

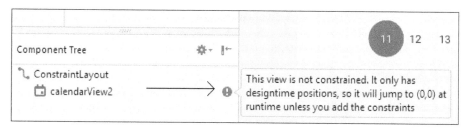

The error says **This view is not constrained. It only has designtime positions, so it will jump to (0,0) at runtime unless you add the constraints**. Remember when we first added buttons to the screen in *Chapter 2, First Contact: Java, XML and the UI Designer*, that they simply disappeared off to the top-left corner?

 Run the app now and click on the **Load ConstraintLayout** button if you want to be reminded of this problem.

Now, we could fix this by clicking the **Infer constraints**; button that we used in *Chapter 2, First Contact – Java, XML, and the UI Designer*. Here it is again as a reminder:

But learning to add the constraints manually is worthwhile because it offers us more options and flexibility. And, as your layouts get more complex, there is always an item or two that doesn't behave as you want it to, and fixing it manually is nearly always necessary.

Adding constraints manually

Make sure that the `CalenderView` is selected and observe the four small circles at the top, bottom, left, and right:

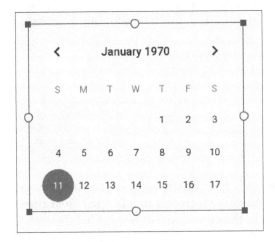

These are the constraint handles. We can click and drag them to anchor them with other parts of the UI or the sides of the screen. By anchoring the `CalenderView` with the four edges of the screen, we can lock it into position when the app is run.

One at a time, click and drag the top handle to the top of the design, the right to the right of the design, the bottom to the bottom of the design, and the left to the left of the design.

Observe that the `CalenderView` is now constrained in the centre. Left-click and drag the `CalenderView` back to the upper part of the screen somewhere like in the following diagram. Use the visual cues (also shown in the following diagram) to make sure the `CalenderView` is horizontally central:

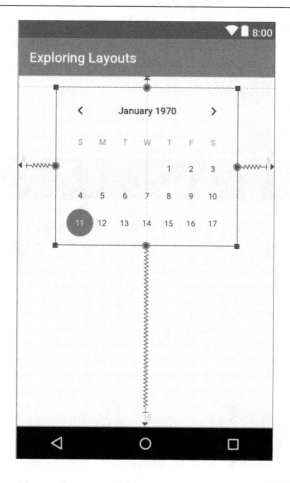

At this stage, you could run the app and the `CalenderView` would be positioned as just pictured.

Let's add a couple more items to the UI and see how to constrain them.

Adding and constraining more UI elements

Drag an `ImageView` from the **Widgets** category of the palette and position it below and to the left of the `CalenderView`. When you place the `ImageView`, a pop-up window will prompt you to choose an image. Select **Project | ic_launcher,** and then click **OK**.

Constrain the left-hand side of the `ImageView` and the bottom of the `ImageView` to the left and bottom of the UI respectively. Here is the position you should be in now:

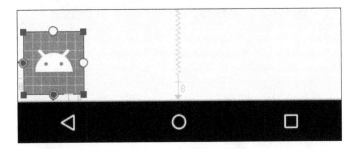

The `ImageView` is constrained in the bottom-left corner. Now grab the top constraint handle on the `ImageView` and drag it to the bottom constraint handle of the `CalenderView`. This is now the current situation:

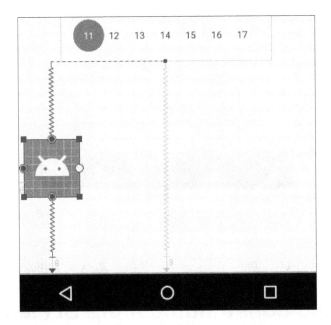

The `ImageView` is only constrained horizontally on one side, so it is pinned/ constrained to the left. It is constrained vertically and equally between the `CalenderView` and the bottom of the UI.

Next, add a `TextView` to the right of the `ImageView`. Constrain the right of the `TextView` to the right of the UI and constrain the left of the `TextView` to the right of the `ImageView`. Constrain the top of the `TextView` to the top of the `ImageView` and constrain the bottom of the `TextView` to the bottom of the UI. Now you will be left with something resembling the following diagram:

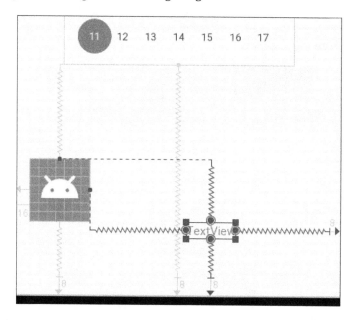

Notice that all the warnings in the **Component Tree** window about unconstrained items are gone.

There are warnings about hardcoded strings because we are adding text directly to the layout instead of the `strings.xml` file and a warning about missing the **contentDescription** attribute. The **contentDescription** attribute should be used to add a textual description so that visually impaired users can get a spoken description of images in the app. For the sake of making rapid progress with the `ConstraintLayout`, we will ignore these two warnings. We will look at adding string resources more correctly in *Chapter 14, Android Dialog Windows*, and you can read about accessibility features in Android Studio on the Android developer's website starting here: `https://developer.android.com/studio/intro/accessibility`

You can move the three UI elements around and line them up neatly and just how you want them. Notice that when you move the `ImageView`, the `TextView` moves with it because the `TextView` is constrained to the `ImageView`. But also notice that you can move the `TextView` independently, and wherever you drop it, this represents its new constrained position relative to the `ImageView`. Whatever an item is constrained to, its position will always be relative to that item. And, as we have seen, the horizontal and vertical constraints are distinct from each other. I positioned mine as in the following diagram:

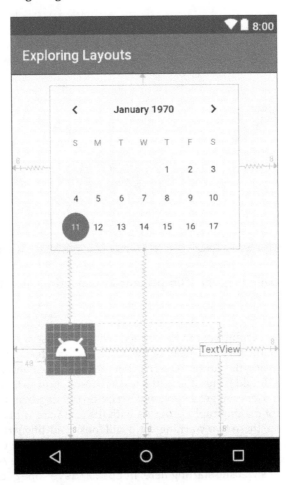

`ConstraintLayout` is the newest layout type and, while it is more complex than the other layouts, it is the most powerful, as well as the one that runs the best on our user's device. It is worth spending more time looking at some more tutorials about `ConstraintLayout`. In particular, look on YouTube, as videos are a great way to learn about tweaking `ConstraintLayout`. We will return to `ConstraintLayout` throughout the book and you do not need to know any more than we have covered already to be able to move on.

Making the text clickable

We are nearly done with our `ConstraintLayout`. We just want to wire up a link back to the main menu screen. This is a good opportunity to demonstrate that `TextView` (and most other UI items) are also clickable. In fact, clickable text is probably more common in modern Android apps than conventional-looking buttons.

Change the `text` attribute of the TextView to `Back to the menu`. Now find the `onClick` attribute and enter `loadMenuLayout`.

Now add the following method to the `MainActivity.java` file just after the `loadTableLayout` method as highlighted here:

```
void loadTableLayout(View v){
    //setContentView(R.layout.my_table_layout);
}

void loadMenuLayout(View v){
    setContentView(R.layout.main_menu);
}
```

Now, whenever the user clicks the text `Back to the menu`, the `loadMenuLayout` method will be called and the `setContentView` method will load the layout in `main_menu.xml`.

You can run the app and click back and forth between the main menu (`LinearLayout`) and the `CalenderView` widget (`ConstraintLayout`).

Let's build the final layout for this chapter.

Laying out data with TableLayout

In the project window, expand the `res` folder. Now right-click the `layout` folder and select **New**. Notice that there is an option for **Layout resource file**.

Select **Layout resource file** and you will see the **New Resource File** dialog window.

In the **File name** field, enter `my_table_layout`. This is the same name we used in the call to `setContentView` within the `loadTableLayout` method.

Notice that it has already selected **LinearLayout** as the **Root** element option. Delete `LinearLayout` and type `TableLayout`.

Click the **OK** button and Android Studio will generate a new `TableLayout` in an XML file called `my_table_layout` and place it in the `layout` folder ready for us to build our new table-based UI. Android Studio will also open the UI designer (if it isn't already) with the palette on the left and the Attributes window on the right.

You can now uncomment the `loadTableLayout` method:

```
void loadTableLayout(View v){
    setContentView(R.layout.my_table_layout);
}
```

You can now switch to the TableLayout screen when you run the app, although at the moment it is blank.

Adding a TableRow to TableLayout

Drag a `TableRow` element from the `Layouts` category on to the UI design. Notice that the appearance of this new `TableRow` is virtually imperceptible, so much so that it is not worth inserting a diagram in the book. There is just a thin blue line at the top of the UI. This is because the `TableRow` has collapsed itself around its content, which is currently empty.

It is possible to drag and drop our chosen UI elements onto this thin blue line, but it is also a little awkward, and even counter-intuitive. Furthermore, once we have multiple `TableRow` elements next to each other, it gets even harder. The solution lies in the **Component Tree** window, which we introduced briefly when building the `ConstraintLayout`.

Using the Component Tree when the visual designer won't do

Look at the **Component Tree** and notice how you can see the `TableRow` as a child of the `TableLayout`. We can drag our UI directly onto the `TableRow` in the **Component Tree**. Drag three `TextView` objects onto the `TableRow` in the **Component Tree** and that should leave you with the following layout. I have photoshopped the following screenshot to show you the **Component Tree** and the regular UI designer in the same diagram:

Now add another two `TableRow` objects (from the **Layouts** category). You can add them via the **Component Tree** window or the UI designer.

 You need to drop them on the far-left of the window, otherwise the new TableRow will become a child of the previous `TableRow`. This will leave the whole table a bit of a muddle. If you accidentally add a `TableRow` as a child of the previous `TableRow`, you can either select it, then tap the *Delete* key and use the *Ctrl | z* keyboard combination to undo it, or drag the dispositioned `TableRow` to the left (in the **Component Tree**) to make it a child of the Table.

Now add three `TextView` objects to each of the new `TableRow`. This will be most easily achieved by adding them via the **Component Tree** window. Check your layout to make sure it is as in the following screenshot:

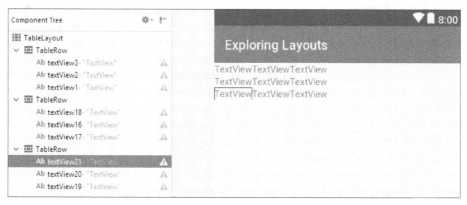

Let's make the table look more like a genuine table of data you might get in an app by changing some attributes.

On the `TableLayout`, set the attributes `layout_width` and `layout_height` to `wrap_content`. This gets rid of extra cells.

Change the color of all the outer (along the top and down the left-hand side) `TextView` objects to black by editing the `textColor` attribute. You achieve this by selecting the first `TextView`, searching for its `color` attribute, and then typing `black` in the `color` attribute values field. You will then be able to select `@android:color/black` from a drop-down list. Do this for each of the outer `TextView`.

Edit the `padding` of each `TextView` and change the `all` attribute to `10sp`.

Organizing the table columns

It might seem at this point that we are done, but we need to organise the data better. Our table, like many tables, will have a blank cell in the top-left to divide the column and row titles. To achieve this, we need to number all the cells. For this, we need to edit the `layout_column` attribute.

 Tip cell numbers are numbered from 0 from the left.

Start by deleting the top-left `TextView`. Notice that the `TextView` from the right has moved into the top-left position.

Next, in the new top-left `TextView`, edit the `layout_column` attribute to be 1 (this assigns it to the second cell because the first is 0 and we want to leave the first one empty) and, for the next cell along, edit the `layout_column` attribute to be 2.

For the next two rows of cells, edit their `layout_column` attributes from 0 to 2 from left to right.

If you want clarification on the precise code for this row after editing, here is a snippet, and remember to look in the download bundle in the `Chapter 4/LayoutExploration` folder to see the whole file in context:

```
<TableRow
    android:layout_width="wrap_content"
    android:layout_height="wrap_content">

    <TextView
        android:id="@+id/textView2"
        android:layout_width="wrap_content"
```

```
        android:layout_height="wrap_content"
        android:layout_column="1"
        android:padding="10sp"
        android:text="India"
        android:textColor="@android:color/black" />

    <TextView
        android:id="@+id/textView1"
        android:layout_width="wrap_content"
        android:layout_height="wrap_content"
        android:layout_column="2"
        android:padding="10sp"
        android:text="England"
        android:textColor="@android:color/black" />

</TableRow>
```

Try to complete this exercise, however, using the **Attributes** window if possible.

Linking back to the main menu

Finally, for this layout, we will add a button that links back to the menu. Add another `TableRow` via the **Component Tree**. Drag a button onto the new `TableRow`. Edit its `layout_column` attribute to 1 so that it is in the middle of the row. Edit its `text` attribute to Menu and edit its `onClick` attribute to match our already existing method `loadMenuLayout`.

You can now run the app and switch back and forth between the different layouts.

If you want to, you can add some meaningful titles and data to the table by editing all the `text` attributes of the `TextView` as I have done in this diagram showing the `TableLayout` running in the emulator:

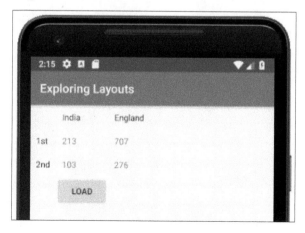

As a final thought, think about an app that presents tables of data. Chances are that data will be added to the table dynamically, not by the developer at design time as we have just done, but more likely by the user or from a database on the web. In *Chapter 16, Adapters, and Recyclers,* we will see how to dynamically add data to different types of layout using adapters and, in *Chapter 27, Android Databases,* we will also see how to create and use databases in our apps.

Summary

We have covered many topics in just a few dozen pages. We have not only built three different types of layout, including `LinearLayout` with nested layouts, `ConstraintLayout` with manually configured constraints, and `TableLayout` (albeit with fake data), but we have also wired all the layouts together with clickable buttons and text that trigger our Java code to switch between all these different layouts.

In the next chapter, we will stick with the topic of layouts. We will review the many attributes we have seen, and we will build our most aesthetically pleasing layout so far by incorporating multiple `CardView` layouts, complete with depth and shadow, into a smooth scrolling `ScrollView` layout.

5

Beautiful Layouts with CardView and ScrollView

This is the last chapter on layouts before we spend some time focusing on Java and object-oriented programming. We will formalize our learning on some of the different attributes we have already met, and we will also introduce two more cool layouts; the `ScrollView` and the `CardView`. To finish the chapter off, we will run the `CardView` project on a tablet emulator.

In this chapter, we will cover the following:

- Compile a quick summary of UI attributes
- Build our prettiest layout so far using `ScrollView` and `CardView`
- Switch and customize themes
- Create and use a tablet emulator

Let's start by recapping some attributes.

Attributes quick summary

In the last few chapters, we have used and discussed quite a few different attributes. I thought it would be worth a quick summary and further investigation of a few of the more common ones.

Sizing using dp

As we know, there are thousands of different Android devices. To try and have a system of measurement that works across different devices, Android uses **density-independent pixels**, or **dp**, as a unit of measurement. The way this works is by first calculating the density of the pixels on the device an app is running on.

 We can calculate density by dividing the horizontal resolution by the horizontal size in inches of the screen. This is all done on-the-fly on the device on which our app is running.

All we must do is use dp in conjunction with a number when setting the size of the various attributes of our widgets. Using density-independent measurements, we can design layouts that scale to create a uniform appearance on as many different screens as possible.

So, problem solved then? We just use dp everywhere and our layouts will work everywhere? Unfortunately, density independence is only part of the solution. We will see more of how we can make our apps look great on a range of different screens throughout the rest of the book.

As an example, we can affect the height and width of a widget, for example, by adding the following code to its attributes:

```
...
android:height="50dp"
android:width="150dp"
...
```

Alternatively, we can use the attributes window and add them through the comfort of the appropriate edit boxes. Which choice you use will depend on your personal preference, but sometimes one way will feel more appropriate than another in a given situation. Either way is correct, and as we go through the book making apps, I will usually point out if one way is *better* than another.

We can also use the same dp units to set other attributes, such as margin and padding. We will look more closely at margin and padding in a minute.

Sizing fonts using sp

Another device-dependent unit of measurement used for sizing Android fonts is **scalable pixels**, or **sp**. The sp unit of measurement is used for fonts and is pixel density-dependent in the exact same way that dp is.

The extra calculation that an Android device will use when deciding how big your font will be, based on the value of sp you use, is the user's own font size settings. So, if you test your app on devices and emulators with normal-sized fonts, then a user who has a sight impairment (or just likes big fonts) and has their font setting set to large will see something different to what you saw during testing.

If you want to try playing with your Android device's font size settings, you can do so by selecting **Settings | Display | Font size**:

As we can see in the preceding diagram, there are a quite a number of settings, and if you try it on **Huge,** the difference is, well, huge!

We can set the size of fonts using sp in any widget that has text. This includes Button, TextView, and all the UI elements under the **Text** category in the palette, as well as some others. We do so by setting the textSize property as follows:

```
android:textSize="50sp"
```

As usual, we can also use the Attributes window to achieve the same thing.

Determining size with wrap or match

We can also decide how the size of UI elements and many other UI elements behave in relation to the containing/parent element. We can do so by setting the layoutWidth and layoutHeight attributes to either wrap_content or match_parent.

For example, we can set the attributes of a lone button on a layout to the following:

```
. . .
android:layout_width="match_parent"
android:layout_height="match_parent"
. . . .
```

Then the button will expand in both height and width to **match** the **parent**. We can see that the button in the next image fills the entire screen:

More common for a button is `wrap_content`, as shown next:

```
. . . .
android:layout_width="wrap_content"
android:layout_height="wrap_content"
. . . .
```

This causes the button to be as big as it needs to be to **wrap** its **content** (width and height in dp and text in sp).

Using padding and margin

If you have ever done any web design, then you will be very familiar with the next two attributes. **Padding** is the space from the edge of the widget to the start of the content in the widget. **Margin** is the space outside of the widget that is left between other widgets—including the margin of other widgets, should they have any. Here is a visual representation:

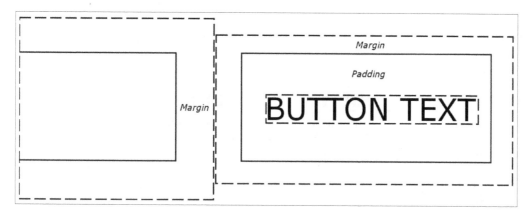

We can set padding and margin in a straightforward way, and equally for all sides, like this:

```
. . .
android:layout_margin="43dp"
android:padding="10dp"
. . .
```

Look at the slight difference in naming convention for the margin and the padding. The padding is just called `padding`, but the margin is referred to as `layout_margin`. This reflects the fact that padding only affects the UI element itself, but margin can affect other widgets in the layout.

Or we can specify different top, bottom, left, and right margin and padding, as follows:

```
android:layout_marginTop="43dp"
android:layout_marginBottom="43dp"
android:paddingLeft="5dp"
android:paddingRight="5dp"
```

Specifying margin and padding values for a widget is optional, and a value of zero will be assumed if nothing is specified. We can also choose to specify some of the different sides' margins and padding but not others, as in the earlier example.

It is probably becoming obvious that the way we design our layouts is extremely flexible, but also that it is going to take some practice to achieve precise results with these many options. We can even specify negative margin values to create overlapping widgets.

Let's look at a few more attributes, and then we will go ahead and play around with a stylish layout—CardView.

Using the layout_weight property

Weight refers to a relative amount compared to other UI elements. So, for layout_weight to be useful, we need to assign a value to the layout_weight property on two or more elements.

We can then assign portions that add up to 100% in total. This is especially useful for dividing up screen space between parts of the UI in which we want the relative space they occupy to remain the same regardless of screen size.

Using layout_weight in conjunction with sp and dp units can make for a simple and flexible layout. For example, look at this code:

```
<Button
        android:layout_width="match_parent"
        android:layout_height="0dp"
        android:layout_weight=".1"
        android:text="one tenth" />


<Button
        android:layout_width="match_parent"
        android:layout_height="0dp"
        android:layout_weight=".2"
        android:text="two tenths" />


<Button
        android:layout_width="match_parent"
        android:layout_height="0dp"
        android:layout_weight=".3"
        android:text="three tenths" />
```

```
<Button
        android:layout_width="match_parent"
        android:layout_height="0dp"
        android:layout_weight=".4"
        android:text="four tenths" />
```

Here is what this code will do:

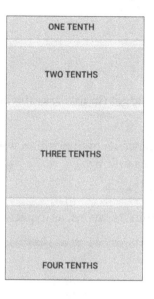

Notice that all the `layout_height` attributes are set to `0dp`. Effectively, the `layout_weight` is replacing the `layout_height` property. The context in which we use `layout_weight` is important (or it won't work), and we will see this in a real project soon. Also note that we don't have to use fractions of 1; we can use whole numbers, percentages, and any other number. As long as they are relative to each other, they will probably achieve the effect you are after. Note that `layout_weight` only works in certain contexts, and we will get to see where as we build more layouts.

Using Gravity

Gravity can be our friend, and can be used in so many ways in our layouts. Just like gravity in the solar system, it affects the position of items by moving them in a given direction, like they were being acted upon by gravity. The best way to see what gravity can do is to look at some example code and diagrams.

If the `gravity` property on a button (or another widget) is set to
`left|center_vertical` as follows, it will have an effect that looks like this:

```
android:gravity="left|center_vertical"
```

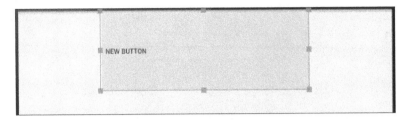

Notice that the content of the widget (in this case the button's text) is indeed aligned
left and centrally vertical.

In addition, a widget can influence its own position within a layout element with
the `layout_gravity` element, as follows:

```
android:layout_gravity="left"
```

This would set the widget within its layout, as expected, like this:

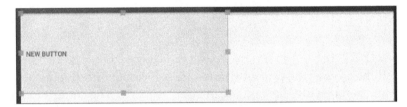

The previous code allows different widgets within the same layout to be affected as
if the layout has multiple different gravities.

The content of all the widgets in a layout can be affected by the `gravity` property of
their parent layout by using the same code as a widget:

```
android:gravity="left"
```

There are, in fact, many more attributes than those we have discussed. Many we
won't need in this book, and some are quite obscure, so you might never need them
in your entire Android career. But others are quite commonly used and include
`background`, `textColor`, `alignment`, `typeface`, `visibility`, and `shadowColor`.
Let's explore some more attributes and layouts now.

Building a UI with CardView and ScrollView

Create a new project in the usual way. Name the project `CardView Layout`. Leave the **Target Android Devices** section on the default settings and choose the **Empty Activity** project template. On the **Configure Activity** screen, uncheck the option to **Generate Layout File** because we will handle that ourselves. The activity name can be left as the default of **MainActivity**. The following screenshot shows these final settings:

Creates a new empty activity	
Activity Name:	MainActivity
	☐ Generate Layout File
	☑ Backwards Compatibility (AppCompat)

To be able to edit our theme and properly test the result, we need to generate our layout file and edit the Java code to display it by calling the `setContentView` method from the `onCreate` method. We will design our `CardView` masterpiece inside a `ScrollView` layout, which, as the name suggests, allows the user to scroll through the content of the layout.

Expand the folders in the project explorer window so you can see the `res` folder. Expand the `res` folder and you will notice that there is no `layout` folder. It is perfectly possible to build an app without using layout files and, as we selected not to generate a layout file, Android Studio didn't generate the `layout` folder either. We will add one now.

 We will build a game in *Chapter 28, Coding a Snake Game, using everything we have learned so far*, but which doesn't need any layout files.

Right-click the `res` folder and select **New | Android Resource Directory**. In the **Directory name** field, enter `layout` and, in the **Resource type** dropdown, choose **layout**. I have shown these options in the following screenshot. The other options can be left as their defaults. Click **OK** to complete the directory creation:

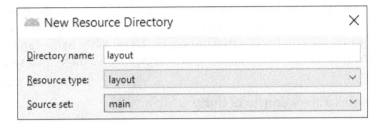

Right-click the newly created `layout` folder and select **New**. Notice that there is an option for **Layout resource file**. Select **Layout resource file** and you will see the **New Resource File** dialog window.

In the **File name** field, enter `main_layout`. The name is arbitrary, but this layout is going to be our main layout, so the name makes that plain.

Notice that it is set to **LinearLayout** as the **Root** element option. Change it to `ScrollView`. This layout type appears to work just like a `LinearLayout`, except that when there is too much content to display on screen, it will allow the user to scroll the content by swiping with their finger.

Click the **OK** button, and then Android Studio will generate a new `ScrollView` in an XML file called `main_layout` and place it in the newly generated `layout` folder ready for us to build our `CardView` based UI.

You can see our new file in our new directory in this next image:

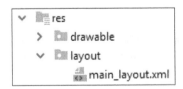

Android Studio will also open the UI designer ready for action.

Setting the view with Java code

As we have done before, we will now load the `main_layout.xml` file as the layout for our app by calling the `setContentView` method in the `MainActivity.java` file.

Select the `MainActivity.java` tab. In the unlikely event the tab isn't there by default, you can find it in the project explorer under `app/java/your_package_name`, where `your_package_name` is equal to the package name that was auto-generated when you created the project.

Amend the code in the `onCreate` method to look exactly like this next code. I have highlighted the line that you need to add:

```
@Override
protected void onCreate(Bundle savedInstanceState) {
    super.onCreate(savedInstanceState);

    setContentView(R.layout.main_layout);
}
```

You could now run the app, but there is nothing to see except an empty `ScrollView`.

Adding image resources

We are going to need some images for this project. This is so we can demonstrate how to add them into the project (this section) and neatly display and format them in a `CardView` (next section).

It doesn't really matter where you get your images from. It is the practical hands-on experience that is the purpose of this exercise. To avoid copyright and royalty issues, I am going to use some book images from the Packt Publishing website. This also makes it easy for me to provide you with all the resources you need to complete the project should you not want to go to the bother of acquiring your own images. Feel free to swap the images in the `Chapter 5/CardViewLayout/res/drawable` folder

There are three: `image_1.png`, `image_2.png`, and `image_3.png`. To add them to the project, follow these steps.

1. Find the image files using your operating system's file explorer.
2. Highlight them all and press *Ctrl + C* to copy them.
3. In the Android Studio project explorer, select the `res/drawable` folder by left-clicking it.

4. Right-click the `drawable` folder and select **Paste.**

5. In the pop-up window that asks you to **Choose Destination Directory,** click **OK** to accept the default destination, which is the `drawable` folder.

6. Click **OK** again to **Copy Specified Files.**

You should now be able to see your images in the `drawable` folder, along with a couple of other files that Android Studio placed there when the project was created, as shown in this next screenshot:

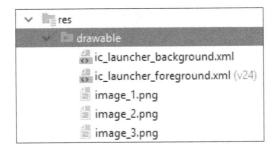

Before we move on to the `CardView`, let's design what we will put inside them.

Creating the content for the cards

The next thing we need to do is create the content for our cards. It makes sense to separate the content from the layout. What we will do is create three separate layouts called `card_contents_1`, `card_contents_2`, and `card_contents_3`. They will each contain a `LinearLayout`, which itself will contain the actual image and text.

Let's create three more layouts with `LinearLayout` at their root:

1. Right-click the `layout` folder and select **New layout resource file.**

2. Name the file `card_contents_1` and make sure that **LinearLayout** is selected as the **Root element**

3. Click **OK** to add the file to the `layout` folder

4. Repeat steps 1 through 3 two more times, changing the filename each time to `card_contents_2` and then `card_contents_3`

Now select the `card_contents_1.xml` tab and make sure you are in design view. We will drag and drop some elements to the layout to get the basic structure, and then we will add some `sp`, `dp`, and gravity attributes to make them look nice.

1. Drag a `TextView` on to the top of the layout
2. Drag an `ImageView` on to the layout below the `TextView`
3. In the **Resources** pop-up window, select **Project | image_1** and then click **OK**
4. Drag another two **TextView** below the image
5. This is how your layout should now appear:

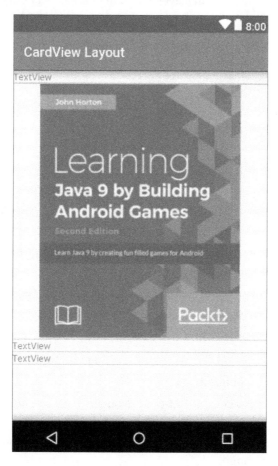

6. Now let's use some material design guidelines to make the layout look more appealing.

It is possible that as you proceed through these modifications, the UI elements on the bottom of the layout might disappear from the bottom of the design view. If this happens to you, remember you can always select any UI element from the **Component Tree** window underneath the palette. Or refer to the next tip.

Another way of minimizing the problem is to use a bigger screen, as explained in the following:

I changed the default device for design view to **Pixel 2 XL** to create the previous image. I will leave this setting for the rest of the book, unless I specifically mention that I am changing it. It allows a few more pixels on the layout and means this layout is easier to complete. If you want to do the same, look at the menu bar above the design view and click the device drop-down and choose your design view device, as shown in the following screenshot:

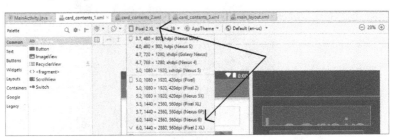

1. Set the `textSize` attribute for the `TextView` at the top to `24sp`.

2. Set the **Layout_Margin | all** attribute to `16dp`.

3. Set the `text` attribute to **Learning Java by Building Android Games** (or whatever title suits your image).

4. On the `ImageView`, set `layout_width` and `layout_height` to `wrap_content`.

5. On the `ImageView`, set `layout_gravity` to `center_horizontal`.

6. On the `TextView` beneath the `ImageView`, set `textSize` to `16sp`.

7. On the same `TextView`, set **Layout_Margin | all** to `16dp`.

8. On the same `TextView`, set the `text` attribute to `Learn Java and Android from scratch by building 6 playable games` (or something that describes your image).

9. On the bottom `TextView`, change the `text` attribute to `BUY NOW`.

10. On the same `TextView`, set the **Layout_Margin | all** to `16dp`.

11. On the same `TextView`, set the `textSize` attribute to `24sp`.

12. On the same `TextView`, set the `textColor` attribute to `@color/ colorAccent`.

13. On the `LinearLayout` holding all the other elements, set `padding` to `15dp`. Note that it is easiest to select `LinearLayout` from the **Component Tree** window.

14. At this point, your layout will look very similar to the following image:

Now lay out the other two files (`card_contents_2` and `card_contents_3`) with the exact same dimensions and colors. When you get the **Resources** pop-up to choose an image, use `image_2` and `image_3` respectively. Also change all the `text` attributes on the first two `TextView` elements so that the titles and descriptions are unique. The titles and descriptions don't really matter; it is layout and appearance that we are learning about.

> Note that all the sizes and colors were derived from the material design website here: `https://material.io/design/introduction`, and the Android-specific UI guideline here: `https://developer.android.com/guide/topics/ui/look-and-feel`. It is well worth studying alongside or soon after you complete this book.

Now we can move on to the `CardView`.

Defining dimensions for CardViews

Right-click the `values` folder and select **New | Values resource file**. In the **New Resource File** pop-up window, name the file `dimens.xml` (short for dimensions) and click **OK**. We will use this file to create some common values that our `CardView` will use by referring to them.

To achieve this, we will edit the XML directly. Edit the `dimens.xml` file to be the same as the following code:

```
<?xml version="1.0" encoding="utf-8"?>
<resources>
    <dimen name="card_corner_radius">16dp</dimen>
    <dimen name="card_margin">10dp</dimen>
</resources>
```

Be sure to make it exactly the same, because a small omission could cause an error and prevent the project from working.

We have defined two resources, the first called `card_corner_radius`, with a value of `16dp`, and the second called `card_margin`, with a value of `10dp`.

We will refer to these resources in the `main_layout` file and use them to consistently configure our three `CardView` elements.

Adding CardViews to our layout

Switch to the `main_layout.xml` tab and make sure you are in the design view. You probably recall that we are now working with a `ScrollView` that will scroll the content of our app, rather like a web browser scrolls the content of a web page that doesn't fit on one screen.

`ScrollView` has a limitation—it can only have one direct child layout. We want it to contain three `CardView` widgets.

To overcome this problem, drag a `LinearLayout` from the `Layouts` category of the palette. Be sure to pick **LinearLayout (vertical),** as represented by this icon in the palette:

We will add our three `CardViews` inside the `LinearLayout`, and then the whole thing will scroll nicely and smoothly without any errors.

`CardView` can be found in the **Containers** category of the palette, so switch to that and locate `CardView`.

Drag a `CardView` onto the `LinearLayout` on the design and you will get a pop-up message appear in Android Studio. This is the message pictured here:

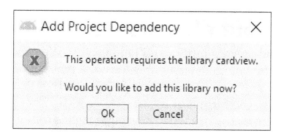

Click the **OK** button, and then Android Studio will do some work behind the scenes and add the necessary parts to the project. Android Studio has added some more classes to the project—specifically, classes that provide `CardView` features to older versions of Android that wouldn't otherwise have them.

You should now have a `CardView` on the design. Until there is some content in it, the `CardView` is only easily visible in the **Component Tree** window.

Select the `CardView` via the **Component Tree** and configure the following attributes:

1. Set `layout_width` to `wrap_content`
2. Set `layout_gravity` to `center`
3. Set **Layout_Margin | all** to `@dimens/card_margin`
4. Set `cardCornerRadius` to `@dimens/card_corner_radius`
5. Set `cardEleveation` to `2dp`

Now switch to the **Text** tab, and you will find you have something very similar to this next code:

```
<androidx.cardview.widget.CardView
    android:layout_width="wrap_content"
    android:layout_height="wrap_content"
    android:layout_gravity="center"
    android:layout_margin="@dimen/card_margin"
    app:cardCornerRadius="@dimen/card_corner_radius"
    app:cardElevation="2dp" />
```

The previous code listing only shows the code for the `CardView`.

The problem at the moment is that our `CardView` is empty. Let's fix that by adding the content of `card_contents_1.xml`. Here is how to do it.

Including layout files inside another layout

We need to edit the code very slightly, and here is why. We need to add an `include` element to the code. The `include` element is the code that will insert the content from the `card_contents_1.xml` layout. The problem is that to add this code, we need to slightly alter the format of the `CardView` XML. The current format starts and concludes the `CardView` with one single tag, as follows:

```
<androidx.cardview.widget.CardView
...
.../>
```

We need to change the format to a separate opening and closing tag like this (don't change anything just yet):

```
<androidx.cardview.widget.CardView
...
...
</androidx.cardview.widget.CardView>
```

This change in format will enable us to add the `include…` code, and then our first `CardView` will be complete. With this in mind, edit the code of the `CardView` to be exactly the same as the following code. I have highlighted the two new lines of code, but also note that the forward slash that was after the `cardElevation` attribute has also been removed:

```
<androidx.cardview.widget.CardView
    android:layout_width="wrap_content"
    android:layout_height="wrap_content"
    android:layout_gravity="center"
    android:layout_margin="@dimen/card_margin"
    app:cardCornerRadius="@dimen/card_corner_radius"
    app:cardElevation="2dp" >

    <include layout="@layout/card_contents_1" />

</androidx.cardview.widget.CardView>
```

You can now view the `main_layout` in the visual designer and see the layout inside the `CardView`. The visual designer does not reveal the real aesthetics of `CardView`. We will see all the `CardView` scrolling nicely in the completed app shortly. Here is an image of where we are up to so far:

Add two more `CardView` widgets to the layout and configure them to be the same as the first, but with one exception. On the second `CardView`, set the `cardElevation` to `22dp` and, on the third `CardView`, set the `cardElevation` to `42dp`. Also change the `include` code to reference `card_contents_2` and `card_contents_3`, respectively.

> You could do this very quickly by copying and pasting the `CardView` XML and simply amending the elevation and the `include` code, as mentioned in the previous paragraph.

Now we can run the app and see our three beautiful, elevated `CardView` in action. In this next image, I have photoshopped two screenshots side by side so you can see one full `CardView` in action (on the left) and, in the image on the right, the effect the elevation setting has, which creates a very pleasing depth with a shadow effect:

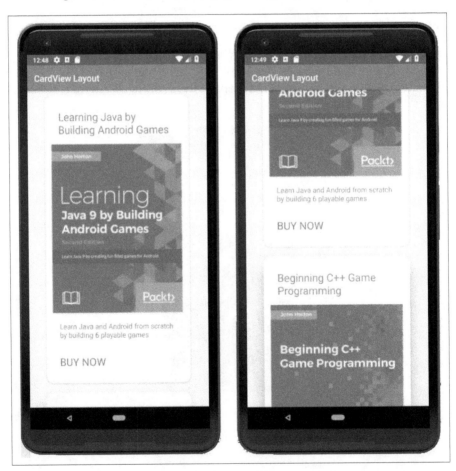

The image will likely be slightly unclear in the black and white printed version of this book. Be sure to build and run the app for yourself to see this cool effect.

Now we can play around with editing the theme of the app.

Themes and material design

Creating a new theme, technically speaking, is very easy, and we will see how to do it in a minute. From an artistic point of view, however, it is more difficult. Choosing which colors work well together, let alone suit your app and the imagery, is much more difficult. Fortunately, we can turn to material design for help.

Material design has guidelines for every aspect of UI design, and all the guidelines are very well documented. Even the sizes for text and padding that we used for the `CardView` project were all taken from material design guidelines.

Not only does material design make it possible for you to design your very own color schemes, it also provides palettes of ready-made color schemes.

 This book is not about design, although it is about implementing design. To get you started, the goal of our designs might be to make our UI unique and to stand out at the exact same time as making it comfortable for, even familiar to, the user.

Themes are constructed from XML `style` items. We saw the `styles.xml` file in *Chapter 3, Exploring Android Studio and the project structure*. Each item in the styles file defined the appearance and gave it a name such as `colorPrimary` or `colorAccent`.

The questions that remain are how do we choose our colors, and how do we implement them into our theme? The answer to the first question has two possible options. The first answer is to enrol on a design course and spend the next few years studying UI design. The more useful answer is to use one of the built-in themes and make customizations based on the material design guidelines discussed in depth for every UI element here: `https://developer.android.com/guide/topics/ui/look-and-feel/`.

We will do the latter now.

Using the Android Studio theme designer

From the Android Studio main menu, select **Tools | Theme Editor**. On the left-hand side, notice the UI examples that show what the theme will look like, and on the right are the controls to edit aspects of the theme:

As mentioned, the easiest way to create your own theme is to start with and then edit an existing theme. In the **Theme** drop-down, select a theme you like the look of. I chose **AppCompat Dark**:

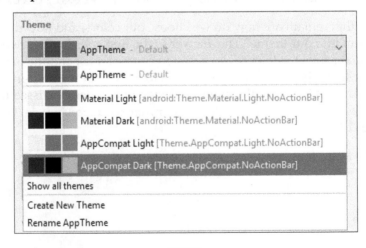

Select any items on the right-hand side that you want to change the color of, and then choose a color in the screen that follows:

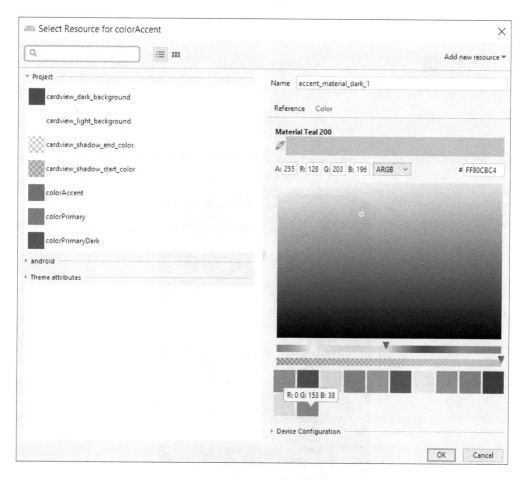

You will be prompted to choose a name for your new theme. I called mine `Theme.AppCompat.MyDarkTheme`:

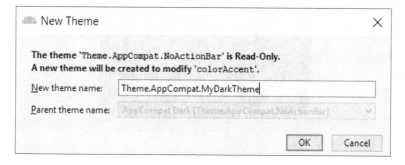

Now click the **fix** text to apply your theme to the current app, as indicated in the following screenshot:

You can then run your app on the emulator to see the theme in action:

So far, all our apps have been run on a phone. Obviously, a huge part of the Android device ecosystem is tablets. Let's see how we can test our apps on a tablet emulator, as well as get an advanced look at some of the problems this diverse eco system is going to cause us that we can then learn to overcome.

Creating a tablet emulator

Select **Tools | AVD Manager** and then click the **Create Virtual Device...** button on the **Your Virtual Devices** window. You will see the **Select Hardware** window, which pictured next:

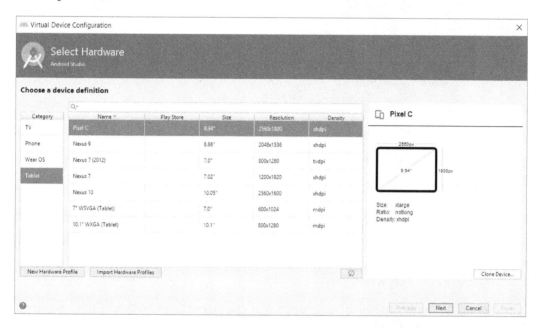

Select the **Tablet** option from the **Category** list, and then highlight the **Pixel C** tablet from the choice of available tablets. These choices are highlighted in the previous screenshot.

If you are reading this sometime in the future, the Pixel C option might have been updated. The choice of tablet is less important than practicing this process of creating a tablet emulator and then testing our apps.

Click the **Next** button. On the **System Image** window that follows, just click **Next**, because this will select the default system image. It is possible that choosing your own image will cause the emulator not to work properly.

Finally, on the **Android Virtual Device** screen, you can leave all the default options as they are. Feel free to change the **AVD Name** for your emulator or the **Startup Orientation** (portrait or landscape) if you want to:

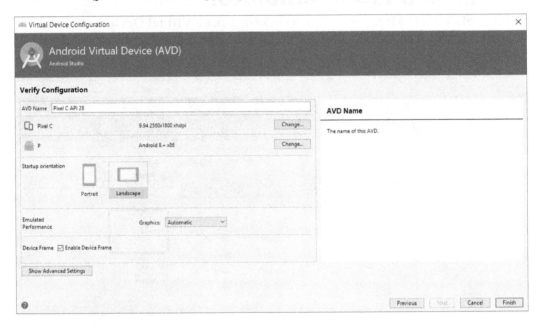

Click the **Finish** button when you are ready.

Now, whenever you run one of your apps from Android Studio, you will be given the option to choose **Pixel C** (or whatever tablet you created). Here is an image of my Pixel C emulator running the CardView app:

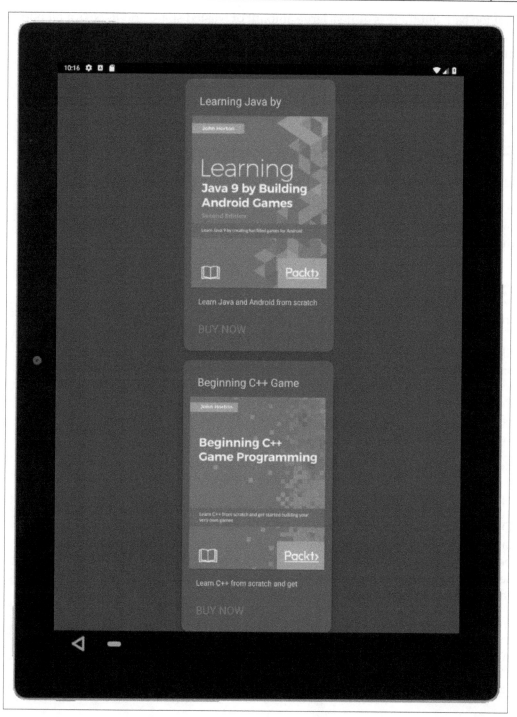

Not too bad, but there is quite a large amount of wasted space and it looks a bit odd. Let's try it in landscape mode. If you try running the app with the tablet in landscape mode, the results are worse. What we can learn from this is that we are going to have to design our layouts for differently sized screens and for different orientations. Sometimes, these will be clever designs that scale to suit different sizes or orientations, but often they will be completely different designs.

Frequently asked questions

Q) Do I need to master all this stuff about material design?

A) No. Unless you want to be a professional designer. If you just want to make your own apps and sell them or give them away on the Play Store, then knowing just the basics is good enough.

Summary

In this chapter, we built aesthetically pleasing `CardView` layouts and put them in a `ScrollView` so that the user can swipe through the content of the layout a bit like browsing a Web page. To conclude the chapter, we launched a tablet emulator and saw that we are going to need to get smart with how we design our layouts if we want to cater for different device sizes and orientations. In *Chapter 24, Design Patterns, Multiple Layouts and Fragments*, we will begin to take our layouts to the next level and learn how to cope with such a diverse array of devices using Android Fragments.

Before we do so, however, it will serve us well to learn more about Java and how we can use it to control our UI and interact with the user. This will be the focus of the next seven chapters.

Of course, the elephant in the room at this point is that despite learning lots about layouts, project structure, the connection between Java and XML and much more besides, our UIs, no matter how pretty, don't actually do anything! We need to seriously upgrade our Java skills while also learning more about how to apply them in an Android context.

In the next chapter, we will do exactly that. We will see how to add Java code that executes at exactly the moment we need it to by working with the **Android Activity lifecycle**.

6
The Android Lifecycle

In this chapter, we will get familiar with the lifecycle of an Android app. At first, this might sound a bit strange, that a computer program has a lifecycle, but it will make sense soon.

The lifecycle is the way that all Android apps interact with the Android OS. Just like the lifecycle of humans interacts with the world around them, we have no choice but to interact with it, and we must be prepared to handle different events without notice if we want our apps to survive.

We will see the phases of the lifecycle that an app goes through, from creation to destruction, and how this helps us know *where* to put out Java code, depending on what we are trying to achieve.

In brief, in this chapter, we will look at the following:

- The life and times of an Android app
- What is method overriding? And the @Override keyword
- The phases of the Android lifecycle
- What exactly we need to know and do to code our apps
- A lifecycle demonstration mini app
- Code structure, ready to get Java coding in the next chapter

Let's start learning about the Android lifecycle.

The life and times of an Android app

We have talked a bit about the structure of our code: we know that we can write classes, and within those classes we have methods, and these methods contain our code that gets things done. We also know that when we want the code within a method to run (be **executed**), we **call** that method by using its name.

Also, in *Chapter 2, First Contact: Java, XML and the UI Designer*, we learned that Android itself calls the onCreate method just before the app is ready to start. We saw this when we output to the logcat and used the Toast class to send a pop up message to the user.

What we will look at in this chapter is what happens throughout the lifecycle of every app we write; when it starts and ends, as well as a few stages in-between as well. And what we will see is that Android interacts with our app on numerous occasions each time it is run.

How Android interacts with our apps

It does so by calling methods that are contained within the Activity class. Even if the method is not visible within our Java code, it is still being called by Android at the appropriate time. If this doesn't seem to make any sense, then read on.

Did you ever wonder why the onCreate method had the strange-looking line of code just before it?

```
@Override
```

What is going on here is that we are saying to Android, when you call onCreate, please use our overridden version because we have some things to do at that time.

Furthermore, you might remember the odd-looking first line of code in the onCreate method:

```
super.onCreate(savedInstanceState)
```

This is telling Android to call the original/official version of onCreate before proceeding with our overridden version. This is not just a quirk of Android; **method overriding** is built in to Java.

There are also many other methods that we can optionally override, and they allow us to add our code at appropriate times within the lifecycle of our Android app. Just as onCreate is called right before the app is shown to the user, so there are more methods that are called at other times. We haven't seen them yet, we haven't overridden them yet, but they are there, they are called, and their code executes.

The reason we need to care about the methods of *our* app that Android calls whenever it wants is because they control the very life and death of our code. For instance, what if our app allows the user to type an important reminder. Then, halfway through typing the reminder, their phone rings, our app disappears, and the data (the reminder) is gone.

It is vital, and thankfully quite straightforward, that we learn when, why, and which methods Android will call as part of the lifecycle of our app. We can then know where we need to override methods to add our own code and where to add the real functionality (code) that defines our app.

Let's examine the Android lifecycle. We can then move on to the ins and outs of Java and will know exactly where to put the code that we write.

A simplified explanation of the Android lifecycle

If you have ever used an Android device, you have probably noticed it works quite differently to many other operating systems. For example, you might be using an app—say you're checking what people are doing on Facebook.

Then you get an email notification and you tap the notification to read it. Midway through reading the email, you might get a Twitter notification, and because you are waiting on important news from someone you follow, you interrupt your email reading and change apps to Twitter with just a touch.

After reading the tweet, you fancy a game of *Angry Birds*, but midway through the first fling, you suddenly remember that Facebook post. So, you quit Angry Birds and tap the Facebook icon.

Then you resume Facebook, probably at the exact same point at which you left it. You could have resumed reading the email, decided to reply to the tweet, or started an entirely new app.

All this toing and froing takes quite a lot of management on the part of the operating system, independent from the individual apps themselves.

The difference between, for example, a Windows PC and Android in the context we have just discussed is this: with Android, although the user decides which app they are using, the OS decides when to close down (destroy) an application and **our user's data** (like the hypothetical note) along with it. We just need to consider this when coding our apps. Just because we might write code to do some cool thing with our user's input doesn't mean that Android will let the code execute.

The lifecycle phases demystified

The Android system has multiple distinct phases that any given app can be in. Depending upon the phase, the Android system decides how the app is viewed by the user, or whether it is viewed at all.

Android has these phases, so it can decide which app is in current use and then allocate the correct amount of resources, such as memory and processing power.

In addition, as the user interacts with the device, for example, by touching the screen, Android must give the details of that interaction to the correct app. For instance, a drag and release movement in *Angry Birds* means take a shot, but in a messaging app, it might mean delete a text message.

We have already raised the issue of when the user quits our app to answer a phone call; will they lose their progress/data/important note?

Android has a system which when simplified a little for the purposes of explanation, means that every app on an Android device is in one of the following phases:

- Being created
- Starting
- Resuming
- Running
- Pausing
- Stopping
- Being destroyed

The list of phases will hopefully appear logical. As an example, the user presses the Facebook app icon and the app is **created**. Then it is **started**. All straightforward so far, but next in the list is **resuming**.

It is not as illogical as it might first appear. If, for a moment, we can just accept that the app resumes after it starts, then all will become clear as we continue.

After **resuming,** the app is **running**. This is when the Facebook app has control of the screen and the greater share of system memory and processing power, and is receiving the details of the user's input.

Now, what about our example in which we switched from the Facebook app to the email app?

As we tap to go to read our email, the Facebook app will have entered the **paused** phase, followed by the stopping phase, and the email app will enter the being **created** phase, followed by **resuming** and then **running**.

If we decide to revisit Facebook, as in the scenario earlier, the Facebook app will probably skip being created and go straight to **resume** and then be **running** again, most likely at the exact same place we left it.

Note that at any time, Android can decide to **stop** and then **destroy** an app, in which case, when we run the app again, it will need to be **created** at the first phase all over again.

So, had the Facebook app been inactive long enough, or Angry Birds had needed so many system resources that Android had **destroyed** the Facebook app, then our experience of finding the exact post we were previously reading might have been different.

If all this phase stuff is starting to get confusing, then you will be pleased to know that the only reason to mention it is so that:

- You know it exists
- We occasionally need to interact with it
- We will take things step by step when we do

How we handle the lifecycle phases

When we are programming an app, how do we interact with this complexity? The good news is that the Android code that was auto-generated when we created our first project does most of it for us.

As we have discussed, we just don't see the methods that handle this interaction, but we do have the opportunity to **override** them and add our own code to that phase **if** we need to.

This means we can get on with learning Java and making Android apps until we come to one of the occasional instances in which we need to do something in one of the phases.

 If our app has more than one Activity, they will each have their own lifecycle. This doesn't have to complicate things and, overall, it will make things easier for us.

The following is a quick explanation of the methods provided by Android, for our convenience, to manage the lifecycle phases. To clarify our discussion of lifecycle methods, they are listed next to their corresponding phases which we have been discussing. However, as you will see, the method names make it clear on their own where they fit in.

There is also a brief explanation or suggestion when we might use a given method, and thereby interact during a specific phase. We will meet most of these methods as we progress through the book. We have, of course, already seen `onCreate`:

- `onCreate`: This method is executed when the Activity is being *created*. Here, we get everything ready for the app, including the UI (such as calling `setContentView`), graphics, and sound.

- `onStart`: This method is executed when the app is in the *starting* phase.

- `onResume`: This method runs after `onStart`, but can also be entered (most logically) after our Activity is resuming after being previously paused. We might reload previously saved user data (such as an important note) from when the app had been interrupted, perhaps by a phone call or the user running another app.

- `onPause`: This occurs when our app is *pausing*. Here, we might save unsaved data (such as the note) that could be reloaded in `onResume`. Activities always transition into a paused state when another UI element is displayed on top of the current activity (for example, a pop up dialog) or when the activity is about to stopped (for example, when the user navigates to a different activity).

- `onStop`: This relates to the *stopping* phase. This is where we might undo everything we did in `onCreate`, such as releasing system resources or writing information to a database. If we reach here, we are probably going to get destroyed sometime soon.

- `onDestroy`: This is when our activity is finally being *destroyed*. There is no turning back at this phase. This is our last chance to dismantle our app in an orderly manner. If we reach this stage, we will be going through the lifecycle phases from the beginning next time.

This diagram shows the likely flows of execution between the methods:

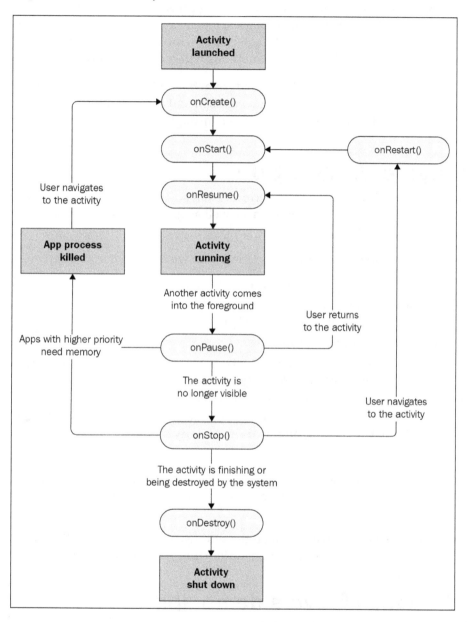

All the method descriptions and their related phases should appear straightforward. The only real question is what about the running phase? As we will see when we write our code in the other methods/phases, the `onCreate`, `onStart`, and `onResume` methods will prepare the app, which then persists, forming the running phase. Then, the `onPause`, `onStop`, and `onDestroy` methods will occur afterward.

Now we can look at these lifecycle methods in action with a mini app. We will do so by overriding them all and adding a `Log` message and a `Toast` message to each. This will visually prove the phases our app passes through.

Lifecycle demo app

In this section, we will do a quick experiment that will help familiarize ourselves with the lifecycle methods our app uses, as well as give us a chance to play around with a bit more Java code.

Follow these steps to start a new project, and then we can add some code:

1. Start a new project and call it **Lifecycle Demo**. Of course, the code is in the download bundle in the `Chapter 6/Lifecycle Demo` folder should you wish to refer to it or copy and paste it.
2. Accept the default target devices.
3. Choose **Basic Activity** and don't worry about customizing the activity options on the **Configure Activity** screen.
4. Wait for Android Studio to generate the project files, and then open the `MainActivity.java` file in the code editor (if it is not opened for you by default) by left-clicking on the **Main Activity** tab above the editor.

 If the preceding steps were not detailed enough, check back to any of the other occasions in which we created a new project for further details.

You have created a new project with all the settings on default. We will only need the `MainActivity.java` file for this demonstration and will not be building a UI.

Coding the lifecycle demo app

In the `MainActivity.java` file, find the `onCreate` method and add these two lines of code just before the closing curly brace } that marks the end of the `onCreate` method:

```
Toast.makeText(this, "In onCreate", Toast.LENGTH_SHORT).show();
Log.i("info", "In onCreate");
```

The entire `onCreate` method should now look like this next code, wherein the highlighted code is the two lines we just added and the ... is where we have skipped some lines of auto-generated code to make the book more readable. For full code listings, check the `MainActivity.java` file in the download bundle. Here is the code:

```
@Override
protected void onCreate(Bundle savedInstanceState) {
    super.onCreate(savedInstanceState);
    setContentView(R.layout.activity_main);




            Toast.makeText(this, "In onCreate",
                Toast.LENGTH_SHORT).show();


            Log.i("info", "In onCreate");
}
```

 Remember you will need to use the *Alt* | *Enter* keyboard combination twice to import the classes needed for `Toast` and `Log`.

After the closing curly brace, }, of the `onCreate` method, leave one clear line and add the following five lifecycle methods and their contained code. Also note that it doesn't matter in which order we add our overridden methods. Android will call them in the correct order, regardless of the order in which we type them:

```
@Override
public void onStart() {
    // First call the "official" version of this method
    super.onStart();

    Toast.makeText(this, "In onStart",
        Toast.LENGTH_SHORT).show();

    Log.i("info", "In onStart");
}

@Override
public void onResume() {
    // First call the "official" version of this method
    super.onResume();
```

```
        Toast.makeText(this, "In onResume",
            Toast.LENGTH_SHORT).show();

        Log.i("info", "In onResume");
    }

    @Override
    public void onPause() {
        // First call the "official" version of this method
        super.onPause();

        Toast.makeText(this, "In onPause",
            Toast.LENGTH_SHORT).show();

        Log.i("info", "In onPause");
    }

    @Override
    public void onStop() {
        // First call the "official" version of this method
        super.onStop();

        Toast.makeText(this, "In onStop",
            Toast.LENGTH_SHORT).show();

        Log.i("info", "In onStop");
    }

    @Override
    public void onDestroy() {
        // First call the "official" version of this method
        super.onDestroy();

        Toast.makeText(this, "In onDestroy",
            Toast.LENGTH_SHORT).show();

        Log.i("info", "In onDestroy");
    }
```

First, let's talk about the code itself. Notice that the method names all correspond to the lifecycle methods and phases we discussed earlier in this chapter. Notice that all the method declarations are preceded by the @Override line of code. Also see that the first line of code inside each method is super.on.....

What exactly is going on here is the following:

- Android calls our methods at the various times we have already discussed.

- The @Override keyword shows that these methods replace/override the original version of the method that is provided as part of the Android API. Note that we don't see these overridden methods but they are there, and if we didn't override them, these original versions would be called by Android instead of ours.

super.on..., which is the first line of code within each of the overridden methods, then calls these original versions. So, we don't simply override these original methods in order to add our own code; we also call them, and their code is executed too.

 For the curious, the keyword super is for super-class. We will explore method overriding and super classes in several chapters as we progress.

Finally, the code that you added will make each of the methods output one Toast message and one Log message. However, the messages that are output vary, as can be seen by the text between the double quote marks, "". The messages that are output will make it clear which method produced them.

Running the lifecycle demo app

Now that we have looked at the code, we can play with our app and learn about the lifecycle from what happens:

1. Run the app on either a device or an emulator.

2. Watch the screen of the emulator and you will see the following appear one after the other as Toast messages on the screen: **In onCreate, In onStart,** and **In onResume**.

3. Notice the following messages in the logcat window. If there are too many messages, remember that you can filter them by setting the **Log level** dropdown to **Info**:

   ```
   info:in onCreate
   info:in onStart
   info:in onResume
   ```

4. Now tap the **Back** button on the emulator or the device. Notice that you get the following three Toast messages in exactly this order: **In onPause, In onStop,** and **In onDestroy**. Verify that we have matching output in the logcat window.

5. Next, run a different app. Perhaps the Hello Android app from *Chapter 1, Beginning Android and Java*, (but any app will do) by tapping its icon on the emulator/device screen.

6. Now try the following: Open the task manager on the emulator.

 See *Chapter 3, Exploring Android Studio and the project structure*, and the section *Using the emulator as a real device* for how to do this on the emulator if you are unsure.

7. You should now see all the recently run apps on the device.

8. Tap the **Lifecycle Demo** app and notice that the usual three starting messages are shown. This is because our app was previously destroyed.

9. Now, however, tap the task manager button again and switch to the **Hello Android** app. Notice that this time, only the **In onPause** and **In onStop** messages are shown. Verify that we have matching output in the logcat. The app has **not** been destroyed.

10. Now, again using the task manager button, switch to the **Lifecycle Demo** app. You will see that only the **In onStart** and **In onResume** messages are shown, indicating that onCreate was not required to get the app running again. This is as expected because the app was not previously destroyed; it was merely stopped.

Next, let's talk about what we saw when we ran the app.

Examining the Lifecycle Demo app output

When we started the Lifecycle Demo app for the first time, we saw that the onCreate, onStart, and onResume methods were called. Then, when we closed the app using the back button, the onPause, onStop, and onDestroy methods were called.

Furthermore, we know from our code that the original versions of all these methods are also called because we are calling them ourselves with the super.on... code, which is the first thing we do in each of our overridden methods.

The quirk in our app's behaviour came when we used the task manager to switch between apps, and when switching away from the Lifecycle Demo, it was not destroyed, and subsequently, when switching back, it was not necessary to run onCreate.

Where's my Toast?

The opening three and closing three `Toast` messages are queued and the methods have already completed by the time they are shown. You can verify this by running the experiments again to see that all three starting/closing log messages are output before even the second `Toast` message is shown. However, the `Toast` messages do reinforce our knowledge about the order, if not the timing.

It is entirely possible (but not that likely) that you got slightly different results when you followed the preceding steps. What is for sure is that when our apps are run on thousands of different devices by millions of different users who have different preferences for interacting with their devices, Android will be calling the lifecycle methods at times we cannot easily predict.

For example, what happens when the user exits the app by pressing the home button? When we open two apps one after the other and then use the back button to switch to the earlier app, will that destroy or just stop the app? What happens when the user has a dozen apps in his task manager and the operating system needs to destroy some apps that were previously only stopped; will our app be one of the 'victims'?

You can, of course, test out all the above scenarios on the emulator. But the results will only be true for the one time you test it. It is not guaranteed that the same behavior will be exhibited every time, and certainly not on every different Android device.

At last, some good news! The solution to all this complexity is to follow a few simple rules:

- Set up your app ready to run in the `onCreate` method.
- Load your user's data in the `onResume` method.
- Save your user's data in the `onPause` method.
- Tidy up your app and make it a good Android citizen in the `onDestroy` method.
- Watch out throughout the book for a couple of occasions in which we might like to use `onStart` and `onStop`.

If we do these things, and we will see over the course of the book how to do so, we can just stop worrying about all this lifecycle stuff and let Android handle it!

There are a few more methods we can override as well. So let's look at them.

Some other overridden methods

Almost certainly, you will have noticed that there are two other auto-generated methods in the code of all our projects using the Basic Activity template. They are `onCreateOptionsMenu` and `onOptionsItemSelected`. Most Android apps have a pop up menu, so Android Studio generates one by default, including the basic code to make it work.

You can see the XML that describes the menu in `res/menu/menu_main.xml` from the project explorer. The key line of XML code is this:

```
<item
        android:id="@+id/action_settings"
        android:orderInCategory="100"
        android:title="@string/action_settings"
        app:showAsAction="never" />
```

This describes a menu **item** with the text **Settings**. If you run any of the apps built with the Basic Activity template we have created so far, you can see the button as shown in the following screenshot:

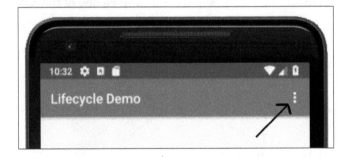

If you tap the button, you can see it in action, as shown next:

So how do the `onCreateOptionsMenu` and `onOptionsItemSelected` methods produce these results?

The `onCreateOptionsMenu` method loads the menu from the `menu_main.xml` file with this line of code:

```
getMenuInflater().inflate(R.menu.menu_main, menu);
```

It is called by the default version of the `onCreate` method, which is why we don't see it happen.

We will use the pop up menu in *Chapter 17, Data Persistence and Sharing* to switch between different screens of our app.

The `onOptionsItemSelected` method is called when the user taps the menu button. This method handles what will happen when an item is selected. Now, nothing happens; it just `returns true`.

Feel free to add `Toast` and `Log` messages to these methods to test out the order and timing I have just described. I just thought it a good time to quickly introduce these two methods because they have been lurking around in our code without an introduction and I didn't want them to feel left out.

Now that we have seen how the Android lifecycle works and have been introduced to a whole bunch of methods we can override to interact with the lifecycle, we had better learn the fundamentals of Java so that we can write some code to go in these methods, as well as our own methods.

The structure of Java code – revisited

We have already seen that each time we create a new Android project, we also create a new Java **package** as a kind of container for the code we write.

We have also learned about and played around with **classes**. We have imported and taken direct advantage of classes from the Android API, such as `Log` and `Toast`. We have also used the `AppCompatActivity` class, but in a different manner to that of `Log` and `Toast`. You might recall that the first line of code in all our projects so far, after the `import` statements, used the `extends` keyword:

```
public class MainActivity extends AppCompatActivity {
```

When we extend a class, as opposed to just importing it, we are making it our own. In fact, if you take another look at the line of code, you can see that we are making a new class with a new name, `MainActivity`, but basing it on the `AppCompatActivity` class from the Android API.

> `AppCompatActivity` is a slightly modified version of `Activity`. It gives extra features to older versions of Android that would otherwise not be present. Everything we have discussed about `Activity` is equally true for `AppCompatActivity`. We will see some more variations on the `Activity` class as we progress. It is entirely possible that you have a different class in place of `AppCompatActivity`, dependent upon changes that have taken place since this was written. Updates to Android Studio will sometimes change the default `Activity` class that it uses when it creates a new project. If the name ends in ...`Activity`, it doesn't matter because everything we have discussed and will discuss is equally true. I will usually just refer to this class simply as `Activity`.

In summary:

- We can import classes to use them
- We can extend classes to use them
- We will eventually make our own classes

The crucial point here is this:

> Classes, in their various forms, are the foundations of every single line of code in Java. Everything in Java is, or is part of, a class.

Our own classes, and those written by others, are the building blocks of our code, and the methods within the classes wrap the functional code—the code that does the work.

We can write methods within the classes that we extend, as we did with `topClick` and `bottomClick` in *Chapter 2, First Contact: Java, XML and the UI*. Furthermore, we overrode methods that are already part of classes written by others, such as `onCreate` and `onPause`.

The only code, however, that we put in these methods was a few calls using `Toast` and `Log`. We aren't going to code the next killer app with just that. But now we can take some more steps.

Summary

We have seen that it is not only us that can call our code. The operating system can also call the code contained within the methods we have overridden. By adding the appropriate code to the various overridden lifecycle methods, we can be sure that the right code will be executed at the right time.

What we need to do now is learn how to write some more Java code. In the next chapter, we will start to focus on Java and, because we have such a good grounding already in Android, we will have no problem practicing and using everything we learn.

7
Java Variables, Operators, and Expressions

In this chapter and the next, we are going to learn and practice the core fundamentals of Java data and manipulating that data. In this chapter, we will focus on the creation and understanding of the data itself, and in the next, we will see how to manipulate and respond it.

We will also quickly recap what we learned in the earlier chapters about Java, and then dive into learning how to write our very own Java code. The principles we are about to learn are not limited to Java, but are also applicable to other programming languages as well.

By the end of the chapter, you will be comfortable writing Java code that creates and uses data within Android. This chapter takes you through the following:

- Java syntax and jargon
- Variables
- Operators
- Expressions

Let's learn some Java.

Java is everywhere

The core Java fundamentals that we are about to learn apply when working within classes that we inherit from (such as `Activity`/`AppCompatActivity`), as well as classes that we write ourselves (as we will start to do in *Chapter 10, Object-Oriented Programming*).

As it is more logical to learn the basics before we write our own classes, we will be using the extended `Activity` class, `AppCompatActivity`, to add lots of different code in a whole bunch of mini-projects in the next few chapters to learn and practice Java. We will use `Log` and `Toast` again to see the results of our coding. In addition, we will use more methods that we will write ourselves (called from buttons), as well as the overridden methods of the `Activity` class to trigger the execution of our code. We will finally get the full details on methods in *Chapter 9, Java Methods*.

When, however, we move onto *Chapter 10, Object-Oriented Programming*, and start to write our own classes, as well as understand more about how classes written by others work, everything we have learned here will apply then too. In fact, this applies to all the Java that you learn in this chapter and the next, if you strip it out of the `Activity` class and paste it into another Java environment, such as any of the following:

- Any of the major desktop operating systems
- Many modern televisions
- Satellite navigation systems
- Smart fridges
- and more...

The Java will work there too!

Calling all Java gurus!

If you have already done some Java programming and understand the following words: **if**, **else**, **while**, **do while**, **switch** and **for**, you can probably skip to *Chapter 10, Object-Oriented programming*. Or you might like to skim over this information as a refresher.

Let's get on with learning how to code in Java.

Syntax and jargon

Throughout this book, we will use plain English to discuss some technical things. You will never be asked to read the technical explanation of a Java or Android concept that has not been previously explained in non-technical language.

So far, on a few occasions, I have asked that you accept a simplified explanation to offer a fuller explanation at a more appropriate time, like I have with classes and methods.

Having said that, the Java and Android communities are full of people who speak in technical terms, and to join in and learn from these communities, you need to understand the terms they use. So, the approach this book takes is to learn a concept or appreciate an idea using entirely plain-speaking language, but at the same time introduce the jargon/technical term as part of the learning.

Java syntax is the way we put together the language elements of Java to produce code that works in the Dalvik virtual machine. The Java syntax is a combination of the words we use and the formation of those words into sentence-like structures that is our code.

These Java "words" are many in number, but taken in small chunks, they are certainly easier to learn than any human spoken language. We call these words **keywords**.

I am confident that, if you can read, then you can learn Java, because learning Java is much easier. What, then, separates someone who has finished an elementary Java course and an expert programmer?

The exact same things that separate a student of language and a master poet. Expertise in Java comes not in the number of Java keywords we know how to use, but in the way we use them. Mastery of the language comes through practice, further study, and using the keywords more skillfully. Many consider programming an art as much as a science, and there is some truth to this.

More code comments

As you become more advanced at writing Java programs, the solutions you use to create your programs will become longer and more complicated. Furthermore, as we will see in later chapters, Java was designed to manage complexity by having us divide up our code into separate classes, very often across multiple files.

Code comments are a part of the Java program that do not have any function in the program execution itself. The compiler ignores them. They serve to help the programmer to document, explain, and clarify their code to make it more understandable to themselves later, or to other programmers who might need to use or change it.

We have already seen a single-line comment:

```
// this is a comment explaining what is going on
```

The preceding comment begins with the two forward slash characters, //. The comment ends at the end of the line. So, anything on that line is for humans only, whereas anything on the next line (unless it's another comment) needs to be syntactically correct Java code:

```
// I can write anything I like here
but this line will cause an error
```

We can use multiple single-line comments:

```
// Below is an important note
// I am an important note
// We can have as many single line comments like this as we like
```

Single-line comments are also useful if we want to temporarily disable a line of code. We can put // in front of the code and it will not be included in the program. Remember this code, which tells Android to load our layout?:

```
// setContentView(R.layout.activity_main);
```

In this situation, the layout will not be loaded and the app will have a blank screen when run, as the entire line of code is ignored by the compiler.

 We saw this in *Chapter 4, Getting Started with Layouts and Material Design*, when we temporarily commented out one of our methods.

There is another type of comment in Java known as the **multi-line comment**. The multi-line comment is useful for longer comments that span across multiple lines and for adding things such as copyright information at the top of a code file. Like the single-line comment, a multi-line comment can be used to temporarily disable code; in this case, usually across multiple lines.

Everything in between the leading /* and the ending */ is ignored by the compiler. Here are some examples:

```
/*
    You can tell I am good at this because my
    code has so many helpful comments in it.
*/
```

There is no limit to the number of lines in a multi-line comment. Which type of comment is best to use will depend upon the situation. In this book, I will always explain every line of code explicitly in the text, but you will often find liberally sprinkled comments within the code itself which add further explanation, insight or context. So, it's always a good idea to read all the code thoroughly too:

```
/*
    The winning lottery numbers for next Saturday are
    9,7,12,34,29,22
    But you still want to make Android apps?
*/
```

[All the best Java programmers liberally sprinkle their code with comments!]

Storing and using data with variables

We can think of a **variable** as a named storage box. We choose a name, perhaps variableA. These names are like our programmer's window into the memory of the user's Android device.

Variables are values in memory ready to be used or altered when necessary by using their name.

Computer memory has a highly complex system of addressing that, fortunately, we do not need to interact with. Java variables allow us to devise our own convenient names for all the data we need our program to work with. The DVM will handle all the technicalities to interact with the operating system and the operating system will in turn interact with the physical memory.

So, we can think of our Android device's memory as a huge warehouse just waiting for us to add our variables to it. When we assign names to our variables, they are stored in the warehouse ready for when we need them. When we use our variable's name, the device knows exactly what we are referring to. We can then tell it to do things such as the following:

- Assign a value to variableA
- Add variableA to variableB
- Test the value of variableB and take an action based on the result
- And more, as we will soon see

In a typical app, we might have a variable named `unreadMessages`; perhaps to hold the number of unread messages the user has. We could add to it when a new message arrives, take away from it when the user reads a message, and show it to the user somewhere in the app layout so they know how many unread messages they have.

Situations that might arise could include the following:

- User gets 3 new messages, so add 3 to the value of `unreadMessages`.
- User logs into the app, so use `Toast` to display a message along with the value stored in `unreadMessages`.
- User sees that a bunch of the messages are from someone she doesn't like and deletes 6 messages. We could then subtract 6 from `unreadMessages`.

These are arbitrary examples of names for variables, and if you don't use any of the characters or keywords that Java restricts, you can actually call your variables whatever you like.

In practice,however, it is best to adopt a **naming convention** so that your variable names will be consistent. In this book, we will use a loose convention of variable names starting with a lowercase letter. When there is more than one word in the variable's name, the second word will begin with an uppercase letter. This is called **camel casing**.

Here are some examples of camel casing:

`unreadMessages`

`contactName`

`isFriend`

Before we look at some real Java code with some variables, we need to first look at the **types** of variables we can create and use.

Types of variables

It is not hard to imagine that even a simple app will have quite a few variables. In the previous section, we introduced the `unreadMessages` variable as a hypothetical example. What if the app has a list of contacts and needs to remember each of their names? We might then need variables for each contact.

And what about when an app needs to know whether a contact is also a friend, or just a regular contact? We might need code that tests for friend status and then adds messages from that contact into an appropriate folder so the user knows whether they were messages from a friend or not.

Another common requirement in a computer program, including Android apps, is the right or wrong test. Computer programs represent right or wrong calculations using true or false.

To cover these and many other types of data you might want to store or manipulate, Java has **types**.

Primitive types

There are many types of variables, and we can even invent our own types as well. But, for now, we will look at the most used built-in Java types. And, to be fair, they cover just about every situation which we are likely to run into for a while. Some examples are the best way to explain types.

We have already discussed the hypothetical unreadMessages variable. This variable is, of course, a number, so we have to tell the Java compiler this by giving it an appropriate type.

On the other hand, the hypothetical contactName will, of course, hold the characters that make up a contact's name.

The type that holds a regular number is called an **int**, and the type that holds name-like data is called a **String**. And if we try and store a contact name – perhaps "Ada Lovelace" – in an int such as unreadMessages – meant for numbers – we will certainly run into trouble, as we can see from the next screenshot:

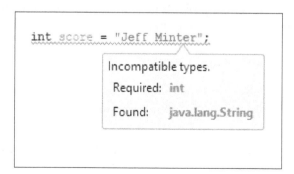

As we can see, Java was designed to make it impossible for such errors to make it into a running program.

Here are the main types of variables in Java:

- `int`: The `int` type is for storing integers, or whole numbers. This type uses 32 pieces (**bits**) of memory and can therefore store values with a size a little in excess of 2 billion, including negative values too.

- `long`: As the name suggests, `long` data types can be used when even larger numbers are needed. A `long` uses 64 bits of memory and can store numbers up to 9,223,372,036,854,775,807. Perhaps surprisingly, there are uses for long variables, but the point is if a smaller variable will do, we should use it because our program will use less memory.

 You might be wondering when you might use numbers of this size. The obvious examples would be math or science applications that do complex calculations, but another use might be for timing. When you time how long something takes, the Java `Date` class uses the number of milliseconds since January 1, 1970. A millisecond is one thousandth of a second, so there are quite a few of them since 1970.

- `float`: This is for floating point numbers. That is, numbers in which there is precision beyond the decimal point. As the fractional part of a number takes memory space just as the whole number part does, the range of a number possible in a `float` is therefore decreased compared to non-floating-point numbers. So, unless our variable will use the extra precision, `float` would not be our data type of choice.

- `double`: When the precision in a `float` is not enough, we have `double`.

- `boolean`: We will be using plenty of Booleans throughout the book. The `boolean` variable type can be either `true` or `false`; nothing else. Booleans answer questions such as the following:
    - Is the contact a friend?
    - Are there any new messages?
    - Are two examples for Boolean enough?

- `char`: Stores a single alphanumeric character in a `char`. It's not going to change the world on its own, but could be useful if we put lots of them together.

I have kept this discussion of data types to a practical level that is useful in the context of this book. If you are interested in how a data type's value is stored and why the limits are what they are, then have a look on the Oracle Java tutorials site here: `http://docs.oracle.com/javase/tutorial/java/nutsandbolts/datatypes.html`. Note that you do not need any more information than we have already discussed to continue with this book.

As we just learned, each type of data that we might want to store will need a specific amount of memory. For this reason, we must let the Java compiler know the type of the variable before we begin to use it.

The preceding variables are known as the **primitive** types. They use predefined amounts of memory and so, using our warehouse storage analogy, fit into predefined sizes of storage box.

As the "primitive" label suggests, they are not as sophisticated as **reference** types.

Reference types

You might have noticed that we didn't cover the `String` variable type, which we previously used to introduce the concept of variables that hold alpha-numeric data such as a contact's name.

Strings

Strings are one of a special type of variable known as a **reference** type. They quite simply refer to a place in memory wherein storage of the variable begins but the reference type itself does not define a specific amount of memory. The reason for this is straightforward.

It's because we don't always know how much data will need to be stored in it until the program is run.

We can think of Strings and other reference types as continually expanding and contracting storage boxes. So, won't one of these `String` reference types bump into another variable eventually?

As we are thinking about the device's memory as a huge warehouse full of racks of labeled storage boxes, then you can think of the DVM as a super-efficient forklift truck driver that puts the different types of storage boxes in the most appropriate place.

And, if it becomes necessary, the DVM will quickly move stuff around in a fraction of a second to avoid collisions. Also, when required, Dalvik, the fork truck driver, will even vaporize any unnecessary storage boxes.

This all happens at the same time as constantly unloading new storage boxes of all types and placing them in the best place for that type of variable. Dalvik keeps reference variables in a different part of the warehouse to the primitive variables. We will learn more details about this in *Chapter 12, The Stack, the Heap, and the Garbage Collector*.

Strings can be used to store any keyboard character. Like a `char`, but of almost any length. Anything from a contact's name to an entire book can be stored in a single `String`. We will be using Strings regularly, including in this chapter.

There are a couple more reference types that we will explore as well.

Arrays

Arrays are a way to store lots of variables of the same type ready for quick and efficient access. We will look at arrays in *Chapter 15, Arrays, ArrayList, Map and Random Numbers*.

Think of an array as an aisle in our warehouse with all the variables of a certain type lined up in a precise order. Arrays are reference types, so Dalvik keeps these in the same part of the warehouse as Strings. We might, for example, use an array to store dozens of contacts in.

Classes

The other reference type is the class that we have already discussed but not explained properly. We will be getting familiar with classes in *Chapter 10, Object-Oriented programming*.

Now we know that each type of data that we might want to store will require an amount of memory. Hence, we must let the Java compiler know the type of the variable before we begin to use it. We do this with a variable **declaration**.

Using variables

That's enough theory. Let's see how we would use our variables and types. Remember that each primitive type needs a specific amount of real device memory. This is one of the reasons that the compiler needs to know what type a variable will be.

Variable declaration

We must first **declare** a variable and its type before we try to do anything with it. To declare a variable of type `int` with name `unreadMessages`, we would type:

```
int unreadMessages;
```

That's it – simply state the type, in this case, `int`, then leave a space and type the name you want to use for this variable. Note also that the semicolon, `;`, at the end of the line will tell the compiler that we are done with this line and what follows, if anything, is not part of the variable declaration.

Similarly, for almost all the other variable types, declaration would occur in the same way. Here are some examples. The variable names in the examples are arbitrary. This is like reserving a labeled storage box in the warehouse:

```
long millisecondsElapsed;
float accountBalance;
boolean isFriend;
char contactFirstInitial;
String messageText;
```

Notice I said almost all the other variable types. One of the exceptions is variables of the class type. We have already seen some code declaring variables of the class type. Do you remember this from *Chapter 3, Exploring Android Studio and the project structure*, in the `MainActivity.java` file?:

```
FloatingActionButton fab…
```

This edited snippet of code is declaring a variable called `fab` of the type `FloatingActionButton`. But we are off track a little and will come back to classes in *Chapter 10, Object-Oriented programming*.

Variable initialization

Initialization is the next step. Here, for each type, we initialize a value to the variable. This is like placing a value inside the storage box in the warehouse:

```
unreadMessages = 10;
millisecondsElapsed = 14381651168411;// 29th July 2016 11:19am
accountBalance = 129.52f;
isFriend = true;
contactFirstInitial = 'C';
messageText = "Hi reader, I just thought I would let you know that
Charles Babbage was an early computing pioneer and he invented the
difference engine. If you want to know more about him, you can click
find look here: www.charlesbabbage.net.";
```

Notice that the char variable uses the single quotes, ', around the initialized value, while the String uses the double quotes, ".

We can also combine the declaration and initialization steps. In the following code snippet, we declare and initialize the same variables as we have previously, but in one step:

```
int unreadMessages = 10;
long millisecondsElapsed = 1438165116841l;//29th July 2016 11:19am
float accountBalance = 129.52f;
boolean isFriend = true;
char contactFirstInitial = 'C';
String messageText = " Hi reader, I just thought I would let you know
that Charles Babbage was an early computing pioneer and he invented
the difference engine. If you want to know more about him, you can
click this link www.charlesbabbage.net.";
```

Whether we declare and initialize separately or together is dependent upon the specific situation. The important thing is that we must do both at some point:

```
int a;
// That's me declared and ready to go?
// The line below attempts to output a to the console
Log.i("info", "int a = " + a);
// Oh no I forgot to initialize a!!
```

This would cause the following:

Compiler Error: Variable a might not have been initialized

There is a significant exception to this rule. Under certain circumstances, variables can have **default values**. We will see this in *Chapter 10, Object-Oriented programming*; however, it is good practice to both declare and initialize variables.

Changing values in variables with operators

Of course, in almost any program, we are going to need to "do things" with these variables' values. We manipulate (change) variables with **operators**. Here is a list of perhaps the most common Java operators that allow us to manipulate variables. You do not need to memorize them as we will look at every line of code as and when we use them for the first time. We already saw the first operator when we initialized our variables, but we will see it again when being a bit more adventurous.

The assignment operator

This is the assignment operator:

```
=
```

It makes the variable to the left of the operator the same as the value to the right; for example, as in this line of code:

```
unreadMessages = newMessages;
```

After the previous line of code has executed, the value stored in `unreadMessages` will be the same as the value stored in `newMessages`.

The addition operator

This is the addition operator:

```
+
```

It will add together values on either side of the operator. It's usually used in conjunction with the assignment operator. For example, it can add together two variables that have numeric values, as in this next line of code:

```
unreadMessages = newMessages + unreadMessages;
```

Once the previous code has executed, the combined value of the values held by `newMessages` and `unreadMessages` will be stored in `unreadMessages`. As another example of the same thing, look at this line of code:

```
accountBalance = yesterdaysBalance + todaysDeposits;
```

Notice it is perfectly acceptable to use the same variable simultaneously on both sides of an operator.

The subtraction operator

This is the subtraction operator:

```
-
```

It will subtract the value on the right side of the operator from the value on the left. This is usually used in conjunction with the assignment operator, as in this example code:

```
unreadMessages = unreadMessages - 1;
```

Here's another example:

```
accountBalance = accountBalance - withdrawals;
```

After the previous line of code has executed, `accountBalance` will hold its original value, minus whatever the value held in `withdrawals` is.

The division operator

This is the division operator:

```
/
```

It will divide the number on the left by the number on the right. Again, it's usually used in conjunction with the assignment operator. Here is an example line of code:

```
fairShare = numSweets / numChildren;
```

If, in the previous line of code, `numSweets` held 9 and `numChildren` held 3, then `fairShare` would now hold the value of 3.

The multiplication operator

This is the multiplication operator:

```
*
```

It will multiply variables and numbers together and, as with many of the other operators, is usually used in conjunction with the assignment operator. For example, look at this line of code:

```
answer = 10 * 10;
```

Here's another example:

```
biggerAnswer = 10 * 10 * 10;
```

After the previous two lines of code have executed, `answer` holds the value 100 and `biggerAnswer` holds the value 1000.

The increment operator

This is the increment operator:

```
++
```

The increment operator is a quick way to add 1 to something. For example, look at this next line of code, which uses the addition operator:

```
myVariable = myVariable + 1;
```

The previous line of code has the same result as this much more compact code:

```
myVariable ++;
```

The decrement operator

This is the decrement operator:

```
--
```

The decrement operator (you probably guessed) is a quick way to subtract 1 from something. For example, look at this next line of code, which uses the subtraction operator:

```
myVariable = myVariable -1;
```

The previous line of code is the same as `myVariable --;`.

> The formal names for these operators are slightly different to those just given. For example, the division operator is one of the multiplicative operators. But the names given here are far more useful for the purpose of learning Java, and if you used the term division operator while conversing with someone from the Java community, they would know exactly what you mean.

There are even more operators than this in Java. We will meet some of them in the next chapter when we learn about making decisions in Java.

> If you are curious about operators, there is a complete list of them on the Java website here: http://docs.oracle.com/javase/tutorial/java/nutsandbolts/operators.html. All the operators needed to complete the projects in this book will be fully explained in this book. The link is provided for the curious among us.

Expressions

Let's try using some declarations, assignments, and operators. When we bundle these elements together into some meaningful syntax, we call it an **expression**. Let's write a quick app to try some out. We will then use `Toast` and `Log` to check our results.

Expressing yourself demo app

Create a new project called `Expressing Yourself`, use a **Basic Activity**, and leave all the other settings at their defaults. The completed code that we will write in this project can be found in the `Chapter 7/Expressing Yourself` folder of the download bundle.

Switch to the **MainActivity** tab in the editor and we will write some code. In the `onCreate` method, just before the closing curly brace, }, add this code:

```
int numMessages;
```

Directly below the previous line of code, we will initialize a value to `numMessages`. But as you begin to type `nu....`, notice that we get a little pop up message like this:

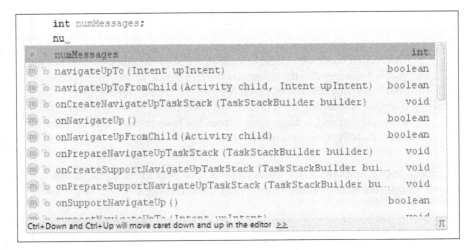

If you look at the first choice in the pop up message, you'll notice that it is, in fact, **numMessages**. Android Studio is offering to complete our typing for us. We can either left-click **numMessages** to have the variable name auto-completed, or simply select it (because it is already highlighted) by pressing *Enter* on the keyboard. Whenever Android Studio thinks it might know what we want to type, it will pop up some options. It is an excellent time-saving habit to get into.

Add this line of code using auto-complete:

```
numMessages = 10;
```

Now we have introduced the handy code completion feature, we will add a larger chunk of code. Immediately after the previous line of code and before the closing } of onCreate, add the following code:

```
// Output the value of numMessages
Log.i("numMessages = ", "" + numMessages);

numMessages++;
numMessages = numMessages + 1;
Log.i("numMessages = ", "" + numMessages);

// Now a boolean (just true or false)
boolean isFriend = true;
Log.i("isFriend = ", "" + isFriend);

// A contact and an important message
String contact = "James Gosling";
String message = "Dear reader, I invented Java.";

// Now let's play with those String variables
Toast.makeText(this, "Message from" + contact, Toast.LENGTH_SHORT).
show();

Toast.makeText(this, "Message is:" + message, Toast.LENGTH_SHORT).
show();
```

Run the app, and then we can examine the output and then the code. In the **logcat** window, you will see the following output:

numMessages =: 10

numMessages =: 12

isFriend =: true

On the screen, you will see two pop-up Toast messages. The first says **Message from James Gosling**. The second says **Message is: Dear Reader, I invented Java.** and is shown in the next screenshot:

Let's step through the code and make sure that each line is clear before moving on.

First, we declared and initialized an `int` type variable called `numMessages`. We could have done it on one line, but we did it like this:

```
int numMessages;
numMessages = 10;
```

Next, we used `Log` to output a message. Instead of simply typing the message between the double quote marks, `""`, this time we used the + operator to add `numMessages` onto the output. And, as we saw in the console, the actual value of `numMessages` was returned:

```
// Output the value of numMessages
Log.i("numMessages = ", "" + numMessages);
```

Just to further prove that our `numMessages` variable is as versatile as it should be, we use the ++ operator, which should increase its value by one, and then add `numMessages` to itself using +1. We then return the new value of `numMessages` and, indeed, find its value has increased to 12 from 10:

```
numMessages ++;
numMessages = numMessages + 1;
Log.i("numMessages = ", "" + numMessages);
```

Next, we created a `boolean` type variable called `isFriend` and output that to the console. We saw from the output that **true** was displayed. This variable type will fully prove its usefulness when we look at decision making in the next chapter:

```
// Now a boolean (just true or false)
boolean isFriend = true;
Log.i("isFriend = ", "" + isFriend);
```

After this, we declared and initialized two `String` type variables:

```
// A contact and an important message
String contact = "James Gosling";
String message = "Dear reader, I invented Java.";
```

Finally, we output the `String` variables using `Toast`. We used a hardcoded part of the message, `"Message from "`, and added the variable part of the message with `+` `contact`. We used the same technique to form the second `Toast` message as well:

 When we add two Strings together to make a longer `String`, it is called **concatenation**.

```
// Now let's play with those String variables
Toast.makeText(this, "Message from " + contact, Toast.LENGTH_SHORT).
show();

Toast.makeText(this, "Message is:" + message, Toast.LENGTH_SHORT).
show();
```

Now we can declare variables, initialize them to a value, change them around a bit, and output them using `Toast` or `Log`.

Summary

At last, we have used some serious Java. We learned about variables, declaration, and initialization. We saw how to use operators to change the value of variables.

It doesn't matter if you don't remember everything straight away, as we will constantly be using these techniques and keywords throughout the book.

In the next chapter, let's look at how we can make decisions based on the value of these variables and find out how this is useful to us.

8
Java Decisions and Loops

We have just learned about variables. We know how we can change the values that they hold with expressions, but how can we take a course of action that's dependent upon the value of a variable?

We can certainly add a number of new messages to the number of previously unread messages, but how might we, for example, trigger an action within our app when the user has read all their messages?

The first problem is that we need a way to test the value of a variable and then respond when the value falls within a range of values or is a specific value.

Another problem that is common in programming of all sorts is that we need sections of our code to be executed a certain number of times (more than once or sometimes not at all) depending on the value of variables.

To solve the first problem, we will look at making decisions in Java with `if`, `else`, and `switch`. To solve the latter, we will look at loops in Java with `while`, `do - while`, `for`, and `break`.

We will cover the following topics in this chapter:

- Making decisions with `if`, `else`, `else - if`, and `switch`
- The `switch` demo app
- Java `while` loops and `do - while` loops
- Java `for` loops
- Loops demo app

Now, let's learn some more Java.

Making decisions in Java

Our Java code will constantly be making decisions. For example, we might need to know whether the user has new messages or whether they have a certain number of friends. We need to be able to test our variables to see whether they meet certain conditions and then execute a certain section of code depending upon whether it did or not.

In this section, as our code gets more in-depth, it helps to present it in a way that makes it more readable. Let's look at code indenting to make our discussion about decisions easier.

Indenting code for clarity

You have probably noticed that the Java code in our projects is indented. For example, the first line of code inside the `MainActivity` class is indented by one tab, and that the first line of code is indented inside each method. Here is an annotated diagram to make this clear by way of another quick example:

```
public class MainActivity extends AppCompatActivity {

TAB @Override
    protected void onCreate(Bundle savedInstanceState) {
    TAB super.onCreate(savedInstanceState);
        setContentView(R.layout.activity_main);
        Toolbar toolbar = (Toolbar) findViewById(R.id.toolbar);
        setSupportActionBar(toolbar);

        FloatingActionButton fab = (FloatingActionButton) findViewById(R.id.fab);
        fab.setOnClickListener((view) → {
            Snackbar.make(view,  text: "Replace with your own action", Snackbar.LENGTH_LONG)
                    .setAction( text: "Action",  listener: null).show();
        });
    }
```

Also notice that when the indented block has ended, often with a closing curly brace } that }, it is indented to the same extent as the line of code that began the block.

We do this to make the code more readable. It is not part of the Java syntax, however, and the code will still compile if we don't bother doing this.

As our code gets more complicated, indenting, along with comments, helps keep the meaning and structure of our code clear. I mention this now because when we start to learn the syntax for making decisions in Java, indenting becomes especially useful and it is recommended that you indent your code in the same way.

Much of this indenting is done for us by Android Studio, but not all of it.

Now that we know how to present our code more clearly, let's learn some more operators and then we can really get to work making decisions with Java.

More operators

We can already add (+), take away (-), multiply (*), divide (/), assign (=), increment (++), and decrement (--) with operators. Let's introduce some more super-useful operators, and then we will go straight on to actually understanding how to use them in Java.

Don't worry about memorizing each of the following operators. Glance over them and their explanations and then move quickly on to the next section. There, we will put a number of operators to use and they will become much clearer as we see a few examples of what they allow us to do. They are presented here in a list just to make the variety and scope of operators plain from the start. The list will also be more convenient to refer to when not intermingled with the discussion about implementation that follows it.

We use operators to create an expression that is either true or false. We wrap that expression in parentheses, like this: (expression goes here).

The comparison operator

This is the comparison operator. It tests for equality and is either true or false:

```
==
```

An expression such as (10 == 9), for example, is false. 10 is obviously not equal to 9. However, an expression such as (2 + 2 == 4) is obviously true.

Except in 1984 when 2 + 2 == 5: https://en.wikipedia.org/wiki/Nineteen_Eighty-Four.

The logical NOT operator

This is the logical NOT operator:

```
!
```

It is used to test the negation of an expression. If the expression is false, then the NOT operator causes the expression to be true. An example will help.

The expression `(!(2+2 == 5))` evaluates to true because 2 + 2 *is NOT* 5. But a further example of `(!(2 + 2 = 4))` would be false. This is because 2 + 2 obviously *is* 4.

The NOT equal operator

This is the NOT equal operator and it is another comparison operator:

```
!=
```

The NOT equal operator tests whether something is NOT equal. For example, the expression `(10 != 9)` is true. 10 is not equal to 9. On the other hand, `(10 != 10)` is false because 10 clearly is equal to 10.

The greater than operator

Another comparison operator (and there are a few more as well) is the greater than operator. Here it is:

```
>
```

This operator tests whether something is greater than something else. The expression `(10 > 9)` is true, but the expression `(9 > 10)` is false.

The less than operator

You can probably guess that this operator tests for values less than others. This is what the operator looks like:

```
<
```

The expression `(10 < 9)` is false because 10 is not less than 9, while the expression `(9 < 10)` is true.

The greater than or equal to operator

This operator tests whether one value is greater than or equal to the other, and if either is true, the result is true. This is what the operator looks like:

```
>=
```

As an example, the expression (10 >= 9) is true; the expression (10 >= 10) is also true, but the expression (10 >= 11) is false because 10 is neither greater than nor equal to 11.

The less than or equal to operator

Like the previous operator, this one tests for two conditions, but this time, less than or equal to. Look at the operator shown here and then we will see some examples:

```
<=
```

The expression (10 <= 9) is false, the expression (10 <= 10) is true, and the expression (10 <= 11) is also true.

The logical AND operator

This operator is known as logical AND. It tests two or more separate parts of an expression, and all parts must be true for the entire expression to be true:

```
&&
```

Logical AND is usually used in conjunction with the other operators to build more complex tests. The expression ((10 > 9) && (10 < 11)) is true because both parts are true. On the other hand, the expression ((10 > 9) && (10 < 9)) is false because only one part of the expression is true— (10 > 9), and the other is false— (10 < 9).

The logical OR operator

This operator is called logical OR and it is just like logical AND, except that only one of two or more parts of an expression need to be true for the expression to be true:

```
||
```

Let's look at the last example we used for logical AND, but replace && with ||. The expression ((10 > 9) || (10 < 9)) is now true because one part of the expression is true.

Seeing these operators in a more practical context, in this chapter and throughout the rest of the book, will help clarify their different uses. Now, we know how to form expressions with operators, variables, and values. Next, we can look at a way of structuring and combining expressions to make a number of deep decisions.

How to use all of these operators to test variables

All of these operators are virtually useless without a way of properly using them to make real decisions that affect real variables and code.

Now that we have all the information we need, we can look at a hypothetical situation and then actually see some code for decision making.

Using the Java if keyword

As we saw previously, operators serve very little purpose on their own, but it was probably useful to see just part of the wide and varied range available to us. Now, when we look at putting the most common operator, `==`, to use, we can start to see the powerful yet fine control that they offer us.

Let's make the previous examples less abstract. Meet the Java **if** keyword. We will use `if` and a few conditional operators along with a small story to demonstrate their use. What follows is a made-up military situation that will hopefully be less abstract than the previous examples.

The captain is dying and, knowing that his remaining subordinates are not very experienced, he decides to write a Java program to convey his last orders after he has died. The troops must hold one side of a bridge while awaiting reinforcements, but with a few rules that determine their actions.

The first command the captain wants to make sure his troops understand is this:

If they come over the bridge, shoot them.

So, how do we simulate this situation in Java? We need a Boolean variable-`isComingOverBridge`. The next bit of code assumes that the `isComingOverBridge` variable has been declared and initialized to either true or false.

We can then use `if` like this:

```
if(isComingOverBridge){

    // Shoot them

}
```

If the `isComingOverBridge` Boolean is true, the code inside the opening and closing curly braces will execute. If `isComingOverBridge` is false, the program continues after the `if` block and without running the code within it.

Else do this instead

The captain also wants to tell his troops what to do if the enemy is not coming over the bridge. In this situation, he wants them to stay where they are and wait.

Now, we introduce another Java keyword, `else`. When we want to explicitly do something when the `if` value does not evaluate to true, we can use `else`.

For example, to tell the troops to stay put if the enemy is not coming over the bridge, we could write the following code:

```
if(isComingOverBridge){

    // Shoot them

}else{

    // Hold position

}
```

The captain then realized that the problem wasn't as simple as he first thought. What if the enemy comes over the bridge, but has too many troops? His squad would be overrun and slaughtered.

So, he came up with the following code (we'll use some variables as well this time):

```
boolean isComingOverBridge;
int enemyTroops;
int friendlyTroops;

// Code that initializes the above variables one way or another

// Now the if
```

```
if(isComingOverBridge && friendlyTroops > enemyTroops){

    // shoot them

}else if(isComingOveBridge && friendlyTroops < enemyTroops) {

    // blow the bridge

}else{


    // Hold position


}
```

The preceding code has three possible paths of execution. First, if the enemy is coming over the bridge and the friendly troops are greater in number:

```
if(isComingOverBridge && friendlyTroops > enemyTroops)
```

Second, if the enemy troops are coming over the bridge but outnumber the friendly troops:

```
else if(isComingOveBridge && friendlyTroops < enemyTroops)
```

Then the third and final possible outcome that will execute if neither of the others is true is captured by the final `else` without an `if` condition:

Can you spot a flaw with the above code? One that might leave a bunch of inexperienced troops in complete disarray? The possibility of the enemy troops and friendly troops being exactly equal in number has not been handled explicitly and would therefore be handled by the final `else` which is meant for when there are no enemy troops. I guess any self-respecting captain would expect his troops to fight in this situation and he could have changed the first `if` statement to accommodate this possibility.

```
if(isComingOverBridge && friendlyTroops >=  enemyTroops)
```

And finally, the captain's last concern was that if the enemy came over the bridge waving the white flag of surrender and were promptly slaughtered, then his men would end up as war criminals. The Java code needed was obvious. Using the `wavingWhiteFlag` Boolean variable, he wrote the following test:

```
if (wavingWhiteFlag){

    // Take prisoners

}
```

But where to put this code was less clear. In the end, the captain opted for the following nested solution and changing the test for `wavingWhiteFlag` to logical NOT, as follows:

```
if (!wavingWhiteFlag){

    // not surrendering so check everything else

    if(isComingOverTheBridge && friendlyTroops >= enemyTroops){

        // shoot them
    }else if(isComingOverTheBridge && friendlyTroops <
            enemyTroops) {

        // blow the bridge

    }

}else{

    // this is the else for our first if
    // Take prisoners

}

// Holding position
```

This demonstrates that we can nest `if` and `else` statements inside one another in order to create quite deep and detailed decisions.

We could go on making more and more complicated decisions with `if` and `else`, but what we have seen is more than sufficient as an introduction.

It is probably worth pointing out that very often, there is more than one way to arrive at a solution to a problem. The *right* way will usually be the way that solves the problem in the clearest and simplest manner.

Let's look at some other ways to make decisions in Java and then we can put them all together in an app.

Switching to make decisions

We have seen the vast and virtually limitless possibilities of combining the Java operators with `if` and `else` statements. But sometimes, a decision in Java can be better made in other ways.

When we must decide based on a clear list of possibilities that doesn't involve complex combinations, then `switch` is usually the way to go.

We start a `switch` decision like this:

```
switch (argument) {

}
```

In the previous example, an `argument` could be an expression or a variable. Within the curly braces { }, we can make decisions based on the argument with `case` and `break` elements:

```
case x:
    // code for case x
    break;

case y:
    // code for case y
    break;
```

You can see in the previous example that each `case` states a possible result and each `break` denotes the end of that case, and the point at which no further `case` statements should be evaluated.

The first `break` that's encountered breaks out of the `switch` block to proceed with the next line of code after the closing brace } of the entire switch block.

We can also use `default` without a value to run some code in case none of the `case` statements evaluate to true, as follows:

```
default:// Look no value
    // Do something here if no other case statements are true
    break;
```

Let's write a quick demo app that uses `switch`.

Switch Demo app

To get started, create a new Android project called `Switch Demo`, use an **Empty Activity,** and leave all the other settings as their default settings. Switch to the `MainActivity.java` file by left-clicking the **MainActivity.java** tab above the editor and we can start coding.

Let's pretend we are writing an old fashioned text adventure game, the kind of game where the player types commands such as "Go East", "Go West", and "Take Sword".

In this case, `switch` could handle that situation like it does in the following example code, and we could use `default` to handle the player typing a command that is not specifically handled.

Enter the following code in the `onCreate` method just before the closing curly brace }:

```java
// get input from user in a String variable called command
String command = "go east";

switch(command){

    case "go east":
        Log.i("Player: ", "Moves to the East" );
        break;

    case "go west":
        Log.i("Player: ", "Moves to the West" );
        break;

    case "go north":
        Log.i("Player: ", "Moves to the North" );
        break;

    case "go south":
        Log.i("Player: ", "Moves to the South" );
        break;

    case "take sword":
        Log.i("Player: ", "Takes the silver sword" );
        break;

    // more possible cases
```

```
default:
    Log.i("Message: ", "Sorry I don't speak Elfish" );
    break;

}
```

Run the app a few times. Each time, change the initialization of command to something new. Notice that when you initialize command to something that is explicitly handled by a case statement, we get the expected output. Otherwise, we get the default **Sorry I don't speak Elfish**.

If we had a lot of code to execute for a case, we could contain it all in a method, just like in the following piece of code. I have highlighted the new line:

```
case "go west":
    goWest();
    break;
```

Of course, we would then need to write the new goWest method. Then, when the command was initialized to "go west", the goWest method would be executed and execution would return to the break statement that would cause the code to continue after the switch block.

Of course, one of the things this code seriously lacks is interaction with a UI. We have seen how we can call methods from button clicks, but even that isn't enough to make this code worthwhile in a real app. We will see how we can solve this problem in *Chapter 12, The Stack, the Heap, and the Garbage Collector*.

The other problem we have is that after the code has been executed, that's it! We need it to continually ask the player for instructions; not just once, but over and over. We will look at a solution to this problem next.

Repeating code with loops

Here, we will learn how to repeatedly execute portions of our code in a controlled and precise way by looking at several types of **loops** in Java. These include while loops, do while loops, and for loops. We will also learn about the most appropriate situations to use the different types of loops.

It would be completely reasonable to ask what loops have to do with programming, but they are exactly what the name implies. They are a way of repeating the same part of the code more than once, or looping over the same part of code, although potentially for a different outcome each time.

This can simply mean doing the same thing until the code being looped over (**iterated**) prompts the loop to end. It could be a predetermined number of iterations, as specified by the loop code itself. It might be until a predetermined situation or **condition** is met. Or, it could be a combination of more than one of these things. Along with `if`, `else`, and `switch`, loops are part of the Java **control flow statements**.

We will look at all the major types of loops that Java offers us to control our code, and we will use some of them to implement a working mini-app to make sure that we understand them completely. Let's look at the first and simplest loop type in Java called the `while` loop.

While loops

Java `while` loops have the simplest syntax. Think back to the `if` statements for a moment. We could put virtually any combination of operators and variables in the conditional expression of the `if` statement. If the expression evaluated to true, then the code in the body of the `if` block is executed. With the `while` loop, we also use an expression that can evaluate to true or false. Look at the following code:

```
int x = 10;

while(x > 0){
    x--;
    // x decreases by one each pass through the loop
}
```

What happens here is this:

1. Outside of the `while` loop, an `int` named x is declared and initialized to 10.
2. Then, the `while` loop begins. Its condition is x > 0. So, the `while` loop will execute the code in its body.
3. The code in its body will continue to execute until the condition evaluates to false.

So, the preceding code will execute 10 times.

On the first pass, x = 10, the second pass is 9, then 8, and so on. But once x is equal to 0, it is, of course, no longer greater than 0. At this point, the program will exit the `while` loop and continue with the first line of code after the `while` loop.

Just like an `if` statement, it is possible that the `while` loop will not execute even once. Look at the following example, where the code in the `while` loop will not execute:

```java
int x = 10;

while(x > 10){
    // more code here.
    // but it will never run
    // unless x is greater than 10.
}
```

Moreover, there is no limit to the complexity of the conditional expression or the amount of code that can go in the loop body. Here is another example:

```java
int newMessages = 3;
int unreadMessages = 0;

while(newMessages > 0 || unreadMessages > 0){
    // Display next message
    // etc.
}

// continue here when newMessages and unreadMessages equal 0
```

The preceding `while` loop will continue to execute until both `newMessages` and `unreadMessages` was equal to, or less than, zero. As the condition uses the logical OR operator `||`, either one of those conditions being true will cause the `while` loop to continue executing.

It is worth noting that once the body of the loop has been entered, it will always complete, even if the expression evaluates to false part way through, as it is not tested again until the code tries to start another pass. For example:

```java
int x = 1;

while(x > 0){
    x--;
    // x is now 0 so the condition is false
    // But this line still runs
    // and this one
    // and me!
}
```

The preceding loop body will execute exactly once. We can also set a `while` loop that will run forever! This, perhaps unsurprisingly, is called an **infinite loop**. Here is an example of an infinite loop:

```
int x = 0;

while(true){
    x++; // I am going to get very big!
}
```

Breaking out of a loop

We might use an infinite loop like this so that we can decide when to exit the loop from a test contained within its body. We would do this by using the `break` keyword when we are ready to leave the loop body. Here is an example:

```
int x = 0;

while(true){
    x++; //I am going to get very big!
    break; // No, you're not- ha!
    // code doesn't reach here
}
```

And you might have been able to guess that we can combine any of the decision-making tools, such as `if`, `else`, and `switch` within our `while` loops, and all the rest of the loops we will look at in a minute. For example:

```
int x = 0;
int tooBig = 10;

while(true){
    x++; // I am going to get very big!
    if(x == tooBig){
        break;
    } // No, you're not- ha!

    // code reaches here only until x = 10
}
```

It would be simple to go on for many more pages demonstrating the versatility of `while` loops but, at some point, we want to get back to doing some real programming. So, here is one last concept combined with `while` loops.

The continue keyword

The **continue** keyword acts in a similar way to `break` — up to a point. The `continue` keyword will break out of the loop body but will also check the condition expression afterward so that the loop *could* run again. The following example will help:

```
int x = 0;
int tooBig = 10;
int tooBigToPrint = 5;

while(true){
    x++; // I am going to get very big!
    if(x == tooBig){
        break;
    } // No, you're not- ha!

    // code reaches here only until x = 10

    if(x >= tooBigToPrint){
        // No more printing but keep looping
        continue;
    }
    // code reaches here only until x = 5

    // Print out x

}
```

Do while loops

A `do while` loop is very much the same as a `while` loop, with the exception that a `do while` loop evaluates its expression *after* the body. This means that a `do while` loop will always execute at least once before checking the loop condition:

```
int x= 1
do{
    x++;
}while(x < 1);
// x now = 2
```

In the previous code, the loop executed, even though the test was false because the test is done after the execution of the loop. The test did, however, prevent the loop body being executed a second time. This caused x to be incremented once, and x now equals 2.

Note that break and continue can also be used in do while loops.

For loops

A for loop has a slightly more complicated syntax than a while or do while loop as they take three parts to initialize. Have a look at the following code first, and then we will break it apart:

```
for(int i = 0; i < 10;  i++){

    //Something that needs to happen 10 times goes here

}
```

The slightly more complicated form of the for loop is clearer when put like this:

```
for(declaration and initialization; condition; change after each pass
through loop).
```

To clarify further, we have the following:

- **Declaration and initialization**: We create a new int variable, i, and initialize it to zero.

- **Condition**: Just like the other loops, it refers to the condition that must evaluate to true for the loop to continue.

- **Change after each pass through the loop**: In the preceding example, i++ means that 1 is added/incremented to i on each pass. We could also use i-- to reduce/decrement i each pass:

```
for(int i = 10; i > 0;  i--){
    // countdown
}
// blast off i = 0
```

 Note that break and continue can also be used in for loops.

The for loop takes control of initialization, condition evaluation, and the control variable by itself.

Loops demo app

To get started, create a new Android project called `Loops`, use **Empty Activity,** and leave all the other settings as their default settings.

Let's add a few buttons to our UI to make this more fun. Switch to the `activity_main.xml` file, make sure you are on the **Design** tab, and then follow these steps:

1. Drag a button onto the UI and center it horizontally near the top.

2. In the properties window, change the **text** property to `countUp`.

3. In the properties window, change the **onClick** property to `countUp`.

4. Place a new button just below the previous one and repeat steps 2 and 3, but this time use `countDown` for the **text** property and the **onClick** property.

5. Place a new button just below the previous one and repeat steps 2 and 3, but this time use **nested** for the **text** property and the **onClick** property.

6. Click the **Infer Constraints** button to constrain the three buttons in position.

Looks are not important for this demo, but run the app and check that the layout looks something like it does in the following image:

I also deleted the Hello World `TextView`, but this is not necessary.

What is important is that we have three buttons labeled **COUNTUP,** **COUNTDOWN,** and **NESTED,** which call methods named `countUp`, `countDown`, and `nested`.

Switch to the `MainActivity.java` file by left-clicking the **MainActivity.java** tab above the editor and then we can start coding our methods.

After the closing curly brace of the `onCreate` method, add the `countUp` method, as follows:

```java
public void countUp(View v){
    Log.i("message:","In countUp method");

    int x = 0;

    // Now an apparently infinite while loop
    while(true){

        // Add 1 to x each time
        x++;
        Log.i("x =", "" + x);

        if(x == 3){
            // Get me out of here
            break;
        }
    }
}
```

 Import the `Log` and `View` classes using your preferred method:
```java
import android.util.Log;
import android.view.View;
```

We will be able to call the method we have just written from the appropriately labeled button.

After the closing curly brace of the countUp method, add the countDown method:

```
public void countDown(View v){
    Log.i("message:","In countDown method");

    int x = 4;
    // Now an apparently infinite while loop
    while(true){

        // Add 1 to x each time
        x--;
        Log.i("x =", "" + x);

        if(x == 1){
            // Get me out of here
            break;
        }
    }
}
```

We will be able to call the method we have just written from the appropriately labeled button.

After the closing curly brace of the countDown method, add the nested method:

```
public void nested(View v){
    Log.i("message:","In nested method");

    // a nested for loop
    for(int i = 0; i < 3; i ++){

        for(int j = 3; j > 0; j --){

            // Output the values of i and j
            Log.i("i =" + i,"j=" + j);

        }
    }
}
```

We will be able to call the method we have just written from the appropriately labeled button.

Now, let's run the app and start tapping buttons. If you tap each of the buttons once from top to bottom, this is the console output you will see:

```
message:: In countUp method
x =: 1
x =: 2
x =: 3
message:: In countDown method
x =: 3
x =: 2
x =: 1
message:: In nested method
i =0: j=3
i =0: j=2
i =0: j=1
i =1: j=3
i =1: j=2
i =1: j=1
i =2: j=3
i =2: j=2
i =2: j=1
```

We can see that the countUp method does exactly that. The int x variable is initialized to zero, an infinite while loop is entered, and x is incremented with the increment ++ operator. Fortunately, on each iteration of the loop, we test for x being equal to 3 with if (x == 3) and break when this is true.

Next, in the countDown method, we do the same in reverse. The int x variable is initialized to 4, an infinite while loop is entered, and x is decremented with the decrement -- operator. This time, on each iteration of the loop, we test for x being equal to 1 with if (x == 1) and break when this is true.

Finally, we nest two for loops within each other. We can see from the output that for each time i (which is controlled by the outer loop) is incremented, j (which is controlled by the inner loop) is decremented from 3 to 1.

Look carefully at this image, which shows where the start and end of each `for` loop is, to help you fully understand this:

```
// a nested for loop
for(int i = 0; i < 3; i ++){

    for(int j = 3; j > 0; j --){

        // Output the values of i and j
        Log.i("i =" + i,"j=" + j);

    }
}
```

You can, of course, keep tapping to observe each button's output for as long as you like. As an experiment, try making the loops longer; perhaps use 1,000.

Summary

We used `if`, `else`, and `switch` to make decisions with expressions and branch our code. We saw and practiced `while`, `for`, and `do while` to repeat parts of our code. Then, we put it all together in two quick demo apps.

It doesn't matter if you don't remember everything straight away, as we will constantly be using these techniques and keywords throughout this book.

In the next chapter, we will take a much closer look at Java methods, which is where all our code will go.

9
Java Methods

As we are starting to get comfortable with Java programming, in this chapter, we will take a closer look at methods. Although we know that you can **call** them to make them execute their code, there is more to them than we have discussed so far.

In this chapter, we will look at the following topics:

- Method structure
- Method overloading versus overriding
- A method demo mini app
- How methods affect our variables

First, let's go through a quick method recap.

Methods revisited

The following diagram sums up where our understanding of methods is at the moment:

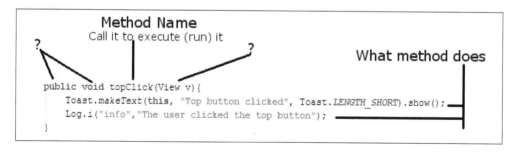

As we can see in the preceding diagram, there are still a couple of question marks surrounding methods. We will totally take the lid off of methods and see how they work, and what exactly the other parts of the method are doing for us, later in this chapter. In *Chapter 10, Object-Oriented programming*, and *Chapter 11, More Object-Oriented Programming*, we will clear up the last few parts of the mystery of methods.

What exactly are Java methods?

A method is a collection of variables, expressions, and control flow statements bundled together inside an opening and closing curly brace, preceded by a name. We have already been using lots of methods, but we just haven't looked very closely at them yet.

Let's start with the method structure.

Method structure

The first part of a method that we write is called the **signature**. Here is a hypothetical method signature:

```
public boolean addContact(boolean isFriend, string name)
```

If we add an opening and closing pair of curly braces {} with some code that the method performs, then we have a complete method – a **definition**. Here is another made-up, yet syntactically correct, method:

```
private void setCoordinates(int x, int y){
    // code to set coordinates goes here
}
```

As we have seen, we could then use our new method from another part of our code, like this:

```
// I like it here

setCoordinates(4,6);// now I am going off to setCoordinates method

// Phew, I'm back again - code continues here
```

At the point where we **call** setCoordinates, our program's execution would branch to the code contained within that method. The method would execute all the statements inside it, step by step, until it reaches the end and returns control to the code that called it – or sooner if it hits a return statement. Then, the code would continue running from the first line after the method call.

Here is another example of a method, complete with the code to make the method return to the code that called it:

```
int addAToB(int a, int b){
    int answer = a + b;
    return answer;
}
```

The call to use the preceding method could look like this:

```
int myAnswer = addAToB(2, 4);
```

Clearly, we don't need to write methods to add two int variables together, but the preceding example helps us see a little more into the workings of methods. First, we pass in the values 2 and 4. In the method signature, the value 2 is assigned to int a, and the value 4 is assigned to int b.

Within the method body, the variables a and b are added together and used to initialize the new variable, int answer. The line return answer returns the value stored in answer to the calling code, causing myAnswer to be initialized with the value 6.

Notice that each of the method signatures in the earlier examples varies a little. The reason for this is that the Java method signature is quite flexible, allowing us to build exactly the methods we need.

Exactly how the method signature defines how the method must be called, and how the method must return a value, deserves further discussion. Let's give each part of the signature a name so that we can break it into chunks and learn about the parts.

 Here is a method signature with its parts labeled up ready for discussion. Also have a look at the table that follows to further clarify which part of the signature is which. This will make the rest of our discussions on methods straightforward:

modifier | return-type | name of method (parameters)

And here are a few examples that we have used so far so that you can clearly find the part of the signature under discussion:

Part of signature	Examples
Modifier	`public`, `private`, `protected`, package-private (without modifier specified)
Return-type	`int` – you can also use any of the Java primitive types (such as `boolean`, `float`, and `long`) or any predefined reference types (such as `String` and class types)
Name of method	`addContact`, `setCoordinates`, `addAToB`
Parameters	`(boolean isFriend, String name)`, `(int x, int y)`, `(int a, int b)`

Modifier

In our earlier examples, we only used a modifier on a couple of occasions, partly because the method doesn't have to use the modifier. The modifier is a way of specifying what code can use (call) your method by using modifiers such as **public** and **private**.

Variables can have modifiers too. For example:

```
// Most code can see me
public int a;

// Code in other classes can't see me
private String secret = "Shhh! I am private";
```

Modifiers (for methods and variables) are an essential Java topic, but they are best dealt with when we are discussing the other vital Java topic we have skirted around a few times already – classes. We will do so in the next chapter.

As we can see from our example methods, and the fact that all the code we have written so far works just fine, modifiers are not necessary to ease our learning, although they will be a big part of our future learning from *Chapter 10, Object-Oriented programming*, onward.

Return type

Next up is the return type. Like a modifier, a return type is optional, so let's look a bit closer. We have seen that our methods do stuff. But what if we need the results from what they have done? The simplest example of a return type we have seen so far was the following:

```
int addAToB(int a, int b){
    int answer = a + b;
    return answer;
}
```

Here, the return type in the signature is highlighted in the preceding code block. So, the return type is an `int`. The method `addAToB` sends back (returns) to the code that called it a value, that will then fit in an `int` variable.

The return type can be any Java type we have seen so far. The method does not have to return a value at all, however.

In this case, the signature must use the `void` keyword as the return type. When the `void` keyword is used, the method body must not try to return a value as this will cause a compiler error. It can, however, use the `return` keyword without a value.

Here are some combinations of the return type and use of the `return` keyword that are valid:

```
void doSomething(){
    // our code

    // I'm done going back to calling code here
    // no return is necessary
}
```

Another combination is as follows:

```
void doSomethingElse(){
    // our code

    // I can do this as long as I don't try and add a value
    return;
}
```

The following code is yet another combination:

```
void doYetAnotherThing(){
    // some code
    if(someCondition){

        // if someCondition is true returning to calling code
        // before the end of the method body
        return;
    }

    // More code that might or might not get executed

    return;
    /*
        As I'm at the bottom of the method body
        and the return type is void, I'm
        really not necessary but I suppose I make it
        clear that the method is over.
    */
}

String joinTogether(String firstName, String lastName){
    return firstName + lastName;
}
```

We could call each of the preceding methods in turn, like this:

```
// OK time to call some methods

doSomething();
doSomethingElse();
doYetAnotherThing();
String fullName = joinTogether("Alan ","Turing")

// fullName now = Alan Turing
// continue with code from here
```

The preceding code would execute all the code in each method in turn.

Name of a method

When we design our own methods, the method name is arbitrary. But it is convention to use verbs that clearly explain what the method will do. Also, it is convention for the first letter of the first word of the name to be lowercase, and the first letter of subsequent words to be uppercase. This is called camel case, as we learned while learning about variable names. For example:

```
XGHHY78802c(){
    // code here
}
```

The preceding method is perfectly legal and will work. However, let's look at a much clearer example that uses the following conventions:

```
doSomeVerySpecificTask(){
    // code here
}

getMyFriendsList(){
    // code here
}

startNewMessage(){
    // code here
}
```

This is much clearer.

Now, let's have a look at parameters in methods.

Parameters

We know that a method can return a result to the calling code. But what if we need to share some data values *from* the calling code *with* the method?

Parameters allow us to share values with the method. We have already seen an example with parameters when we looked at return types. We will look at the same example, but a little more closely at the parameters:

```
int addAToB(int a, int b){
    int answer = a + b;
    return answer;
}
```

In the preceding code, the parameters are highlighted. Parameters are contained in parentheses (parameters go here), immediately after the method name.

Notice that in the first line of the method body, we use a + b as if they are already declared and initialized variables. That is because they are. The parameters of the method signature are their declaration and the code that calls the method initializes them, as highlighted in the following line of code:

```
int returnedAnswer = addAToB(10,5);
```

Also, as we have partly seen in earlier examples, we don't have to just use int in our parameters. We can use any Java type, including types we design ourselves.

What's more, we can mix and match types as well. We can also use as many parameters as is necessary to solve our problem. An example might help:

```
void addToAddressBook(char firstInitial, String lastName, String
city, int age){

    /*
            all the parameters are now living, breathing,
            declared and initialized variables.

            The code to add details to address book goes here.
    */
}
```

Now, we will look at the method body — what goes inside the method.

The body

The body is the part we have been partly avoiding, with comments such as the following:

```
// code here
```

as well as the following:

```
// some code
```

And finally the addToAddressBook method:

```
    /*
            all the parameters are now living, breathing,
            declared and initialized variables.

            The code to add details to address book goes here.
    */
```

But, we know exactly what to do in the body already. Any Java syntax we have learned so far will work in the body of a method. In fact, if we think back, all the code we have written in this book so far *has* been in a method.

The best thing we can do next is write a few methods that do something in the body.

Using methods demo apps

Here, we will quickly build two apps to explore methods a bit further. First, we will explore the fundamentals with the `Real World Methods` app, and then we will glimpse a new topic, **method overloading,** in action with the `Exploring Method Overloading` app.

As we normally do, you can open the ready-typed code files in the usual way. The following two examples on methods can be found in the PACKT download in the `chapter 8` folder and the `Real World Methods` and `Exploring Method Overloading` sub-folders.

Real world methods

First, let's make ourselves some simple working methods, complete with return type parameters and fully functioning bodies.

To get started, create a new Android project called `Real World Methods`, use an **Empty Activity,** and leave all the other settings at their default settings. Switch to the `MainActivity.java` file by left-clicking the **MainActivity.java** tab above the editor and we can start coding.

First, add these three methods to `MainActivity`. Add them just after the closing curly brace } of the `onCreate` method:

```
String  joinThese(String a, String b, String c){
    return a + b + c;
}

float getAreaCircle(float radius){
    return 3.141f * radius * radius;
}

void changeA(int a){
    a++;
}
```

The first method we added is called joinThese. It will return a String and needs three String variables passed into it. In the method body, there is only one line of code. The code return a + b + c will concatenate the three strings that are passed into it and return the joined strings as the result.

The next method, getAreaCircle, takes a float variable as an argument and then returns a float variable too. The body of the method simply uses the formula for the area of a circle, incorporating the passed-in radius, and then returns the answer to the calling code. The odd-looking f on the end of 3.141 is used to let the compiler know that the number is of the float type. Any floating point number is assumed to be of the double type unless it has the trailing f.

The third and final method is the simplest of all the methods. Notice that it doesn't return anything; it has a void return type. We have included this method to make an important point clear: we want to remember about methods. But let's see it in action before we talk about it.

Now, in onCreate, after the call to setContentView, add the following code, which calls our methods and outputs some text to the logcat:

```
String joinedString = joinThese("Methods ", "are ", "cool ");
Log.e("joinedString = ","" + joinedString);

float area  = getAreaCircle(5f);
Log.e("area = ","" + area);

int a = 0;
changeA(a);
Log.e("a = ","" + a);
```

Run the app and see the output in the logcat window, which is provided here for your convenience:

```
joinedString =: Methods are cool
area =: 78.525
a =: 0
```

In the logcat output, the first thing we can see is the value of the joinedString string. As expected, it is the concatenation of the three words we passed into the joinThese method.

Next, we can see that the getAreaCircle has indeed been calculated and returned the area of a circle based on the length of the radius passed in.

Discovering variable scope

The final line of output is the most interesting: a=: 0. In the onCreate method, we declared and initialized int a to zero, and then we called changeA. In the body of changeA, we incremented a with the code a++. Yet, back in onCreate, we can see that when we use Log to print the value of a to the logcat window, it is still 0.

So, when we passed in a to the changeA method, we were actually passing the *value stored in* a, not the actual variable a. This is referred to as passing by value in Java.

> When we declare a variable in a method, it can only be *seen* in that method. When we declare a variable in another method, even if it has the exact same name, it is NOT the same variable. A variable only has **scope** within the method it was declared.

With all primitive variables, this is how passing them to methods works. With reference variables, it works slightly different, and we will see how in the next chapter.

> I have talked about this scope concept with a number of people new to Java. To some it seems blindingly obvious, even natural. To others, however, it is a cause of constant confusion. Should you fall into the latter category, don't worry, because we will talk a bit more about this later in this chapter, and, in future chapters, we will explore scope in greater depth and make sure that it is no longer an issue.

Let's look at another practical example of methods and learn something new at the same time.

Exploring method overloading

As we are learning, methods are quite deep as a topic. But, hopefully, taking them a step at a time, we will see that they are not daunting in any way. We will also be returning to methods in the next chapter. For now, let's create a new project to explore **method overloading**.

Create a new Empty Activity project called Exploring Method Overloading, and then we will get on with writing three methods, but with a slight twist.

As we will now see, we can create more than one method with the same name, provided that the parameters are different. The code in this project is very simple. It is how it works that might appear slightly curious until we analyze it subsequently.

In the first method, we will simply call it printStuff and pass in an int variable via a parameter to be printed. Insert this method after the closing } of onCreate, but before the closing } of MainActivity. Remember to import the Log class in the usual way:

```
void printStuff(int myInt){
    Log.i("info", "This is the int only version");
    Log.i("info", "myInt = "+ myInt);
}
```

In this second method, we will also call it printStuff, but pass in a String variable to be printed. Insert this method after the closing } of onCreate, but before the closing } of MainActivity:

```
void printStuff(String myString){
    Log.i("info", "This is the String only version");
    Log.i("info", "myString = "+ myString);
}
```

In this third method, we will also call it printStuff, but pass in a String variable and an int to be printed. Insert this method after the closing } of onCreate, but before the closing } of MainActivity:

```
void printStuff(int myInt, String myString){
    Log.i("info", "This is the combined int and String version");
    Log.i("info", "myInt = "+ myInt);
    Log.i("info", "myString = "+ myString);
}
```

Now, insert this code just before the closing } of the onCreate method to call the methods and print some values to the logcat:

```
// Declare and initialize a String and an int
int anInt = 10;
String aString = "I am a string";

// Now call the different versions of printStuff
// The name stays the same, only the parameters vary
printStuff(anInt);
printStuff(aString);
printStuff(anInt, aString);
```

Now, we can run the run the app on the emulator or a real device.

Here is the console output:

```
info: This is the int only version
info: myInt = 10
info: This is the String only version
info: myString = I am a string
info: This is the combined int and String version
info: myInt = 10
info: myString = I am a string
```

As you can see, Java has treated three methods with the same name as different methods. This, as we have just shown, can be useful. It is called **method overloading**.

> **Method overloading and overriding confusion**
>
> **Overloading** is when we have more than one method with the same name but different parameters.
>
> **Overriding** is when we replace a method with the same name and the same parameter list.
>
> We know enough about overloading and overriding to complete this book, but if you are brave and your mind is wandering, yes, you can override an overloaded method, but that is something for another time.

This is how it all works. In each of the steps where we wrote code, we created a method called printStuff. But each printStuff method has different parameters, so each is actually a different method that can be called individually:

```
void printStuff(int myInt){
    ...
}

void printStuff(String myString){
    ...
}

void printStuff(int myInt, String myString){
    ...
}
```

The body of each of the methods is trivial and just prints out the passed-in parameters and confirms which version of the method is being called.

The next important part of our code is when we make it plain what we mean to call by using the specific arguments that match the parameters in the signature. In the final step, we call each in turn by using the matching parameters so that Java knows the exact method required:

```
printStuff(anInt);
printStuff(aString);
printStuff(anInt, aString);
```

We now know all we need to about methods, so let's take a quick second look at the relationship between methods and variables and then get our heads around this scope phenomenon a bit more.

Scope and variables revisited

You might remember that in the `Real World Methods` project, the slightly disturbing anomaly was that variables in one method were not apparently the same as those from another, even if they do have the same name. If you declare a variable in a method, whether that is one of the life cycle methods or one of our own methods, it can only be used within that method.

It is no use doing this in `onCreate`:

```
int a = 0;
```

And then trying to do this in `onPause` or some other method:

```
a++;
```

We will get an error because `a` is only visible within the method it was declared. At first, this might seem like a problem but surprisingly, it is actually a very useful feature of Java.

I have already mentioned that the term used to describe this is **scope**. A variable is said to be in scope when it is usable and out of scope when it is not. The topic of scope is best discussed along with classes, and we will do so in *Chapter 10, Object-Oriented programming*, and *Chapter 11, More Object-Oriented Programming*, but as a sneak peek look at what lies ahead, you might like to know that a class can have its very own variables and when it does, they have scope for the whole class; that is, all its methods can see and use them. We call them **member** variables or **fields**.

To declare a member variable, you simply use the usual syntax after the start of the class, outside of any method declared in the class. If our app started like this:

```
public class MainActivity extends AppCompatActivity {

    int mSomeVariable = 0;
    // Rest of code and methods follow as usual
    // ...
```

We could use `mSomeVariable` anywhere, inside any method in this class. Our new variable, `mSomeVariable`, has **class scope**. We append an `m` to the variable name simply to remind us when we see it that it is a member variable. This is not required by the compiler, but it is a useful convention.

Here are a couple of hypothetical method questions to try and make some of what we have learned stick a little more in our minds. Try and answer them yourself.

Frequently asked questions

Q- What is wrong with this method definition?

```
doSomething(){
    // Do something here
}
```

A- No return type is declared. You do not have to return a value from a method, but its return type must be `void` in this case. This is what the method should look like:

```
void doSomething(){
    // Do something here
}
```

Q- What is wrong with the following method definition?

```
float getBalance(){
    String customerName = "Linus Torvalds";
    float balance = 429.66f;
    return userName;
}
```

A- The method returns a string (userName), but the signature states that it must return a float. With a method name like getBalance, this code is what was likely intended:

```
float getBalance(){
    String customerName = "Linus Torvalds";
    float balance = 429.66f;
    return balance;
}
```

Q- When do we call the onCreate method? Trick question alert!

A- We don't. Android decides when to call onCreate, as well as all the other methods that make up the life cycle of an Activity. We just override the ones that are useful to us. We do, however, call super.onCreate, so that our overridden version and the original version both get executed.

> For the sake of complete disclosure, it is technically possible to call the life cycle methods from our code, but we will never need to in the context of this book. It is best to leave these things to Android.

Further reading

We have learned enough Java to proceed with this book. It is always beneficial, however, to see more examples of Java in action and to go beyond the minimum necessary to proceed. If you want a good source to learn Java in greater depth, then the official Oracle website is good. Note that you do not need to study this website to continue with this book. Also note that the tutorials on the Oracle website are not set in an Android context, but the site is a useful resource to bookmark and browse all the same:

The official Java tutorials can be found at https://docs.oracle.com/javase/tutorial/.

Summary

In the first five chapters, we got quite proficient with a whole array of widgets and other UI elements. We also built a broad selection of UI layouts. In this chapter and the previous three, we have explored Java and the Android Activity life cycle in quite significant depth, especially considering how quickly we have done it.

We have, to a small extent, interacted between our Java code and our UI. We have called our methods by setting the `onClick` attribute and we have loaded our UI layouts using the `setContentView` method. We haven't, however, really made a proper connection between our UI and our Java code.

What we really need to do now is bring these things together so that we can begin to display and manipulate our data using the Android UI. To achieve this, we need to understand a bit more about classes.

Classes have been lurking in our code since *Chapter 1, Beginning Android and Java*, and we have even used them a bit. Hitherto, however, we haven't tackled them properly other than constantly referring to *Chapter 10, Object-Oriented Programming*. In the next chapter (number 10), we will quickly get to grips with classes and then we can finally start to build apps where the UI designs and our Java code work in perfect harmony.

10
Object-Oriented programming

In this chapter, we will discover that in Java, classes are fundamental to just about everything. We will begin to understand why the software engineers at Sun Microsystems back in the early 1990s made Java the way they did.

We have already talked about reusing other people's code, specifically the Android API, but in this chapter, we will really get to grips with how this works and learn about object-oriented programming and how to use it.

In summary, we will cover the following topics:

- What is OOP, including **encapsulation**, **inheritance,** and **polymorphism**
- How to write and use our first class in an app

Before we get to what exactly OOP is, a quick warning.

Important memory management warning

I'm referring to our brain's memories for a change. If you try to memorize this chapter (or the next), you will have to make a lot of room in your brain and you will probably forget something really important in its place, such as going to work or thanking the author for telling you not to try and memorize this stuff.

A good goal will be to try and *just-about get it*. This way, our understanding will become more rounded. You can then refer to this chapter (or the next) for a refresher when needed.

[It doesn't matter if you don't completely understand everything in this chapter straight away! Keep on reading and make sure to complete all the apps.]

Object-oriented programming

In *Chapter 1, Beginning Android and Java,* we mentioned that Java was an object-oriented language. An object-oriented language requires us to use **object-oriented programming (OOP)**. It isn't an optional extra like a racing spoiler on a car or pulsating LEDs in a gaming PC. It's part of Java and, therefore, Android as well.

Let's find out a little bit more.

What is OOP exactly

OOP is a way of programming that involves breaking our requirements down into chunks that are more manageable than the whole.

Each chunk is self-contained, yet potentially reusable, by other programs, while working together as a whole with the other chunks.

These chunks are what we have been referring to as objects. When we plan/code an object, we do so with a class. A class can be thought of as the blueprint of an object.

We implement an object *of* a class. This is called an **instance** of a class. Think about a house blueprint. You can't live in it, but you can build a house from it; you build an instance of it. Often, when we design classes for our apps, we write them to represent real world *things*.

However, OOP is more than this. It is also a *way* of doing things—a methodology that defines best practices.

The three core principles of OOP are **encapsulation, polymorphism,** and **inheritance**. This might sound complex but, taken a step at a time, is reasonably straightforward.

Encapsulation

Encapsulation means keeping the internal workings of your code safe from interference from the code that uses it, by allowing only the variables and methods you choose to be accessed.

This means that your code can always be updated, extended, or improved without affecting the programs that use it, as long as the exposed parts are still accessed in the same way.

Remember this line of code from *Chapter 1, Beginning Android and Java*?

```
locationManager.getLastKnownLocation(LocationManager.GPS_PROVIDER)
```

With proper encapsulation, it doesn't matter if the satellite company or the Android API team need to update the way their code works. If the `getLastKnownLocation` method signature remains the same, we don't have to worry about what goes on inside. Our code written before the update will still work after the update.

If the manufacturer of a car gets rid of the wheels and makes it an electrically-powered hover car, as long as it still has a steering wheel, accelerator, and brake pedal, driving it should not be a challenge.

When we use the classes of the Android API, we are doing so in the way that the Android developers designed their classes to allow us to.

Polymorphism

Polymorphism allows us to write code that is less dependent on the *types* we are trying to manipulate, making our code clearer and more efficient. Polymorphism means *different forms*. If the objects that we code can be more than one type of thing, then we can take advantage of this. Some examples later in this chapter will make this clear. An analogy will give you a more real-world perspective. If we have car factories that can make vans and small trucks just by changing the instructions given to the robots and the parts that go onto the production line, then the factory is using polymorphism.

Wouldn't it be useful if we could write code that can handle different types of data without starting again? We will see some examples of this in *Chapter 11, More Object-Oriented Programming*.

Inheritance

Just like it sounds, **inheritance** means that we can harness all the features and benefits of other peoples' classes, including encapsulation and polymorphism, while further refining their code specifically to our situation. Actually, we have done this already, every time we used the `extends` keyword:

```
public class MyActivity extends AppCompatActivity {
```

The `AppCompatActivity` class itself inherits from `Activity`. So, we inherited from `Activity` every time we created a new Android project. We can go further than this and we will see how it is useful.

Imagine if the strongest man in the world gets together with the smartest woman in the world. There is a good chance that their children will have serious benefits from gene inheritance. Inheritance in Java lets us do the same thing with another person's code and our own.

Why do it like this?

When written properly, all of this OOP allows you to add new features without worrying as much about how they interact with existing features. When you do have to change a class, its self-contained (encapsulated) nature means less or perhaps even zero consequences for other parts of the program. This is the encapsulation part.

You can use other people's code (like the Android API) without knowing or perhaps even caring how it works: think about the android life cycle, Toast, Log, all the UI widgets, listening to satellites, and so on. For example, the Button class has nearly 50 methods – do we really want to write all that ourselves, just for a button? It would be much better to use someone else's Button class.

OOP allows you to write apps for highly complex situations without breaking a sweat.

You can create multiple, similar, yet different versions of a class without starting the class from scratch by using inheritance; and you can still use the methods intended for the original type of object with your new object because of polymorphism.

It makes, sense really. And Java was designed from the start with all of this in mind, so we are forced into using all this OOP; however, this is a good thing. Let's have a quick class recap.

Class recap

A class is a bunch of code that can contain methods, variables, loops, and all the other Java syntax we have learned. A class is part of a Java package, and most packages will normally have multiple classes. Usually, although not always, each new class will be defined in its own .java code file with the same name as the class, as with all of our activity classes so far.

Once we have written a class, we can use it to make as many objects from it as we want. Remember, the class is the blueprint, and we make objects based on the blueprint. The house isn't the blueprint, just as the object isn't the class; it is an object made from the class. An object is a reference variable, just like a string, and later we will discover exactly what being a reference variable means. For now, let's look at some actual code.

Looking at the code for a class

Let's say we are making an app for the military. It is to be used by senior officers to micro-manage their troops in battle. Among other things, we would probably need a class to represent a soldier.

Class implementation

Here is some real code for our hypothetical class. We call it a class **implementation**. As the class is called `Soldier`, if we implement this for real, we would do so in a file called `Soldier.java`:

```
public class Soldier {

    // Member variables
    int health;
    String soldierType;

    // Method of the class
    void shootEnemy(){
            // Bang! Bang!
    }

}
```

What we have here is a class implementation for a class called `Soldier`. There are two **member variables** or **fields**, an `int` variable called `health`, and a `String` variable called `soldierType`.

There is also a method called `shootEnemy`. The method has no parameters and a `void` return type, but class methods can be of any shape or size, which is what we discussed in *Chapter 9, Java Methods*.

To be precise about member variables and fields, when the class is instantiated into a real object, the fields become variables of the object itself and we call them **instance** or **member** variables.

They are just variables of the class, regardless of whichever fancy name they are referred to by, although the difference between fields and variables declared in methods (called **local** variables) does become more important as we progress.

We briefly discussed variable scope at the end of *Chapter 9, Java Methods*. We will look at all types of variables again later in the next chapter. Let's concentrate on coding and using a class here.

Declaring, initializing, and using an object of the class

Remember that Soldier is just a class, not an actual usable object. It is a blueprint for a soldier, not an actual soldier object, just like int, String, and boolean are not variables; they are just types we can make variables of. This is how we make an object of the Soldier type from our Soldier class:

```
Soldier mySoldier = new Soldier();
```

In the first part of the code, Soldier mySoldier declares a new variable of type Soldier called mySoldier. The last part of the code, new Soldier(), calls a special method called a **constructor** that is automatically made for all classes by the compiler.

It is this constructor method that creates an actual Soldier object. As you can see, the constructor method has the same name as the class. We will look at constructors in more depth later in this chapter.

And, of course, the assignment operator = in the middle of the two parts assigns the result of the second part to that of the first. The following diagram summarizes all of this information:

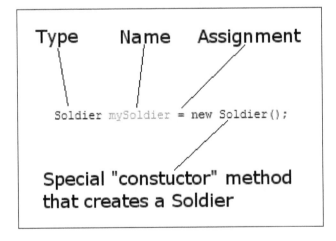

This is not far off how we deal with a regular variable, except for the constructor/ method call instead of a value on the end of the line of code. To create and use a very basic class, we have done enough.

As we will see when we explore further, we can write our own constructors rather than rely on the auto-generated constructor. This gives us lots of power and flexibility, but we will just continue to explore the simplest case for now.

Just like regular variables, we could also have done it in two parts, like this:

```
Soldier mySoldier;
mySoldier = new Soldier();
```

This is how we might assign to and use the variables of our hypothetical class:

```
mySoldier.health = 100;
mySoldier.soldierType = "sniper";

// Notice that we use the object name mySoldier.
// Not the class name Soldier.
// We didn't do this:
// Soldier.health = 100;
// ERROR!
```

In the preceding code, the dot operator . is used to access the variables of the class. This is how we would call the method – again, by using the object name and not the class name, followed by the dot operator:

```
mySoldier.shootEnemy();
```

We can summarize the use of the dot operator with a diagram, like so:

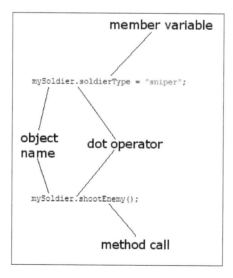

We can think of a class's methods as what it can *do,* and its instance/ member variables as what it *knows* about itself.

We can also go ahead and make another `Soldier` object and access its methods and variables:

```
Soldier mySoldier2 = new Soldier();
mySoldier2.health = 150;
mySoldier2.soldierType = "special forces";
mySoldier2.shootEnemy();
```

It is important to realize that `mySoldier2` is a totally separate object with completely distinct instance variables to `mySoldier`, as demonstrated in the following diagram:

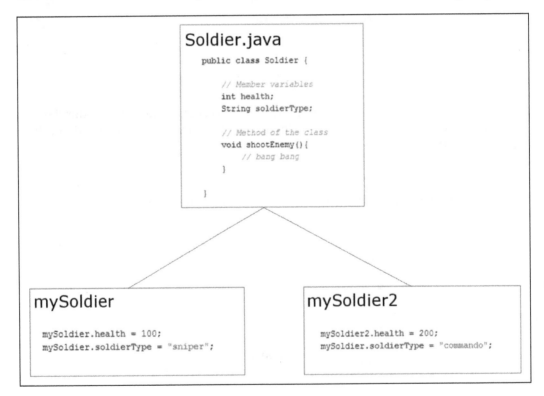

What is also key here is that this previous code would not be written within the class itself. For example, we could create the `Soldier` class in an external file called `Soldier.java` and then use the code that we have just seen, perhaps in our `MainActivity` class.

This will become clearer when we write our first class in an actual project in a minute.

Also notice that everything is done *on* the object itself. We must create objects of classes to make them useful.

 As always, there are exceptions to this rule, but they are in the minority, and we will look at these exceptions in the next chapter. In fact, we have already seen two exceptions in this book so far. The exceptions we have seen are the `Toast` and `Log` classes. Exactly what is going on with them will be explained soon.

Let's explore basic classes a little more deeply by writing one for real.

Basic classes app

The generals who will be using our app will need more than one `Soldier` object. In our app that we are about to build, we will instantiate and use multiple objects. We will also demonstrate using the dot operator on variables and methods to show that different objects have their very own instance variables.

You can get the completed code for this example in the code download. It is in the `chapter 10/Basic Classes` folder. However, it is most useful to read on to create your own working example.

Create a project with the Empty Activity template. Call the application `Basic Classes`. Now, we will create a new class called `Soldier`:

1. Right-click the `com.gamecodeschool.basicclasses` (or whatever your package name is) folder in the project explorer window.
2. Select **New | Java Class** in the **Name:** field.
3. Type `Soldier` and click **OK**.

The new class is created for us with a code template, ready for us to put our implementation in, as demonstrated in the following screenshot:

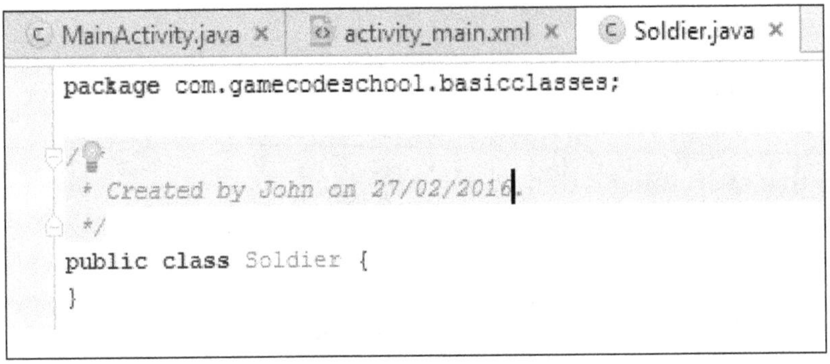

```
C MainActivity.java ×    ◇ activity_main.xml ×    C Soldier.java ×

    package com.gamecodeschool.basicclasses;

    /**
     * Created by John on 27/02/2016.
     */
    public class Soldier {

    }
```

Notice that Android Studio has put the class in the same package/folder as the rest of our app's Java files.

And now we can write its implementation.

Write the class implementation code that follows within the opening and closing curly braces of the Soldier class, as shown. The new code to type is highlighted:

```
public class Soldier {
    int health;
    String soldierType;

    void shootEnemy(){
        //let's print which type of soldier is shooting
        Log.i(soldierType, " is shooting");
    }
}
```

Now that we have a class and a blueprint for our future objects of the Soldier type, we can start to build our army. In the editor window, left-click the **MainActivity. java tab**. We will write this code, as so often, within the onCreate method, just after the call to setContentView. Type the following code:

```
// First, we make an object of type soldier
Soldier rambo = new Soldier();
rambo.soldierType = "Green Beret";
rambo.health = 150;
// It takes allot to kill Rambo
```

```
// Now we make another Soldier object
Soldier vassily = new Soldier();
vassily.soldierType = "Sniper";
vassily.health = 50;
// Snipers have less health

// And one more Soldier object
Soldier wellington = new Soldier();
wellington.soldierType = "Sailor";
wellington.health = 100;
// He's tough but no green beret
```

If you aren't doing so already, this is a really appropriate time to start taking advantage of the auto-complete feature in Android Studio. Notice after you have declared and created a new object, all you must do is begin typing the object's name and all the auto-complete options present themselves.

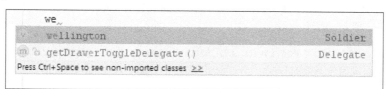

Now that we have our extremely varied and somewhat unlikely army, we can use it and also verify the identity of each object.

Type the following code beneath the code from the previous step:

```
Log.i("Rambo's health = ", "" + rambo.health);
Log.i("Vassily's health = ", "" + vassily.health);
Log.i("Wellington's health = ", "" + wellington.health);

rambo.shootEnemy();
vassily.shootEnemy();
wellington.shootEnemy();
```

Now, we can run our app. All the output will be in the **logcat** window.

This is how it works. First, we created a template for our new `Soldier` class. Then, we implemented our class, including declaring two fields (member variables), an `int`, and a `String` called `health` and `soldierType`.

We also have a method in our class called `shootEnemy`. Let's look at it again and examine what is going on:

```
void shootEnemy(){
        //let's print which type of soldier is shooting
        Log.i(soldierType, " is shooting");
}
```

In the body of the method, we print to the console; first, the `soldierType` string and then the arbitrary `" is shooting"`. What's neat here is that the `soldierType` string will be different, depending upon which object we call the `shootEnemy` method on.

Next, we declared and created three new objects of the `Soldier` type. They were `rambo`, `vassily`, and `wellington`.

Finally, we initialized each with a different value for `health`, as well as `soldierType`.

Here is the output:

```
Rambo's health =: 150
Vassily's health =: 50
Wellington's health =: 100
Green Beret: is shooting
Sniper: is shooting
Sailor: is shooting
```

Notice that each time we access the `health` variable of each `Soldier` object, it prints the value we assigned it, proving that although the three objects are of the same type, they are completely separate, individual instances/objects.

Perhaps more interesting is the three calls to `shootEnemy`. One by one, each of our `Soldier` object's `shootEnemy` methods is called and we print the `soldierType` variable to the logcat. The method has the proper value for each individual object, proving further that we have three distinct objects (instances of the class), albeit created from the same `Soldier` class.

We saw how each object is completely independent of the other objects. However, if we imagine whole armies of `Soldier` objects in our app, then we realize that we are going to need to learn new ways of handling large numbers of objects (and regular variables, too).

Think about managing just 100 separate `Soldier` objects. What about when we have thousands of objects? In addition, this isn't very dynamic. The way we are writing the code now relies on us (the developers) knowing the exact details of the soldiers that the generals (the user) will be commanding. We will see the solution for this in *Chapter 15, Arrays, ArrayList, Map, and Random Numbers*.

More things that we can do with our first class

We can treat a class much like we can other variables. We can use a class as a parameter in a method signature, like in the following code:

```
public void healSoldier(Soldier soldierToBeHealed){
    // Use soldierToBeHealed here

    // And because it is a reference the changes
    // are reflected in the actual object passed into
    // the method.
}
```

And when we call the method, we must, of course, pass an object of that type. Here is a hypothetical call to the `healSoldier` method:

```
healSoldier(rambo);
```

Of course, the preceding example might raise questions like, should the `healSoldier` method be a method of a class?

```
fieldhospital.healSoldier(rambo);
```

It could be, or not, as the case may be. It would depend upon what is the best solution for the situation. We will look at OOP some more, and then the best solution for lots of similar conundrums should present themselves more easily.

And, as you might guess, we can also use an object as the return value of a method. Here is what the updated hypothetical `healSoldier` signature and implementation might look like now:

```
Soldier healSoldier(Soldier soldierToBeHealed){
    soldierToBeHealed.health++;

    return soldierToBeHealed;
}
```

In fact, we have already seen classes being used as parameters. For example, here is our `topClick` method from *Chapter 2, First Contact – Java, XML and the UI Designer,*. It receives an object called `v` of type `View`:

```
public void topClick(View v){
```

However, in the case of `topClick`, we didn't do anything with the passed-in object of the type `View`, partly because we didn't need to and partly because we don't know what we can do with an object of the type `View`, yet.

As I mentioned at the start of this chapter, you don't need to understand or remember everything in this chapter. The only way to get good at OOP is to keep using it. Like learning a spoken language, studying it and pouring over grammatical rules will help, but nowhere near as much as having a conversation verbally (or in writing). If you just about get it, move on to the next chapter, but make sure to do all the practical apps in Android Studio.

Frequently asked questions

Q- I just can't wait any longer. What is a reference already?!

A- It literally is the same thing as a reference in normal (non-programming) language. It is a value that identifies/points to the data rather than the actual data itself. One way of thinking about it is that a reference is a memory location/address. It identifies and gives access to the actual data at that location/address in memory.

Q- If it is not the actual object, but just a reference, how come we can do things like call methods on it, such as `mySoldier.shootEnemy()`.

A- Java works out the exact details under the hood, but you can think of a reference as being the controller of an object, and anything you want to do to the object you must do through the controller, because the actual object/memory itself cannot be directly accessed. More on this will be covered in *Chapter 12, The Stack, the Heap, and the Garbage Collector*.

Summary

We have at last written our first class. We have seen that we can implement a class in a Java file of the same name as the class. The class itself doesn't do anything until we instantiate an object/instance of the class. Once we have an instance of the class, we can use its variables and methods. As we proved in the Basic Classes app, each and every instance of a class has its own distinct variables. Just as when you buy a car made in a factory, you get your very own steering wheel, Sat Nav, and go-faster stripes.

All this information will raise more questions. OOP is like that. So, let's try and consolidate all of this class stuff by taking another look at variables and encapsulation, polymorphism, and inheritance in action in the next chapter. We can then go further with classes and explore topics such as static classes (like Log and Toast), as well as the more advanced concepts of abstract classes and interfaces.

11
More Object-Oriented Programming

This chapter is the second part of our whirlwind tour (theoretical and practical) of OOP. We have already briefly discussed the concepts of encapsulation, inheritance, and polymorphism, but in this chapter, we will get to see them in action in some demo apps. While the working examples will show these concepts in their simplest forms, it will still be a significant stepping stone toward taking control of our layouts via our Java code.

In this chapter, we will explore the following topics:

- Encapsulation in depth and how it helps us
- Inheritance in depth and how to take full advantage of it
- Polymorphism explained in greater detail
- Static classes and how we have been using them already
- Abstract classes and interfaces

First, we will handle encapsulation.

Remember that encapsulation thing?

So far, what we have really seen is what amounts to a kind of code-organizing convention where we write classes, full of variables and methods. We did discuss the wider goals of all this OOP stuff, but now we will take things further and begin to see how we actually manage to achieve encapsulation with OOP.

Definition of encapsulation

Keeping the internal workings of your code safe from interference from the programs that use it, allowing only the variables and methods you choose to be accessed. This means your code can always be updated, extended, or improved without affecting the programs that use it— provided the exposed parts are still made available in the same way. It also allows the code that uses your encapsulated code to be much simpler and easier to maintain because much of the complexity of the task is encapsulated in your code.

"But didn't you say we don't have to know what is going on inside?" So, you might question what we have seen so far like this: if we are constantly setting the instance variables like this: `rambo.health = 100;`, isn't it possible that eventually things could start to go wrong, perhaps like this:

```
rambo.soldierType = "fluffy bunny";
```

Encapsulation protects your class/objects of your class/code from being used in a way that it wasn't meant to be. By controlling the way that your code is used, it can only ever do what you want it to do and with value ranges that you can control.

It can't be forced into errors or crashes. Also, you are then free to make changes to the way your code works internally, without breaking the rest of your program or any programs that are using an older version of the code:

```
weightlifter.legstrength = 100;
weightlifter.armstrength = 1;
weightlifter.liftHeavyWeight();

// one typo and weightlifter rips own arms off
```

Encapsulation is not just vital for writing code that other people will use (like the Android API that we use); it is also essential when writing code we will reuse ourselves, as it will save us from our own mistakes. Furthermore, a team of programmers will use encapsulation extensively so that different members of the team can work on the same program without all members of the team knowing how the other team member's code works. We can encapsulate our classes for this same advantage, and here is how.

Controlling class use with access modifiers

The designer of the class controls what can be seen and manipulated by any program that uses their class. We can add an **access modifier** before the class keyword, like this:

```
public class Soldier{
    //Implementation goes here
}
```

Class access modifiers

There are two main access modifiers for classes in the context we have discussed so far. Let's briefly look at each in turn:

- **public**: This is straightforward. A class declared as public can be seen by all other classes.

- **default**: A class has default access when no access modifier is specified. This will make it public, but only to classes in the same package, and inaccessible to all others.

So, now we can make a start at this encapsulation thing. But even at a glance, the access modifiers described thus far are not very fine-grained. We seem to be limited to complete lockdown to anything outside the package or a complete free-for-all.

Actually, the benefits here are easily taken advantage of. The idea would be to design a package of classes that fulfills a set of tasks. Then, all the complex inner workings of the package – the stuff that shouldn't be messed with by anybody but our package – should be default access (only accessible to classes within the package). We can then make a careful choice of public classes available that can be used by others (or other distinct parts of our program).

> For the size and complexity of the apps in this book, creating multiple packages is overkill. We will, of course, be using other people's packages and classes, so this stuff is worth knowing.

Class access in summary

A well-designed app will probably consist of one or more packages, each containing only default or default and public classes.

In addition to class-level privacy controls, Java gives us programmers very fine-grained controls, but to use these controls, we have to look into variables with a little more detail.

Controlling variable use with access modifiers

To build on the class visibility controls, we have variable access modifiers. Here is a variable with the `private` access modifier being declared:

```
private int myInt;
```

Also note that all our discussion of variable access modifiers applies to object variables, too. For example, here is an instance of our `Soldier` class being declared, created, and assigned. As you can see, the access specified in this case is public:

```
public Soldier mySoldier = new Soldier();
```

Before you apply a modifier to a variable, you must first consider class visibility. If class *a* is not visible to class *b* – say, because class *a* has default access and class *b* is in another package – then it doesn't make any difference what access modifiers you use on the variables in class *a*: class *b* can't see any of them.

So, it makes sense to show a class to another class when necessary, but only to expose the variables that are needed – not everything.

Here is an explanation of the different variable access modifiers.

Variable access modifiers

Variable access modifiers are more numerous and finely grained than the class access modifiers. The depth and complexity of access modification is not so much in the range of modifiers, but rather in the smart ways we can combine them to achieve the worthy goals of encapsulation. Here are the variable access modifiers:

- **public**: You guessed it: any class or method from any package can see this variable. Use public only when you are sure that this is what you want.
- **protected**: This is the next least restrictive after public. Protected variables can be seen by any class and any method as long as they are in the same package.

- **default**: Default doesn't sound as restrictive as protected, but it is more so. A variable has default access when no access is specified. The fact that default is restrictive perhaps implies that we should be thinking on the side of hiding our variables more than we should be exposing them. At this point, we need to introduce a new concept. Do you remember that we briefly discussed inheritance and how we can quickly take on the attributes of a class and yet refine it by using the `extends` keyword? Just for the record, default access variables are not visible to subclasses; that is, when we `extend` a class like we did with Activity, we cannot see its default variables. We will look at inheritance in more detail later in this chapter.

- **private**: Private variables can only be seen within the class they are declared. As with default access, they cannot be seen by subclasses (classes that inherit from the class in question).

Variable access summary

A well-designed app will probably consist of one or more packages, each containing only default or default and public classes. Within these classes, variables will have carefully chosen and varied access modifiers, chosen with a view to achieving our goal of encapsulation.

There's one more twist in all this access modification stuff that we must look at before we get practical with it.

Methods have access modifiers too

We already briefly mentioned in *Chapter 9, Java Methods*, that methods have access modifiers. This makes sense since methods are the things that our classes can *do*. We will want to control what users of our class can and can't do.

The general idea here is that some methods will do things internally only and are therefore not needed by users of the class. Some methods will be fundamental to how users of the class use your class.

Method access modifiers

The access modifiers for methods are the same as for the class variables. This makes things easy to remember but suggests, again, that successful encapsulation is a matter of design rather than of following any specific set of rules.

As an example, this method, provided it is in a public class, could be used by any other class:

```
public useMeEverybody(){
    //do something everyone needs to do here
}
```

On the other hand, this method could only be used internally by the class that created it:

```
private secretInternalTask(){
    /*
            do something that helps the class function internally
            Perhaps, if it is part of the same class,
            useMeEverybody could use this method...
            On behalf of the classes outside of this class.
            Neat!
    */
}
```

And the following method with no access specified has default visibility. It can be used only by other classes in the same package. If we extend the class, holding this default access method, the class will not have access to this method:

```
fairlySecretTask(){
    // allow just the classes in the package
    // Not for external use
}
```

As a last example before we move on, here is a protected method, only visible to the package, but usable by our classes that extend it – just like onCreate:

```
protected packageTask(){
    // Allow just the classes in the package
    // And you can use me if you extend me too
}
```

Let's have a quick recap on method encapsulation. Remember, you don't need to memorize everything.

Method access summary

Method access should be chosen to best enforce the principles we have already discussed. It should provide the users of your class with just the access they need and preferably nothing more. That way, we achieve our encapsulation goals, such as keeping the internal workings of our code safe from interference from the programs that use it, for all the reasons we have discussed.

Accessing private variables with getters and setters

Now we need to consider, if it is a best practice to hide our variables away as private, how would we allow access to them without spoiling our encapsulation. What if an object of the `Hospital` class wanted access to the `health` member variable from an object of the `Soldier` type so that it could increase it? The health variable should be private because we don't want just any piece of code changing it.

To be able to make as many member variables as possible private and yet still allow some kind of limited access to some of them, we use **getters** and **setters**. Getters and setters are just methods that get and set variable values.

This is not some special new Java thing that we have to learn. It is just a convention for using what we already know. Let's have a look at getters and setters by using our `Soldier` and `Hospital` class example.

In this example, each of our two classes are created in their own file but in the same package. First of all, here is our hypothetical `Hospital` class:

```
class Hospital{

    private void healSoldier(Soldier soldierToHeal){
        int health = soldierToHeal.getHealth();
        health = health + 10;
        soldierToHeal.setHealth(health);
    }

}
```

Our implementation of the `Hospital` class has just one method, `healSoldier`. It receives a reference to a `Soldier` object as a parameter. So, this method will work on whichever `Soldier` object is passed in: `vassily`, `wellington`, `rambo`, or whoever.

It also has a local `health` variable, which it uses to temporarily hold and increase the soldier's health. In the same line, it initializes the `health` variable to the `Soldier` object's current health. The `Soldier` object's health is private, so the public getter method, `getHealth`, is used instead.

Then, `health` is increased by `10` and the `setHealth` setter method loads up the new revived health value, back to the `Soldier` object.

The key here is that although a `Hospital` object can change a `Soldier` object's health, it only does so within the bounds of the getter and setter methods. The getter and setter methods can be written to control and check for potentially mistaken – even harmful – values.

Next, let's look at our hypothetical `Soldier` class with the simplest implementation possible of its getter and setter methods:

```
public class Soldier{

    private int health;

    public int getHealth(){
        return health;
    }

    public void setHealth(int newHealth){

        // Check for stupid values of newHealth
        health = newHealth;

    }
}
```

We have one instance variable called `health`, and it is private. Private means that it can only be changed by methods of the `Soldier` class. We then have a public `getHealth` method, which returns the value held in the private `health` int variable. As this method is public, any code with access to an object of the `Soldier` type can use it.

Next, the `setHealth` method is implemented. Again, it is public, but this time it takes an int as a parameter and assigns whatever is passed in to the private `health` variable. In a more life-like example, we would write some more code here to make sure that the value passed in is within the bounds we expect.

Now, we declare, create, and assign to make an object of each of our two new classes and see how our getters and setters work:

```
Soldier mySoldier = new Soldier();
// mySoldier.health = 100;//Doesn't work, private

// we can use the public setter setHealth() instead
mySoldier.setHealth(100); //That's better

Hospital militaryHospital = new Hospital();

// Oh no mySoldier has been wounded
mySoldier.setHealth(10);

/*
    Take him to the hospital.
    But my health variable is private
    And Hospital won't be able to access it
    I'm doomed - tell Laura I love her

    No wait- what about my public getters and setters?
    We can use the public getters and setters
    from another class
*/

militaryHospital.healSoldier(mySoldier);

// mySoldiers private variable health has been increased
// by 10. I'm feeling much better thanks!
```

We can see that we can call our public `setHealth` and `getHealth` methods directly on our object of the `Soldier` type. Not only that, we can call the `healSoldier` method of the `Hospital` object, passing in a reference to the `Soldier` object, which too can use the public getters and setters to manipulate the private `health` variable.

We can see that the private `health` variable is simply accessible, yet totally within the control of the designer of the `Soldier` class.

If you want to play around with this example, there is the code for a working app in the code bundle in the `Chapter 11` folder called `GettersAndSetters`. I have added a few lines of code to print to the console. We deliberately covered this the way we did to keep the key parts of the code as clear as possible.

[Getters and setters are sometimes referred to by their more correct names, **Accessors** and **Mutators**. We will stick to getters and setters. I just thought you might like to know the jargon.]

Yet again, our example and the explanation are probably raising more questions. That's good.

By using encapsulation features (such as access control), it is like signing a really important deal about how to use and access a class, its methods, and variables. The contract is not just an agreement about now, but an implied guarantee for the future. We will see that, as we go ahead through this chapter, there are more ways that we refine and strengthen this contract.

[Use encapsulation where it is needed or, of course, if you are being paid to use it by an employer. Often, encapsulation is overkill on small learning projects, such as some of the examples in this book – except, of course, when the topic you are learning is encapsulation itself.

We are learning this Java OOP stuff under the assumption that you will one day want to write much more complex apps, whether on Android or some other platform which uses OOP. In addition, we will be using classes from the Android API that use it extensively, and this will help us understand what is happening then as well. Typically, throughout this book, we will use encapsulation when implementing full projects and often overlook it when showing small code samples to demonstrate a single idea or topic.]

Setting up our objects with constructors

With all these private variables and their getters and setters, does it mean that we need a getter and a setter for every private variable? What about a class with lots of variables that need initializing at the start. Think about the following:

```
mySoldier.name
mysoldier.type
mySoldier.weapon
mySoldier.regiment
    . . .
```

Some of these variables might need getters and setters, but what if we just want to set things up when the object is first created to make the object function correctly?

Surely, we don't need two methods (a getter and a setter) for each?

Fortunately, this is unnecessary. For solving this potential problem, there is a special method called a **constructor**. We briefly mentioned the existence of a constructor when we discussed instantiating an object from a class in *Chapter 10, Object-Oriented programming*. Let's look at constructors once more.

Here, we create an object of the `Soldier` type and assign it to an object called `mySoldier`:

```
Soldier mySoldier = new Soldier();
```

Nothing new here, but look at the last part of that line of code:

```
...Soldier();
```

This looks suspiciously like a method.

All along, we have been calling a special method called a constructor that has been created, behind the scenes, automatically, by the compiler.

However – and this is getting to the point now – as with a method, we can *override* it, which means we can do useful things to set up our new object *before* it is used. The following code shows how we could do this:

```
public Soldier(){
    // Someone is creating a new Soldier object

    health = 200;
    // more setup here
}
```

The constructor has a lot of syntactical similarities to a method. It can, however, only be called with the use of the `new` keyword, and it is created for us automatically by the compiler – unless we create our own, as in the previous code.

Constructors have the following features:

- They have no return type
- They have the exact same name as the class
- They can have parameters
- They can be overloaded

One more piece of Java syntax that is useful to introduce at this point is the Java `this` keyword.

The this keyword is used when we want to be explicit about exactly which variables we are referring to. Look at this example constructor, again for a hypothetical variation of the Soldier class:

```
public class Soldier{

    String name;
    String type;
    int health;

    // This is the constructor
    // It is called when a new instance is created
    public Soldier(String name, String type, int health){

        // Someone is creating a new Soldier object

        this.name = name;
        this.type = type;
        this.health = health;

        // more setup here

    }
}
```

This time, the constructor has a parameter for each of the variables we want to initialize. By using the this keyword, it is clear when we mean the member variable or the parameter.

There are more twists and turns to be learned about variables and this, and they make much more sense when applied to a practical project. In the next app, we will explore all we have learned so far in this chapter and some more new ideas too.

First, let's look at a bit more OOP.

Static methods

We know quite a lot about classes already. For example, we know how to turn them into objects and use their methods and variables. But something isn't quite right. Since the very start of this book, we have been using two classes more than any other. We have repeatedly used Log and Toast to output to the logcat or the users screen, but have not instantiated them once! How can this be? We never did this:

```
Log myLog   = new Log();
Toast myToast = new Toast();
```

We just went ahead and used the classes directly, like this:

```
Log.i("info","our message here");
Toast.makeText(this, "our message",
Toast.LENGTH_SHORT).show();
```

The **static** methods of classes can be used *without* first instantiating an object of the class. We can think of this as a static method belonging to the class and all other methods belonging to an object/instance of a class.

And, as you have probably realized by now, Log and Toast both contain static methods. To be clear: Log and Toast *contain* static methods; they themselves are still classes.

Classes can have both static and regular methods as well, but the regular methods would need to be used in the regular way, via an instance/object of the class.

Let's take another look at Log.i in action:

```
Log.i("info","our message here");
```

Here, i is the method being statically accessed, and the method takes two parameters, both of type String.

Next, we can see the makeText static method of the Toast class in use:

```
Toast.makeText(this, "our message",
        Toast.LENGTH_SHORT).show();
```

The makeText method of the Toast class takes three arguments.

First is this, which takes some explaining. We saw when talking about constructors that to explicitly refer to the member variables of the current instance of an object, we can use this.health, this.regiment, and so on.

When we use this as we do in the previous line of code, we are referring to the instance of the class itself. Not the Toast class, but the this in the previous line of code is a reference to the class the method is being used *from*. In our case, we have used it from MainActivity.

Many things in Android require a reference to an instance of Activity to do its job. We will – fairly regularly throughout this book – pass in this (a reference to the Activity) in order to help a class/object from the Android API do its work. We will also write classes that need this as an argument in one or more of its methods. So, we will see how to handle this when it is passed in as well.

The second argument is, of course, a `String`.

The third argument is accessing a `final` variable, LENGTH_SHORT, again via the class name, not an instance of the class. This is achieved if we declare a variable like we do in the following line of code:

```
public static final int LENGTH_SHORT = 1;
```

If the variable was declared in a class called `MyClass`, we could access the variable like this: `MyClass.LENGTH_SHORT`, and use it like any other variable, but the `final` keyword makes sure that the value of the variable can never be changed. This type of variable is called a **constant**.

The `static` keyword also has another consequence for a variable, especially when it is not a constant (can be changed), and we will see this in action in our next app.

Now, if you look carefully at the very end of the line of code that shows a `Toast` message to the user, you will see something else new, `.show()`.

This is called **chaining,** and all we are doing is calling a second method of the `Toast` class but using just one line of code. It is the `show` method that actually triggers the message.

We will see some more chaining as we proceed through this book, like in *Chapter 14, Android Dialog Windows*, when we make pop-up dialogs.

> If you want to read about the `Toast` class and some of its other methods in detail, you can do so here: `http://developer.android.com/reference/android/widget/Toast.html`.

Static methods are often provided in classes that have uses that are so generic that it doesn't make sense to have to create an object of the class. Another really useful class with static methods is `Math`. This class is actually a part of the Java API, not the Android API.

> Want to write a calculator app? It's easier than you think with the static methods of the `Math` class. You can look at them here: `http://docs.oracle.com/javase/7/docs/api/java/lang/Math.html`.

If you try this out, you will need to import the `Math` class in the same way that we imported all the other classes we have used.

Encapsulation and static methods mini-app

We have looked at the intricate way that access to variables and their scope is controlled, and it would serve us well to look at an example of them in action. These will not so much be practical real-world examples of variable use, but more a demonstration to help understand access modifiers for classes, methods, and variables alongside the different types of variable, such as reference or primitive and local or instance, along with the new concepts of static and final variables and the **this** keyword.

The completed code is in the `chapter 11` folder of the download bundle. It is called `Access Scope This And Static`.

Create a new Empty Activity project and call it `Access Scope This And Static`.

Create a new class by right-clicking on the existing `MainActivity` class in the project explorer and clicking **New | Class**. Name the new class `AlienShip`.

Now, we will declare our new class and some member variables. Note that `numShips` is `private` and `static`. We will see how this variable is the same across all instances of the class soon. The `shieldStrength` variable is `private` and `shipName` is `public`:

```
public class AlienShip {

    private static int numShips;
    private int shieldStrength;
    public String shipName;
```

Next is the constructor. We can see that the constructor is public, has no return type, and has the same name as the class – as per the rules. In it, we increment the private static `numShips` variable. Remember that this will happen each time we create a new object of type `AlienShip`. Also, the constructor sets a value for the `shieldStrength` private variable using the private `setShieldStrength` method:

```
public AlienShip(){
    numShips++;

    /*
            Can call private methods from here because I am part
            of the class.
            If didn't have "this" then this call
            might be less clear
            But this "this" isn't strictly necessary
            Because of "this" I am sure I am setting
```

```
                  the correct shieldStrength
   */

   this.setShieldStrength(100);


}
```

Here is the public static getter method so that classes outside of `AlienShip` can find out how many `AlienShip` objects there are. We will also see the way in which we use static methods:

```
      public static int getNumShips(){
            return numShips;


      }
```

And this is our private `setShieldStrength` method. We could have just set `shieldStrength` directly from within the class, but the following code shows how we distinguish between the `shieldStrength` local variable/parameter and the `shieldStrength` member variable by using the `this` keyword:

```
      private void setShieldStrength(int shieldStrength){

            // "this" distinguishes between the
            // member variable shieldStrength
            // And the local variable/parameter of the same name
            this.shieldStrength = shieldStrength;


      }
```

The following method is the getter so that other classes can read but not alter the shield strength of each `AlienShip` object:

```
      public int getShieldStrength(){
            return this.shieldStrength;
      }
```

Now, we have a public method that can be called every time an `AlienShip` object is hit. It just prints to the console and then detects whether that object's `shieldStrength` is zero. If it is, it calls the `destroyShip` method, which we can see in the following code:

```
      public void hitDetected(){

            shieldStrength -=25;
            Log.i("Incomiming: ","Bam!!");
            if (shieldStrength == 0){
```

```
            destroyShip();
     }


  }
```

And lastly for our `AlienShip` class, we will code the `destroyShip` method. We print a message that indicates which ship has been destroyed based on its `shipName`, as well as decrement the `numShips` static variable so that we can keep track of how many objects of type `AlienShip` we have:

```
     private void destroyShip(){
            numShips--;
            Log.i("Explosion: ", ""+this.shipName + " destroyed");
     }
} // End of the class
```

Now, we switch over to our `MainActivity` class and write some code that uses our new `AlienShip` class. All the code goes in the `onCreate` method after the call to `setContentView`. First, we create two new `AlienShip` objects called `girlShip` and `boyShip`:

```
// every time we do this the constructor runs
AlienShip girlShip = new AlienShip();
AlienShip boyShip = new AlienShip();
```

In the following code, look how we get the value in `numShips`. We use the `getNumShips` method, as we might expect. However, look closely at the syntax. We are using the class name and not an object. We can also access static variables with methods that are not static. We did it this way to see a static method in action:

```
// Look no objects but using the static method
Log.i("numShips: ", "" + AlienShip.getNumShips());
```

Now, we assign names to our public `shipName` String variables:

```
// This works because shipName is public
girlShip.shipName = "Corrine Yu";
boyShip.shipName = "Andre LaMothe";
```

In the following code, we try to assign a value directly to a private variable. It won't work. Then, we use the public `getShieldStrength` getter method to print out the `shieldStrength` that was assigned in the constructor:

```
// This won't work because shieldStrength is private
// girlship.shieldStrength = 999;

// But we have a public getter
```

```
    Log.i("girlShip shieldStrength: ", "" + girlShip.getShieldStrength());

    Log.i("boyShip shieldStrength: ", "" + boyShip.getShieldStrength());

    // And we can't do this because it's private
    // boyship.setShieldStrength(1000000);
```

Finally, we get to blow some stuff up by playing with the `hitDetected` method and occasionally checking the `shieldStrength` of our two objects:

```
    // let's shoot some ships
    girlShip.hitDetected();
    Log.i("girlShip shieldStrength: ", "" + girlShip.getShieldStrength());

    Log.i("boyShip shieldStrength: ", "" + boyShip.getShieldStrength());

    boyShip.hitDetected();
    boyShip.hitDetected();
    boyShip.hitDetected();

    Log.i("girlShip shieldStrength: ", "" + girlShip.getShieldStrength());

    Log.i("boyShip shieldStrength: ", "" + boyShip.getShieldStrength());

    boyShip.hitDetected();//Ahhh!

    Log.i("girlShip shieldStrength: ", "" + girlShip.getShieldStrength());

    Log.i("boyShip shieldStrength: ", "" + boyShip.getShieldStrength());
```

When we think we have destroyed a ship, we again use our static `getNumShips` method to see whether our static `numShips` variable was changed by the `destroyShip` method:

```
    Log.i("numShips: ", "" + AlienShip.getNumShips());
```

Run the demo and look at the console output:

```
numShips: 2
girlShip shieldStrength: 100
boyShip shieldStrength: 100
Incomiming: Bam!!
girlShip shieldStrength:: 75
boyShip shieldStrength:: 100
```

```
Incomiming: Bam!!
Incomiming: Bam!!
Incomiming: Bam!!
girlShip shieldStrength:: 75
boyShip shieldStrength:: 25
Incomiming: Bam!!
Explosion: Andre LaMothe destroyed
girlShip shieldStrength: 75
boyShip shieldStrength: 0
numShips: 1
boyShip shieldStrength: 0
numShips: 1
```

In the previous example, we saw that we can distinguish between local and member variables of the same name by using the `this` keyword. We can also use the `this` keyword to write code that refers to whatever the current object being acted upon is.

We saw that a static variable – in this case, `numShips` – is consistent across all instances; moreover, by incrementing it in the constructor and decrementing it in our `destroyShip` method, we can keep track of the number of `AlienShip` objects we currently have.

We also saw that we can use static methods by using the class name with the dot operator instead of an actual object.

 Yes, I know it is like living in the blueprint of a house – but it's quite useful too.

Finally, we proved how we could hide and expose certain methods and variables using an access specifier.

OOP and inheritance

We have seen how we can use other people's code by instantiating/creating objects from the classes of an API like Android. But this whole OOP thing goes even further than that.

What if there is a class that has loads of useful functionality in it but not exactly what we want? We can inherit from the class and then further refine or add to how it works and what it does.

You might be surprised to hear that we have done this already. In fact, we have done this with every single app we have created. When we use the extends keyword, we are inheriting. Remember this:

```
public class MainActivity extends AppCompatActivity ...
```

Here, we are inheriting from the AppCompatActivity class, along with all its functionality – or more specifically, all the functionality that the class designers want us to have access to. Here are some of the things we can do to classes we have extended.

We can even override a method *and* still rely in part on the overridden method in the class we inherit from. For example, we overrode the onCreate method every time we extended the AppCompatActivity class. But we also called on the default implementation provided by the class designers when we did this:

```
super.onCreate(...
```

And in *Chapter 6, The Android Life Cycle*, we overrode just about all of the Activity class' life cycle methods.

We have discussed inheritance mainly so that we can understand what is going on around us and as the first step toward being able to eventually design useful classes that we or others can extend.

With this in mind, let's look at some example classes and see how we can extend them, just to see the syntax as a first step, and also to be able to say we have done it.

When we look at the final major topic of this chapter, polymorphism, we will also dig a little deeper into inheritance at the same time. Here is some code that's using inheritance.

This code would go in a file named Animal.java:

```
public class Animal{

    // Some member variables
    public int age;
    public int weight;
    public String type;
    public int hungerLevel;

    public void eat(){
```

```
                hungerLevel--;
        }

        public void walk(){
                hungerLevel++;
        }

}
```

Then, in a separate file named `Elephant.java`, we could do this:

```
public class Elelphant extends Animal{

        public Elephant(int age,  int weight){
                this.age = 57;
                this.weight = 1000;
                this.type = "Elephant";
                int hungerLevel = 0;
        }

}
```

We can see in the previous code that we have implemented a class called `Animal` and that it has four member variables: `age`, `weight`, `type`, and `hungerLevel`. It also has two methods: `eat` and `walk`.

We then extended `Animal` with `Elephant`. Now, `Elephant` can do anything `Animal` can and it also has all its variables.

We initialized the variables from `Animal` that `Elephant` has in the `Elephant` constructor. Two variables (`age` and `weight`) are passed into the constructor when an `Elephant` object is created and two variables (`type` and `hungerLevel`) are assigned the same for all `Elephant` objects.

We could go ahead and write a bunch of other classes that extend `Animal`, perhaps `Lion`, `Tiger`, and `ThreeToedSloth`. Each would have an `age`, `weight`, `type`, and `hungerLevel`, and each would be able to `walk` and `eat`.

As if OOP were not useful enough already, we can now model real-world objects. We have also seen that we can make OOP even more useful by sub-classing/extending/inheriting from other classes. The terminology we might like to learn here is that the class that is extended from is the **superclass** and the class that inherits from the superclass is the **sub class**. We can also say parent and child class.

As usual, we might find ourselves be asking this question about inheritance. Why? The reason is something like this: if we write common code in the parent class, then we can update that common code, and all classes that inherit from it will also be updated. Furthermore, a subclass only gets to use public/protected instance variables and methods. So, designed properly, this also further enhances the goals of encapsulation.

Let's take a closer look at the final major OOP concept. Then, we will be able to do some more practical things with the Android API.

Inheritance example app

We have looked at the way we can create hierarchies of classes to model the system that fits our app. So, let's try out some simple code that uses inheritance. The completed code is in the `chapter 11` folder of the code download. It is called `Inheritance Example`.

Create a new project called `Inheritance Example` using the Empty Activity template and then add three new classes in the usual way. Name one `AlienShip`, another `Fighter`, and the last one `Bomber`.

Here is the code for the `AlienShip` class. It is very similar to our previous class demo `AlienShip`. The differences are that the constructor now takes an `int` parameter, which it uses to set the shield strength.

The constructor also outputs a message to the logcat so that we can see when it is being used. The `AlienShip` class also has a new method, `fireWeapon`, which is declared `abstract`.

Declaring a class as abstract guarantees that any class that are subclasses of `AlienShip` must implement their own version of `fireWeapon`. Notice that the class has the `abstract` keyword as part of its declaration. We have to do this because one of its methods also uses the `abstract` keyword. We will explain the `abstract` method when discussing this demo and the `abstract` class when we talk about polymorphism. Create a class called `AlienShip` and type the following code:

```
public abstract class AlienShip {
    private static int numShips;
    private int shieldStrength;
    public String shipName;

    public AlienShip(int shieldStrength){
```

```
        Log.i("Location: ", "AlienShip constructor");
        numShips++;
        setShieldStrength(shieldStrength);
    }


    public abstract void fireWeapon();
    // Ahh my body where is it?

    public static int getNumShips(){
        return numShips;
    }

    private void setShieldStrength(int shieldStrength){
        this.shieldStrength = shieldStrength;
    }


    public int getShieldStrength(){
        return this.shieldStrength;
    }

    public void hitDetected(){
        shieldStrength -=25;
        Log.i("Incomiming: ", "Bam!!");
        if (shieldStrength == 0){
            destroyShip();
        }

    }

    private void destroyShip(){
        numShips--;
        Log.i("Explosion: ", "" + this.shipName + " destroyed");
    }

}
```

Now, we will implement the `Bomber` class. Notice the call to `super(100)`. This calls the constructor of the superclass with the value for `shieldStrength`. We could do further specific `Bomber` initialization in this constructor, but for now we just print out the location so that we can see when the `Bomber` constructor is being executed. We also, because we must, implement a `Bomber`-specific version of the abstract `fireWeapon` method. Create a class called `Bomber` and type the following code:

```java
public class Bomber extends AlienShip {

    public Bomber(){
        super(100);
        // Weak shields for a bomber
        Log.i("Location: ", "Bomber constructor");
    }

    public void fireWeapon(){
        Log.i("Firing weapon: ", "bombs away");
    }

}
```

Now, we will implement the `Fighter` class. Notice the call to `super(400)`. This calls the constructor of the superclass with the value for `shieldStrength`. We could do further specific `Fighter` initialization in this constructor, but for now we just print out the location so that we can see when the `Fighter` constructor is being executed. We also do this because we must implement a `Fighter`-specific version of the abstract `fireWeapon` method. Create a class called `Fighter` and type the following code:

```java
public class Fighter extends AlienShip{

    public Fighter(){
        super(400);
        // Strong shields for a fighter
        Log.i("Location: ", "Fighter constructor");
    }

    public void fireWeapon(){
        Log.i("Firing weapon: ", "lasers firing");
    }

}
```

And here is our code in the `onCreate` method of `MainActivity`. As usual, enter this code after the call to `setContentView`. This is the code that uses our three new classes. The code looks quite ordinary, nothing new – it is the output that is interesting:

```
Fighter aFighter = new Fighter();
Bomber aBomber = new Bomber();

// Can't do this AlienShip is abstract -
// Literally speaking as well as in code
// AlienShip alienShip = new AlienShip(500);

// But our objects of the subclasses can still do
// everything the AlienShip is meant to do

aBomber.shipName = "Newell Bomber";
aFighter.shipName = "Meier Fighter";

// And because of the overridden constructor
// That still calls the super constructor
// They have unique properties
Log.i("aFighter Shield:", ""+ aFighter.getShieldStrength());
Log.i("aBomber Shield:", ""+ aBomber.getShieldStrength());

// As well as certain things in certain ways
// That are unique to the subclass
aBomber.fireWeapon();
aFighter.fireWeapon();

// Take down those alien ships
// Focus on the bomber it has a weaker shield
aBomber.hitDetected();
aBomber.hitDetected();
aBomber.hitDetected();
aBomber.hitDetected();
```

Run the app and you will get the following output in the logcat window:

```
Location:: AlienShip constructor
Location:: Fighter constructor
Location:: AlienShip constructor
Location:: Bomber constructor
aFighter Shield:: 400
```

```
aBomber Shield:: 100
Firing weapon:: bombs away
Firing weapon:: lasers firing
Incomiming:: Bam!!
Incomiming:: Bam!!
Incomiming:: Bam!!
Incomiming:: Bam!!
Explosion:: Newell Bomber destroyed
```

We can see how the constructor of the subclass can call the constructor of the superclass. We can also clearly see that the individual implementations of the `fireWeapon` method work exactly as expected.

Polymorphism

We already know that polymorphism means *different forms*. But what does it mean to us?

 Boiled down to its simplest form, it means the following:
Any subclass can be used as part of the code that uses the superclass.

This means that we can write code that is simpler and easier to understand, and easier to change.

Also, we can write code for the superclass and rely on the fact that no matter how many times it is subclassed, within certain parameters, the code will still work. Let's discuss an example.

Suppose we want to use polymorphism to help write a zoo management app. We will probably want to have a method, such as `feed`. We will probably want to pass a reference to the animal to be fed into the `feed` method. This might seem like we need to write a feed method for each and every type of Animal.

However, we can write polymorphic methods with polymorphic return types and arguments:

```
Animal feed(Animal animalToFeed){
    // Feed any animal here
    return animalToFeed;
}
```

The preceding method has `Animal` as a parameter, which means that any object that is built from a class that `extends Animal` can be passed into it. And, as you can see in the preceding code, the method also returns `Animal`, which has exactly the same benefits.

There is a small gotcha with polymorphic return types, and that is that we need to be aware of what is being returned and make it explicit in the code that calls the method.

For example, we could handle `Elephant` being passed into the `feed` method like this:

```
someElephant = (Elephant) feed(someElephant);
```

Notice the highlighted `(Elephant)` in the previous code. This makes it plain that we want `Elephant` from the returned `Animal`. This is called **casting**. We will use casting with methods from the Android API in the next chapter and throughout the rest of this book, when we look at how to interact with our UI from our Java code.

So, you can even write code *today* and make another subclass in a week, month, or year, and the very same methods and data structures will still work.

Also, we can enforce upon our subclasses a set of rules as to what they can and cannot do, as well as how they do it. So, clever design in one stage can influence it at other stages.

But will we ever really want to instantiate an actual Animal?

Abstract classes

An abstract class is a class that cannot be instantiated; it cannot be made into an object. So, it's a blueprint that will never be used, then? But that's like paying an architect to design your home and then never building it! You might be saying to yourself, "I kind of get the idea of an abstract method, but abstract classes are just silly."

If we or the designer of a class wants to force us to inherit *before* we use their class, they can declare a class as `abstract`. Then, we cannot make an object from it; therefore, we must extend it first and make an object from the subclass.

We can also declare a method as `abstract` and then that method must be overridden in any class that extends the class with the abstract method.

Let's look at an example, as it will help. We make a class `abstract` by declaring it with the `abstract` keyword, like this:

```
abstract class someClass{
    /*
            All methods and variables here.
            As usual!
            Just don't try and make
            an object out of me!
    */
}
```

Yes, but why?

Sometimes, we want a class that can be used as a polymorphic type, but we need to guarantee that it can never be used as an object. For example, Animal doesn't really make sense on its own.

We don't talk about animals, we talk about *types* of animals. We don't say, "Ooh, look at that lovely fluffy, white animal". Or, "yesterday we went to the pet shop and got an animal and an animal bed". It's just too, well, *abstract*.

So, an abstract class is kind of like a template to be used by any class that `extends` it (inherits from it).

We might want a `Worker` class and extend it to make, `Miner`, `Steelworker`, `OfficeWorker`, and, of course, `Programmer`. But what exactly does a plain `Worker` do? Why would we ever want to instantiate one?

The answer is that we wouldn't want to instantiate one; but we might want to use it as a polymorphic type, so we can pass multiple worker subclasses between methods and have data structures that can hold all types of `Worker`.

We call this type of class an abstract class, and when a class has even one abstract method, it must be declared abstract itself. All abstract methods must be overridden by any class that extends it.

This means that the abstract class can give some of the common functionality that would be available in all its subclasses. For example, the `Worker` class might have the `height`, `weight`, and `age` member variables.

It might also have the `getPayCheck` method, which is not abstract and is the same in all the subclasses, but a `doWork` method, which is abstract and must be overridden, because all the different types of worker `doWork` very differently.

This leads us neatly to another area of polymorphism that is going to make life easier for us throughout this book.

Interfaces

An interface is like a class. Phew! Nothing complicated here then. But it's like a class that is always abstract and with only abstract methods.

We can think of an interface as an entirely abstract class with all its methods being abstract and no member variables either.

OK, so you can just about wrap your head around an abstract class because at least it can pass on some functionality in its methods that are not abstract and serve as a polymorphic type.

But, seriously, this interface seems a bit pointless. Let's look at the simplest possible generic example of an interface, and then we can discuss it further.

To define an interface, we type the following:

```
public interface myInterface{
    void someAbstractMethod();
    // omg I've got no body

    int anotherAbstractMethod();
    // Ahh! Me too

    // Interface methods are always abstract and public implicitly
    // but we could make it explicit if we prefer

    public abstract explicitlyAbstractAndPublicMethod();
    // still no body though


}
```

The methods of an interface have no body because they are abstract, but they can still have return types and parameters, or not.

To use an interface, we use the `implements` keyword after the class declaration:

```
public class someClass implements someInterface{

    // class stuff here

    /*
```

```
            Better implement the methods of the interface
            or we will have errors.
            And nothing will work
    */

    public void someAbstractMethod(){
            // code here if you like
            // but just an empty implementation will do
    }

    public int anotherAbstractMethod(){
            // code here if you like
            // but just an empty implementation will do

            // Must have a return type though
            // as that is part of the contract
            return 1;

    }
}
```

This enables us to use polymorphism with multiple different objects that are from completely unrelated inheritance hierarchies. If a class implements an interface, the whole thing can be passed along or used as if it is that thing, because it is that thing. It is polymorphic (many things).

We can even have a class implement multiple different interfaces at the same time. Just add a comma between each interface and list them after the `implements` keyword. Just make sure to implement all the necessary methods.

In this book, we will use the interfaces of the Android API more often than we write our own. In *Chapter 13, Anonymous Classes – Bringing Android Widgets to Life*, one such interface we will use in the Java Meet UI app is the `OnClickListener` interface.

Many things might like to know when they are being clicked. Perhaps a `Button` or a `TextView`. So, using an interface, we don't need different methods for every type of UI element we might like to click.

Frequently asked questions

Q1) What is wrong with the following class declaration:

```
    private class someClass{
            // class implementation goes here
    }
```

A) There are no private classes. Classes can be public or default. Public is public, while default is like being private within its own package.

Q2) What is encapsulation?

A) Encapsulation is how we contain our variables, code, and methods in a manner that exposes just the parts and functionality we want to other code.

Summary

In this chapter, we covered more theory than in any other chapter. If you haven't memorized everything or some of the code seemed a bit too in-depth, then you have still succeeded completely.

If you just understand that OOP is about writing reusable, extendable, and efficient code through encapsulation, inheritance, and polymorphism, then you have the potential to be a Java master.

Simply put, OOP enables us to use other people's code, even when those other people were not aware of exactly what we would be doing at the time they did the work.

All you must do is keep practicing because we will constantly be using these same concepts over and over again throughout this book, so you do not need to have even begun mastering them at this point.

In the next chapter, we will be revisiting some concepts from this one, as well as looking at some new aspects of OOP and how it enables our Java to interact with our XML layouts.

But first, there is an important incoming news flash! Apparently, all the UI elements – `TextView`, `ConstraintLayout`, `CalenderView`, `Button`, all of them – are classes too. Their attributes are member variables and they have loads of methods that we can use to do all sorts of things with the UI. This could prove useful.

There will much more on this revelation in the next two chapters, but first we will see how Android handles the trash.

12
The Stack, the Heap, and the Garbage Collector

By the end of this chapter, the missing link between Java and our XML layouts will be fully revealed, leaving us with the power to add all kinds of widgets to our apps as we have done before. However, this time, we will be able to control them through our Java code.

In this chapter, we will get to take control of some fairly simple UI elements, such as Button and TextView, and, in the next chapter, we will take things further and manipulate a whole range of UI elements.

To enable us to understand what is happening, we need to find out a bit more about the memory in an Android device and two areas of it – the **Stack** and the **Heap**.

In this chapter, we will learn about the following topics:

- Android UI elements are classes
- Garbage collection
- Our UI is on the Heap
- Special types of class, including Inner and Anonymous

Back to that news flash.

All the Android UI elements are classes too

When our app is run and the `setContentView` method is called from `onCreate`, the layout is **inflated** from XML UI classes and loaded into memory as usable objects. They are stored in a part of the DVM's memory, called the **Heap**.

Re-introducing references

But where are all these UI objects/classes? We certainly can't see them in our code. And how on earth do we get our hands on them?

The DVM inside every Android device takes care of memory allocation to our apps. In addition, it stores different types of variables in different places.

Variables that we declare and initialize in methods are stored on an area of memory known as the **Stack**. We can stick to our existing warehouse analogy when talking about the Stack – almost. We already know how we can manipulate variables on the Stack with straightforward expressions. So, let's talk about the Heap and what is stored there.

 Important fact: **All objects of classes are reference type variables and are just references to the actual objects that are stored on the Heap** – they are not the actual objects.

Think of the Heap as a separate area of the same warehouse. The Heap has lots of floor space for odd shaped objects, racks for smaller objects, lots of long rows with smaller sized cubby holes, and so on. This is where objects are stored. The problem is that we have no direct access to the Heap. Think of it as a restricted access part of the warehouse. You can't actually go there, but you can *refer* to what is stored there. Let's look at what a reference variable actually is.

It is a variable that we refer to and use via a reference. A reference can be loosely, but usefully, defined as an address or location. The reference (address or location) of the object is on the Stack.

So, when we use the dot operator, we are asking Dalvik to perform a task *at* a specific location – a location that is stored in the reference.

 Reference variables are just that – a reference. They are used as a way to access and manipulate the object (variables and methods), but they are not the actual variable itself.

Why oh why would we ever want a system like this? Just give me my objects on the Stack already. Here is why.

A quick break to throw out the trash

This is what the whole Stack and Heap thing does for us.

As we know, the DVM keeps track of all our objects for us and stores them in a devoted area of our warehouse called the **Heap**. Regularly, while our app is running, the DVM will scan the Stack, the regular racks of our warehouse, and match up references to objects that are on the Heap, and any objects it finds without a matching reference, it destroys – or, in Java terminology, it **garbage collects**.

Think of a very discerning refuse vehicle driving through the middle of our Heap, scanning objects to match up to references (on the Stack). No reference means it is garbage now.

If an object has no reference variable, we can't possibly do anything with it anyway because we have no way to access it/refer to it. This system of garbage collection helps our apps run more efficiently by freeing up unused memory.

If this task was left to us, our apps would be much more complicated to code.

So, variables declared in a method are local, on the Stack, and only visible within the method where they were declared. A member variable (in an object) is on the Heap and can be referenced from anywhere where there is a reference to it and the access specification (encapsulation) allows.

Seven facts about the Stack and the Heap

Let's take a quick look at what we learned about Stack and Heap:

1. You don't delete objects, but the VM sends the garbage collector when it thinks it is appropriate. This is usually when there is no active reference to the object.

2. Local variables and methods are on the Stack and the local variables are local to the specific method within which they were declared.

3. Instance/class variables are on the Heap (with their objects), but the reference *to* the object (its address) is a local variable on the Stack.

4. We control what goes onto the Stack. We can use the objects on the Heap, but only by referencing them.

5. The Heap is kept clear and up-to-date by the garbage collector.

6. An object is garbage collected when there is no longer a valid reference to it. So, when a reference variable is removed from the Stack, then its related object becomes viable for garbage collection. And when the DVM decides the time is right (usually very promptly), it will free up the RAM memory to avoid running out.

7. If we try to reference an object that doesn't exist, we will get a **NullPointerException** and the app will crash.

Let's move on and see exactly what this information buys us in terms of taking control of our UI.

So how does this Heap thing help me?

Any UI element that has its `id` attribute set in the XML layout can have its reference retrieved from the Heap using the `findViewById` method, which is part of the Activity/`AppCompatActivity` class. As it is part of the class that we extend in all our apps, we have access to it, just like the following code shows:

```
myButton = (Button) findViewById(R.id.myButton);
```

The preceding code assumes that `myButton` has been declared previously to an appropriate type, in this case, `Button`. The code also assumes that within the XML layout is a `Button` with an `id` attribute set to `myButton`.

Notice that `findViewById` is also polymorphic. We know this because we use a cast, `(Button)`, to be explicit about making the returned object a `Button` from its `View` parent type, just like we did with our object of type `Elephant` with the `feed` method in the last chapter.

This is quite exciting because it implies we can grab a reference to a whole bunch of stuff from our layout. We can then start using all the methods that these objects have. Here are some examples of the methods we can use for `Button` objects:

```
myButton.setText
myButton.setHeight
myButton.setOnCLickListener
myButton.setVisibility
```

 The `Button` class alone has around 50 methods!

If you think that after eleven chapters, we are finally going to start doing some neat stuff with Android, you would be right!

Using Buttons and TextView widgets from our layout

To follow along with this project, create a new Android Studio project, call it `Java Meet UI`, choose the **Empty Activity** template, and leave all the other options at their defaults. As usual, you can find the Java code and the XML layout code in the `Chapter 12/Java Meet UI` folder.

First, let's build a simple UI by observing the following steps:

1. In the editor window of Android Studio, switch to `activity_main.xml` and make sure that you are on the **Design** tab.

2. Delete the auto-generated `TextView`, the one that reads "Hello world!".

3. Add a **TextView** widget to the top center of the layout.

4. Set its **text** property to `0`, its `id` property to `txtValue`, and its `textSize` to `40sp`. Pay careful attention to the case of the `id`. It has an uppercase `V`.

5. Now, drag and drop six buttons on the layout so that it looks a bit like the following diagram. The exact layout isn't important:

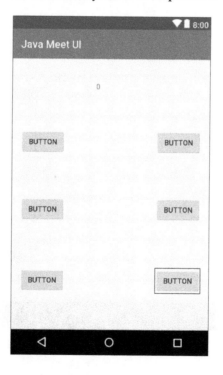

6. When the layout is how you want it, click the **Infer Constraints** button to constrain all the UI items.

7. Double left-click on each button in turn (left to right, and then top to bottom) and set the `text` and `id` properties, as shown in the following table:

The `text` property	The `id` property
add	btnAdd
take	btnTake
grow	btnGrow
shrink	btnShrink
hide	btnHide
reset	btnReset

When you're done, your layout should look like the following diagram:

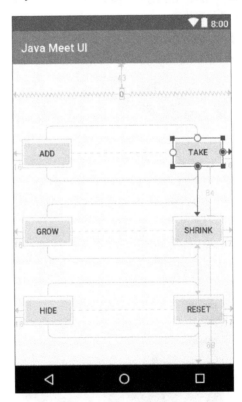

The precise position and text on the buttons is not very important, but the values given to the id properties must be the same. The reason for this is that we will be using these ids to get a reference to the buttons and the `TextView` in this layout from our Java code.

Switch to the **MainActivity.java** tab in the editor and we will write the code.

Amend the following line:

```
public class MainActivity extends AppCompatActivity{
```

To the following:

```
public class MainActivity extends AppCompatActivity implements
    View.OnClickListener{
```

 You will need to import the `View` class. Be sure to do this before continuing with the next step or you will get confusing results.
```
import android.view.View;
```

Notice that the entire line we just amended is underlined in red, showing an error. Now, because we have made `MainActivity` into an `OnClickListener` by adding it as an interface, we must implement the abstract method of `OnClickListener`. The method is called `onClick`. When we add the method, the error will be gone.

We can get Android Studio to add it for us by left-clicking anywhere on the line containing an error and then using the keyboard combination *Alt + Enter*. Left-click **Implement methods,** as shown in the following screenshot:

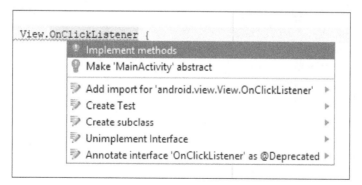

Now, left-click **OK** to confirm that we want Android Studio to add the onClick method. The error is gone, and we can carry on adding code. We also have an onClick method and we will soon see what we will do with that.

Now, we will declare an int variable called value and initialize it to 0. We will also declare six Button objects and a TextView object. We will give them the exact same names we gave the id property values in our UI layout. This name association is not mandatory, but it is useful to keep track of which Button in our Java code will be holding a reference to which Button from our UI.

Furthermore, we are declaring them all with the private access specification because we know they will not be needed outside of this class.

Before you go ahead and type the code, note that all these variables are members of the MainActivity class. This means that we enter all the code shown next, immediately after the class declaration that we amended in the previous step.

Making all these variables into members/fields means that they have class scope and that we can access them from anywhere within the MainActivity class. This will be essential for this project because we will need to use them all in onCreate and in our new onClick method.

Enter the following code that we have just discussed after the opening curly brace { of the MainActivity class and before the onCreate method:

```
// An int variable to hold a value
private int value = 0;

// A bunch of Buttons and a TextView
private Button btnAdd;
private Button btnTake;
private TextView txtValue;
private Button btnGrow;
private Button btnShrink;
private Button btnReset;
private Button btnHide;
```

Remember to use the *ALT* + *Enter* keyboard combination to import new classes.
```
import android.widget.Button;
import android.widget.TextView;
```

Next, we want to prepare all our variables ready for action. The best place for this to happen is in the `onCreate` method because we know that will be called by Android just before the app is shown to the user. This code uses the `findViewById` method to associate each of our Java objects with an item from our UI.

It does so by returning a reference to the object associated with the UI widget on the Heap. It "knows" which one we are after because we use the proper `id` as an argument. For example . . . `(R.id.btnAdd)` will return the `Button` with the text **ADD** that we created in our layout.

 As a reminder, we use the odd looking `=  (Button)` syntax because the method is polymorphic and could potentially return any object type that is a subclass of the `View` class. This is called casting.

Enter the following code, just after the call to `setContentView` in the `onCreate` method:

```
// Get a reference to all the buttons in our UI
// Match them up to all our Button objects we declared earlier
btnAdd = (Button) findViewById(R.id.btnAdd);
btnTake = (Button) findViewById(R.id.btnTake);
txtValue = (TextView) findViewById(R.id.txtValue);
btnGrow = (Button) findViewById(R.id.btnGrow);
btnShrink = (Button) findViewById(R.id.btnShrink);
btnReset = (Button) findViewById(R.id.btnReset);
btnHide = (Button) findViewById(R.id.btnHide);
```

Now that we have a reference to all our `Button` objects and our `TextView`, we can start using their methods. In the code that follows, we use the `setOnClickListener` method on each of the `Button` references to make Android pass any clicks from the user onto our `onClick` method.

This works because when we implemented the `View.OnClickListener` interface, our `MainActivity` class effectively *became* an `OnClickListener`.

So, all we have to do is call `setOnClickListener` on each button in turn. As a reminder, the `this` argument is a reference to `MainActivity`. So, the method call says, "hey Android, I want an `OnClickListener` and I want it to be the `MainActivity` class."

Android now knows on which class to call `onClick`. The following code wouldn't work if we hadn't implemented the interface first. Also, we must set up these listeners before the Activity starts, which is why we do it in `onCreate`.

We will add code to `onClick` to actually handle what happens soon.

Add the following code after the previous code, inside the `onCreate` method:

```
// Listen for all the button clicks
btnAdd.setOnClickListener(this);
btnTake.setOnClickListener(this);
txtValue.setOnClickListener(this);
btnGrow.setOnClickListener(this);
btnShrink.setOnClickListener(this);
btnReset.setOnClickListener(this);
btnHide.setOnClickListener(this);
```

Now, scroll down to the `onClick` method that Android Studio added for us after we implemented the `OnClickListener` interface. Add the `float size;` variable declaration and an empty switch block inside it so that it looks like the following code snippet. The new code to add is highlighted here:

```
public void onClick(View view)

        // A local variable to use later
        float size;

        switch(view.getId()){


        }
    }
}
```

Remember that `switch` will check for a `case` to match the condition inside the `switch` statement.

In the previous code, the `switch` condition is `view.getId()`. Let's step through and explain this. The view variable is a reference to an object of the `View` type that was passed into the `onClick` method by Android:

```
public void onClick(View view)
```

`View` is the parent class for `Button`, `TextView`, and more. So, perhaps, as we might expect, calling `v.getId()` will return the `id` attribute of the UI widget that has been clicked and triggered the call to `onClick` in the first place.

All we need to do then is provide a `case` statement (and appropriate action) for each of the `Button` references we want to respond to.

The following code we will see is the first three `case` statements. They handle `R.id.btnAdd`, `R.id.btnTake`, and `R.id.btnReset`.

The code in the `R.id.btnAdd` case simply increments the `value` variable, and then it does something new.

It calls the `setText` method on the `txtValue` object. Here is the argument – `(""+ value)`. This argument uses an empty string and adds (concatenates) whatever value is stored in `value` to it. This has the effect of causing our `TextView txtValue` to display whatever value is stored in `value`.

The **TAKE** button (`R.id.btnTake`) does exactly the same, only it subtracts one from `value` instead of adding one.

The third case statement handles the **RESET** button and sets `value` to zero, again updating the `text` attribute of `txtValue`.

Then, at the end of each `case`, there is a `break` statement. At this point, the `switch` block is exited, the `onClick` method returns, and life goes back to normal, until the user's next click.

Enter the following code that we have just discussed inside the `switch` block after the opening curly brace `{`:

```
case R.id.btnAdd:
    value ++;
    txtValue.setText(""+ value);

    break;

case R.id.btnTake:
    value--;
    txtValue.setText(""+ value);

    break;

case R.id.btnReset:
    value = 0;
    txtValue.setText(""+ value);

    break;
```

The next two `case` statements handle the **SHRINK** and **GROW** buttons from our UI. We can confirm this from the id's `R.id.btnGrow` and `R.id.btnShrink` methods. What is new and more interesting are the two new methods that are used.

The `getTextScaleX` method returns the horizontal scale of the text within the object it is used on. We can see that the object it is used on is our `TextView` `txtValue`. The `size` = at the start of the line of code assigns that returned value to our `float` variable `size`.

The next line of code in each `case` statement changes the horizontal scale of the text using `setTextScaleX`. When the **GROW** button is pressed, the scale is set to `size` + `1`, and when the **SHRINK** button is pressed, the scale is set to `size` - `1`.

The overall effect is to allow these two buttons to grow and shrink the text in `txtValue` by a scale of `1` on each click.

Enter the following two `case` statements that we have just discussed, below the previous code:

```
case R.id.btnGrow:
    size = txtValue.getTextScaleX();
    txtValue.setTextScaleX(size + 1);

    break;

case R.id.btnShrink:
    size = txtValue.getTextScaleX();
    txtValue.setTextScaleX(size - 1);

    break;
```

In our final case statement that we will code next, we have an `if-else` block. The condition takes a little bit of explaining, so here is advance sight of it:

```
if(txtValue.getVisibility() == View.VISIBLE)
```

The condition to be evaluated is `txtValue.getVisibility()` `==` `View.VISIBLE`. The first part of that before the `==` operator returns the `visibility` attribute of our `txtValue` `TextView`. The return value will be one of three possible constant values as defined in the `View` class. They are `View.VISIBLE`, `View.INVISIBLE`, and `View.GONE`.

If the `TextView` is visible to the user on the UI, the method returns `View.VISIBLE`, the condition is evaluated as `true`, and the `if` block is executed.

Inside the `if` block, we use the `setVisibility` method on `txtValue` and make it invisible to the user with the `View.INVISIBLE` argument.

In addition to this, we change the text on the `btnHide` to **SHOW** using the `setText` method.

After the `if` block has executed, `txtValue` is invisible, and we have a button on our UI that says **SHOW**. When the user clicks on it in this state, the `if` statement will be false and the `else` block will execute. In the `else` block, we reverse the situation. We set `txtValue` back to `View.VISIBLE` and the `text` property on `btnHide` back to **HIDE**.

If this is in any way unclear, just enter the code, run the app, and revisit this final piece of code and explanation once you have seen it in action:

```
case R.id.btnHide:
    if(txtValue.getVisibility() == View.VISIBLE)
    {
            // Currently visible so hide it
            txtValue.setVisibility(View.INVISIBLE);

            // Change text on the button
            btnHide.setText("SHOW");

    }else{
            // Currently hidden so show it
            txtValue.setVisibility(View.VISIBLE);

            // Change text on the button
            btnHide.setText("HIDE");
    }


    break;
```

We have the UI and the code in place, so it is time to run the app and try out all the buttons. Notice that the **ADD** and **TAKE** buttons change the value of value by one in either direction and then display the result in the TextView. In the following diagram, I have clicked the **ADD** button three times:

Notice that the **SHRINK** and **GROW** buttons increase the width of the text, and **RESET** sets the value variable to 0 and displays it on the TextView. In the following diagram, I have clicked the **GROW** button eight times:

Finally, the **HIDE** button not only hides the `TextView`, but changes its own text to **SHOW** and will indeed re-show the `TextView` if tapped again.

 I will not bother you by showing you an image of something that is hidden. Make sure to try the app in Android Studio as well as following along with the book.

Notice that there was no need for `Log` or `Toast` in this app as we are finally manipulating the UI by using our Java code.

The Inner and Anonymous classes

Before we go ahead to the next chapter and build apps with loads of different widgets that will put into practice and reinforce everything we have learned in this chapter, we will have a very brief introduction to **Anonymous** and **Inner** classes.

When we implemented our Basic classes demo app in *Chapter 10, Object-Oriented programming,* we declared and implemented the class in a separate file to our `MainActivity` class. That file had to have the same name as the class. This is the way to create a regular class.

We can also declare and implement classes within a class. The only question remaining, of course, is why would we do this?

When we implement an inner class, the inner class can access the member variables of the enclosing class and the enclosing class can access the members of the inner class.

This often makes the structure of our code more straightforward. Therefore, inner classes are sometimes the way to go.

In addition, we can also declare and implement an entire class within a method of one of our classes. When we do so, we use a slightly different syntax and do not use a name with the class. This is an **anonymous** class.

We will see both inner and anonymous classes in action throughout the rest of this book and we will thoroughly discuss them when we use them.

Frequently asked questions

Q1 - I don't get all of what we've covered and actually I have more questions now than I had at the start of this chapter. What should I do?

A - You know enough about OOP to make considerable progress with Android and any other type of Java programming. If you are desperate to know more OOP right now, there are plenty of highly-rated books that discuss nothing but OOP. However, practice and familiarity with the syntax will go a long way to achieving the same thing and will be more fun. This is exactly what we will do for the rest of this book.

Summary

In this chapter, we finally had some real interaction between our code and our UI. It turns out that every time we add a widget to our UI, we are adding a Java object of a class that we can access with a proper reference in our Java code. All of these objects are stored in a separate area of memory called the Heap, along with any classes of our own.

We are now in a position where we can learn about and do cool things with some of the more interesting widgets. We will look at loads of them in the next chapter, *Chapter 13, Anonymous Classes - Bringing Android Widgets to Life,* and then keep introducing further new widgets throughout the rest of the book as well.

13
Anonymous Classes – Bringing Android Widgets to Life

This chapter could have been called "Even More OOP," as anonymous classes are very much still part of that subject, but as we will see, anonymous classes offer us so much flexibility, especially when it comes to interacting with the UI, that I thought they deserved a chapter title dedicated to them and one of their key uses in Android.

Now that we have a good overview of both the layout and coding of an Android app, as well as our newly acquired insight into object-oriented programming and how we can manipulate the UI from our Java code, we are ready to experiment with more widgets from the palette, alongside anonymous classes.

OOP is a tricky thing at times, and anonymous classes are known to sometimes be a bit awkward for beginners but, by gradually learning these new concepts and then practicing them repeatedly, over time, they will become our friend.

In this chapter, we will diversify a lot by going back to the Android Studio palette and looking around at half a dozen widgets that we have either not seen at all or have not used fully yet.

Once we have done so, we will put them all into a layout and practice manipulating them with Java code.

In this chapter, we will cover the following topics:

- Refreshing our memories on declaring and initializing layout widgets
- How to create widgets with just Java code
- Looking at the `EditText`, `ImageView`, `RadioButton` (and `RadioGroup`), `Switch`, `CheckBox`, and `TextClock` widgets
- How to use an anonymous class
- Making a widget demo mini app using all of the preceding widgets and plenty of anonymous classes

Let's start with a quick recap.

Declaring and initializing the objects

We know that when we call `setContentView` in the `onCreate` method, Android inflates all the widgets and layouts, and turns them into *real* Java objects on the Heap.

We know that to use a widget from the heap, we must first declare an object of the correct type and then use it to get a reference to the UI widget object on the heap by using its unique `id` property.

For example, we get a reference to a `TextView` with an `id` property of `txtTitle` and assign it to a new Java object called `myTextView`, as follows:

```
// Grab a reference to an object on the heap
TextView myTextView = (TextView) findViewById(R.id.txtTitle);
```

Now, using our `myTextView` instance variable, we can do anything that the `TextView` class was designed to do. For example, we can set the text to appear as follows:

```
myTextView.setText("Hi there");
```

Make it disappear like this:

```
// Bye bye
myTextView.setVisibility(View.GONE)
```

And then change its text again and make it reappear:

```
myTextView.setText("BOO!");

// Surprise
myTextView.setVisibility(View.VISIBLE)
```

It is worth mentioning that we can manipulate any property in Java that we set using XML in the previous chapters. Furthermore, we have hinted at, but not actually seen, that we can create widgets from nothing, using just Java code.

Creating UI widgets from pure Java without XML

We can also create widgets from Java objects that are not a reference to an object in our layout. We can declare, instantiate, and set a widget's attributes, all in code, like this:

```
Button myButton = new Button();
```

The preceding code creates a new `Button` by using `new()`. The only warning is that the `Button` has to be part of a layout before it can be shown. So, we could either get a reference to a layout element from our XML layout or create a new one, in code.

If we assume that we have a `LinearLayout` in our XML with an `id` property equal to `linearLayout1`, we could incorporate our `Button` from the earlier line of code in it, as follows:

```
// Get a reference to the LinearLayout
LinearLayout linearLayout = (LinearLayout)
    findViewById(R.id.linearLayout);

// Add our Button to it
linearLayout.addView(myButton);
```

We could even create an entire layout in pure Java code by first creating a new layout and then all the widgets we want to add, and finally calling `setContentView` on the layout that has our widgets.

In the following piece of code, we are creating a layout in pure Java, albeit a very simple one with a single `Button` inside a `LinearLayout`:

```
// Create a new LinearLayout
LinearLayout linearLayout = new LinearLayout();

// Create a new Button
Button myButton = new Button();

// Add myButton to the LinearLayout
```

```
linearLayout.addView(myButton);

// Make the LinearLayout the main view
setContentView(linearLayout);
```

It is probably obvious, but well worth pointing out as well, that designing a detailed and nuanced layout in only Java is significantly more awkward, harder to visualize, and not the way it is most commonly done. There are times, however, when we will find it useful to do things this way.

We are getting quite advanced now with layouts and widgets. It is plain to see, however, that there are a whole bunch of other widgets (and UI elements) from the palette that we have not explored or interacted with (other than just dumping them in a layout and done nothing with them). So, let's fix that.

Exploring the palette – part 1

Let's take a whirlwind tour of some of those previously unexplored/unused items from the palette, and then we can drag a bunch of them onto a layout and see some of the methods they have that might be useful. We can then implement a project to put them all to use.

We already explored `Button` and `TextView` in the last chapter. Let's take a closer look at some more alongside them.

The EditText widget

The `EditText` widget does what the name suggests. If we make an `EditText` widget available to our users, then they will indeed be able to *edit* the *text* in it. We saw this in an earlier chapter, but we didn't actually achieve anything with it. What we didn't see was how to capture the information from within it, or where we would type this text-capturing code.

The following block of code assumes that we have declared an object of type `EditText` and used it to get a reference to `EditText` in our XML layout. We might write code like the following for a button click, perhaps a submit button for a form, but it could go anywhere we deem it necessary for our app:

```
String editTextContents = editText.getText()
// editTextContents now contains whatever the user entered
```

We will see it in a real context in the next mini app.

The ImageView widget

We have already put an image onto our layout a couple of times so far, but we have never got a reference to one from our Java code or done anything with it before. The process is the same getting a reference to an `ImageView` as it is to any other widget:

1. Declare an object.
2. Get a reference using the `findViewById` method and a valid `id` property.

You can do this like this:

```
ImageView imageView = (ImageView) findViewById(R.id.imageView);
```

Then, we can go on to do some quite neat things with our image by using code like this:

```
// Make the image 50% TRANSPARENT
imageView.setAlpha(.5f);
```

 The odd-looking f simply lets the compiler know that the value is of type `float`, as required by the `setAlpha` method.

In the preceding code, we used the `setAlpha` method on `imageView`. The `setAlpha` method takes a value between 0 and 1. Zero is completely see-through, while 1 is no transparency at all.

 There is also an overloaded `setAlpha` method that takes an int value from 0 (completely see-through) to 255 (no transparency). We can choose whichever is most appropriate at the time. If you want a reminder about method overloading, see *Chapter 9, Java Methods*.

We will use some of the `ImageView` methods in our next app.

Radio button and group

A RadioButton is used when there are two or more mutually exclusive options for the user to choose from. This means that when one option is chosen, the other options are not, like on an old-fashioned radio. You can see a simple RadioGroup with a few RadioButtons in the following diagram:

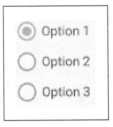

When the user makes a choice, the other options will automatically be deselected. We control RadioButton widgets by placing them within a RadioGroup in our UI layout. We can, of course, use the visual designer to simply drag a bunch of RadioButtons onto a RadioGroup. When we do, the XML will look something like this:

```
<RadioGroup
    android:layout_width="match_parent"
    android:layout_height="match_parent"
    android:layout_alignParentTop="true"
    android:layout_alignParentLeft="true"
    android:layout_alignParentStart="true"
    android:id="@+id/radioGroup">

    <RadioButton
        android:layout_width="wrap_content"
        android:layout_height="wrap_content"
        android:text="Option 1"
        android:id="@+id/radioButton1"
        android:checked="true" />

    <RadioButton
        android:layout_width="wrap_content"
        android:layout_height="wrap_content"
        android:text="Option 2"
        android:id="@+id/radioButton2"
        android:checked="false" />

    <RadioButton
        android:layout_width="wrap_content"
```

```
android:layout_height="wrap_content"
android:text="Option 3"
                android:id="@+id/radioButton3"
android:checked="false" />
```

```
<RadioGroup/>
```

Notice, as highlighted in the previous code, that each `RadioButton` and the `RadioGroup` has objects that have an appropriate `id` attribute set. We can then get a reference to them, as we might expect, as the following code shows us:

```
// Get a reference to all our widgets
RadioGroup radioGroup =
(RadioGroup) findViewById(R.id.radioGroup);

RadioButton rb1 =
(RadioButton) findViewById(R.id.radioButton1);

RadioButton rb2 =
(RadioButton) findViewById(R.id.radioButton2);

RadioButton rbnew3 =
(RadioButton) findViewById(R.id.radioButton3);
```

In practice, however, as we will see, we can manage almost everything from the `RadioGroup` reference alone.

You might be thinking: how do we know when they have been clicked or that keeping track of which one is selected might be awkward? We need some help from the Android API and Java in the form of anonymous classes.

Anonymous classes

In the last chapter, we briefly introduced anonymous classes. Here, we will learn a little more about them and see how they can help us. When a `RadioButton` is part of a `RadioGroup`, the visual appearance of them all is coordinated for us. All we need to do is react when any given `RadioButton` is pressed. Of course, as with any other button, we need to know when they have been clicked.

A `RadioButton` behaves differently to a regular `Button`, and simply listening for clicks in `onClick` (after implementing `OnClickListener`) will not work because `RadioButton` is not designed that way.

What we need to do is use another Java feature. We need to implement a class, an anonymous class, for the sole purpose of listening for clicks on the `RadioGroup`. The following block of code assumes that we have a reference to a `RadioGroup` called `radioGroup`. Here is the code:

```
radioGroup.setOnCheckedChangeListener(
    new RadioGroup.OnCheckedChangeListener() {

        @Override
        public void onCheckedChanged(RadioGroup group,
                int checkedId) {

            // Handle clicks here

        }

    }
);
```

The preceding code, specifically `RadioGroup.OnCheckedChangeListener` from its opening { to closing }, is what is known as an **anonymous** class because it has no name.

The actual class code does not run when `onCreate` is called; it simply prepares the class ready to handle any clicks on `radioGroup`. We will now discuss this in more detail.

This class is more technically known as an **anonymous inner** class because it is inside another class. Inner classes can be anonymous or have names. We will see an inner class with a name in *Chapter 16, Adapters and Recyclers*.

I remember the first time I saw an anonymous class and it almost made me want to hide in a cupboard, but it is not as complex as it might look at first.

What we are doing is adding a listener to `radioGroup`, which has very much the same effect as when we implemented the `View.OnClickListener` in *Chapter 12, The Stack, the Heap, and the Garbage Collector*. Only this time, we are declaring and instantiating a listener class, and preparing it to listen to `radioGroup`, while simultaneously overriding the required method, which in this case is `onCheckedChanged`. This is like the `RadioGroup` equivalent of `onClick`.

Let's step through it. We call the `setOnCheckedChangeListener` method on our `radioGroup` as follows:

```
radioGroup.setOnCheckedChangeListener(
```

We pass in a new anonymous class, along with the details of its overridden method, as the argument, as follows:

```
new RadioGroup.OnCheckedChangeListener() {

    @Override
    public void onCheckedChanged(RadioGroup group,
            int checkedId) {

        // Handle clicks here
    }
}
```

Finally, we have the closing parenthesis of the method. And, of course, the semi-colon to mark the end of the line. The only reason we present it on multiple lines is to make it more readable. As far as the compiler is concerned, it could all be lumped together:

```
);
```

If we use the preceding code to create and instantiate a class that listens for clicks to our `RadioGroup`, perhaps in the `onCreate` method, it will listen and respond for the entire life of the Activity. All we need to learn now is to handle the clicks in the `onCheckedChanged` method that we override.

Notice that one of the parameters of this method that is passed in when the `radioGroup` is pressed is `int checkedId`. This holds the `id` of the currently selected `RadioButton`. This is just what we need – almost.

It might be surprising that `checkedId` is an `int`. Android stores all ids as `int`, even though we declare them with alphanumeric characters such as `radioButton1` or `radioGroup`.

All our human-friendly names are converted to `int` when the app is compiled. So, how do we know which `int` refers to an `id`, such as `radioButton1` or `radioButton2` and so on?

What we need to do is get a reference to the actual object that the `int` is an id for, using the `int id`, and then ask the object for its human-friendly `id`. We would do so like this:

```
RadioButton rb = (RadioButton) group.findViewById(checkedId);
```

Now, we can retrieve the familiar `id` that we used for the currently selected `RadioButton`, for which we now have a reference stored in `rb`, with the `getId` method, as follows:

```
rb.getId();
```

We could therefore handle `RadioButton` clicks by using a `switch` block with a `case` for each possible `RadioButton` that could be pressed, and `rb.getId()` as the `switch` block's expression.

The following code shows the entire contents of the `onCheckedChanged` method we just discussed:

```
// Get a reference to the RadioButton
// that is currently checked
RadioButton rb = (RadioButton) group.findViewById(checkedId);

// Switch based on the 'friendly' id
switch (rb.getId()) {

    case R.id.radioButton1:
            // Do something here
            break;

    case R.id.radioButton2:
            // Do something here
            break;


    case R.id.radioButton3:
            // Do something here
            break;


}
// End switch block
```

Seeing this in action in the next working mini-app, where we can press the buttons for real, will make this clearer.

Let's continue with our palette exploration.

Exploring the palette – Part 2, and more anonymous classes

Now that we have seen how anonymous classes work, specifically with `RadioGroup` and `RadioButton`, we can now continue exploring the palette and look at how anonymous classes work with some more UI widgets.

Switch

The `Switch` (not to be confused with the lowercase `switch` Java keyword) widget is just like a `Button` except that it has two possible states that can be read and responded to.

An obvious use for the `Switch` widget would be to show and hide something. Remember in our *Java meet UI* app in *Chapter 12, The Stack, the Heap, and the Garbage Collector*, that we used a `Button` to show and hide a `TextView`?

Each time we hid/showed the `TextView`, we changed the `Text` property on the `Button` to make it plain what would happen if it was clicked again. What might have been more logical for the user and more straightforward for us as programmers would have been to use a `Switch`, as illustrated here:

The following code assumes that we already have an object called `mySwitch` with a reference to a `Switch` object in the layout. We could show and hide a `TextView` just like we did in our *Java Meet UI* app in *Chapter 12, The Stack, the Heap, and the Garbage Collector*.

To listen for and respond to clicks, we again use an anonymous class. This time, however, we use the `CompoundButton` version of `OnCheckedChangeListener` instead of `RadioGroup`.

We need to override the `onCheckedChanged` method, and that method has a Boolean parameter, `isChecked`. The `isChecked` variable is simply false for off and true for on.

Here is how we could more intuitively replace that text hiding/showing code:

```
mySwitch.setOnCheckedChangeListener(
    new CompoundButton.OnCheckedChangeListener() {

        public void onCheckedChanged(
                CompoundButton buttonView, boolean isChecked) {

            if(isChecked){
                // Currently visible so hide it
                txtValue.setVisibility(View.INVISIBLE);

            }else{
                // Currently hidden so show it
                txtValue.setVisibility(View. VISIBLE);
            }
        }
    }
);
```

If the anonymous class code still looks a little odd, don't worry, because it will get more familiar the more often we use it. We will do this again now when we look at CheckBox.

CheckBox

With a CheckBox, we simply detect its state (checked or unchecked) at a given moment – perhaps at the moment when a specific button is clicked. The following code gives us a glimpse at how this might happen, again using an inner class to act as a listener:

```
myCheckBox.setOnCheckedChangeListener(
    new CompoundButton.OnCheckedChangeListener() {

        public void onCheckedChanged(
                CompoundButton buttonView, boolean isChecked) {

            if (myCheckBox.isChecked()) {
                // It's checked so do something
            } else {
                // It's not checked do something else
            }

        }
    }
);
```

In the previous code, we assume that `myCheckBox` has been declared and initialized, and then use exactly the same type of anonymous class as we did for `Switch` to detect and respond to clicks.

TextClock

In our next app, we will use the `TextClock` widget to show off some of its features. We will need to add the XML directly as this widget is not available to drag and drop from the palette. This is what the `TextClock` looks like:

As an example of using `TextClock`, this is how we would set its time to the same time as it is in Brussels, Europe:

```
tClock.setTimeZone("Europe/Brussels");
```

The previous code assumes that `tClock` is a reference to a `TextClock` in the layout.

With all this extra information, let's make an app to use the Android widgets more practically than what we have so far.

Widget exploration app

We have just talked about six Widgets – the `EditText`, `ImageView`, `RadioButton` (and `RadioGroup`), `Switch`, `CheckBox`, and `TextClock` widgets. Let's make a working app and do something real with each of them. We will also use a `Button` and a `TextView` again as well.

In this layout, we will use `LinearLayout` as the layout type that holds everything, and within `LinearLayout`, we will use multiple `RelativeLayout`.

`RelativeLayout` has been superseded by `ConstraintLayout`, but they are still very commonly used and well worth playing around with. You will see as you build layouts within `RelativeLayout` that the UI elements behave very much the same as `ConstraintLayout` but that the underlying XML is different. It is not necessary to learn this XML in detail, rather, using `RelativeLayout` will allow us to show the neat way Android Studio enables you to convert these layouts to `ConstraintLayout`.

Remember that you can refer to the completed code in the download bundle. This app can be found in `Chapter 13/Widget Exploration`.

Setting up the widget exploration project and UI

First, we will set up a new project and prepare the UI layout. These steps will get all the widgets on the screen and the id properties set, ready to grab a reference to them. It will help to look at the target layout up and running before we get started, as shown in the following screenshot:

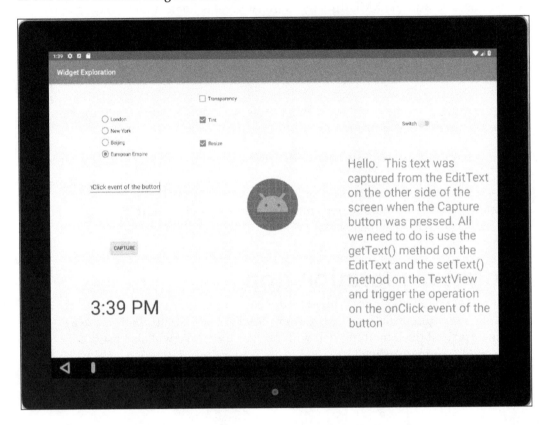

Here is how this app will demonstrate these widgets:

- The radio buttons allow the user to change the time displayed on the clock to a choice of four time zones.
- The **Capture** button, when clicked, will change the text of the TextView (on the right) to whatever is currently in the EditText widget (on the left).

- The three CheckBoxes will add and remove visual effects from the Android robot image. In the previous image, the image is resized and has a color tint applied.

- The Switch will turn the TextView that displays information entered in the EditText on and off. This is captured on the click of a button.

The exact layout positions are not essential, but the id properties specified must match exactly. If you just want to see/use the code, you can find all the files in the Chapter 13/Widget Exploration folder of the download bundle.

So, let's observe the following steps to set up a new project and prepare the UI layout:

1. Create a new project called Widget Exploration, set the **Minimum API** to 17, use **Empty Activity**, and keep all the other settings at their defaults. We are using API 17 because one of the features of the TextClock widget requires us to. We still support in excess of 97% of all Android devices.

2. Let's create a new layout file as we want our new layout to be based on LinearLayout. Right-click the layout folder in the project explorer and select **New | Layout resource file** from the pop-up menu.

3. In the **New resource file** window, enter exploration_layout.xml in the **File name** field and then enter LinearLayout in the **Root element** field. Now, press **OK**.

4. In the **Attributes** window, change the orientation property of the LinearLayout to **horizontal**.

5. Using the drop-down controls above the design view, make sure that you have selected a tablet in landscape orientation.

 For a reminder of how to make a tablet emulator, see *Chapter 3, Exploring Android Studio and the project structure*. For advice on how to manipulate the orientation of the emulator, see *Chapter 5, Beautiful Layouts with CardView and ScrollView*.

6. We can now begin creating our layout. Drag and drop three **RelativeLayout** layouts from the **Legacy** category of the palette onto the design to create the three vertical divisions of our design. You will probably find it easiest to use the **Component Tree** window for this step.

7. Set the **weight** property of each `RelativeLayout` in turn to `.33`. We now have three equal vertical divisions, just like in the following diagram:

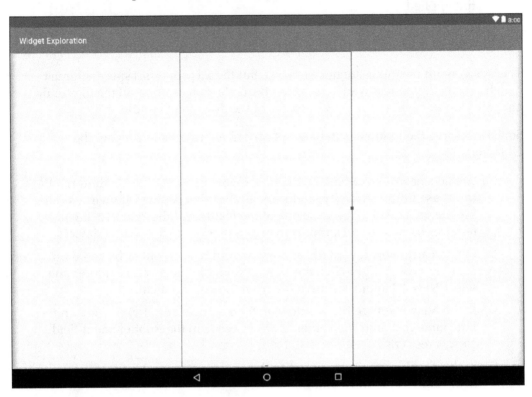

8. The **Component Tree** window should also look like it does in the following screenshot:

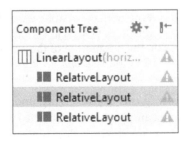

If you want to use `ConstraintLayout` instead of `RelativeLayout`, then the following instructions will be nearly identical. Just remember to set the final position of your UI by clicking the **Infer Constraints** button or by setting the constraints manually as discussed in *Chapter 4, Getting Started with Layouts and Material Design*. Alternatively, you can build the layout exactly as detailed in this tutorial and later you can use the **Convert to Constraint layout** feature discussed later in this chapter. This is excellent for using layouts that you have and want to use, but you should prefer to use the faster-running `ConstraintLayout`.

9. Drag a **Switch** near the top-center of the right-hand `RelativeLayout` and just below, drag a **TextView** from the palette. The right-hand side of your layout should now look like it does in the following diagram:

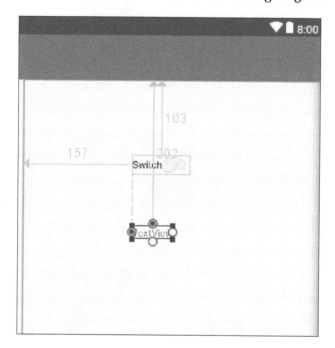

10. Drag three **CheckBox** widgets, one above the other, and then an **ImageView** below them onto the central `RelativeLayout`. In the resulting pop-up **Resources** dialog window, choose **Project | ic_launcher** to use the Android icon as the image for the `ImageView`. The central column should now appear as follows:

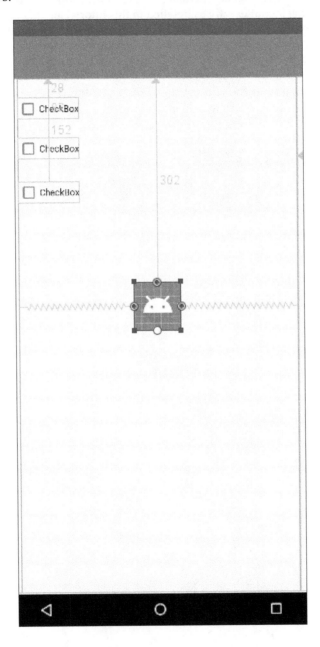

11. Drag a **RadioGroup** to the left-hand `RelativeLayout`.

12. Add four **RadioButton** widgets within the **RadioGroup**. This step will be easiest when using the **Component Tree** window.

13. Underneath the **RadioGroup,** drag a **Plain Text** widget from the **Text** category of the palette. Remember, despite its name, this is a widget that allows the user to type some text into it. Soon, we will see how to capture and use the entered text.

14. Add a **Button** widget to the right of the **Plain Text** widget. Your left-hand `RelativeLayout` should look like it does in the following diagram:

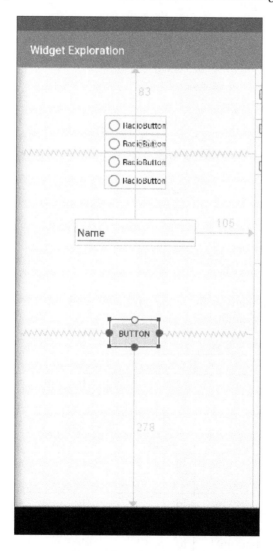

15. And the **Component Tree** window will look like it does in the following screenshot:

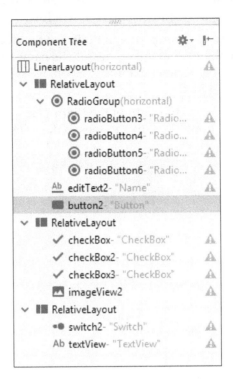

16. Now, add the following attributes to the widgets we have just laid out:

 Note that some of the attributes might already be correct by default.

Widget type	Property	Value to set to
RadioGroup	Id	radioGroup
RadioButton (top)	Id	radioButtonLondon
RadioButton (top)	Text	London
RadioButton (top)	checked	Select the "tick" icon for true
RadioButton (second)	Id	radioButtonBeijing
RadioButton (second)	Text	Beijing
RadioButton (third)	Id	radioButtonNewYork
RadioButton (third)	Text	New York
RadioButton (bottom)	id	radioButtonEuropeanEmpire

Widget type	Property	Value to set to
RadioButton (bottom)	text	European Empire
EditText	id	editText
Button	id	button
Button	text	Capture
CheckBox (top)	text	Transparency
CheckBox (top)	id	checkBoxTransparency
CheckBox (middle)	text	Tint
CheckBox (middle)	id	checkBoxTint
CheckBox (bottom)	text	Resize
CheckBox (bottom)	id	checkBoxReSize
ImageView	id	imageView
Switch	id	switch1
Switch	enabled	Select the "tick" icon for true
Switch	clickable	Select the "tick" icon for true
TextView	id	textView
TextView	textSize	34sp
TextView	layout_width	match_parent
TextView	layout_height	match_parent

17. Now, switch to the **Text** tab to view the XML for the layout. Find the end of the first (left-hand) `RelativeLayout` column, as shown in the following code listing. I have added an XML comment and highlighted it in the following code:

```
. . .
. . .
    </RadioGroup>

    <EditText
        android:id="@+id/editText2"
        android:layout_width="wrap_content"
        android:layout_height="wrap_content"
        android:layout_alignParentTop="true"
        android:layout_alignParentEnd="true"
        android:layout_marginTop="263dp"
        android:layout_marginEnd="105dp"
```

```
        android:ems="10"
        android:inputType="textPersonName"
        android:text="Name" />

    <Button
        android:id="@+id/button2"
        android:layout_width="wrap_content"
        android:layout_height="wrap_content"
        android:layout_alignParentBottom="true"
        android:layout_centerHorizontal="true"
        android:layout_marginBottom="278dp"
        android:text="Button" />

    <!-- Insert TextClock here-->

</RelativeLayout>
```

18. After the comment `<!--Insert TextClock Here-->`, insert the following XML for the `TextClock`. Note that the comment was added by me in the previous listing to show where to put the code. The comment will not be present in your code. We did things this way because `TextClock` is not available directly from the palette. Here is the code to add after the comment:

```
<TextClock
    android:id="@+id/textClock"
    android:layout_width="wrap_content"
    android:layout_height="wrap_content"
    android:layout_alignParentBottom="true"
    android:layout_centerHorizontal="true"
    android:layout_gravity="center_horizontal"
    android:layout_marginBottom="103dp"
    android:textSize="54sp" />
```

19. Switch to the **Design** tab and tweak your layout to resemble the reference diagram that follows as closely as possible, but if you have the appropriate types of UI with the correct `id` attributes, then the code will still work, even if the layout isn't identical:

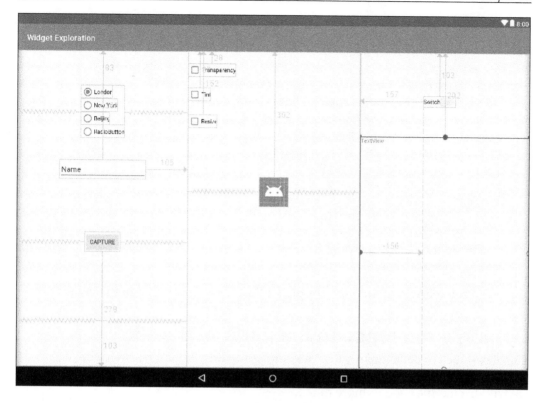

We have just laid out and set the required attributes for our layout. There is nothing new that we haven't done before, except that some of the widget types are new to us and the layout is slightly more intricate.

Now we can get on with using all these widgets in our Java code.

Coding the widget exploration app

The first part of the Java code we need to change is to make sure our new layout is displayed. We can do so by changing the call to setContentView in onCreate to look like this:

```
setContentView(R.layout.exploration_layout);
```

There are many import statements needed for this app, so let's add them all up front to save mentioning them all the time. Add the following import statements:

```
import android.graphics.Color;
import android.graphics.PorterDuff;
import androidx.appcompat.app.AppCompatActivity;
```

```
import android.os.Bundle;
import android.util.Log;
import android.view.Menu;
import android.view.MenuItem;
import android.view.View;
import android.widget.AnalogClock;
import android.widget.Button;
import android.widget.CheckBox;
import android.widget.CompoundButton;
import android.widget.EditText;
import android.widget.ImageView;
import android.widget.RadioButton;
import android.widget.RadioGroup;
import android.widget.Switch;
import android.widget.TextClock;
import android.widget.TextView;
```

Let's get a reference to all the parts of the UI that we will be using in the Java code.

Getting a reference to the parts of the UI

This next block of code looks quite long and sprawling, but all we are doing is getting a reference to each of the widgets in our layout. When we come to use them, we will discuss the code in more detail.

The only thing that is new in this next block of code is that some of the objects are declared as `final`. This is needed as they are going to be used within an anonymous class.

But doesn't final mean that the object can't be changed?

If you remember back in *Chapter 11, More Object-Oriented Programming*, we saw that variables declared as final cannot be changed; they are a constant. So, how are we going to change the attributes of these objects? Remember that objects are reference type variables. That is, they refer to an object on the heap. They are not the object themselves. We can think of them as holding an address of an object. It is the address that cannot change. We can still use the address to reference the object on the heap and change the actual object as much as we like.

Enter the following code just after the call to `setContentView` in the `onCreate` method:

```
// Get a reference to all our widgets

RadioGroup radioGroup = (RadioGroup)
findViewById(R.id.radioGroup);

final EditText editText =
(EditText) findViewById(R.id.editText);

final Button button =
(Button) findViewById(R.id.button);

final TextClock tClock =
(TextClock) findViewById(R.id.textClock);

final CheckBox cbTransparency =
(CheckBox) findViewById(R.id.checkBoxTransparency);

final CheckBox cbTint =
(CheckBox) findViewById(R.id.checkBoxTint);
final CheckBox cbReSize =
(CheckBox) findViewById(R.id.checkBoxReSize);

final ImageView imageView =
(ImageView) findViewById(R.id.imageView);

Switch switch1 = (Switch) findViewById(R.id.switch1);
Final TextView textView =
(TextView) findViewById(R.id.textView);

// Hide the TextView at the start of the app
textView.setVisibility(View.INVISIBLE);
```

We now have a reference in our Java code to all the UI elements in our layout that we need to manipulate.

Coding the checkboxes

Now, we can create an anonymous class to listen for and handle clicks on the checkboxes. The next three blocks of code each implement an anonymous class for each of the checkboxes in turn. What is different in each of them, however, is how we respond to a click, and we will discuss each in turn.

Changing transparency

The first checkbox is labeled **Transparency**, and we use the `setAlpha` method on `imageView` to change how transparent (see-through) it is. The `setAlpha` method takes a floating point value between 0 and 1 as an argument.

0 is invisible and 1 has no transparency at all. So, when this checkbox is checked, we set the alpha to `.1` so that the image is barely visible, and when it is unchecked, we set it to `1`, which is completely visible with no transparency. The `boolean` `isChecked` parameter of `onCheckedChanged` contains true or false as to whether the checkbox is checked or not.

Add the following code after the previous block of code in `onCreate`:

```
// First the check boxes using an anonymous class
cbTransparency.setOnCheckedChangeListener(new
CompoundButton.OnCheckedChangeListener(){

    public void onCheckedChanged(
            CompoundButton buttonView, boolean isChecked){

            if(cbTransparency.isChecked()){
                    // Set some transparency
                imageView.setAlpha(.1f);
        }else{
                imageView.setAlpha(1f);
        }

    }
});
```

In the next anonymous class, we handle the checkbox labeled **Tint**.

Changing color

In the `onCheckedChanged` method, we use the `setColorFilter` method on `imageView` to overlay a color layer on the image. When `isChecked` is true, we layer a color, and when `isChecked` is false, we remove it.

The `setColorFilter` method takes a color in **ARGB (Alpha, Red, Green**, and **Blue)** format as an argument. The color is provided by the static method `argb` of the `Color` class. The four arguments of the `argb` method are, as you might expect, values for alpha, red, green, and blue. These four values create a color. In our case, the value `150`, `255`, `0`, `0` creates a strong red tint, while the value `0`, `0`, `0`, `0` creates no tint at all.

To understand more about the Color class, check out the Android developer site at `http://developer.android.com/reference/android/graphics/Color.html`, and to understand the RGB color system more, take a look on Wikipedia here: `https://en.wikipedia.org/wiki/RGB_color_model`.

Add this code after the previous block of code in `onCreate`:

```
// Now the next checkbox
cbTint.setOnCheckedChangeListener(new
    CompoundButton.OnCheckedChangeListener() {

    public void onCheckedChanged(CompoundButton
            buttonView, boolean isChecked) {

        if (cbTint.isChecked()) {
            // Checked so set some tint
            imageView.setColorFilter(
                    Color.argb(150, 255, 0, 0));

    } else {
            // No tint needed
            imageView.setColorFilter(Color.argb(0, 0, 0, 0));
    }

    }
});
```

Now, we will see how to scale the UI.

Changing size

In the anonymous class that handles the **Resize** labeled checkbox, we use the `setScaleX` method to resize the robot image. When we call `setScaleX(2)` and `setScaleY(2)` on `imageView`, we will double the size of the image, and `setScaleX(1)` and `setScaleY(1)` will return it to normal.

Add this code after the previous block of code in `onCreate`:

```
// And the last check box
cbReSize.setOnCheckedChangeListener(
        new CompoundButton.OnCheckedChangeListener() {

    public void onCheckedChanged(
```

```
                    CompoundButton buttonView, boolean isChecked) {

        if (cbReSize.isChecked()) {
                // It's checked so make bigger
                imageView.setScaleX(2);
                imageView.setScaleY(2);
        } else {
                // It's not checked make regular size
                imageView.setScaleX(1);
                imageView.setScaleY(1);
        }


    }
});
```

Now we will handle the three radio buttons.

Coding the RadioButtons

As they are part of a `RadioGroup`, we can handle them much more succinctly than we did the `CheckBox` objects. Here is how we do it.

First, we make sure that they are clear to start with by calling `clearCheck()` on `radioGroup`. Then, we create our anonymous class of the `OnCheckedChangedListener` type and override the `onCheckedChanged` method.

This method will be called when any `RadioButton` from the `RadioGroup` is clicked. All we need to do is get the id of the `RadioButton` that was clicked and respond accordingly. We will achieve this by using a `switch` statement with the three possible cases, one for each `RadioButton`.

Remember from when we first talked about `RadioButton` that the id supplied in the `checkedId` parameter of `onCheckedChanged` is an `int`. This is why we must first create a new `RadioButton` object from `checkedId`:

```
RadioButton rb =
(RadioButton) group.findViewById(checkedId);
```

Then, we can call `getId` on the new `RadioButton` as the condition for the `switch`, as follows:

```
switch (rb.getId())
```

Then, in each `case`, we use the `setTimeZone` method with the proper Android time zone code as an argument.

 You can see all the Android time zone codes here: https://gist.github.com/arpit/1035596.

Then, add the following code, which incorporates everything we have just discussed. Add it in `onCreate` after the previous code that we entered for handling the checkboxes:

```
// Now for the radio buttons
// Uncheck all buttons
radioGroup.clearCheck();

radioGroup.setOnCheckedChangeListener(new RadioGroup.
OnCheckedChangeListener() {
@Override
public void onCheckedChanged(
RadioGroup group, int checkedId) {

        RadioButton rb = (RadioButton)
group.findViewById(checkedId);


            switch (rb.getId()) {

                case R.id.radioButtonLondon:
                    tClock.setTimeZone("Europe/London");
                    break;

                case R.id.radioButtonBeijing:
                    tClock.setTimeZone("CST6CDT");
                    break;

                case R.id.radioButtonNewYork:

                    tClock.setTimeZone(
                        "America/New_York");
                    break;

                case R.id.radioButtonEuropeanEmpire:
```

```
                            tClock.setTimeZone(
                                    "Europe/Brussels");
                            break;



                    }// End switch block
        }
    });
```

Now for something a little bit new.

Using an anonymous class for a regular button

In this next block of code that we will write, we use an anonymous class to handle the clicks on a regular Button. We call button.setOnclickListener, as we have done previously. This time, however, instead of passing this as an argument, we create a brand-new class of the type View.OnClickListener and override onClick as the argument, just like we did with our other anonymous classes.

 This method is preferable in this situation because there is only one button. If we had lots of buttons, then having MainActivity implement View.OnClickListener and then overriding onClick to handle all clicks in one method would probably be preferable, as we have done previously.

In the onClick method, we use setText to set the text property on textView and the getText method of editText to get whatever text is currently in the EditText widget.

Add this code after the previous block of code in onCreate:

```
/*
    Let's listen for clicks on our "Capture" Button.
    We can do this with an anonymous class as well.
    An interface seems a bit much for one button.
*/
button.setOnClickListener(new View.OnClickListener() {
    @Override
    public void onClick(View v) {
            // We only handle one button
            // So, no switching required

            // Change the text on the TextView
```

```
        // to whatever is currently in the EditText
        textView.setText(editText.getText());
    }
});
```

Coding the Switch

Next, we create yet another anonymous class to listen for and handle changes to our Switch widget.

When the isChecked variable is true, we show textView, and when it is false, we hide it.

Add this code after the previous block of code in onCreate:

```
// Show or hide the TextView
switch1.setOnCheckedChangeListener(
    new CompoundButton.OnCheckedChangeListener() {

    public void onCheckedChanged(
            CompoundButton buttonView, boolean isChecked) {

        if(isChecked){
            textView.setVisibility(View.VISIBLE);
        }else{
            textView.setVisibility(View.INVISIBLE);
        }
    }
});
```

Now, we can run our app and try out all the features.

 The Android emulators can be rotated into landscape mode by pressing the *Ctrl + F11* keyboard combination on a PC, or *Ctrl + fn+ F11* on a mac.

Running the Widget Exploration app

Try checking the radio buttons to see the time zone change on the clock. In the following screenshot, I have photoshopped a few cropped screenshots together to show that the time changes when a new time zone is selected:

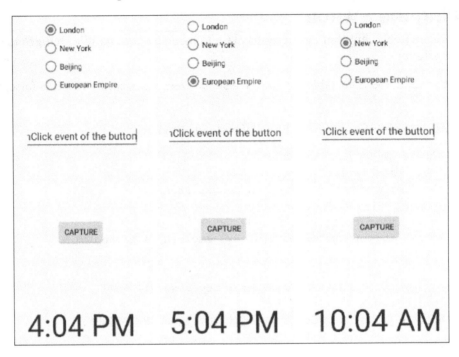

Enter different values into EditText and then click the button to see it grab the text and display it on itself, as follows:

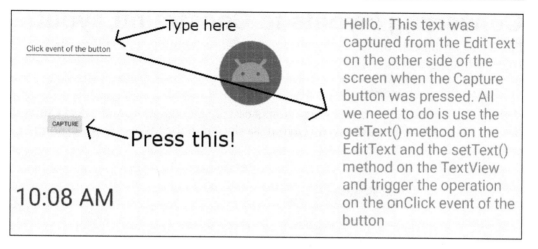

Change what the image in the app looks like with different combinations of checked and unchecked checkboxes and hide and show the TextView by using the switch above it. The following screenshot is two combinations of the checkboxes and the switch photoshopped together for demonstration purposes:

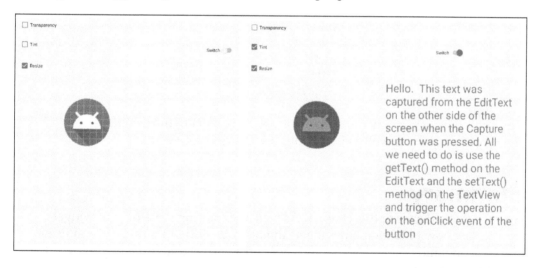

 Transparency doesn't show very clearly in a print book, so I didn't check that box. Make sure to try this out on an emulator or actual device.

Converting layouts to ConstraintLayout

Finally, as promised, this is how we can convert `RelativeLayout` to the faster-running `ConstraintLayout`:

1. Switch back to the **Design** tab
2. Right-click the parent layout – in this case, `LinearLayout`, and select **Convert LinearLayout to ConstraintLayout**, as shown in the following screenshot:

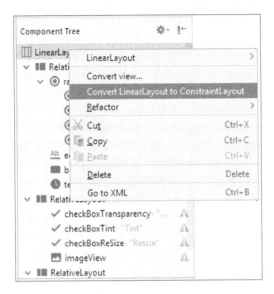

Now, you can convert any old `RelativeLayout` layouts to the new faster `ConstraintLayout` as well as build your own `RelativeLayout`.

Summary

We have learned a lot in this chapter. As well as exploring a plethora of widgets, we also saw how to implement widgets in Java code without any XML, and used our first anonymous classes to handle clicks on a widget and put all our new widget prowess into a working app.

Now, let's move on and look at another way that we can significantly enhance our UIs.

In the next chapter, we will see a totally new UI element that we can't just drag and drop from the palette, but we will still have plenty of help from the Android API. Next up are the dialog windows. We will also make a start on our most significant app to date, the Note to self, memo, and to-do and personal note app.

Android Dialog Windows

14

In this chapter, we will see how to present the user with a pop-up dialog window. We can then put all that we know into the first phase of our first app, *Note to self*. We will then learn about new Android and Java features in this chapter and the four that follow (up to *Chapter 18, Localization*) as well, and then use our newly acquired knowledge to enhance the Note to Self app each time.

In each chapter, we will also build a selection of smaller apps that are separate from this main app. So, what does *Chapter 14, Android Dialog Windows*, hold in store for you? The following topics will be covered:

- Implementing a simple app with a pop-up dialog box
- Learning how to use `DialogFragment` to begin the Note to self app
- Learning how to add string resources in our projects instead of hardcoding text in our layouts
- Using Android naming conventions for the first time to make our code more readable
- Implementing more complex dialog boxes to capture input from the user

Let's get started.

Dialog windows

In many situations in our apps, we will want to show the user some information, or perhaps ask for confirmation of an action in a pop-up window. This is known as a **dialog** window. If you quickly scan the palette in Android Studio, you might be surprised to see no mention whatsoever of dialogs.

Dialogs in Android are more advanced than a simple widget or even a whole layout. They are classes that can themselves have layouts and other UI elements of their own.

The best way to create a dialog window in Android is to use the `FragmentDialog` class.

 Fragments are an extensive and vital topic in Android and we will spend much of the second half of this book exploring and using them.

Creating a neat pop-up dialog (using `FragmentDialog`) for our user to interact with is, however, a great introduction to fragments and not too complicated at all.

Creating the Dialog Demo project

We previously mentioned that the best way to create a dialog in Android is with the `FragmentDialog` class. In Android, there is another way to create dialogs that is arguably a little bit simpler. The problem with this slightly simpler `Dialog` class is that it is not as well supported in the Activity life cycle. It is even possible that `Dialog` could accidentally crash the app.

If you were writing an app with one fixed orientation layout that only needed one simple pop-up dialog, it could be argued that the simpler `Dialog` class should be used. But as we are aiming to build modern, professional apps with advanced features, we will benefit from ignoring this class. More specifically, we will be using the `DialogFragment` class.

Create a new project in Android Studio using the Empty Activity template and call it `Dialog Demo`. Tell Android Studio to generate a layout file and use backward compatibility by leaving those options selected as the defaults. Any settings I haven't mentioned can be left as their defaults. As you have come to expect, the completed code for this project is in the `Chapter 14/Dialog Demo` folder of the download bundle.

Coding a DialogFragment class

Create a new class in Android Studio by right-clicking on the folder with the name of your package (the one that has the `MainActivity.java` file). Select **New | Java class** and name it `MyDialog`. Left-click **OK** to create the class.

The first thing to do is change the class declaration to extend `DialogFragment`. When you have done so, your new class will look like this:

```
public class MyDialog extends DialogFragment {
}
```

Now, let's add code to this class a bit at a time and explain what is happening at each step. Now, we need to import the `DialogFragment` class. You can do so, as we have done so frequently, by holding *Alt* and then tapping *Enter*, or by adding the following line of highlighted code after the package declaration at the top of the `MyDialog.java` file:

```
package com.gamecodeschool.dialogdemo;

import androidx.fragment.app.DialogFragment;

public class MyDialog extends DialogFragment {
}
```

Just like so many classes in the Android API, `DialogFragment` provides us with methods that we can override to interact with the different events that will occur with the class.

Add the following highlighted code that overrides the `onCreateDialog` method. Study it carefully and then we will examine what is happening:

```
public class MyDialog extends DialogFragment {

    @Override
    public Dialog onCreateDialog(Bundle savedInstanceState) {

        // Use the Builder class because this dialog
        // has a simple UI
        AlertDialog.Builder builder =
                new AlertDialog.Builder(getActivity());
    }
}
```

You will need to import the `Dialog`, `Bundle`, and `AlertDialog` classes in the usual way or by adding the following highlighted code manually:

```
import android.app.Dialog;
import android.os.Bundle;

import androidx.appcompat.app.AlertDialog;
import androidx.fragment.app.DialogFragment;
```

[There is still one error in the code because we are missing the return statement, which we will add when we have finished coding the rest of the method in a minute.]

In the code we just added, first, we add the overridden `onCreateDialog` method, which will be called by Android when we later show the dialog with code from the `MainActivity` class.

Then, inside the `onCreateDialog` method, we get our hands on a new class. We declare and initialize an object of the `AlertDialog.Builder` type that needs a reference to `MainActivity` passed into its constructor. This is why we use `getActivity()` as the argument.

The `getActivity` method is part of the `Fragment` class (and therefore `DialogFragment` too) and it returns a reference to the `Activity` that will create the `DialogFragment`. In this case, this is our `MainActivity` class.

Let's see what we can do with `builder` now that we have declared and initialized it.

Using chaining to configure the DialogFragment

Now, we can use our `builder` object to do the rest of the work. There is something slightly odd in the next three blocks of code. If you quickly scan them, you will notice that there is a distinct lack of semi-colons `;`. This shows us that these three blocks of code are, in fact, just one line to the compiler.

What is going on here is something we have seen before, but in a less pronounced situation. When we created a `Toast` message and added a `.show()` method to the end of it, we were **chaining**. That is, we were calling more than one method, in sequence, on the same object. This is equivalent to writing multiple lines of code; it is just clearer and shorter this way.

Add the following code, which utilizes chaining, right after the previous code we added in `onCreateDialog`, examine it, and then we will discuss it:

```
// Dialog will have "Make a selection" as the title

builder.setMessage("Make a selection")

// An OK button that does nothing

.setPositiveButton("OK", new DialogInterface.OnClickListener() {
```

```
            public void onClick(DialogInterface dialog, int id) {

                    // Nothing happening here
            }
    })

    // A "Cancel" button that does nothing
    .setNegativeButton("Cancel", new DialogInterface.OnClickListener() {

            public void onClick(DialogInterface dialog, int id) {

                    // Nothing happening here either

            }

    });
```

At this point, you will need to import the `DialogInterface` class. Use your preferred method or add this line of code among the other import statements:

```
import android.content.DialogInterface;
```

Here is an explanation to each of the three parts of the code we just added:

1. In the first of the three blocks that uses chaining, we call `builder.setMessage`, which sets the main message the user will see in the dialog box. Note also that it is fine to have comments in-between parts of the chained method calls, as these are ignored entirely by the compiler.

2. Then, we add a button to our dialog with the `setPositiveButton` method, and the first argument sets the text on it to `OK`. The second argument is an anonymous class called `DialogInterface.OnClickListener` that handles clicks on the button. Notice that we are not going to add any code to the `onClick` method. We just want to see this simple dialog and we will take things a step further in the next project.

3. Next, we call yet another method on the same `builder` object. This time, it's the `setNegativeButton` method. Again, the two arguments set `Cancel` as the text for the button and an anonymous class to listen for clicks. Again, for the purposes of this demo, we are not taking any action in the overridden `onClick` method. After the call to `setNegativeButton`, we finally see a semi-colon, marking the end of the line of code.

We then code the `return` statement to complete the method and remove the error. Add the `return` statement shown next to the end (but inside the final curly brace) of the `onCreateDialog` method:

```
...
// Create the object and return it
return builder.create();

}// End of onCreateDialog
```

This last line of code has the effect of returning to `MainActivity` (which called/will call `onCreateDialog` in the first place) our new, fully configured, dialog window. We will see and add this calling code quite soon.

Now that we have our `MyDialog` class that extends `FragmentDialog`, all we have to do is declare an instance of `MyDialog`, instantiate it, and call its overridden (by us just now) `createDialog` method.

Using the DialogFragment class

Before we turn to the code, let's add a button to our layout by observing the following steps:

1. Switch to the `activity_main.xml` tab and then switch to the **Design** tab.

2. Drag a **Button** onto the layout and make sure its `id` attribute is set to `button`.

3. Click the **Infer Constraints** button to constrain the button exactly where you place it, but the position isn't important; how we will use it to create an instance of our `MyDialog` class is the key lesson.

Now, switch to the `MainActivity.java` tab and we will handle a click on this new button by using an anonymous class as we did in *Chapter 13, Anonymous Classes – Bringing Android Widgets to Life*, during the Widget Exploration app. We do it this way as we only have one button in the layout and it seems sensible and more compact than implementing the alternative (implementing the `OnClickListener` interface and then overriding `onClick` for the entire `MainActivity` class as we did in *Chapter 12, The Stack, the Heap, and the Garbage Collector*).

Notice in the following code that the anonymous class is exactly the same type that we previously implemented an interface for. Add this code to the `onCreate` method:

```
/*
    Let's listen for clicks on our regular Button.
```

We can do this with an anonymous class.
```
*/


Button button = (Button) findViewById(R.id.button);

button.setOnClickListener(
    new View.OnClickListener() {

        @Override
        public void onClick(View v) {
            // We only handle one button
            // So no switching required
            MyDialog myDialog = new MyDialog();
            myDialog.show(getSupportFragmentManager(), "123");
            // This calls onCreateDialog
            // Don't worry about the strange looking 123
            // We will find out about this in chapter 24

        }
    }
);
```

 The following import statements are needed for this code:
```
import android.view.View;
import android.widget.Button;
```

Notice that the only thing that happens in the code is that the onClick method creates a new instance of MyDialog and calls its show method, which unsurprisingly will show our dialog window just as we configured it in the MyDialog class.

The show method needs a reference to a FragmentManager, which we get with getSupportFragmentManager. This is the class that tracks and controls all Fragment instances for an Activity. We also pass in an id ("123").

More details on the FragmentManager will be revealed when we look more deeply at Fragments, starting in *Chapter 24, Design Patterns, Multiple Layouts and Fragments.*

 The reason we use the getSupportFragmentManager method is because we are supporting older devices by extending AppCompatActivity. If we simply extended Activity, then we could use the getFragmentManager class. The downside is that the app wouldn't run on as many devices.

Now, we can run the app and admire our new dialog window that appears when we click the button in the layout. Notice that clicking either of the buttons in the dialog window will close it. This is default behavior. The following close-up screenshot shows our dialog in action on the Pixel C tablet emulator:

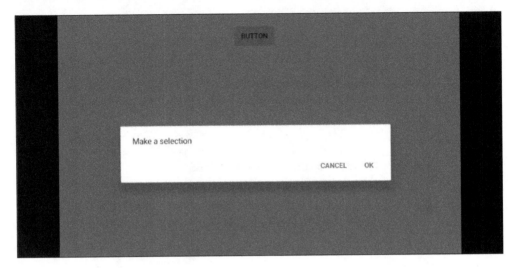

Next in this chapter, we will make two more classes that implement dialogs as the first phase of our multi-chapter Note to self app. We will see that a dialog window can have almost any layout we choose, and that we don't have to rely on the simple layouts that the `Dialog.Builder` class provides us with.

The Note to self app

Welcome to the first of four major apps we will implement in this book. When we do these projects, we will do them more professionally than we do the smaller apps. We will use Android naming conventions, string resources, and proper encapsulation.

Sometimes, these things are overkill when trying to learn a new Android/Java topic, but they are useful and important to start using as soon as possible in real projects. They become like second nature, and the quality of our apps will benefit from it.

Using naming conventions and String resources

In *Chapter 3, Exploring Android Studio and the Project Structure*, we talked about using String resources instead of hardcoding text in our layout files. There were a few benefits to doing things this way, but it was also slightly long-winded.

As this is our first real-world project, it would be a good time to do things the right way so that we can get experience of doing so. If you want a quick refresher on the benefits of String resources, go back to *Chapter 3, Exploring Android Studio and the Project Structure.*

Naming conventions are the conventions or rules used for naming the variables, methods, and classes in our code. Throughout this book, we have loosely applied the Android naming conventions. As this is our first real-world app, we will be slightly stricter in applying these naming conventions.

Most notably, when a variable is a member of a class, we will prefix the name with a lowercase m.

 More information about Android naming conventions and code style is available here: `https://source.android.com/source/code-style.html`.

In general, throughout this book, we will be relaxed about naming conventions and String resources when learning new things or building mini-apps, but apply them fairly strictly when building the main apps.

How to get the code files for the Note to self app

The fully completed app, including all the code and resources, can be found in the `Chapter 18/Note to self` folder within the download bundle. As we are implementing this app over the next five chapters, it will probably be useful to see the part-completed, runnable app at the end of every chapter as well. The part completed runnable apps and all their associated code and resources can be found in their respective folders:

`Chapter 14/Note to self`

`Chapter 16/Note to self`

`Chapter 17/Note to self`

`Chapter 18/Note to self`

 There is no Note to Self code in *Chapter 15, Arrays, ArrayList, Map and Random Numbers*, because although we will learn about topics we use in Note to Self, we don't make the changes to it until *Chapter 16, Adapters and Recyclers.*

Be aware that each of these is a separate, runnable project, and each is contained within its own unique Java package. This is so that you can easily see the app running as it would be having completed a given chapter. When copying and pasting the code, be careful not to include the package name because it will likely be different from yours and cause the code not to compile.

If you are following along and intend to build Note to Self from start to finish, we will build a project simply called `Note to self`. There is still nothing stopping you, however, from dipping into the code files of the projects from each chapter to do a bit of copying and pasting at any time. Just don't copy the package directive from the top of a file and be aware that at a couple points in the instructions, you will be asked to remove/replace the occasional line of code from a previous chapter.

So, even if you are copying and pasting more than you are typing the code, make sure to read the instructions in full and look at the code in the book for extra comments that might be useful.

In each chapter, the code will be presented as if you have completed the last chapter in full, showing code from earlier chapters, where necessary, as context for our new code.

Each chapter will not be solely devoted to the Note to Self app. We will learn about other, usually related things, and build some smaller/simpler apps as well. So, when we come to the Note to Self implementation, we will be technically prepared for it.

The completed app

The following features and screenshots are from the completed app. It will obviously look slightly different to this at the various stages of development. Where necessary, we will look at more images, either as a reminder, or to see the differences throughout the development process.

The completed app will allow the user to tap the **floating button** in the bottom-right corner of the app to open a dialog window to add a new note. Here is the screenshot that shows this feature being highlighted:

The screenshot on the left shows the button to tap, and the screenshot on the right shows the dialog window where the user can add a new note.

Eventually, as the user adds more notes, they will have a list of all the notes they have added on the main screen of the app, as shown in the following screenshot. The user can select whether the note is **important**, an **idea,** and/or a **to do**:

They will be able to scroll the list and tap on a note to see it shown in another dialog window dedicated to that note. Here is that dialog window showing a note:

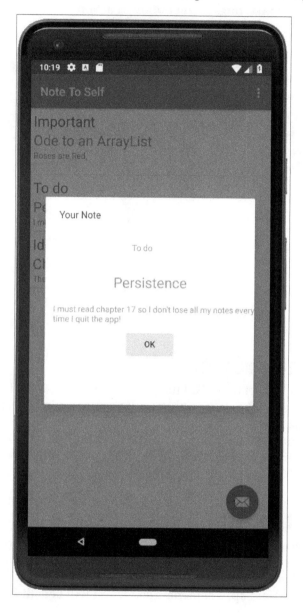

There will also be a simple (very simple) Settings screen that's accessible from the menu that will allow the user to configure whether the note list is formatted with a dividing line. Here is the settings menu option in action:

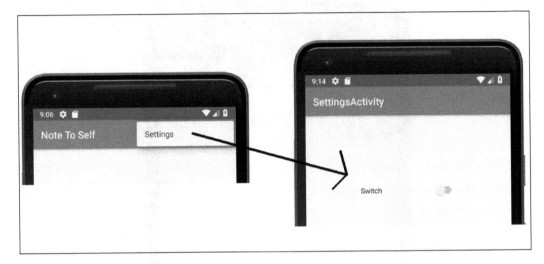

Now that we know exactly what we are going to build, we can go ahead and start to implement it.

Building the project

Let's create our new project now. Call the project Note to Self. Use the Basic Activity template. Remember from *Chapter 3, Exploring Android Studio and the Project Structure*, that this template will generate a simple menu as well as a floating action button that are both used in this project. Leave the other settings at their defaults, including the options to generate a layout file, and make the app backward compatible.

Preparing the String resources

Here, we will create all the String resources that we will refer to from our layout files instead of hardcoding the text property, as we have been doing up until now. Strictly speaking, this is a step that could be avoided. However, if you are looking to make in-depth Android apps sometime soon, you will benefit from learning to do things this way.

To get started, open the `strings.xml` file from the `res/values` folder in the project explorer. You will see the auto-generated resources. Add the following highlighted string resource. We will be using these in our app throughout the rest of the project. Add this code before the closing `</resources>` tag:

```
    . . .
    <resources>
        <string name="app_name">Note To Self</string>
        <string name="hello_world">Hello world!</string>
        <string name="action_settings">Settings</string>

        <string name="action_add">add</string>
        <string name="title_hint">Title</string>
        <string name="description_hint">Description</string>
        <string name="idea_text">Idea</string>
        <string name="important_text">Important</string>
        <string name="todo_text">To do</string>
        <string name="cancel_button">Cancel</string>
        <string name="ok_button">OK</string>

        <string name="settings_title">Settings</string>
        <string name="theme_title">Theme</string>
        <string name="theme_light">Light</string>
        <string name="theme_dark">Dark</string>

    </resources>
```

Observe in the preceding code that each string resource has a `name` attribute that is unique and distinguishes it from all the others, as well as providing a meaningful and hopefully memorable clue as to the actual string value it represents. It is these name values that we will use to refer to the String that we want to use from within our layout files.

We will not need to revisit this file for the rest of the app.

Coding the Note class

This is the fundamental data structure of the app. It is a class we will write ourselves from scratch and has all the member variables we need to represent a single user note. In *Chapter 15, Arrays, ArrayList, Map, and Random Numbers,* we will learn some new Java to see how we can let the user have dozens, hundreds, or even thousands of notes.

Create a new class by right-clicking on the folder with the name of your package, as usual, the one that contains the `MainActivity.java` file. Select **New | Java class** and name it `Note`. Left-click **OK** to create the class.

Add the following highlighted code to the new `Note` class:

```
public class Note {

    private String mTitle;
    private String mDescription;
    private boolean mIdea;
    private boolean mTodo;
    private boolean mImportant;


}
```

Notice that our member variable names are prefixed with `m`, as per the Android convention. Furthermore, we don't want any other class to access these variables directly, so they are all declared as `private`.

We will therefore need a getter and a setter method for each of our members. Add the following getter and setter methods to the `Note` class:

```
public String getTitle() {
    return mTitle;
}

public void setTitle(String mTitle) {
    this.mTitle = mTitle;
}

public String getDescription() {
    return mDescription;
}

public void setDescription(String mDescription) {
    this.mDescription = mDescription;
}

public boolean isIdea() {
    return mIdea;
}

public void setIdea(boolean mIdea) {
    this.mIdea = mIdea;
```

```
    }

    public boolean isTodo() {
        return mTodo;
    }

    public void setTodo(boolean mTodo) {
        this.mTodo = mTodo;
    }

    public boolean isImportant() {
        return mImportant;
    }

    public void setImportant(boolean mImportant) {
        this.mImportant = mImportant;
    }
```

There is quite a lot of code in that previous list, but there is nothing complicated. Each of the methods has `public` access specified, so it can be used by any other class that has a reference to an object of type `Note`. Furthermore, for each variable, there is a method with the name `get...`, and a method with the name `set...`. The getters for the Boolean-type variables are named `is...`. This is a logical name if you think about it because the returned answer will be either true or false.

Each of the getters simply returns the value of the related variable, and each of the setters sets the value of the related variable to whatever value/parameter is passed in to the method.

> In fact, we should really enhance our setters a little by doing a bit of checking to make sure that the values passed in are within reasonable limits. For example, we might want to check on and enforce a maximum or minimum length for the `String mTtile` and `String mDescription`. We won't do so here, however, as this extraneousness will only serve to cloud the real learning objectives of this project.

Let's now design the layout of the two dialog windows.

Implementing the Dialog designs

Now, we will do something we have done many times before, but this time, for a new reason. As we know, we will have two dialog windows – one for the user to enter a new note, and one for the user to view a note of their choice.

We can design the layouts of these two dialog windows in the same way we have designed all our previous layouts. When we come to create the Java code for the `FragmentDialog` classes, we will then see how we incorporate these layouts.

First, let's add a layout for our "new note" dialog by following these steps:

1. Right-click the `layout` folder in the project explorer and select **New | Layout resource file**. Enter `dialog_new_note` in the **File name:** field and then start typing `Constrai` for the **Root element:** field. Notice that there is a drop-down list with multiple options that start with **Constrai...**. Select **androidx. constraintlayout.widget.ConstraintLayout** . Left-click **OK** to generate the new layout file that will have the `ConstraintLayout` type as its root element.

2. Refer to the target design in the following screenshot while following the rest of these instructions. I have photoshopped together the finished layout, including the constraints we will soon auto-generate, next to the layout, with the constraints hidden for a bit of extra clarity:

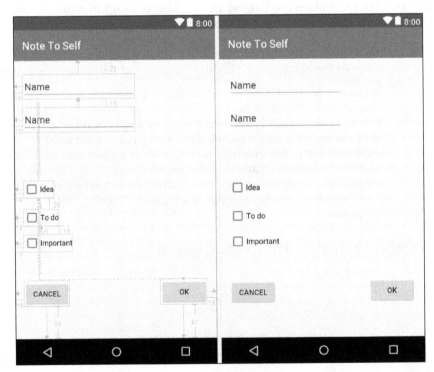

3. Drag and drop a **Plain Text** (from the **Text** category) to the very top and left of the layout, and then add another **Plain Text** below it. Don't worry about any of the attributes for now.

4. Drag and drop three **CheckBox** widgets from the **Button** category, one below the other. Look at the previous reference screenshot for guidance. Again, don't worry about any attributes for now.

5. Drag and drop two **Buttons** onto the layout, the first directly below the last **CheckBox** from the previous step, and the second horizontally in line with the first **Button,** but hard over to the right of the layout.

6. Tidy up the layout so that it resembles the reference screenshot as closely as possible, and then click the **Infer Constraints** button to fix the positions you have chosen.

7. Now, we can set up all our `text`, `id`, and `hint` properties. You can do so by using the values from the following table. Remember, we are using our string resources for the `text` and `hint` properties:

 When you edit the first id property (in a moment), you will be shown a pop-up window asking for confirmation of your changes. Check the box for **Don't ask again during this session** and click **Yes** to continue, as shown in the following screenshot:

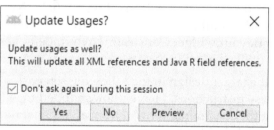

Widget type	Property	Value to set to
Plain Text (top)	id	`editTitle`
Plain Text (top)	hint	`@string/title_hint`
Plain Text (bottom)	id	`editDescription`
Plain Text (bottom)	hint	`@string/description_hint`
Plain Text (bottom)	inputType	`textMultiLine` (uncheck any other options)
CheckBox (top)	id	`checkBoxIdea`

Widget type	Property	Value to set to
CheckBox (top)	text	@string/idea_text
CheckBox (middle)	id	checkBoxTodo
CheckBox (middle)	text	@string/todo_text
CheckBox (bottom)	id	checkBoxImportant
CheckBox (bottom)	text	@string/important_text
Button (left)	id	btnCancel
Button (left)	text	@string/cancel_button
Button (right)	id	btnOK
Button (right)	text	@string/ok_button

We now have a nice neat layout ready for our Java code to display. Make sure to keep in mind the id of the different widgets because we will see them in action when we write our Java code. The important thing is that our layout looks nice and has an id for every relevant item so that we can get a reference to it.

Let's lay out our dialog box to "show note" to the user:

1. Right-click the **layout** folder in the project explorer and select **New | Layout resource file**. Enter dialog_show_note for the **File name:** field and then start typing Constrai... for the **Root element:** field. Notice that there is a drop-down list with multiple options that start with **Constrai...**. Select **androidx. constraintlayout.widget.ConstraintLayout**. Left-click **OK** to generate the new layout file that will have the ConstraintLayout type as its root element.

2. Refer to the target design in the following screenshot, while following the rest of these instructions. I have photoshopped together the finished layout, including the constraints we will soon auto-generate next to the layout, with the constraints hidden for a bit of extra clarity:

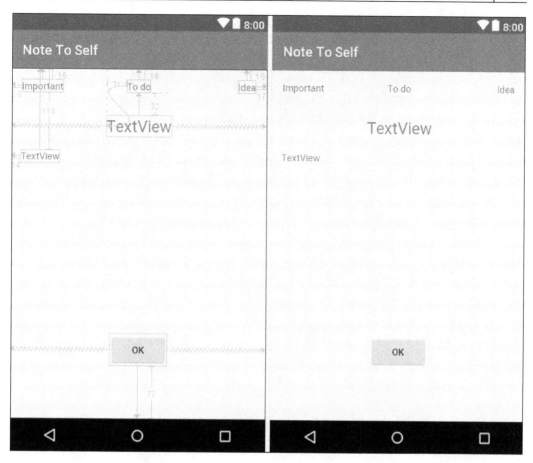

3. First of all, drag and drop three **TextView** widgets, vertically aligned across the top of the layout.

4. Next, drag and drop another **TextView** widget just below the center of the three previous TextView widgets.

5. Add another **TextView** widget just below the previous one, but over to the left.

6. Now, add a **Button** horizontally and centrally, and near the bottom of the layout. This is what it should look like so far:

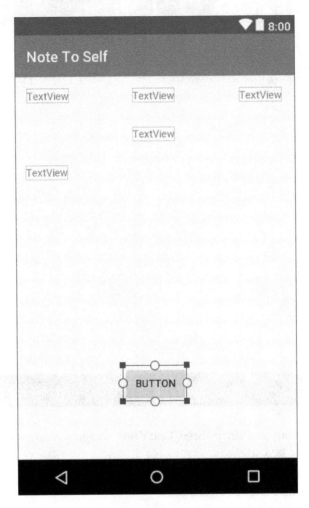

7. Tidy up the layout so that it resembles the reference screenshot as closely as possible, and then click the **Infer Constraints** button to fix the positions you have chosen.

8. Configure the attributes from the following table:

Widget type	Attribute	Value to set to
TextView (top-left)	id	`textViewImportant`
TextView (top-left)	text	`@string/important_text`
TextView (top-center)	id	`textViewTodo`
TextView (top-center)	text	`@string/todo_text`
TextView (top-right)	id	`textViewIdea`
TextView (top-right)	text	`@string/idea_text`
TextView (center, second row)	id	`txtTitle`
TextView (center, second row)	textSize	`24sp`
TextView (last one added)	id	`txtDescription`
Button	id	`btnOK`
Button	text	`@string/ok_button`

 You might want to tweak the final positions of some of the UI elements by dragging them about a bit since we have adjusted their size and contents. First, click **Clear all Constraints**, then get the layout how you want it, and finally click **Infer Constraints** to constrain the positions again.

Now, we have a layout we can use for showing a note to the user. Notice that we get to reuse some string resources. The bigger our apps get, the more beneficial it is to do things this way.

Coding the dialog boxes

Now that we have a design for both of our dialog windows ("show note" and "new note"), we can use what we know about the `FragmentDialog` class to implement a class to represent each of the dialog windows that the user can interact with.

We will start with the "new note" screen.

Coding the DialogNewNote class

Create a new class by right-clicking the project folder that has all the `.java` files and choose **New | Java class**. Name the class `DialogNewNote`.

First, change the class declaration and extend `DialogFragment`. Also override the `onCreateDialog` method, which is where all the rest of the code in this class will go. Make your code the same as the following in order to achieve this:

```
public class DialogNewNote extends DialogFragment {

    @Override
    public Dialog onCreateDialog(Bundle savedInstanceState) {

        // All the rest of the code goes here

    }
}
```

You will need to add these new imports as well:

```
import androidx.fragment.app.DialogFragment;
import android.app.Dialog;
import android.os.Bundle;
```

We temporarily have an error in the new class because we need a `return` statement, but we will get to that in just a moment.

In the next block of code, which we will add in a moment, first we declare and initialize an `AlertDialog.Builder` object as we have done before when creating dialog windows. This time, however, we will use this object much less than previously.

Next, we initialize a `LayoutInflater` object, which we will use to inflate our XML layout. "Inflate" simply means to turn our XML layout into a Java object. Once this has been done, we can then access all our widgets in the usual way. We can think of `inflater.inflate` replacing `setContentView` for our dialog. In the second line, we do just that with the `inflate` method.

Add the three lines of code we have just discussed:

```
AlertDialog.Builder builder =
    new AlertDialog.Builder(getActivity());

LayoutInflater inflater =
    getActivity().getLayoutInflater();

View dialogView =
    inflater.inflate(R.layout.dialog_new_note, null);
```

To support the new classes in the previous three lines of code, you will need to add the following import statements:

```
import androidx.appcompat.app.AlertDialog;
import android.view.View;
import android.view.LayoutInflater;
```

We now have a `View` object called `dialogView` that has all the UI from our `dialog_new_note.xml` layout file.

Immediately after the previous block, we will add the code that we will talk about in a moment.

This code will get a reference to each of the UI widgets in the usual way. Many of the objects in the forthcoming code are declared `final` because they will be used in an anonymous class and, as we learned previously, this is required. Remember that it is the reference that is `final` (cannot change); we can still change the objects on the heap to which they refer.

Add the following code just after the previous block of code:

```
final EditText editTitle = (EditText) dialogView.findViewById(R.
id.editTitle);
final EditText editDescription = (EditText) dialogView.findViewById(R.
id.editDescription);
final CheckBox checkBoxIdea = (CheckBox) dialogView.findViewById(R.
id.checkBoxIdea);
final CheckBox checkBoxTodo = (CheckBox) dialogView.findViewById(R.
id.checkBoxTodo);
final CheckBox checkBoxImportant = (CheckBox) dialogView.
findViewById(R.id.checkBoxImportant);
Button btnCancel = (Button) dialogView.findViewById(R.id.btnCancel);
Button btnOK = (Button) dialogView.findViewById(R.id.btnOK);
```

Make sure to add the following import code to make the code you just added error-free:

```
import android.widget.Button;
import android.widget.CheckBox;
import android.widget.EditText;
```

In the next code block, we will set the message of the dialog using `builder`. Then, we will write an anonymous class to handle clicks on `btnCancel`. In the overridden `onClick` method, we will simply call `dismiss()`, which is a public method of `DialogFragment`, to close the dialog window. This is just what we need should the user click **Cancel**.

Add the following code that we have just discussed:

```
builder.setView(dialogView).setMessage("Add a new note");

// Handle the cancel button
btnCancel.setOnClickListener( new View.OnClickListener() {
    @Override
    public void onClick(View v) {
            dismiss();
    }
});
```

Now, we will add an anonymous class to handle what happens when the user clicks the **OK** button (`btnOK`).

First, we create a new `Note` called `newNote`. Then, we set each of the member variables from `newNote` to the appropriate content of the form.

After this, we do something new. We create a reference to `MainActivity` using the `getActivity` method and then use that reference to call the `createNewNote` method in `MainActivity`.

 Note that we have not written this `createNewNote` method yet and it will show an error until we do so later in this chapter.

The argument sent in this method is our newly initialized `newNote` object. This has the effect of sending the user's new note back to `MainActivity`. We will see what we do with this later in this chapter.

Finally, we call `dismiss` to close the dialog window.

Add the code we have been discussing after the last block:

```
btnOK.setOnClickListener(new View.OnClickListener() {

    @Override
    public void onClick(View v) {

        // Create a new note
```

```
Note newNote = new Note();

// Set its variables to match the
// user's entries on the form
newNote.setTitle(editTitle.
        getText().toString());

newNote.setDescription(editDescription.
        getText().toString());

newNote.setIdea(checkBoxIdea.isChecked());
newNote.setTodo(checkBoxTodo.isChecked());
newNote.setImportant(checkBoxImportant.
        isChecked());

// Get a reference to MainActivity
MainActivity callingActivity = (
        MainActivity) getActivity();

// Pass newNote back to MainActivity
callingActivity.createNewNote(newNote);

// Quit the dialog
dismiss();
    }
});

return builder.create();
```

That's our first dialog done. We haven't wired it up to appear from `MainActivity` yet and we need to implement the `createNewNote` method too. We will do this right after we create the next dialog.

Coding the DialogShowNote class

Create a new class by right-clicking the project folder that contains all the `.java` files and choose **New | Java class**. Name the class `DialogShowNote`.

First, change the class declaration, extend `DialogFragment`, and override the `onCreateDialog` method. As most of the code for this class goes in the `onCreateDialog` method, implement the signature and empty body, as shown next. We will revisit this in a minute.

Notice that we declare a member variable, mNote, of the Note type. Also add the sendNoteSelected method and its single line of code that initializes mNote. This method will be called by MainActivity and it will pass in the Note object the user has clicked on.

Add the code we have just discussed and then we can look at and code the details of onCreateDialog, as follows:

```
public class DialogShowNote extends DialogFragment {

    private Note mNote;

    @Override
    public Dialog onCreateDialog(Bundle savedInstanceState) {

        // All the other code goes here


    }


    // Receive a note from the MainActivity
    public void sendNoteSelected(Note noteSelected) {
        mNote = noteSelected;
    }

}
```

At this point, you will need to import the following classes:
```
import android.app.Dialog;
import android.os.Bundle;
import androidx.fragment.app.DialogFragment;
```

Coming up next, as usual, we declare and initialize an instance of AlertDialog.Builder. Next, as we did for DialogNewNote, we declare and initialize a LayoutInflater and then use it to create a View object that has the layout for the dialog. In this case, it is the layout from dialog_show_note.xml.

Finally, in the following block of code, we get a reference to each of the UI widgets and set the text attributes on txtTitle and textDescription from the appropriate member variables of mNote, which was initialized in sendNoteSelected.

Add the code we have just discussed within the `onCreateDialog` method:

```
// All the other code goes here
AlertDialog.Builder builder =
        new AlertDialog.Builder(getActivity());

LayoutInflater inflater =
        getActivity().getLayoutInflater();

View dialogView =
        inflater.inflate(R.layout.dialog_show_note, null);

TextView txtTitle =
        (TextView) dialogView.findViewById(R.id.txtTitle);

TextView txtDescription =
        (TextView) dialogView.findViewById(R.id.txtDescription);

txtTitle.setText(mNote.getTitle());
txtDescription.setText(mNote.getDescription());

TextView txtImportant =
        (TextView) dialogView.findViewById(R.id.textViewImportant);

TextView txtTodo =
        (TextView) dialogView.findViewById(R.id.textViewTodo);

TextView txtIdea =
        (TextView) dialogView.findViewById(R.id.textViewIdea);
```

 Add the following import statements to make all the classes in the previous code available:

```
import android.view.LayoutInflater;
import android.view.View;
import android.widget.TextView;
import androidx.appcompat.app.AlertDialog;
```

The following code is also in the `onCreateDialog` method. It checks whether the note being shown is "important" and then shows or hides the `txtImportant` `TextView` accordingly. We then do exactly the same for `txtTodo` and `txtIdea`.

Add the following code after the previous block of code, while still in the onCreateDialog method:

```
if (!mNote.isImportant()){
    txtImportant.setVisibility(View.GONE);
}

if (!mNote.isTodo()){
    txtTodo.setVisibility(View.GONE);
}

if (!mNote.isIdea()){
    txtIdea.setVisibility(View.GONE);
}
```

All we need to do now is dismiss (close) the dialog window when the user clicks the **OK** button. This is done with an anonymous class, as we have seen several times already. The onClick method simply calls the dismiss method that closes the dialog window.

Add the following code to the onCreateDialog method after the previous block of code:

```
Button btnOK = (Button) dialogView.findViewById(R.id.btnOK);

builder.setView(dialogView).setMessage("Your Note");

btnOK.setOnClickListener(new View.OnClickListener() {
    @Override
    public void onClick(View v) {
            dismiss();
    }
});

return builder.create();
```

Import the Button class with this line of code:
```
import android.widget.Button;
```

We now have two dialog windows ready to roll. We just have to add some code to MainActivity to finish the job.

Showing our new dialogs

Add a new temporary member variable just after the `MainActivity` declaration. This won't be in the final app – it is just so that we can test our dialog windows as soon as possible:

```
// Temporary code
Note mTempNote = new Note();
```

Now, add this method so that we can receive a new note from the `DialogNewNote` class:

```
public void createNewNote(Note n){
    // Temporary code
    mTempNote = n;
}
```

Now, to send a note to the `DialogShowNote` method, we need to add a button with the id `button` to the `layout_main.xml` layout file.

Just so that it is clear what this button is for, we will change its `text` attribute to `Show Note`, as follows:

- Drag a Button onto `layout_main.xml` and configure its `id` as `button` and `text` as `Show Note`.

- Click the **Infer Constraints** button so that the button stays where you put it. The exact position of this button is not important at this stage.

 Just to clarify, this is a temporary button for testing purposes and will not be in the final app. At the end of development, we will click on a note's title from a list.

Now, in the `onCreate` method, we will set up an anonymous class to handle clicks on our temporary button. The code in `onClick` will do the following:

- Create a new `DialogShowNote` instance simply called `dialog`.

- Call the `sendNoteSelected` method on `dialog` to pass in as a parameter our `Note` object, `mTempNote`.

- Finally, it will call `show`, which breathes life into our new dialog.

Add the code just described to onCreate:

```
// Temporary code
Button button = (Button) findViewById(R.id.button);
button.setOnClickListener(new View.OnClickListener() {
    @Override
    public void onClick(View v) {

        // Create a new DialogShowNote called dialog
        DialogShowNote dialog = new DialogShowNote();

        // Send the note via the sendNoteSelected method
        dialog.sendNoteSelected(mTempNote);

        // Create the dialog
        dialog.show(getSupportFragmentManager(), "123");
    }
});
```

Make sure to import the Button class with the following line of code:

```
import android.widget.Button;
```

We can now summon our DialogShowNote dialog window at the click of a button. Run the app and click the **SHOW NOTE** button to see the DialogShowNote dialog with the dialog_show_note.xml layout, as demonstrated in the following screenshot:

Admittedly, this is not much to look at considering how much coding we have done in this chapter, but when we get the DialogNewNote working, we will see how MainActivity interacts and shares data between the two dialogs.

Let's make the DialogNewNote dialog useable.

Coding the floating action button

This is going to be really easy. The floating action button was provided for us in the layout. By way of a reminder, this is the floating action button:

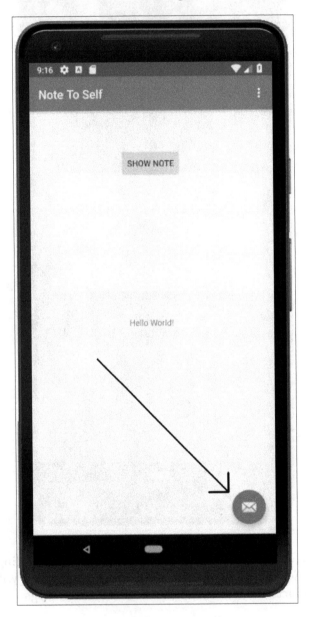

It is located in the `activity_main.xml` file. This is the XML code that positions and defines its appearance:

```
<com.google.android.material.floatingactionbutton
.FloatingActionButton

    android:id="@+id/fab"
    android:layout_width="wrap_content"
    android:layout_height="wrap_content"
    android:layout_gravity="bottom|end"
    android:layout_margin="@dimen/fab_margin"
    app:srcCompat="@android:drawable/ic_dialog_email" />
```

Android Studio has even provided an anonymous class to handle clicks on the floating action button. All we need to do is add some code to the `onClick` method of this already provided class and we can use the `DialogNewNote` class.

The floating action button is usually used for a core action of an app. For example, in an email app, it would probably be used to start a new email or, in a note-keeping app, it would probably be used to add a new note. So, let's do that now.

In `MainActivity.java`, find the auto-generated code provided by Android Studio in the `MainActivity.java` class in the `onCreate` method. Here it is in its entirety:

```
fab.setOnClickListener(new View.OnClickListener() {
    @Override
    public void onClick(View view) {
            Snackbar.make(view, "Replace with your own action",
                    Snackbar.LENGTH_LONG)
                .setAction("Action", null).show();

    }
});
```

In the previous code, note the highlighted line and delete it. Now, add the following code in place of the deleted code:

```
DialogNewNote dialog = new DialogNewNote();
dialog.show(getSupportFragmentManager(), "");
```

The new code creates a new dialog window of the `DialogNewNote` variety and then shows it to the user.

We can now run the app. Tap the floating action button and add a note along the lines of the following screenshot:

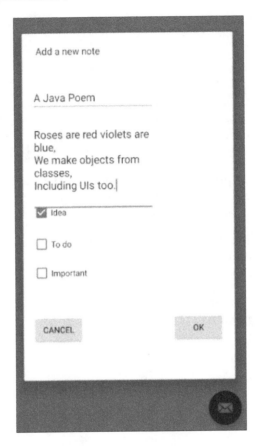

Then, we can tap the **Show Note** button to see it in a dialog window, like in the following screenshot:

Be aware that if you add a second note, it will overwrite the first because we only have one Note object. We need to learn some more Java in order to solve this problem.

Summary

In this chapter, we have seen and implemented a common user interface design with dialog windows by using the DialogFragment class.

We went a step further when we started the Note to self app by implementing more complicated dialogs that can capture information from the user. We saw that DialogFragment enables us to have any UI we like in a dialog box.

In the next chapter, we will begin to deal with the obvious problem whereby the user can only have one note by exploring Java arrays and their close cousin, ArrayList, as well as another data-related class, Map.

15
Arrays, ArrayList, Map and Random Numbers

In this chapter, we will learn about Java arrays that allow us to manipulate a potentially huge amount of data in an organized and efficient manner. We will also use a close Java relation to arrays, the `ArrayList`, and see the differences between them.

In addition, we will see how to handle data which can be logically linked to an identifier as part of a pair using a Map and we will also build some mini apps to practice these new concepts.

Furthermore we will see how to generate random numbers.

The topics we will cover in this chapter include the following:

- The Random class
- Handling data with arrays
- Arrays mini app
- Dynamic arrays, including mini app
- Multi-dimensional arrays, including mini app
- The `ArrayList` class
- The enhanced `for` loop
- Java `HashMap`

But first, let's learn about the `Random` class.

A random diversion

Sometimes in our apps, we will want a random number and Java provides us with the Random class for these occasions. There are many possible uses for this class; perhaps our app wants to show a random tip-of-the-day or a game that has to choose between scenarios, or a quiz that asks random questions.

The Random class is part of the Java API and is fully compatible in our Android apps.

Let's have a look at how we can create random numbers, and later in the chapter we will put it to practical use. All the hard work is done for us by the Random class. First, we need to create an object of type Random.

```
Random randGenerator = new Random();
```

Then we use our new object's nextInt method to generate a random number between a certain range.

This line of code generates the random number using our Random object and stores the result in the ourRandomNumber variable:

```
int ourRandomNumber = randGenerator.nextInt(10);
```

The number that we enter for the range starts from zero. So the preceding line will generate a random number between 0 and 9. If we want a random number between 1 and 10, we just do this:

```
ourRandomNumber ++;
```

We can also use the Random object to get other types of random number using nextLong, nextFloat, and nextDouble.

We will put the Random class to practical use later in the chapter with a quick geography quiz app.

Handling large amounts of data with arrays

You might be wondering what happens when we have an app with lots of variables to keep track of. What about our Note to Self app with 100 notes, or a high score table in a game with the top 100 scores? We could declare and initialize 100 separate variables as follows:

```
Note note1;
Note note2;
```

```
Note note3;
// 96 more lines like the above
Note note100;
```

or

```
int topScore1;
int topScore2;
int topScore3;
// 96 more lines like the above
int topScore100;
```

Straight away, this can seem unwieldy, but what about when someone gets a new top score or we want to let our users sort the order their notes are displayed in? Using the high scores scenario, we have to shift the scores in every variable down one place? A nightmare begins.

```
topScore100 = topScore99;
topScore99 = topScore98;
topScore98 = topScore97;
// 96 more lines like the above
topScore1 = score;
```

There must be a better way. When we have a whole array of variables, what we need is a Java **array**. An array is a reference variable that holds up to a predetermined fixed maximum number of elements. Each element is a variable with a consistent type.

The following code declares an array that can hold `int` type variables; perhaps a high score table or a series of exam grades:

```
int [] intArray;
```

We could also declare arrays of other types, including classes such as `Note`, as follows:

```
String [] classNames;
boolean [] bankOfSwitches;
float [] closingBalancesInMarch;
Note [] notes;
```

Each of these arrays would need to have a fixed maximum amount of storage space allocated before it was used. Just like other objects, we must initialize arrays before we use them, as follows:

```
intArray = new int [100];
```

The preceding code allocates up to a maximum of `100` int sized storage spaces. Think of a long aisle of 100 consecutive storage spaces in our variable warehouse. The spaces would probably be labelled `intArray[0]`, `intArray[1]`, `intArray[2]`, and so on, with each space holding a single int value. Perhaps the slightly surprising thing here is that the storage spaces start off at zero, not 1. Therefore, in a 100 *wide* array, the storage spaces would run from 0 to 99.

We could initialize some of these storage spaces like this:

```
intArray[0] = 5;
intArray[1] = 6;
intArray[2] = 7;
```

But note that we can only ever put the pre-declared type into an array and that the type that an array holds can never change, as demonstrated in the following:

```
intArray[3]= "John Carmack"; // Won't compile String not int
```

So, when we have an array of int types, what are each of these int variables called? What are the names of these variables, and how do we access the values stored in them? The array notation syntax replaces the name. And we can do anything with a variable in an array that we could do with a regular variable with a name, demonstrated as follows:

```
intArray [3] = 123;
```

Here is another example:

```
intArray[10] = intArray[9] - intArray[4];
```

This also includes assigning the value from an array to a regular variable of the same type, like this:

```
int myNamedInt = intArray [3];
```

Note, however, that `myNamedInt` is a separate and distinct primitive variable and any changes to it do not affect the value stored in the `intArray` reference. It has its own space in the warehouse and is unconnected to the array. To be more specific, the array is on the heap and the int is on the stack.

Arrays are objects

We said that arrays are reference variables. Think of an array variable as an address to a group of variables of a given type. Perhaps, using the warehouse analogy, `someArray` is an aisle number. So `someArray[0]`, `someArray[1]`, and so on, are the aisle numbers, followed by the position number in the aisle.

Arrays are also objects. That is, they have methods and properties that we can use, as can be seen in the following example:

```
int lengthOfSomeArray = someArray.length;
```

In the preceding, we assigned the length of `someArray` to the `int` variable called `lengthOfSomeArray`.

We can even declare an array of arrays. This is an array in which another array lurks in each of its elements. This is shown as follows:

```
String[][] countriesAndCities;
```

In the preceding array, we could hold a list of cities within each country. Let's not go array crazy just yet though. Just remember that an array holds up to a predetermined number of variables of any predetermined type, and those values are accessed using the following syntax:

```
someArray[someLocation];
```

Let's use some arrays in a real app to try and get an understanding of how to use them in real code and what we might use them for.

Simple array example mini-app

Let's make a simple working array example. You can get the completed code for this example in the downloadable code bundle. It can be found in the `Chapter 15/ Simple Array Example/MainActivity.java` folder.

Create a project with an **Empty Activity** and call it `Simple Array Example`.

First we declare our array, allocate five spaces, and initialize values to each of the elements. Then we output each of the values to the **logcat** console. Add the following code to the `onCreate` method just after the call to `setContentView`:

```
// Declaring an array
int[] ourArray;

// Allocate memory for a maximum size of 5 elements
ourArray = new int[5];

// Initialize ourArray with values
// The values are arbitrary, but they must be int
// The indexes are not arbitrary. 0 through 4 or crash!

ourArray[0] = 25;
```

```
ourArray[1] = 50;
ourArray[2] = 125;
ourArray[3] = 68;
ourArray[4] = 47;

//Output all the stored values
Log.i("info", "Here is ourArray:");
Log.i("info", "[0] = "+ourArray[0]);
Log.i("info", "[1] = "+ourArray[1]);
Log.i("info", "[2] = "+ourArray[2]);
Log.i("info", "[3] = "+ourArray[3]);
Log.i("info", "[4] = "+ourArray[4]);
```

Next, we add each of the elements of the array together, just as we could regular `int` type variables. Notice that when we add the array elements together, we are doing so over multiple lines. This is fine as we have omitted a semi-colon until the last operation, so the Java compiler treats the lines as one statement. Add the code we have just discussed to `MainActivity.java`:

```
/*
    We can do any calculation with an array element
    provided it is appropriate to the contained type
    Like this:
*/
int answer = ourArray[0] +
ourArray[1] +
ourArray[2] +
ourArray[3] +
ourArray[4];

Log.i("info", "Answer = "+ answer);
```

Run the example and see output in the logcat window.

Remember that nothing will happen on the emulator display as all the output will be sent to our **logcat** console window in Android Studio. Here is the output:

```
info: Here is ourArray:
info: [0] = 25
info: [1] = 50
info: [2] = 125
info: [3] = 68
info: [4] = 47
info: Answer = 315
```

We declared an array called `ourArray` to hold `int` variables, and then allocated space for up to 5 of that type.

Next, we assigned a value to each of the five spaces in our array. Remember that the first space is `ourArray[0]` and the last space is `ourArray[4]`.

Next, we simply printed the value in each array location to the console, and from the output, we can see they hold the value we initialized them to be in the previous step. Then, we added together each of the elements in `ourArray` and initialized their value to the `answer` variable. We then printed `answer` to the console and we can see that indeed, all the values were added together, just as if they were plain old `int` types, which they are, but just stored in a different manner.

Getting dynamic with arrays

As we discussed at the beginning of all this array stuff, if we need to declare and initialize each element of an array individually, there isn't a huge amount of benefit to an array over regular variables. Let's look at an example of declaring and initializing arrays dynamically.

Dynamic array example

Let's make a simple dynamic array example. You can get the working project for this example in the download bundle. It can be found in the `Chapter 15/Dynamic Array Example/MainActivity.java` folder.

Create a project with an empty `Activity` and call it `Dynamic Array Example`.

Type the following just after the call to `setContentView` in `onCreate`. See if you can work out what the output will be before we discuss it and analyze the code:

```
// Declaring and allocating in one step
int[] ourArray = new int[1000];

// Let's initialize ourArray using a for loop
// Because more than a few variables is allot of typing!

for(int i = 0; i < 1000; i++){

    // Put the value of our value into ourArray
    // At the position decided by i.
    ourArray[i] = i*5;

    //Output what is going on
```

```
        Log.i("info", "i = " + i);
        Log.i("info", "ourArray[i] = " + ourArray[i]);
    }
```

Run the example app, remembering that nothing will happen on screen as all the output will be sent to our **logcat** console window in Android Studio. Here is the output:

```
info: i = 0
info: ourArray[i] = 0
info: i = 1
info: ourArray[i] = 5
info: i = 2
info: ourArray[i] = 10
```

994 iterations of the loop have been removed for the sake of brevity:

```
info: ourArray[i] = 4985
info: i = 998
info: ourArray[i] = 4990
info: i = 999
info: ourArray[i] = 4995
```

First, we declared and allocated an array called `ourArray` to hold up to `1000 int` values. Notice that this time we performed the two steps in a single line of code:

```
    int[] ourArray = new int[1000];
```

Then we used a `for` loop that was set to loop 1000 times:

```
    (int i = 0; i < 1000; i++){
```

We initialized the spaces in the array, starting at 0 through to 999, with the value of `i` multiplied by 5, as follows:

```
    ourArray[i] = i*5;
```

Then, to demonstrate the value of `i` and the value held in each position of the array, we output the value of `i` followed by the value held in the corresponding position in the array, as follows:

```
    Log.i("info", "i = " + i);
    Log.i("info", "ourArray[i] = " + ourArray[i]);
```

And all this happened 1,000 times, producing the output we have seen. Of course, we have yet to use this technique in a real-world app, but we will use it soon to make our Note to Self app hold an almost infinite number of notes.

Entering the nth dimension with Arrays

We very briefly mentioned that an array can even hold other arrays at each position. And, of course, if an array holds lots of arrays, which in turn hold lots of some other type, how do we access the values in the contained arrays? And why would we ever need this anyway? Look at this next example of where multi-dimensional arrays can be useful.

Multidimensional Array mini app

Let's make a simple multi-dimensional array example. You can get the working project for this example in the download bundle. It can be found in the Chapter 15/ Multidimensional Array Example/MainActivity.java folder.

Create a project with an empty Activity and call it Multidimensional Array Example.

After the call to setContentView in onCreate, declare and initialize a two-dimensional array as follows:

```
// Random object for generating question numbers
Random randInt = new Random();
// a variable to hold the random value generated
int questionNumber;

// declare and allocate in separate stages for clarity
// but we don't have to
String[][] countriesAndCities;
// Now we have a 2 dimensional array

countriesAndCities = new String[5][2];
// 5 arrays with 2 elements each
// Perfect for 5 "What's the capital city" questions

// Now we load the questions and answers into our arrays
// You could do this with less questions to save typing
// But don't do more or you will get an exception
countriesAndCities [0][0] = "United Kingdom";
```

```
countriesAndCities [0][1] = "London";

countriesAndCities [1][0] = "USA";
countriesAndCities [1][1] = "Washington";

countriesAndCities [2][0] = "India";
countriesAndCities [2][1] = "New Delhi";

countriesAndCities [3][0] = "Brazil";
countriesAndCities [3][1] = "Brasilia";

countriesAndCities [4][0] = "Kenya";
countriesAndCities [4][1] = "Nairobi";
```

Now we output the content of the array using a `for` loop and our `Random` object. Note how we ensure that although the question is random, we can always pick the correct answer. Add this following code after the previous block:

```
/*
    Now we know that the country is stored at element 0
    The matching capital at element 1
    Here are two variables that reflect this
*/
int country = 0;
int capital = 1;

// A quick for loop to ask 3 questions
for(int i = 0; i < 3; i++){
    // get a random question number between 0 and 4
    questionNumber = randInt.nextInt(5);

    // and ask the question and in this case just
    // give the answer for the sake of brevity
    Log.i("info", "The capital of "
    +countriesAndCities[questionNumber][country]);

    Log.i("info", "is "
    +countriesAndCities[questionNumber][capital]);

} // end of for loop
```

Run the example, remembering that nothing will happen on screen as all the output will be sent to our **logcat** console window in Android Studio. Here is the output:

```
info: The capital of USA
info: is Washington
info: The capital of India
info: is New Delhi
info: The capital of United Kingdom
info: is London
```

What just happened? Let's go through this chunk by chunk so we know exactly what is going on.

We make a new object of type `Random` called `randInt`, ready to generate random numbers later in the program:

```
Random randInt = new Random();
```

A simple `int` variable to hold a question number.

```
int questionNumber;
```

And here we declare our array of arrays called `countriesAndCities`. The outer array holds arrays as follows:

```
String[][] countriesAndCities;
```

Now we allocate space within our arrays. The first outer array will now be able to hold five arrays, and each of the inner arrays will be able to hold two `Strings`:

```
countriesAndCities = new String[5][2];
```

Now we initialize our arrays to hold countries and their corresponding capital cities. Notice with each pair of initializations that the outer array number stays the same, indicating that each country/capital pair is within one inner array (a `String` array). And, of course, each of these inner arrays is held in one element of the outer array (which holds arrays). This is demonstrated as follows:

```
countriesAndCities [0][0] = "United Kingdom";
countriesAndCities [0][1] = "London";

countriesAndCities [1][0] = "USA";
countriesAndCities [1][1] = "Washington";

countriesAndCities [2][0] = "India";
countriesAndCities [2][1] = "New Delhi";
```

```
countriesAndCities [3][0] = "Brazil";
countriesAndCities [3][1] = "Brasilia";

countriesAndCities [4][0] = "Kenya";
countriesAndCities [4][1] = "Nairobi";
```

To make the upcoming `for` loop clearer, we declare and initialize `int` variables to represent the country and the capital from our arrays. If you glance back at the array initialization, all the countries are held in position 0 of the inner array and all the corresponding capital cities at position 1:

```
int country = 0;
int capital = 1;
```

Now we set up a `for` loop to run three times. Note that this does not simply access the first three elements of our array; it just determines the number of times we go through the loop. We could make it loop one time or a thousand times and the example would still work:

```
for(int i = 0; i < 3; i++){
```

Next, we determine which question to ask or, more specifically, which element of our outer array. Remember that `randInt.nextInt(5)` returns a number between 0 and 4 — just what we need, as we have an outer array with 5 elements: 0 through 4:

```
questionNumber = randInt.nextInt(5);
```

Now we can ask a question by outputting the Strings held in the inner array, which in turn is held by the outer array that was chosen in the previous line by the randomly generated number:

```
Log.i("info", "The capital of "
+countriesAndCities[questionNumber][country]);

Log.i("info", "is "
+countriesAndCities[questionNumber][capital]);

}//end of for loop
```

For the record, we will not be using any multi-dimensional arrays in the rest of this book. So, if there is still a little bit of murkiness around these arrays inside arrays, then that doesn't matter. You know they exist, what they can do, and you can revisit them if necessary.

Array out of bounds exceptions

An array out of bounds exception occurs when we attempt to access an element of an array that does not exist. Sometimes the compiler will catch it for us to prevent the error from making its way into a working app. Take the following code by way of an example:

```
int[] ourArray = new int[1000];
int someValue = 1; // Arbitrary value
ourArray[1000] = someValue;
// Won't compile as compiler knows this won't work.
// Only locations 0 through 999 are valid
```

But what if we do something like this:

```
int[] ourArray = new int[1000];
int someValue = 1;// Arbitrary value
int x = 999;
if(userDoesSomething){
   x++; // x now equals 1000
}

ourArray[x] = someValue;
ourArray[x] = someValue;
// Array out of bounds exception if userDoesSomething evaluates to
// true! This is because we end up referencing position 1000 when
// the array only has positions 0 through 999
// Compiler can't spot it. App will crash!
```

The only way we can avoid this problem is to know the rule; the rule that arrays start at zero and go up to their length -1. We can also use clear, readable code where it is easy to evaluate what we have done and spot problems more easily.

ArrayLists

An `ArrayList` is like a regular Java array on steroids. It overcomes some of the shortfalls of arrays, such as having to predetermine its size. It adds a number of useful methods to make its data easy to manage, and it uses an enhanced version of a `for` loop, which is clearer to use than a regular `for` loop.

Let's look at some code that uses `ArrayList`:

```
// Declare a new ArrayList called myList to hold int variables
ArrayList<int> myList;

// Initialize the myList ready for use
myList = new ArrayList<int>();
```

In the previous code, we declared and initialized a new `ArrayList` called `myList`. We can also do this in a single step, as demonstrated by the following code:

```
ArrayList<int> myList = new ArrayList<int>();
```

Nothing especially interesting so far, so let's take a look at what we can actually do with `ArrayList`. Let's use a `String ArrayList` this time:

```
// declare and initialize a new ArrayList
ArrayList<String> myList = new ArrayList<String>();

// Add a new String to myList in the next available location
myList.add("Donald Knuth");
// And another
myList.add("Rasmus Lerdorf");
// And another
myList.add("Richard Stallman");
// We can also choose 'where' to add an entry
myList.add(1, "James Gosling");

// Is there anything in our ArrayList?
if(myList.isEmpty()){
    // Nothing to see here
}else{
    // Do something with the data
}

// How many items in our ArrayList?
int numItems = myList.size();

// Now where did I put James Gosling?
int position = myList.indexOf("James Gosling");
```

In the previous code, we saw that we can use some really useful methods of the `ArrayList` class on our `ArrayList` object. These methods are as follows:

- We can add an item (`myList.add`)
- Add at a specific location (`myList.add(x, value)`)
- Check if the `ArrayList` is empty (`myList.isEmpty`)
- See how big it is (`myList.size()`) and get the current position of a given item (`myList.indexOf`)

There are even more methods in the `ArrayList` class, and you can read about them here: `http://docs.oracle.com/javase/7/docs/api/java/util/ArrayList.html`.

What we have seen so far is enough to complete this book, however.

With all this functionality, all we need now is a way to handle `ArrayLists` dynamically.

The enhanced for loop

This is what the condition of an enhanced `for` loop looks like:

```
for (String s : myList)
```

The previous example would iterate (step through) all of the items in `myList` one at a time. At each step, `s` would hold the current `String`.

So, this code would print to the console all of our eminent programmers from the previous section's `ArrayList` code sample, as follows:

```
for (String s : myList){
    Log.i("Programmer: ","" + s);
}
```

We can also use the enhanced `for` loop with regular arrays too, demonstrated as follows:

```
int [] anArray = new int [];
// We can initialize arrays quickly like this
anArray {0, 1, 2, 3, 4, 5}

for (int s : anArray){
    Log.i("Contents = ","" + s);
}
```

There's another incoming news flash!

Arrays and ArrayLists are polymorphic

We already know that we can put objects into arrays and `ArrayList`. But being polymorphic means they can handle objects of multiple distinct types as long as they have a common parent type all within the same array or `ArrayList`.

In *Chapter 10, Object-Oriented programming,* we learned that polymorphism means *different forms*. But what does it mean to us in the context of arrays and `ArrayList`?

Boiled down to its simplest form: any subclass can be used as part of the code that uses the super class.

For example, if we have an array of `Animals`, we could put any object that is a type that is a subclass of `Animal` in the `Animal` array — for example, `Cats` and `Dogs`.

This means we can write code that is simpler and easier to understand, as well as easier to change:

```
// This code assumes we have an Animal class
// And we have a Cat and Dog class that extends Animal
Animal myAnimal =  new Animal();
Dog myDog = new Dog();
Cat myCat = new Cat();
Animal [] myAnimals = new Animal[10];
myAnimals[0] = myAnimal; // As expected
myAnimals[1] = myDog; // This is OK too
myAnimals[2] = myCat; // And this is fine as well
```

Also, we can write code for the super class and rely on the fact that no matter how many times it is sub-classed, within certain parameters the code will still work. Let's continue our previous example:

```
// 6 months later we need elephants
// with its own unique aspects
// If it extends Animal we can still do this
Elephant myElephant = new Elephant();
myAnimals[3] = myElephant; // And this is fine as well
```

But when we remove an object from a polymorphic array, we must remember to cast it to the type we want. This is just like we do every time we get a reference to a UI element from our XML using `findViewById`;

```
Cat newCat = (Cat) myAnimals[2];
```

All we have just discussed is true for `ArrayLists` as well. Armed with this new toolkit of arrays, `ArrayLists`, and the fact that they are polymorphic, we can move on to learn about some more Android classes that we will soon use to enhance our Note to Self app.

More Java Collections – Meet Java Hashmap

Java `HashMaps` are neat. They are part of the Java Collections, and they are a kind of cousin to `ArrayList`, which we will use in the Note to Self project during the next chapter. They basically encapsulate useful data storage techniques that would otherwise be quite technical for us to code successfully for ourselves.

I thought it would be worth taking a first look at `HashMap` on its own.

Suppose we want to store the data of lots of characters from a role-playing game, and each different character is represented by an object of type `Character`.

We could use some of the Java tools we already know about, such as arrays or `ArrayList`. However, Java `HashMap` is also like these things, but with `HashMap` we can give a unique key/identifier to each `Character` object and access any such object using that key/identifier.

 The term "hash" comes from the process of turning our chosen key/identifier into something used internally by the `HashMap` class. The process is called hashing.

Any of our `Character` instances can then be accessed with our chosen key/identifier. A good candidate for a key/identifier in the `Character` class scenario would be the character's name.

Each key/identifier has a corresponding object; in this case, of the `Character` type. This is known as a key-value pair.

We just give `HashMap` a key and it gives us the corresponding object. There is no need to worry about which index we stored our characters—perhaps Geralt, Ciri, or Triss—at; just pass the name to `HashMap` and it will do the work for us.

Let's look at some examples. You don't need to type any of this code; just get familiar with how it works.

We can declare a new `HashMap` to hold keys and `Character` instances like this code:

```
Map<String, Character> characterMap;
```

The previous code assumes we have coded a class called `Character`.

We can initialize the `HashMap` as follows:

```
characterMap = new HashMap();
```

We can add a new key and its associated object like this:

```
characterMap.put("Geralt", new Character());
```

And this:

```
characterMap.put("Ciri", new Character());
```

And this:

```
characterMap.put("Triss", new Character());
```

 All the example code assumes that we can somehow give the `Character` instances their unique properties to reflect their internal differences elsewhere.

We can then retrieve an entry from the `HashMap` as follows:

```
Character ciri = characterMap.get("Ciri");
```

Or perhaps use the `Character` class's methods directly, as follows:

```
characterMap.get("Geralt").drawSilverSword();

// Or maybe call some other hypothetical method
characterMap.get("Triss").openFastTravelPortal("Kaer Morhen");
```

The previous code calls the hypothetical methods `drawSilverSword` and `openFastTravelPortal` on the `Character` class.

 The HashMap class also has lots of useful methods like `ArrayList`. See the official Java page for HashMap here: https://docs.oracle.com/javase/tutorial/collections/interfaces/map.html.

Now, let's talk about the Note to Self app.

The Note to Self app

Despite all we have learned, we are not quite ready to apply a solution to the Note to Self app. We could update our code to store lots of notes in an `ArrayList`, but before we do, we also need a way to display the contents of our `ArrayList` in the UI. It won't look good to throw the whole thing into a TextView.

The solution is **Adapters,** and a special UI layout called `RecyclerView`. We will get to them in the next chapter.

Frequently asked questions

Q) How can a computer that can only make real calculations possibly generate a genuinely random number?

A) In reality, a computer cannot create a number that is truly random, but the `Random` class uses a **seed** that produces a number that would stand up as genuinely random under close statistical scrutiny. To find out more about seeds and generating random numbers, look at the following article: `https://en.wikipedia.org/wiki/Random_number_generation`.

Summary

In this chapter, we looked at how to use simple Java arrays to store substantial amounts of data, provided it is of the same type. We also used `ArrayList`, which is like an array with loads of extra features. Furthermore, we found out that both arrays and `ArrayList` are polymorphic, which means that a single array (or `ArrayList`) can hold multiple different objects, as long as they are all derived from the same parent class.

We also learned about the `HashMap` class, which is also a data storage solution, but which allows access in different ways.

In the next chapter, we will learn about `Adapter` and `RecyclerView` to put our theory into practice and enhance our Note to Self app.

16
Adapters and Recyclers

In this brief chapter, we will achieve much. We will first go through the theory of adapters and lists. We will then look at how we can extend RecyclerAdapter in Java code and add RecyclerView, which acts as a list to our UI, and then, through the apparent magic of the Android API, bind them together so that RecyclerView displays the contents of RecyclerAdapter and allows the user to scroll through the contents. You have probably guessed that we will be using this technique to display our list of notes in the Note to Self app.

In this chapter, we will do the following:

- Look at the theory of adapters and binding them to our UI
- Implement the layout with RecyclerView
- Lay out a list item for use in RecyclerView
- Implement the adapter with RecyclerAdapter
- Bind the adapter to RecyclerView
- Store notes in ArrayList and display them in RecyclerView
- Discuss how we can improve the Note to Self app further

Soon, we will have a self-managing layout that holds and displays all our notes, so let's get started.

RecyclerView and RecyclerAdapter

In *Chapter 5, Beautiful Layouts with CardView and ScrollView*, we used ScrollView and we populated it with a few CardView widgets so we could see it scrolling. We could take what we have just learned about arrays and ArrayList and create an array of TextViews, use them to populate ScrollView, and, within each TextView, place the title of a note. This sounds like a perfect solution for showing each note so that it is clickable in the Note to Self app.

We could create the TextViews dynamically in Java code, set their text property to be the title of a note, and then add the TextViews to a LinearLayout contained in a ScrollView. But this is imperfect.

The problem with displaying lots of widgets

This might seem fine, but what if there were dozens, hundreds, or even thousands of notes? We couldn't have thousands of TextViews in memory because the Android device might simply run out of memory, or at the very least grind to a halt, as it tries to handle the scrolling of such a vast amount of data.

Now, also consider if we wanted (which we do) each note in the ScrollView to show whether it was important, a to-do, or an idea. And how about a short snippet from the text of the note as well?

We would need to devise some clever code that loads and destroys Note objects and TextViews from an array/ArrayList. It can be done, but to do it efficiently is far from straightforward.

The solution to the problem with displaying lots of widgets

Fortunately, this is a problem faced so commonly by mobile developers that the Android API has a solution built in.

We can add a single widget called a RecyclerView (like an environmentally friendly ScrollView but with boosters too) to our UI layout. RecyclerView was designed precisely as a solution to the problem we have been discussing. In addition, we need to interact with a RecyclerView with a special type of class that understands how RecyclerView works. We will interact with it using an **adapter**. We will use the RecyclerAdapter class, extend it, customize it, and then use it to control the data from our ArrayList and display it in the RecyclerView.

Let's find out a bit more about how the RecyclerView and RecyclerAdapter classes work.

How to use RecyclerView and RecyclerAdapter

We already know how to store almost unlimited notes—we can do so in an ArrayList, although we haven't implemented it yet. We also know that there is a UI layout called RecyclerView, which is specifically designed to display potentially long lists of data from an ArrayList. We just need to see how to put it all into action.

To add a `RecyclerView` to our layout, we can simply drag and drop it from the palette onto our UI in the usual way.

 Don't do it yet. Let's just discuss it for a bit first.

The `RecyclerView` will look like this in the UI designer:

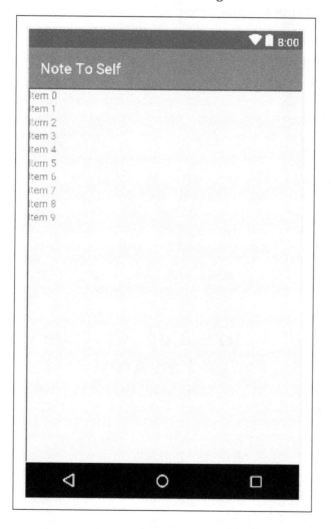

This appearance, however, is more a representation of the possibilities than the actual appearance in an app. If we run the app at once after adding a `RecyclerView`, we just get a blank screen.

The first thing we need to do to make practical use of RecyclerView is decide what each item in the list will look like. It could be just a single TextView; it could be an entire layout. We will use a LinearLayout. To be clear and specific, we will use a LinearLayout that holds three TextView widgets for each item in our RecyclerView. This will allow us to display the note status (important/idea/to-do), the note title, and a short snippet of text from the actual note contents.

A list item needs to be defined in its own XML file, then the RecyclerView can hold multiple instances of this list item layout.

Of course, none of this explains how we overcome the complexity of managing what data is shown in which list item and how it is retrieved from an ArrayList.

This data handling is taken care of by our own customized implementation of RecyclerAdapter. The RecyclerAdapter class implements the Adapter interface. We don't need to know how Adapter works internally; we just need to override the right methods and then RecyclerAdapter will do all the work of communicating with our RecyclerView.

Wiring up an implementation of RecyclerAdapter to a RecyclerView is certainly more complicated than dragging 20 TextViews onto a ScrollView—but once it is done, we can forget about it and it will keep on working and manage itself regardless of how many notes we add to the ArrayList. It also has built in features for handling things like neat formatting and detecting which item in a list was clicked.

We will need to override some methods of RecyclerAdapter and add a little code of our own.

What we will do to set up RecyclerView with RecyclerAdapter and an ArrayList of notes

Look at this outline of the required steps so we know what to expect when we do this next. To get the whole thing up and running, we would do the following:

1. Delete the temporary button and related code and then add a RecyclerView to our layout with a specific id property.

2. Create an XML layout to represent each item in the list. We have already mentioned that each item in the list will be a LinearLayout that contains 3 TextView widgets.

3. Create a new class that extends RecyclerAdapter and add code to several overridden methods to control how it looks and behaves, including using our list item layout and ArrayList full of Note instances.

4. Add code in `MainActivity` to use the `RecyclerAdapter` and the `RecyclerView` and bind it to our `ArrayList` instance.

5. Add an `ArrayList` to `MainActivity` to hold all our notes and update the `createNewNote` method to add any new notes created in the `DialogNewNote` class to this `ArrayList`.

Let's go through each of those steps in detail.

Adding RecyclerView, RecyclerAdapter, and ArrayList to the Note to Self project

Open the Note to Self project. As a reminder, if you want to see the completed code and working app based on completing this chapter, it can be found in the `Chapter 16/Note to self` folder.

 As the required action in this chapter jumps around between different files, classes, and methods, I encourage you to follow along with the files from the download bundle for reference open in your preferred text editor.

Removing the temporary Show Note button and adding the RecyclerView

These next few steps will get rid of the temporary code we added in *Chapter 14, Android Dialog Windows*, and set up our `RecyclerView` ready for binding to the `RecyclerAdapter` later in the chapter:

1. In the `content_main.xml` file, remove the temporary `Button` with an `id` of `button`, which we added previously for testing purposes.

2. In the `onCreate` method of `MainActivity.java`, delete the `Button` declaration and initialization, along with the anonymous class that handles its clicks, as this code now creates an error. We will delete some more temporary code later in this chapter. Delete the code shown next:

```
// Temporary code
Button button = (Button) findViewById(R.id.button);
button.setOnClickListener(new View.OnClickListener() {
    @Override
    public void onClick(View v) {

        // Create a new DialogShowNote called dialog
```

```
                    DialogShowNote dialog = new DialogShowNote();

                    // Send the note via the sendNoteSelected method
                    dialog.sendNoteSelected(mTempNote);

                    // Create the dialog
                    dialog.show(getSupportFragmentManager(), "123");
            }
      });
```

3. Now switch back to `content_main.xml` in design view and drag a **RecyclerView** from the **Common** category of the palette onto the layout.

4. Set its `id` property to `recyclerView`.

5. Now we have removed the temporary UI aspects from our project and we have a `RecyclerView` complete with a unique id ready to be referenced from our Java code shortly.

Creating a list item for the RecyclerView

Next, we need a layout to represent each item in our `RecyclerView`. As previously mentioned, we will use a `LinearLayout` that holds three `TextView` widgets.

These are the steps needed to create a list item for use within our `RecyclerView`:

1. Right-click on the `layout` folder in the project explorer and select **New | Layout resource file**. Enter `listitem` in the **Name:** field and make the **Root element:** `LinearLayout`. The default orientation attribute is vertical, which is just what we need.

2. Look at the next screenshot to see what we are trying to achieve with the remaining steps of this section. I have annotated it to show what each part will be in the finished app:

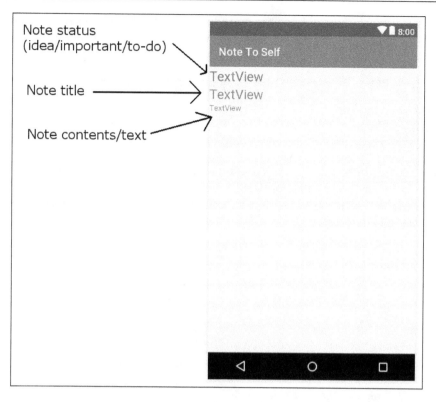

3. Drag three TextView instances onto the layout, one above the other, as per the reference screenshot. The first (top) will hold the note status/type (idea/ important/to do/). The second (middle) will hold the note title, and the third (bottom) the note itself.

4. Configure the various attributes of the LinearLayout and the TextView widgets, as shown in the following table:

Widget type	Property	Value to set to
LinearLayout	layout_height	wrap_contents
LinearLayout	Layout_Margin all	5dp
TextView (top)	id	textViewStatus
TextView (top)	textSize	24sp
TextView (top)	textColor	@color/colorAccent
TextView (middle)	id	textViewTitle
TextView (middle)	textSize	24sp
TextView (top)	id	textViewDescription

Now we have a `RecylerView` for the main layout and a layout to use for each item in the list. We can go ahead and code our `RecyclerAdapter` implementation.

Coding the RecyclerAdapter class

We will now create and code a brand-new class. Let's call our new class `NoteAdapter`. Create a new class called `NoteAdapter` in the same folder as the `MainActivity` class (and all the other classes).

Edit the code for the `NoteAdapter` class by adding these `import` statements and extending with the `RecyclerView.Adapter` class, and add these two important member variables. Edit the `NoteAdapter` class to be the same as the following code that we have just discussed:

```
import android.view.LayoutInflater;
import android.view.View;
import android.view.ViewGroup;
import android.widget.TextView;

import java.util.List;

import androidx.recyclerview.widget.RecyclerView;

public class NoteAdapter extends
    RecyclerView.Adapter<NoteAdapter.ListItemHolder> {

    private List<Note> mNoteList;
    private MainActivity mMainActivity;
}
```

Notice the class declaration is underlined in red, showing there is an error in our code. The error is because the `RecylerView.Adapter` class (which we are extending) needs us to override some of its abstract methods.

 We discussed abstract classes and their methods in *Chapter 11, More Object-Oriented Programming.*

The quickest way to do this is to click the class declaration, hold the *Alt* key, and then tap the *Enter* key. Choose **Implement methods,** as shown in the next screenshot:

This process adds the following three methods:

- The `onCreateViewHolder` method, which is called when a layout for a list item is required.

- The `onBindViewHolder` method, which is called when the `RecyclerAdapter` is bound (connected/associated with) the `RecyclerView` in the layout.

- The `getItemCount` method, which will be used to return the number of Note instances in the `ArrayList`. Now it just returns zero.

We will soon add code to each of these methods to do the required work at the specific time.

Note, however, that we still have multiple errors in our code, including in the auto-generated methods, as well as the class declaration. A screenshot of the code editor at this stage might be useful:

```
public class NoteAdapter extends
            RecyclerView.Adapter<NoteAdapter.ListItemHolder> {

    private List<Note> mNoteList;
    private MainActivity mMainActivity;
                                                    Error

    @NonNull
    @Override
    public NoteAdapter.ListItemHolder onCreateViewHolder(@NonNull ViewGroup parent, int viewType) {
        return null;
    }

    @Override                          Error
    public void onBindViewHolder(@NonNull NoteAdapter.ListItemHolder holder, int position) {

    }
                                                    Error
    @Override
    public int getItemCount() {
        return 0;
    }
}
```

The errors are because the `NoteAdapter.ListItemHolder` class does not exist. `ListItemHolder` was added by us when we extended `NoteAdapter`. It is our chosen class type which will be used as the holder for each list item. At the moment, it doesn't exist – hence the error. The two methods that also have the same error for the same reason were auto-generated when we asked Android Studio to implement the missing methods.

Let's solve the problem by making a start on the required `ListItemHolder` class. It is useful to us for `ListItemHolder` instances to share data/variables with `NoteAdapter`; therefore, we will create `ListItemHolder` as an inner class.

Click the error in the class declaration and select **Create class 'ListItemHolder,'** as shown in this next screenshot:

```
public class NoteAdapter extends
            RecyclerView.Adapter<NoteAdapter.ListItemHolder> {
                                          Create class 'ListItemHolder'
    private List<Note> mNoteList;         Create enum 'ListItemHolder'
    private MainActivity mMainActivity;   Create interface 'ListItemHolder'

)   @NonNull                              Create Test                    ▶
)   @Override                             Create subclass                ▶
:   public NoteAdapter.ListItemHolder onCreateViewH  Unimplement Class   ▶ ent, int viewType) {
        return null;
)   }
```

The following code has been added to the `NoteAdapter` class:

```
public class ListItemHolder {
}
```

But there is still one error with the class declaration, as shown next in this screenshot:

```
14      public class NoteAdapter extends
16              RecyclerView.Adapter<NoteAdapter.ListItemHolder> {
```
Type parameter 'com.gamecodeschool.notetoself.NoteAdapter.ListItemHolder' is not within its bound; should extend 'androidx.recyclerview.widget.RecyclerView.ViewHolder'

The error message reads **... should extend 'android.recylerview.widget. RecyclerView.ViewHolder',** because we may have added `ListItemHolder`, but `ListItemHolder` must also extend `RecyclerView.ViewHolder` in order to be used as the parameterized type.

Amend the declaration of the `ListItemHolder` class to match this code:

```
public class ListItemHolder extends
    RecyclerView.ViewHolder
    implements View.OnClickListener {

}
```

Now the error is gone from the `NoteAdapter` class declaration, but because we implemented `View.OnClickListener`, we need to implement the `onClick` method. Furthermore, `ViewHolder` doesn't provide a default constructor, so we need to do it. Add the following `onClick` method (empty for now) and this constructor method (empty for now) to the `ListItemHolder` class:

```
public ListItemHolder(View view) {
    super(view);
}

@Override
public void onClick(View view) {
}
```

[Be sure you added the code to the inner `ListItemHolder` class and not the `NoteAdapter` class.]

After much tinkering and auto-generating, we finally have an error-free `NoteAdapter` class, complete with overridden methods and inner class that we can code to get our `RecyclerAdapter` working. In addition, we can write code to respond to clicks (in `onClick`) on each of our `ListItemHolder` instances.

Coding the NoteAdapter constructor

Next, we will code the `NoteAdapter` constructor, which will initialize the members of the `NoteAdapter` class. Add this constructor shown next to the `NoteAdapter` class:

```
public NoteAdapter(MainActivity mainActivity,
                        List<Note> noteList) {

    mMainActivity = mainActivity;
    mNoteList = noteList;
}
```

First, notice the parameters of the constructor. It receives a `MainActivity` as well as a `List`. This implies that when we use this class, we will need to send in a reference to the main activity of this app (`MainActivity`), as well as a `List`/`ArrayList`. We will see what use we put the `MainActivity` reference to shortly, but we can sensibly guess that the reference to a `List` with a parameterized type of `<Note>` will be a reference to our `ArrayList` of `Note` instances, which we will soon code in the `MainActivity` class. `NoteAdapter` will then hold a permanent reference to all the users' notes.

Coding the onCreateViewHolder method

Next, we will adapt the auto-generated `onCreateViewHolder`. Add the two highlighted lines of code to the `onCreateViewHolder` method and study the parameters that were auto-generated:

```
@NonNull
@Override
public NoteAdapter.ListItemHolder onCreateViewHolder(
        @NonNull ViewGroup parent, int viewType) {

    View itemView = LayoutInflater.from(parent.getContext())
                .inflate(R.layout.listitem, parent, false);

    return new ListItemHolder(itemView);
}
```

This code works by initializing `itemView` using `LayoutInflater` and our newly designed `listitem` layout. It then returns a new `ListItemHolder` instance, complete with an inflated and ready-to-use layout.

Coding the onBindViewHolder method

Next, we will adapt the `onBindViewHolder` method. Add the highlighted code to make the method the same as this code, and also make sure to study the parameters as well:

```
@Override
public void onBindViewHolder(
@NonNull NoteAdapter.ListItemHolder holder, int position) {

        Note note = mNoteList.get(position);
        holder.mTitle.setText(note.getTitle());
        // Show the first 15 characters of the actual note
// Unless a short note then show half
```

```
if(note.getDescription().length() > 15) {
        holder.mDescription.setText(note.getDescription()
        .substring(0, 15));
}
else{
        holder.mDescription.setText(note.getDescription()
        .substring(0, note.getDescription().length() /2 ));
}


    // What is the status of the note?
    if(note.isIdea()){
            holder.mStatus.setText(R.string.idea_text);
    }
    else if(note.isImportant()){
            holder.mStatus.setText(R.string.important_text);
    }
    else if(note.isTodo()){
            holder.mStatus.setText(R.string.todo_text);
    }
}
```

First, the code checks whether the note is longer than 15 characters, and if it is, it truncates it so it looks sensible in the list.

Then it checks what type of note it is (idea/to-do/important) and assigns the appropriate label from the String resources.

This new code has left some errors in the code with `holder.mTitle`, `holder.mDescription`, and `holder.mStatus` variables, because we need to add them to our `ListItemHolder` inner class. We will do this very soon.

Coding getItemCount

Amend the `return` statement in this auto-generated method to be the same as the highlighted line of code shown next:

```
@Override
public int getItemCount() {
    return mNoteList.size();
}
```

This code is used internally by the class and it supplies the current number of items in the `ArrayList`.

Coding the ListItemHolder inner class

Now we can turn our attention to the inner class, `ListItemHolder`. Adapt the `ListItemHolder` inner class by adding the highlighted code:

```
public class ListItemHolder
    extends RecyclerView.ViewHolder
    implements View.OnClickListener {

    TextView mTitle;
    TextView mDescription;
    TextView mStatus;

    public ListItemHolder(View view) {
            super(view);
            mTitle = (TextView)
                    view.findViewById(R.id.textViewTitle);

            mDescription = (TextView)
                    view.findViewById(R.id.textViewDescription);

            mStatus = (TextView)
                    view.findViewById(R.id.textViewStatus);

            view.setClickable(true);
            view.setOnClickListener(this);
    }

    @Override
    public void onClick(View view) {
            mMainActivity.showNote(getAdapterPosition());
    }
}
```

The `ListItemHolder` constructor just gets a reference to each of the `TextView` widgets in the layout. The final two lines of code set the whole view as clickable so that the OS will call the next method we discuss, `onClick`, when a holder is clicked.

In `onClick`, the call to `mMainActivity.showNote` has an error because the method doesn't exist yet, but we will fix that in the next section. The call will simply show the clicked note in its `DialogFragment`.

Coding MainActivity to use the RecyclerView and RecyclerAdapter classes

Now switch over to the MainActivity class in the editor window. Add these three new members to the MainActivity class and remove the temporary code shown commented out next:

```
// Temporary code
//Note mTempNote = new Note();

private List<Note> noteList = new ArrayList<>();
private RecyclerView recyclerView;
private NoteAdapter mAdapter;
```

These three members are our ArrayList for all our Note instances, our RecyclerView instance, and an instance of our NoteAdapter class.

Adding code to onCreate

Add the following highlighted code in the onCreate method after the code that handles presses on the floating action button (shown again for context):

```
fab.setOnClickListener(new View.OnClickListener() {
    @Override
    public void onClick(View view) {
        DialogNewNote dialog = new DialogNewNote();
        dialog.show(getSupportFragmentManager(), "");
    }
});


recyclerView = (RecyclerView)
    findViewById(R.id.recyclerView);

mAdapter = new NoteAdapter(this, noteList);
RecyclerView.LayoutManager mLayoutManager =
    new LinearLayoutManager(getApplicationContext());

recyclerView.setLayoutManager(mLayoutManager);
recyclerView.setItemAnimator(new DefaultItemAnimator());

// Add a neat dividing line between items in the list
recyclerView.addItemDecoration(
```

```
        new DividerItemDecoration(this, LinearLayoutManager.VERTICAL));

    // set the adapter
    recyclerView.setAdapter(mAdapter);
```

Here we initialize `recyclerView` with the `RecyclerView` in the layout. Our `NoteAdapter` (`mAdapter`) is initialized by calling the constructor we coded. Note that a reference to `MainActivity` (`this`) and the `ArrayList` is passed in, just as required by the class we have coded previously.

Next, we create a new object: a `LayoutManager`. In the next line of code, we call `setLayoutManager` on `recyclerView` and pass in this new `LayoutManager` instance. Now we can configure some properties of `recyclerView`.

The `setItemAnimator` and `addItemDecoration` methods make each list item a little more visually enhanced with a separator line between each item in the list. Later, when we build a settings screen, we will give the user the option to add or remove this separator.

The last thing we do is call `setAdapter`, which combines our adapter with our view.

Now we will make some changes to the `addNote` method.

Modifying the addNote method

In the `addNote` method, delete the temporary code we added in *Chapter 14, Android Dialog Windows,* (shown commented out) and add the new highlighted code shown next:

```
public void createNewNote(Note n){
    // Temporary code
    //mTempNote = n;
    noteList.add(n);
    mAdapter.notifyDataSetChanged();
}
```

The new highlighted code adds a note to the `ArrayList` instead of simply initializing a solitary `Note` object, which has now been commented out. Then we need to call `notifyDataSetChanged`, which lets our adapter know that a new note has been added.

Coding the showNote method

Add this new method, which is called from the `NoteAdapter`, using the reference to this class that was passed into the `NoteAdapter` constructor. Or, more accurately, it is called from the `ListerItemHolder` inner class when one of the items in the `RecyclerView` is tapped by the user. Add the `showNote` method to the `MainActivity` class:

```
public void showNote(int noteToShow){
    DialogShowNote dialog = new DialogShowNote();
    dialog.sendNoteSelected(noteList.get(noteToShow));
    dialog.show(getSupportFragmentManager(), "");
}
```

 All the errors in the `NoteAdapter.java` file are now gone.

The code just added will launch a new instance of `DialogShowNote`, passing in the specific required note as pointed to by `noteToShow`.

Running the app

You can now run the app and enter a new note, as shown in this next screenshot:

After you have entered several notes of several types, the list (`RecyclerView`) will look something like this next screenshot:

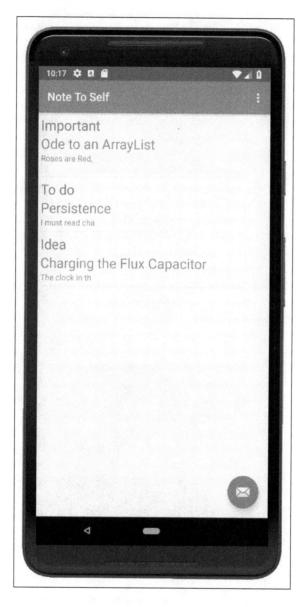

And, if you click to view one of the notes, it will look like this:

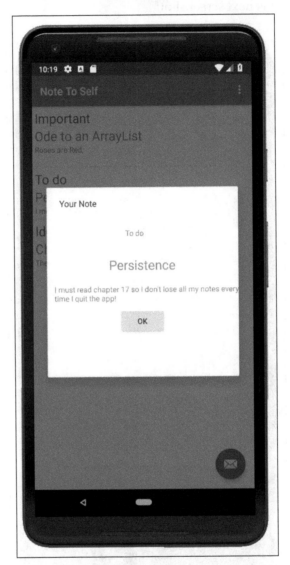

Reader challenge

We could have spent more time formatting the layouts of our two dialog windows. Why not refer to *Chapter 5, Beautiful Layouts with CardView and ScrollView*, as well as the Material Design website, and do a better job than this. Furthermore, you could enhance the `RecyclerView`/list of notes by using `CardView` instead of `LinearLayout`.

Don't spend too long adding new notes, however, because there is a slight problem: close and restart the app. Uh oh, all the notes are gone!

Frequently asked questions

Q1) I still don't understand how `RecyclerAdapter` works...

A) That's because we haven't really discussed it. The reason we have not discussed the behind-the-scenes details is because we don't need to know them. If we override the required methods, as we have just seen, everything will work. This is how `RecyclerAdapter` and most other classes we use are meant to be — hidden implementation with public methods to expose the necessary functionality.

Q2) I feel like I *need* to know what is going on inside `RecyclerAdapter` and other classes as well.

A) It is true that there are more details for `RecyclerAdapter` (and almost every class that we use in this book) that we don't have the space to discuss. It is good practice to read the official documentation of the classes you use. You can read more about it here: `https://developer.android.com/reference/android/support/v7/widget/RecyclerView.Adapter`.

Summary

Now we have added the ability to hold multiple notes and implemented the ability to display them.

We achieved this by learning about and using the `RecyclerAdapter` class, which implements the `Adapter` interface, which allows us to bind together a `RecyclerView` and an `ArrayList`, allowing for the seamless display of data without us (the programmer) having to worry about the complex code that is part of these classes and that we don't even see.

In the next chapter, we will start with making the user's notes persist when they quit the app or switch off their device. In addition, we will create a settings screen and see how we can make the settings persist as well. We will use different techniques to achieve each of these goals.

17
Data Persistence and Sharing

In this chapter, we will look at a couple of different ways to save data to an Android device's permanent storage. Also, for the first time, we will add a second `Activity` to our app. It often makes sense when implementing a separate "screen," such as a settings screen, in our app to do so in a new `Activity`. We could go to the trouble of hiding the original UI and then showing the new UI, but this would quickly lead to confusing and error-prone code. So, we will see how to add an `Activity` and navigate the user between them.

In summary, in this chapter, we will do the following:

- Learn about Android Intents to switch `Activity` and pass data
- Create a simple (very simple) settings screen in a new `Activity`
- Persist the settings screen data using the `SharedPreferences` class
- Learn about **JavaScript Object Notation (JSON)** for serialization
- Explore Java's `try-catch-finally`
- Implement saving data in our Note to Self app

Android Intents

The `Intent` class is appropriately named. It is a class that demonstrates the intent of an `Activity` from our app. It makes intent clear and it also facilitates it.

All our apps so far have had just one `Activity`, but many Android apps are comprised of more than one.

In perhaps its most common use, an `Intent` allows us to switch between Activities. But, of course, Activities are classes. So, what happens to the data when we switch between them? Intents handle this problem for us as well by allowing us to pass data between Activities.

Intents aren't just about wiring up the Activities of our app. They also make it possible to interact with other apps, too. For example, we could provide a link in our app for the user to send an email, make a phone call, interact with social media, or open a web page in a browser, and have the email, dialler, web browser, or relevant social media app do all the work.

There aren't enough pages to really dig deep into interacting with other apps, and so we will mainly focus on switching between Activities and passing data.

Switching Activity

Let's say we have an app with two `Activity`-based classes, because we will soon. We can assume that, as usual, we have an `Activity` called `MainActivity`, which is where the app starts, and a second Activity called `SettingsActivity`. This is how we can swap from `MainActivity` to `SettingsActivity`:

```
// Declare and initialize a new Intent object called myIntent
Intent myIntent = new  Intent(this, SettingsActivity.class);

// Switch to the SettingsActivity
startActivity(myIntent);
```

Look carefully at how we initialized the `Intent` object. `Intent` has a constructor that takes two arguments. The first is a reference to the current `Activity`, `this`. The second parameter is the name of the `Activity` we want to open, `SettingsActivity.class`. The `.class` on the end of `SettingsActivity` makes it the full name of the Activity as declared in the `AndroidManifest.xml` file, and we will peek at that when we experiment with `Intent`s shortly.

The only problem is that `SettingsActivity` doesn't share any of the data of `MainActivity`. In a way, this is a good thing, because if you need all the data from `MainActivity`, then it is a reasonable indication that switching Activities might not be the best way of proceeding with your app's design. It is, however, unreasonable to have encapsulation so thorough that the two Activities know absolutely nothing about each other.

Passing data between Activities

What if we have a sign-in screen for the user and we want to pass the login credentials to each `Activity` of our app? We could do so using Intents.

We can add data to an `Intent` like this:

```
// Create a String called username
// and set its value to bob
String username = "Bob";

// Create a new Intent as we have already seen
Intent myIntent = new Intent(this, SettingsActivity.class);

// Add the username String to the Intent
// using the putExtra method of the Intent class
myIntent.putExtra("USER_NAME", username);

// Start the new Activity as we have before
startActivity(myIntent);
```

In `SettingsActivity`, we could then retrieve the `String` like this:

```
// Here we need an Intent also
// But the default constructor will do
// as we are not switching Activity
Intent myIntent = new Intent();

// Initialize username with the passed in String
String username = intent.getExtra().getStringKey("USER_NAME");
```

In the previous two blocks of code, we switched `Activity` in the same way as we have already seen. But, before we called `startActivity`, we used the `putExtra` method to load a String into the intent.

We add data using **key-value pairs**. Each piece of data needs to be accompanied by an `identifier` that can be used in the retrieving `Activity` to identify and retrieve the data.

The identifier name is arbitrary, but useful/memorable values should be used.

Then, in the receiving `Activity`, we simply create an `Intent` using the default constructor:

```
Intent myIntent = new Intent();
```

We can then retrieve the data using the `getExtras` method and the appropriate identifier from the key-value pair.

Once we want to start sending more than a few values, it is worth considering different tactics.

The `Intent` class can help us send more complex data than this, but the `Intent` class has its limits. For example, we wouldn't be able to send a `Note` object.

Adding a settings page to Note to Self

Now that we are armed with all this knowledge about the Android `Intent` class, we can add another screen (`Activity`) to our Note to Self app – a Settings screen.

We will first create a new `Activity` for our Settings screen and see what effect that has on the `AndroidManifest.xml` file. We will then create a very simple layout for our Settings screen and add the Java code to switch from `MainActivity` to the new one. We will, however, defer wiring up our Settings screen with Java until we have learned how to save the settings to disk. We will do this later this chapter and then come back to the Settings screen to make it persist.

First, let's create that new `Activity`. We will call it `SettingsActivity`.

Creating the SettingsActivity

This will be a screen where the user can turn the decorative divider between each note in the `RecyclerView` on or off. This will not be the most comprehensive settings screen, but it will be a useful exercise, and we will learn how to switch between activities as well as save data to disk. Follow these steps to get started:

1. In the project explorer, right-click the folder that contains all your `.java` files and has the same name as your package. From the pop-up context menu, select **New | Activity | Empty Activity**.
2. In the **Activity Name:** field, enter `SettingsActivity`.
3. Leave all the other options at their defaults and left-click **Finish**.

Android Studio has created a new `Activity` for us and its associated `.java` file. Let's take a quick peek at some of the work that was done behind the scenes for us, because it is useful to know what is going on.

Open the `AndroidManifest.xml` file from within the `manifests` folder in the project explorer. Notice the following few lines of code near the end of this file:

```
<activity
            android:name=".SettingsActivity"
            android:label="@string/title_activity_settings"
            android:theme="@style/AppTheme.NoActionBar">
</activity>
```

This is how an `Activity` is **registered** with the operating system. If an `Activity` is not registered, then an attempt to run it will crash the app. We could create an `Activity` simply by creating a class that extends `Activity` (or `AppCompatActivity`) in a new `.java` file. However, we would then have had to add the preceding code ourselves. Also, by using the new Activity wizard, we got a layout XML file (`activity_settings.xml` and `content_settings.xml`) automatically generated for us.

Designing the Settings screen layout

We will quickly build a user interface for our settings screen; the following steps and screenshot should make this straightforward:

1. Open the `activity_settings.xml` file, switch to the **Design** tab, and we will quickly lay out our settings screen.

2. Delete the floating action button (fab) that was put in automatically.

3. Switch to `SettingsActivity.java` and remove all the code related to the just-deleted floating action button. This is to avoid errors when we run the app. For clarity, here is the code you need to delete (formatted slightly differently):

```
FloatingActionButton fab =
    (FloatingActionButton) findViewById(R.id.fab);

fab.setOnClickListener(new View.OnClickListener() {

@Override
public void onClick(View view) {
        Snackbar.make(view,
        "Replace with your own action",
        Snackbar.LENGTH_LONG)
                    .setAction("Action", null).show();
    }

});
```

4. Switch to the `content_settings.xml` file and again make sure that you are in the design view.

5. Use the following screenshot as a guide while following the rest of these steps:

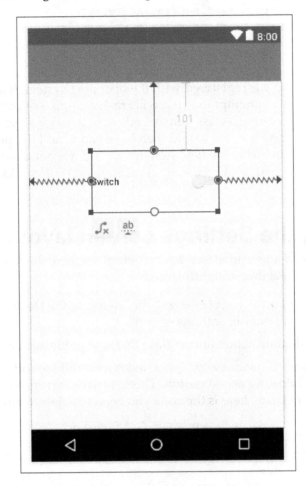

6. Drag and drop a **Switch** onto the center-top of the layout. I stretched mine by dragging the edges to make it nice and clear.

7. Add an `id` attribute of `switch1` (if it isn't there already) so that we can interact with it using Java.

8. Use the constraint handles to fix the position of the switch or click the **Infer Constraints** button to fix it automatically.

We now have a nice (and very simple) new layout for our settings screen and the `id` properties are in place, ready for when we wire it up with our Java code later in this chapter.

Enabling the user to switch to the settings screen

We already know how to switch to SettingsActivity. Also, as we won't be passing any data to it or from it, we can get this working with just two lines of Java.

You might have noticed in the action bar of our app that there is the menu icon. It is shown in the next screenshot:

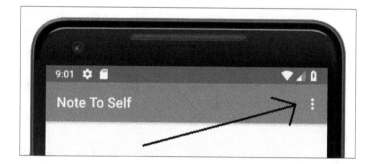

If you tap it, there will already be a menu option in there for **Settings**. This was provided by default when we first created the app. This is what you will see when you tap the menu icon:

All we need to do is place our code to switch to SettingsActivity within the onOptionsItemSelected method in the MainActivity.java file. Android Studio even provides an if block by default for us to paste our code into, on the assumption that we would one day want to add a settings menu. How thoughtful.

Switch to `MainActivity.java` in the editor window and find the following block
of code in the `onOptionsItemSelected` method:

```
//noinspection SimplifiableIfStatement
if (id == R.id.action_settings) {
    return true;
}
```

Add this code into the `if` block shown previously, just before the
`return true` statement:

```
Intent intent = new Intent(this, SettingsActivity.class);
startActivity(intent);
```

 You will need to import the `Intent` class using your preferred
technique to add this line of code:
```
import android.content.Intent;
```

You can now run the app and visit the new Settings screen by tapping the **Settings**
menu option. This screenshot shows the Settings screen running on the emulator:

To return from `SettingsActivity` to `MainActivity`, you can tap the back button on
the device.

Persisting data with SharedPreferences

In Android, there are a few ways to make data persist. By persist, I mean that if the user quits the app, then when they come back to it, their data is still available. What method is the correct one to use is dependent upon the app and the type of data.

In this book, we will look at three ways to make data persist. For saving our user's settings, we only need a simple method. After all, we just need to know whether they want the decorative divider between each of the notes in the `RecyclerView`.

Let's look at how we can make our apps save and reload variables to the internal storage of the device. We need to use `SharedPreferences` objects. `SharedPreferences` is a class that provides access to data that can be accessed and edited by all `Activity` classes of an app. Let's look at how we can use it:

```
// A SharedPreferences for reading data
SharedPreferences prefs;

// A SharedPreferences.Editor for writing data
SharedPreferences.Editor editor;
```

As with all objects, we need to initialize them before we can use them. We can initialize the `prefs` object using the `getSharedPreferences` method and passing in a `String` that will be used to refer to all the data read and written using this object. Typically, we could use the name of the app as this string. In the following code, `Mode_Private` means that any class, in this app only, can access it:

```
prefs = getSharedPreferences("My App", MODE_PRIVATE);
```

We then use our newly initialized `prefs` object to initialize our editor object by calling the `edit` method:

```
editor = prefs.edit();
```

Let's say we wanted to save the user's name, which we have in a String called `username`. We can then write the data to the internal memory of the device like this:

```
editor.putString("username", username);
editor.commit();
```

The first argument used in the `putString` method is a label that can be used to refer to the data, while the second is the actual variable that holds the data we want to save. The second line in the previous code initiates the saving process. So, we could write multiple variables to disk like this:

```
editor.putString("username", username);
editor.putInt("age", age);
```

```
editor.putBoolean("newsletter-subscriber", subscribed);

// Save all the above data
editor.commit();
```

The preceding code demonstrates that you can save other variable types and it, of course, assumes that the `username`, `age`, and `subscribed` variables have previously been declared and then initialized with appropriate values.

Once `editor.commit()` has executed, the data is stored. We can quit the app, even turn off the device, and the data will persist.

Reloading data with SharedPreferences

Let's see how we can reload our data the next time the app is run. This code will reload the three values that the previous code saved. We could even declare our variables and initialize them with the stored values:

```
String username   =
    prefs.getString("username", "new user");

int age   = prefs.getInt("age", -1);

boolean subscribed =
    prefs.getBoolean("newsletter-subscriber", false)
```

In the previous code, we load the data from disk using the method that's appropriate for the data type and the same label we used to save the data in the first place. What is less clear is the second argument to each of the method calls.

The `getString`, `getInt`, and `getBoolean` methods require a default value as the second parameter. If there is no data stored with that label, it will then return the default value.

We could then check for these default values in our code and go about trying to obtain the real values. For example:

```
if (age == -1){
    // Ask the user for his age
}
```

We now know enough to save our user's settings in Note to Self.

Making the Note to Self settings persist

We have already learned how to save data to the device's memory. As we implement saving the user's settings, we will also see how we handle `Switch` input and where exactly the code we have just seen will go to make our app work the way we want it to.

Coding the SettingsActivity class

Most of the action will take place in the `SettingsActivity.java` file. So, click on the appropriate tab and we will add the code a bit at a time.

First, we need some member variables that will give us a working `SharedPreferences` and `Editor` reference. We also want a member variable to represent the user's settings option – whether they want decorative dividers or not.

Add the following member variables to `SettingsActivity`:

```
private SharedPreferences mPrefs;
private SharedPreferences.Editor mEditor;

private boolean mShowDividers;
```

 Import the `SharedPreferences` class:
```
import android.content.SharedPreferences;
```

Now, in `onCreate`, add the highlighted code to initialize `mPrefs` and `mEditor`:

```
mPrefs = getSharedPreferences("Note to self", MODE_PRIVATE);
mEditor = mPrefs.edit();
```

Next, still in `onCreate`, let's get a reference to our switch and load up the saved data, which represents our user's previous choice for whether to show the dividers. We get a reference to the switch in the same way that we did in *Chapter 13, Anonymous Classes – Bringing Android Widgets to Life*. Notice that the default value is `true` in order to show the dividers. We will also set the switch to either on or off as appropriate:

```
mShowDividers  = mPrefs.getBoolean("dividers", true);

Switch switch1 = (Switch) findViewById(R.id.switch1);
// Set the switch on or off as appropriate
switch1.setChecked(mShowDividers)
```

You will need to import the Switch class:

import android.widget.Switch;

Next, we create an anonymous class to listen for and handle changes to our Switch widget.

When the isChecked variable is true, we use prefs to set the dividers label and the mShowDividers variable to true; when it is not checked, we set them both to false.

Add the following code to the onCreate method, which we have just discussed:

```
switch1.setOnCheckedChangeListener(
        new CompoundButton.OnCheckedChangeListener() {

                public void onCheckedChanged(
                        CompoundButton buttonView,
                            boolean isChecked) {

                    if(isChecked){
                            mEditor.putBoolean(
                                        "dividers", true);

                            mShowDividers = true;

                    }else{
                            mEditor.putBoolean(
                                        "dividers", false);

                            mShowDividers = false;
                    }
                }
        }
);
```

You will need to import the CompoundButton class:

import android.widget.CompoundButton;

You might have noticed that at no point in any of that code did we call mEditor. comit to save the user's settings. We could have placed it after we detected a change to the switch, but it is much simpler to put it where it is guaranteed to be called, but only once.

We will use our knowledge of the `Activity` life cycle and override the `onPause` method. When the user leaves the `SettingsActivity` either to go back to `MainActivity` or to quit the app, `onPause` will be called and the settings will be saved. Add this code to override `onPause` and save the users settings. Add the code just before the closing curly brace of the `SettingsActivity` class:

```
@Override
protected void onPause() {
    super.onPause();

    // Save the settings here
    mEditor.commit();
}
```

Finally, we can add some code to `MainActivity` to load the settings when the app starts or when the user switches back from the settings screen to the main screen.

Coding the MainActivity class

Add the following highlighted code to add some member variables after our `NoteAdapter`:

```
private List<Note> noteList = new ArrayList<>();
private RecyclerView recyclerView;
private NoteAdapter mAdapter;
private boolean mShowDividers;
private SharedPreferences mPrefs;
```

 Import the `SharedPreferences` class:
`import android.content.SharedPreferences;`

Now, we have a `boolean` member to decide whether to show the dividers and a `SharedPreferences` instance to read the settings from disk.

Now, we will override the `onResume` method and initialize our `mPrefs` variable, and then load the settings into the `mShowDividers` variable.

Add the overridden `onResume` method, as shown in the following code, to the `MainActivity` class:

```
@Override
protected void onResume(){
    super.onResume();

    mPrefs = getSharedPreferences(
```

```
        "Note to self", MODE_PRIVATE);

    mShowDividers   = mPrefs.getBoolean(
        "dividers", true);
}
```

The user is now able to choose their settings. The app will both save and reload them as necessary, but we need to make MainActivity respond to the user's choice.

Find this code in the onCreate method and delete it:

```
// Add a neat dividing line between items in the list
recyclerView.addItemDecoration(
    new DividerItemDecoration(
    this, LinearLayoutManager.VERTICAL));
```

The previous code is what set the dividers between each note in the list. Add this new code to the onResume method, which is the same line of code surrounded by an if statement, to selectively use dividers only when mShowDividers is true. Add the code after the previous code in onResume:

```
if(mShowDividers) {
    // Add a neat dividing line between list items
    recyclerView.addItemDecoration(
        new DividerItemDecoration(
        this, LinearLayoutManager.VERTICAL));
}else{
    // check there are some dividers
// or the app will crash
if(recyclerView.getItemDecorationCount() > 0) {
        recyclerView.removeItemDecorationAt(0);
}
}
```

Run the app and you'll notice that the dividers are gone; go to the settings screen, switch on the dividers, and return to the main screen (with the back button), and behold: there are now separators. The following screenshot shows the list with and without separators, photoshopped side by side, to illustrate that the switch works, and that the settings persist between the two Activity classes:

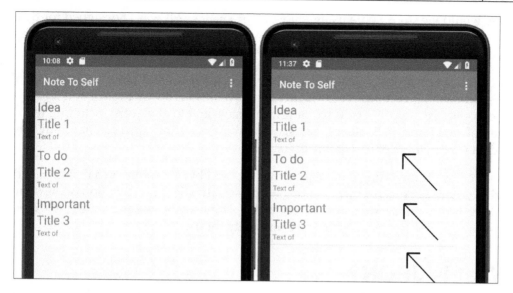

Make sure to try quitting the app and restarting it to verify that the settings are saved to disk. You can even turn the emulator off and back on again and the settings will persist.

Now, we have a neat settings screen and we can permanently save the users choices. Of course, the big missing link with regard to persistence is that the user's fundamental data – their notes – still does not persist.

More advanced persistence

Let's think about what we need to do. We want to save a bunch of notes to the internal storage. Being more specific, we want to store a selection of Strings and related Boolean values. These Strings and Boolean values represent the user's note title, the note's text, and whether it is a to-do, important, or idea.

Given what we already know about the SharedPreferences class, at first glance, this might not seem especially challenging – until we dig a little deeper into our requirements. What if the user loves our app and ends up with 100 notes? We would need 100 identifiers for key-value pairs. Not impossible, but it would start to get awkward.

Now, consider that we want to enhance the app and give the user the ability to add dates to them. Android has a Date class, which is perfect for this. It would be reasonably straightforward to then add neat features such as reminders to our app. But when it comes to saving data, suddenly, things start to get complicated.

How would we store a date using `SharedPreferences`? It wasn't designed for this. We could convert it to a string when we save it and convert it back again when we load it, but this is far from simple.

And, as our app grows in features and our users get more and more notes, the whole persistence thing becomes a nightmare. What we need is a way to save and load objects – actual Java objects. If we can simply save and load objects, including their internal data (Strings, Booleans, dates, or anything else), our apps can have any kind of data we can think of to suit our users.

The process of converting data objects into bits and bytes to store on a disk is called **serialization;** the reverse process is called **de-serialization**. Serialization on its own is a vast topic and far from straightforward. Fortunately, as we are coming to expect, there is a class to handle most of the complexity for us.

What is JSON?

JSON stands for **JavaScript Object Notation,** and it is widely used in fields beyond Android and the Java language. It is perhaps more frequently used for sending data between web applications and servers.

Fortunately, there are JSON classes available for Android that almost entirely hide the complexity of the serialization process. By learning about a few more Java concepts, we can quickly begin to use these classes and start writing entire Java objects to the device storage rather than worry ourselves about what primitive types make up the objects.

The JSON classes, when compared with other classes we have seen so far, undertake operations that have a higher than normal possibility of failure beyond their control. To find out why this is so and what can be done about it, let's look at Java exceptions.

Java exceptions – try, catch, and finally

All this talk of JSON requires us to learn a new Java concept: **exceptions**. When we write a class that performs operations that have a possibility of failure, especially for reasons beyond our control, it is advisable to make this plain in our code so that anyone using our class is prepared for the possibility.

Saving and loading data is one such scenario where failure is possible beyond our control. Think about trying to load data when the SD card has been removed or has been corrupted. Another instance where code might fail is perhaps when we write code that relies on a network connection – what if the user goes offline part of the way through a data transfer?

Java exceptions are the solution and the JSON classes use them, so it is a good time to learn about them.

When we write a class that uses code with a chance of failure, we can prepare the users of our class by using exceptions with `try`, `catch`, and `finally`.

We can write methods in our classes using the `throws` Java keyword at the end of the signature. A bit like this, perhaps:

```
public void somePrecariousMethod() throws someException{
    // Risky code goes here
}
```

Now, any code that uses the `somePrecariousMethod` will need to **handle** the exception. The way that we handle exceptions is by wrapping code in `try` and `catch` blocks. Perhaps like this:

```
try{
    ...
    somePrecariousMethod();
    ...
}catch(someException e){
    Log.e("Exception:" + e, "Uh ohh")
    // Take action if possible
}
```

Optionally, we can also add a `finally` block if we want to take any further action after the `try` and `catch` blocks:

```
finally{
    // More action here
}
```

In our Note to Self app, we will take the minimum of necessary action to handle exceptions and simply output an error to logcat, but you could do things such as notify the user, retry the operation, or put some clever back-up plan into operation.

Backing up user data in Note to Self

So, with our new-found insight into exceptions, let's modify our Note to Self code and then we can be introduced to `JSONObject` and `JSONException`.

First, let's make some minor modifications to our `Note` class.

Add some more members that will act as the key in a key-value pair for each aspect of our Note class:

```
private static final String JSON_TITLE = "title";
private static final String JSON_DESCRIPTION = "description";
private static final String JSON_IDEA = "idea";
private static final String JSON_TODO = "todo";
private static final String JSON_IMPORTANT = "important";
```

Now, add a constructor and empty default constructor that receives a JSONObject and throws a JSONException. The body of the constructor initializes each of the members that define the properties of a single Note object by calling the getString or getBoolean method of the JSONObject, passing in the key as an argument. We also provide an empty default constructor, which is required now that we are providing our specialized constructor:

```
// Constructor
// Only used when new is called with a JSONObject
public Note(JSONObject jo) throws JSONException {

    mTitle =  jo.getString(JSON_TITLE);
    mDescription = jo.getString(JSON_DESCRIPTION);
    mIdea = jo.getBoolean(JSON_IDEA);
    mTodo = jo.getBoolean(JSON_TODO);
    mImportant = jo.getBoolean(JSON_IMPORTANT);
}

// Now we must provide an empty default constructor
// for when we create a Note as we provide a
// specialized constructor.
public Note (){

}
```

> You will need to import the JSONException and
> JSONObject classes:
> ```
> import org.json.JSONException;
> import org.json.JSONObject;
> ```

The next code we will see will load the member variables of a given Note object into a JSONObject. This is where the Note object's members are packed up as a single JSONObject, ready for when the actual serialization takes place.

All we need to do is call `put` with the appropriate key and the matching member variable. This method returns a `JSONObject` (we will see where in a minute) and also throws a `JSONObject` exception. Add the code we have just discussed:

```
public JSONObject convertToJSON() throws JSONException{

    JSONObject jo = new JSONObject();

    jo.put(JSON_TITLE, mTitle);
    jo.put(JSON_DESCRIPTION, mDescription);
    jo.put(JSON_IDEA, mIdea);
    jo.put(JSON_TODO, mTodo);
    jo.put(JSON_IMPORTANT, mImportant);

    return jo;
}
```

Now, let's make a `JSONSerializer` class, which will perform the actual serialization and deserialization. Create a new class and call it `JSONSerializer`.

Let's split it up into a few chunks and talk about what we are doing as we code each chunk.

First, we need to deal with the declaration and a couple of member variables: a String to hold the filename where the data will be saved; and a `Context` object, which is necessary in Android for writing data to a file. Add the following highlighted code inside the class you just created:

```
public class JSONSerializer {

    private String mFilename;
    private Context mContext;

    // All the rest of the code for the class goes here

}// End of class
```

 You will need to import the `Context` class:
`import android.content.Context;`

The previous code shows the closing curly brace of the class, and all the code that follows for this class should be entered inside of it. Here is the very straightforward constructor where we initialize the two member variables that are passed in as parameters to the constructor. Add the constructor for the JSONSerializer, as follows:

```
public JSONSerializer(String fn, Context con){
    mFilename = fn;
    mContext = con;
}
```

Now, we can start coding the real guts of the class. The save method is next. It first creates a JSONArray object, which is a specialized ArrayList for handling JSON objects.

Next, the code uses an enhanced for loop to go through all the Note objects in notes and convert them to JSON objects using the convertToJSON method from the Note class, which we added previously. Then, we load these converted JSONObjects into jArray.

Next, the code uses a Writer instance and an OutputStream instance combined to write the data to an actual file. Notice that the OutputStream instance needed the mContext to be initialized. Add the code we have just discussed:

```
public void save(List<Note> notes)
    throws IOException, JSONException{

    // Make an array in JSON format
    JSONArray jArray = new JSONArray();

    // And load it with the notes
    for (Note n : notes)
        jArray.put(n.convertToJSON());

    // Now write it to the private disk space of our app
    Writer writer = null;
    try {
        OutputStream out = mContext.openFileOutput(mFilename,
            mContext.MODE_PRIVATE);

        writer = new OutputStreamWriter(out);
        writer.write(jArray.toString());
    } finally {
        if (writer != null) {
```

```
                    writer.close();
            }
        }
    }
```

You will need to add the following import statements for these new classes:
```
import org.json.JSONArray;
import org.json.JSONException;
import java.io.IOException;
import java.io.OutputStream;
import java.io.OutputStreamWriter;
import java.io.Writer;
import java.util.List;
```

Now for the de-serialization – loading the data. This time, as we might expect, the method receives no parameters but instead returns an `ArrayList`. An `InputStream` instance is created using `mContext.openFileInput`, and our file containing all our data is opened.

We use a `while` loop to append all the data to a String and use our new `Note` constructor, which extracts JSON data to regular primitive variables, to unpack each `JSONObject` into a `Note` object and add it to the `ArrayList`, which is returned to the calling code:

```
public ArrayList<Note> load() throws IOException, JSONException{
    ArrayList<Note> noteList = new ArrayList<Note>();
    BufferedReader reader = null;
    try {

        InputStream in = mContext.openFileInput(mFilename);
        reader = new BufferedReader(new InputStreamReader(in));
        StringBuilder jsonString = new StringBuilder();
        String line = null;

        while ((line = reader.readLine()) != null) {

            jsonString.append(line);
        }


        JSONArray jArray = (JSONArray) new
            JSONTokener(jsonString.toString()).nextValue();

        for (int i = 0; i < jArray.length(); i++) {
```

```
                    noteList.add(new Note(jArray.getJSONObject(i)));
            }
    } catch (FileNotFoundException e) {
            // we will ignore this one, since it happens
            // when we start fresh. You could add a log here.
    } finally {// This will always run
            if (reader != null)
                    reader.close();
    }

    return noteList;
}
```

> You will need to add these imports:
> ```
> import org.json.JSONTokener;
> import java.io.BufferedReader;
> import java.io.FileNotFoundException;
> import java.io.InputStream;
> import java.io.InputStreamReader;
> import java.util.ArrayList;
> ```

Now all we need to do is put our new class to work in the MainActivity class. Add a new member after the MainActivity declaration, as highlighted in the following code. Also, remove the initialization of noteList to leave just the declaration, as we will now initialize it with some new code in the onCreate method. I have commented out the line you need to delete:

```
public class MainActivity extends AppCompatActivity {

    private JSONSerializer mSerializer;

    //private List<Note> noteList = new ArrayList<>();
    private List<Note> noteList;
```

Now, in the onCreate method, we initialize mSerializer by calling the JSONSerializer constructor with the filename and getApplicationContext(), which is the Context of the application and is required. We can then use the JSONSerializer load method to load any saved data. Add this new highlighted code after the code that handles the floating action button. This new code must come before we handle the RecyclerView:

```
...
FloatingActionButton fab =
        (FloatingActionButton) findViewById(R.id.fab);
```

```
fab.setOnClickListener(new View.OnClickListener() {
        @Override
        public void onClick(View view) {
                DialogNewNote dialog = new DialogNewNote();
                dialog.show(getSupportFragmentManager(), "");
        }
});


    mSerializer = new JSONSerializer("NoteToSelf.json",
getApplicationContext());

    try {
            noteList = mSerializer.load();
    } catch (Exception e) {
            noteList = new ArrayList<Note>();
            Log.e("Error loading notes: ", "", e);
    }

    recyclerView = (RecyclerView)
            findViewById(R.id.recyclerView);
mAdapter = new NoteAdapter(this, noteList);
                ...
```

> I have shown a great deal of context in the previous code
> because its positioning is essential for it to work. If you
> are having any problems getting this to work, make sure
> to compare it to the code in the download bundle in the
> Chapter 17/Note to self folder.

Now, add a new method to our MainActivity class so that that we can call it to
save all our user's data. All this new method does is call the save method of the
JSONSerializer class, passing in the required list of Note objects:

```
public void saveNotes(){
    try{
            mSerializer.save(noteList);

    }catch(Exception e){
            Log.e("Error Saving Notes","", e);
    }
}
```

Now, just as we did when saving our users settings, we will override the `onPause` method to save our user's data. Make sure to add this code in the `MainActivity` class:

```
@Override
protected void onPause(){
    super.onPause();

    saveNotes();

}
```

That's it. We can now run the app and add as many notes as we like. The `ArrayList` will store them all in our running app, our `RecyclerAdapter` will manage displaying them in the `RecyclerView`, and now JSON will take care of loading them from disk and saving them back as well.

Frequently asked questions

Q.1- I didn't understand everything in this chapter, so maybe I am not cut out to be a programmer...?

A- This chapter introduced many new classes, concepts, and methods. If your head is aching a little, that is to be expected. If some of the detail is unclear, don't let it hold you back. Proceed with the next couple of chapters (they are much more straightforward), then revisit this one and especially examine the completed code files.

Q.2- So, how does serialization work in detail?

A- Serialization really is a vast topic. It is possible to write apps your whole life and never really need to understand it. It is the type of topic that would be the subject of a computer science degree. If you are curious to know more, have a look at this article: https://en.wikipedia.org/wiki/Serialization.

Summary

At this point in our journey through the Android API, it is worth taking stock of what we know. We can lay out our own UI designs and choose from a wide and diverse range of widgets to allow the user to interact. We can create multiple screens as well as pop-up dialogs, and we can capture comprehensive user data. Furthermore, we can now make this data persist.

Certainly, there is a lot more to the Android API still to learn, even beyond what this book will teach you, but the point is that we know enough now to plan and implement a working app. You could just get started on your own app right now.

If you have the urge to start your own project right away, then my advice is to go ahead and do it. Don't wait until you consider yourself "expert" or readier. Reading this book and, more importantly, implementing the apps will make you a better Android programmer, but nothing will teach you faster than designing and implementing your own app! It is perfectly possible to complete this book and work on your own project simultaneously.

In the next chapter, we will add the finishing touches to this app by making it multilingual. This is quite quick and easy.

18
Localization

This chapter is quick and simple, but what we will learn to do here can make your app accessible to millions more potential users. We will see how to add additional languages. We will see how adding text the correct way – via String resources – benefits us when it comes to adding multiple languages.

In this chapter, we will do the following:

- Make Note to Self multilingual by adding the Spanish and German languages
- Learn how to use **String resources** more fully

Let's get started.

Making the Note to Self app for Spanish, English, and German speakers

First, we need to add some folders to our project – one for each new language. The text is classed as a *resource* and, consequently, needs to go in the res folder. Follow these steps to add Spanish and German support to the project.

 While the source files for this project are provided in the Chapter 18 folder, they are just for reference. You need to go through the processes described next to achieve multilingual functionality.

Adding Spanish support

Follow these steps to add the Spanish language:

1. Right-click on the `res` folder, then select **New | Android resource directory**. In the **Directory name** field, type `values-es`.

2. Now, we need to add a file in which we can place all our Spanish translations.

3. Right-click on `res`, then select **New | Android resource file** and type `strings.xml` in the **File name** field. Type `values-es` in the **Directory name** field.

4. We now have a `strings.xml` file that any device set to use the Spanish language will refer to. To be clear, we now have two distinct `strings.xml` files.

Adding German support

Follow these steps to add German language support:

1. Right-click on the `res` folder, then select **New | Android resource directory**. In the **Directory name** field, type `values-de`.

2. Now, we need to add a file in which we can place all our German translations.

3. Right-click on `res`, then select **New | Android resource file** and type `strings.xml` in the **File name** field. Type `values-de` in the **Directory name** field.

This is what the `strings.xml` folder looks like. You are probably wondering where the `strings.xml` folder came from as it doesn't correspond to the structure we seemed to be creating in the previous steps.

Android Studio is helping us (apparently) to organize our files and folders, as it is required by the Android operating system in the APK format. You can, however, clearly see the Spanish and German files indicated by their flags as well as their **(de)** and **(es)** postfixes:

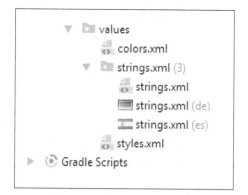

 Depending on your Android Studio settings, you might not see the country flag icons. Provided you can see three `strings.xml` files – one without a postfix, one with **(de)**, and one with **(es)** – you are ready to continue.

Now, we can add the translations to the files we just created.

Adding the string resources

As we know, the `strings.xml` file contains the words that the app will display, such as "important", "to do", "idea", and more. By having a `strings.xml` file for each language we want to support, we can then leave Android to choose the appropriate text depending upon the language settings of the user.

As you go through the following steps, notice that although we place the translation of whatever word we are translating as the value, the `name` attribute remains the same. If you think about it, this is logical, because it is the name attribute that we refer to in our layout files.

Let's provide the translations, see what we have achieved, and then come back and discuss what we will do about text in our Java code.

The simplest way to achieve this code is to copy and paste the code from the original `strings.xml` file and then edit the values of each of the `name` attributes:

1. Open the `strings.xml` file by double-clicking it. Make sure to choose the one next to the Spanish flag or (es) postfix. Edit the file to look like this:

    ```
    <?xml version="1.0" encoding="utf-8"?>
    <resources>
    <string name="app_name">Nota a sí mismo</string>
    ```

```xml
<string name="action_settings">Configuración</string>

<string name="action_add">add</string>
<string name="title_hint">Título</string>
<string name="description_hint">Descripción</string>
<string name="idea_text">Idea</string>
<string name="important_text">Importante</string>
<string name="todo_text">Que hacer</string>
<string name="cancel_button">Cancelar</string>
<string name="ok_button">Vale</string>

<string name="settings_title">Configuración</string>
<string name="title_activity_settings">Configuración</string>

</resources>
```

2. Open the `strings.xml` file by double-clicking it. Make sure to choose the one next to the German flag or (de) postfix. Edit the file to look like this:

```xml
<?xml version="1.0" encoding="utf-8"?>
<resources>
<string name="app_name">Hinweis auf selbst</string>
<string name="action_settings">Einstellungen</string>

<string name="action_add">add</string>
<string name="title_hint">Titel</string>
<string name="description_hint">Beschreibung</string>
<string name="idea_text">Idee</string>
<string name="important_text">Wichtig</string>
<string name="todo_text">zu tun</string>
<string name="cancel_button">Abbrechen</string>
<string name="ok_button">Okay</string>

<string name="settings_title">Einstellungen</string>
<string name="title_activity_settings">Einstellungen</string>
</resources>
```

If you don't provide all the string resources in the extra (Spanish and German) `strings.xml` files, then the missing resources will be taken from the default file.

What we have done is provided two translations. Android knows which translation is for which language because of the folders they are placed in. Furthermore, we have used a **string identifier** (the `name` attribute) to refer to the translations. Look back at the previous code and you will see that the same identifier is used for both translations as well as in the original `strings.xml`.

 You can even localize to different versions of a language; for example, you can have US or United Kingdom English. The complete list of codes can be found here: `http://stackoverflow.com/questions/7973023/what-is-the-list-of-supported-languages-locales-on-android`. You can even localize resources such as images and sound. Find out more about this here: `http://developer.android.com/guide/topics/resources/localization.html`.

The translations were copied and pasted from Google Translate, so it is very likely that some of the translations are far from correct. Doing translation on the cheap like this can be an effective way to get an app with a basic set of string resources onto devices of users who speak different languages to yourself. Once you start having any depth of translation needed, perhaps such as the lines of a story-driven game or a social media app, you will certainly benefit from having the translation done by a human professional.

The purpose of this exercise is to show how Android works, not how to translate.

 My sincere apologies to any Spanish or German speakers who can likely see the limitations of the translations provided here.

Now that we have the translations, we can see them in action – up to a point.

Running Note to Self in German or Spanish

Run the app to see whether it is working as normal. Now, we can change the localization settings to see it in Spanish. Different devices vary slightly in how to do this, but the Pixel 2 XL emulator can be changed by clicking on the **Custom Locale** app:

Next, select **es-ES** and then click the **SELECT 'ES'** button in the bottom-left corner of the screen, as shown in the following screenshot:

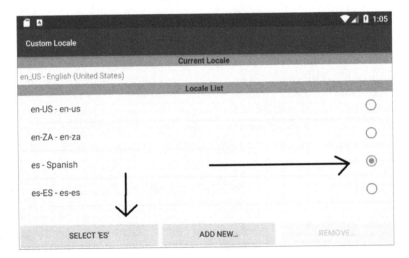

Now, you can run the app in the usual way. Here are some screenshots of the app running in Spanish. I have photoshopped a few screenshots side by side to show a few different screens of the Note to Self app:

In the preceding screenshots, you can clearly see that our app is translated to Spanish – mainly. Obviously, the text that the user enters will be in whatever language they speak – that is not a flaw of our app. However, look at the screenshots closely and notice that I have pointed out a couple of places where the text is still in English. We still have some untranslated text in each of our dialog windows.

This is because the text is contained within our Java code directly. As we have seen, it is easy to use String resources in multiple languages and then refer to them in our layouts, but how do we refer to String resources from our Java code?

Making the translations work in Java code

The first thing to do is create the resources in each of the three `strings.xml` files. Here are the two resources that need adding to the three different files.

In `strings.xml` (without any flag or postfix), add these two resources within the `<resources></resources>` tags:

```
<string name="add_new_note">Add a new note</string>
<string name="your_note">Your note</string>
```

In `strings.xml` with the Spanish flag and/or the **(es)** postfix, add these two resources within the `<resources></resources>` tags:

```
<string name="add_new_note">Agregar una nueva nota</string>
<string name="your_note">Su nota</string>
```

In `strings.xml` with the German flag and/or the **(de)** postfix, add these two resources within the `<resources></resources>` tags:

```
<string name="add_new_note">Eine neue Note hinzufügen</string>
<string name="your_note">Ihre Notiz</string>
```

Next, we need to edit some Java code to refer to a resource instead of a hardcoded String.

Open the `DialogNewNote.java` file and find this line of code:

```
builder.setView(dialogView).setMessage("Add a new note");
```

Edit it as shown in the following code to use the String resource we just added instead of the hardcoded text:

```
builder.setView(dialogView).setMessage(getResources().
getString(R.string.add_new_note));
```

The new code uses the chained `getResources.getString` methods to replace the previously hardcoded `"Add a new note"` text. Look closely and you will see that the argument sent to `getString` is the String identifier `R.string.add_new_note`.

The `R.string` code refers to the String resources in the `res` folder, and `add_new_note` is our identifier. Android will then be able to decide which version (default, Spanish, or German) is appropriate based upon the locale of the device in which the app is running.

We have one more hardcoded String to change.

Open the `DialogShowNote.java` file and find this line of code:

```
builder.setView(dialogView).setMessage("Your Note");
```

Edit it as shown in the following to use the String resource we just added instead of the hardcoded text:

```
builder.setView(dialogView).setMessage(getResources().
getString(R.string.your_note));
```

The new code, again, uses the chained `getResources.getString` methods to replace the previously hardcoded `"Your note"` text. And, again, the argument sent to `getString` is the String identifier; in this case, `R.string.your_note`.

Android can now decide which version (default, Spanish, or German) is appropriate based upon the locale of the device in which the app is running. The following screenshot shows that the New note screen now has the opening text in the appropriate language:

You can add as many string resources as you like. As a reminder from *Chapter 3, Exploring Android Studio and the Project Structure*, note that using string resources is the recommended way to add all text to all projects. The tutorials in this book (apart from Note to Self) will tend to hardcode them to make a more compact tutorial.

Summary

We can now go global with our apps as well as adding the more flexible String resources instead of hardcoding all the text.

In the next chapter, we will see how we can add cool animations to our apps by using Animations and Interpolators.

Animations and Interpolations

19

Here we will see how we can use the `Animation` class to make our UI a little less static and a bit more interesting. As we have come to expect, the Android API will allow us to do some quite advanced things with relatively straightforward code, and the `Animation` class is no different.

This chapter can be approximately divided into these parts:

- An introduction to how animations in Android work and are implemented
- An introduction to a UI widget we haven't explored yet, the `SeekBar`
- A working animation app

First, let's explore how animations in Android work.

Animations in Android

The normal way to create an animation in Android is through XML. We can write XML animations and then load and play them in Java on a specified UI widget. So, for example, we can write an animation that fades in and out five times over three seconds, and then play that animation on an `ImageView` or any other widget. We can think of these XML animations as a script, as they define the type, order, and timing.

Let's explore some of the different properties we can assign to our animations, then how to use them in our Java code, and then finally, we can make a neat animations app to try it all out.

Designing cool animations in XML

We have learned that XML can also be used to describe animations as well as UI layouts, but let's find out exactly how. We can state properties of an animation that describe the starting and ending appearance of a widget. The XML can then be loaded by our Java code by referencing the name of the XML file that contains it and turning it into a usable Java object; again, not unlike a UI layout.

Here is a quick look at some of the animation property pairs we can state to create an animation. Straight after we have looked at some XML, we will see how to use it in our Java.

Fading in and out

Alpha is the measure of transparency. So, by stating the starting `fromAlpha` and ending `toAlpha` values, we can fade items in and out. A value of 0.0 is invisible and 1.0 is an object's normal appearance. Steadily moving between the two makes a fading-in effect:

```
<alpha
    android:fromAlpha="0.0"
    android:toAlpha="1.0" />
```

Move it, move it

We can move an object within our UI by using a similar technique; `fromXDelta` and `toXDelta` can have their values set as a percentage of the size of the object being animated.

The following code would move an object from left to right a distance equal to the width of the object itself:

```
<translate
android:fromXDelta="-100%"
android:toXDelta="0%"/>
```

In addition, there are the `fromYDelta` and `toYDelta` properties for animating up and down.

Scaling or stretching

The `fromXScale` and `toXScale` values will increase or decrease the scale of an object. As an example, the following code will change the object running the animation from normal size to invisible:

```
<scale
android:fromXScale="1.0"
android:fromYScale="0.0"/>
```

As another example, we could shrink the object to a tenth of its usual size using `android:fromYScale="0.1"`, or make it 10 times as big using `android:fromYScale="10.0"`.

Controlling the duration

Of course, none of these animations would be especially interesting if they just instantly arrived at their conclusion. To make our animations more interesting, we can therefore set their duration in milliseconds. A millisecond is one thousandth of a second. We can also make timing easier, especially in relation to other animations, by setting the `startOffset`, also in milliseconds.

The next code would begin an animation one third of a second after we started it, and it would take two thirds of a second to complete:

```
android:duration="666"
android:startOffset="333"
```

Rotate animations

If you want to spin something around, just use `fromDegrees` and `toDegrees`. This next code, probably predictably, will spin a widget around in a complete circle because, of course, there are 360 degrees in a circle:

```
<rotate android:fromDegrees="360"
        android:toDegrees="0"
/>
```

Repeating animations

Repetition might be important in some animations, perhaps a wobble or shake effect, so we can add a `repeatCount` property. In addition, we can specify how the animation is repeated by setting `repeatMode`.

The following code would repeat an animation 10 times, each time reversing the direction of the animation. The `repeatMode` property is relative to the current state of the animation. What this means is that if you, for example, rotated a button from 0 to 360 degrees, the second part of the animation (the first repeat) would rotate the other way, from 360 degrees back to 0. The third part of the animation (the second repeat) would again reverse and rotate from 0 to 360 degrees:

```
android:repeatMode="reverse"
android:repeatCount="10"
```

Combining animation's properties with Set

To combine groups of these effects, we need a `set`. This code shows how we can combine all the previous code snippets we have just seen into an actual XML animation that will compile:

```
<?xml version="1.0" encoding="utf-8"?>
<set xmlns:android="http://schemas.android.com/apk/res/android"
   ...All our animations go here:
</set>
```

We still haven't seen any Java with which to bring these animations to life. Let's fix that now.

Instantiating animations and controlling them with Java code

This next snippet of Java code shows how we would declare an object of the `Animation` type, initialize it with an animation contained in an XML file named `fade_in.xml`, and start the animation on an `ImageView`. Soon we will do this in a project, and see where to put the XML animations as well:

```
// Declare an Animation object
Animation animFadeIn;

// Initialize it
animFadeIn = AnimationUtils.loadAnimation(
getApplicationContext(), R.anim.fade_in);

// Get an ImageView from the UI in the usual way
ImageView (ImageView) findViewById(R.id.imageView);

// Start the animation on the ImageView
imageView.startAnimation(animFadeIn);
```

We already have quite a powerful arsenal of animations and control features for things such as timing. But the Android API gives us a little bit more than this as well.

More animation features

We can listen for the status of animations much like we can listen for clicks on a button. We can also use **interpolators** to make our animations more life-like and pleasing. Let's look at listeners first.

Listeners

If we implement the AnimationListener interface, we can indeed listen to the status of animations by overriding the three methods that tell us when something has occurred. We could then act based on these events.

OnAnimationEnd announces the end of an animation, onAnimationRepeat is called each and every time an animation begins a repeat, and — perhaps predictably — onAnimationStart is called when an animation has started animating. This might not be the same time as when startAnimation is called if a startOffset is set in the animations XML:

```
@Override
public void onAnimationEnd(Animation animation) {
    // Take some action here

}

@Override
public void onAnimationRepeat(Animation animation) {

    // Take some action here

}

@Override
public void onAnimationStart(Animation animation) {

    // Take some action here

}
```

We will see how AnimationListener works in the Animations demo app, as well as putting another widget, SeekBar, into action.

Animation interpolators

If you can think back to high school, you might remember exciting lessons about calculating acceleration. If we animated something at a constant speed, at first glance things might seem OK. If we then compared the animation to another that uses gradual acceleration, then the latter would almost certainly be more pleasing to watch.

It is possible that if we were not told that the only difference between the two animations was that one used acceleration and the other didn't, we wouldn't be able to say *why* we preferred it. Our brains are more receptive to things that conform to the norms of the world around us. This is why adding a bit of real-world physics, such as acceleration and deceleration, improves our animations.

The last thing we want to do, however, is start doing a bunch of mathematical calculations just to slide a button onto the screen or spin some text in a circle.

This is where **interpolators** come in. They are animation modifiers that we can set in a single line of code within our XML.

Some examples of interpolators are `accelerate_interpolator` and `cycle_interpolator`:

```
android:interpolator="@android:anim/accelerate_interpolator"
android:interpolator="@android:anim/cycle_interpolator"/>
```

We will put some interpolators, along with some XML animations and the related Java code, into action next.

> You can learn more about interpolators and the Android Animation class on the developer website here: http://developer.android.com/guide/topics/resources/animation-resource.html.

Animations Demo App – introducing SeekBar

That's enough theory, especially with something that should be so visible. Let's build an animation demo app that explores everything we have just discussed, and a bit more.

This app involves little amounts of code in lots of different files. Therefore, I have tried to make it plain what code is in which file so you can keep track of what is going on. This will make the Java we write for this app more understandable as well.

The app will demonstrate rotations, fades, translations, animation events, interpolations, and controlling duration with SeekBar. The best way to explain what SeekBar does is to build it and then watch it in action.

Laying out the animation demo

Create a new project called `Animation Demo` using the **Empty Activity** template, leaving all the other settings at their defaults. As usual, should you wish to speed things up by copying and pasting the layout, the code, or the animation XML, it can all be found in the `Chapter 19` folder.

Use the following reference screenshot of the finished layout to help guide you through the next steps:

Here is how to lay out the UI for this app:

1. Open `activity_main.xml` in the design view of the editor window.

2. Delete the default **Hello world!** `TextView`.

3. Add an **ImageView** to the top-centre portion of the layout. Use the previous reference screenshot to guide you. Use the `@mipmap/ic_launcher` to show the Android robot in the `ImageView` when prompted to do so by selecting **Project | ic_launcher** in the pop-up **Resources** window.

4. Set the `id` property of the `ImageView` to `imageView`.

5. Directly below the `ImageView`, add a `TextView`. Set the `id` to `textStatus`. I made my `TextView` a little bigger by dragging its edges (not the constraint handles) and changed its `textSize` attribute to `40sp`. The layout so far should look something like this next screenshot:

6. Now we will add a large selection of **Button** widgets to the layout. Exact positioning is not vital, but the exact id property values we add to them later in the tutorial will be. Follow this next screenshot to lay out 12 buttons in the layout. Alter the text attribute so that your buttons have the same text as those in the next screenshot. The text attributes are detailed specifically in the next step in case the image isn't clear enough:

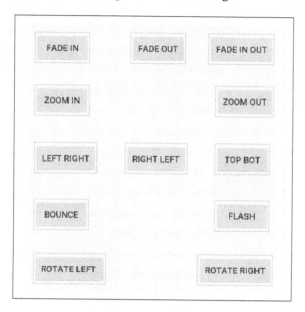

 To make the process of laying out the buttons quicker, lay them out just approximately at first, then add the text attributes from the next step, and then fine-tune the button positions to get a neat layout.

7. Add the text values as they are in the screenshot. Here are all the values from left to right and top to bottom: FADE IN, FADE OUT, FADE IN OUT, ZOOM IN, ZOOM OUT, LEFT RIGHT, RIGHT LEFT, TOP BOT, BOUNCE, FLASH, ROTATE LEFT, and ROTATE RIGHT.

8. Add a `SeekBar` from the **Widgets** category of the palette, which is on the left below the buttons. Set the `id` property to `seekBarSpeed` and the `max` property to `5000`. This means that SeekBar will hold a value between 0 and 5,000 as it is dragged by the user from left to right. We will see how we can read and use this data soon.

9. We want to make the `SeekBar` much wider. To achieve this, you use the exact same technique as with any widget; just drag the edges of the widget. However, as the `SeekBar` is quite small, it is hard to increase its size without accidentally selecting the constraint handles. To overcome this problem, zoom into the design view by holding the *Ctrl* key and rolling the middle mouse wheel forward. You can then grab the edges of the `SeekBar` without touching the constraint handles. I have shown this in action in the next screenshot:

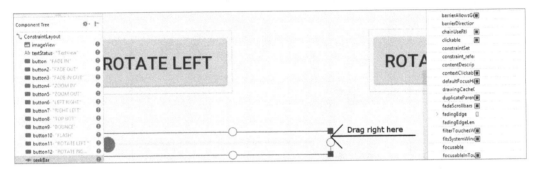

10. Now add a `TextView` just to the right of the `SeekBar` and set its `id` property to `textSeekerSpeed`. This step combined with the previous two should look like this screenshot:

11. Tweak the positions to look like the reference screenshot at the start of these steps, and then click the **Infer Constraints** button to lock the positions. Of course, you can do this manually if you want the practice. Here is a screenshot with all the constraints in place:

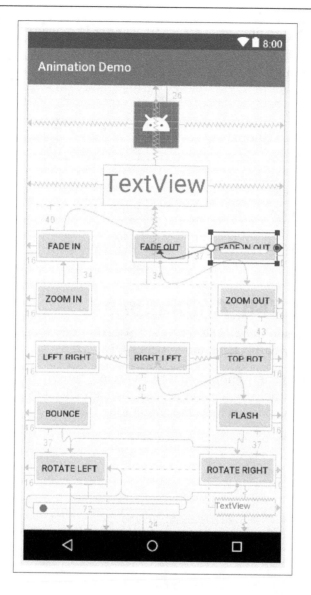

12. Next, add the following `id` properties to the buttons, as identified by the text property that you have already set. If you are asked if you want to **Update usages...** as you enter these values, select **Yes**:

Existing text property	Value of id property to set
Fade In	`btnFadeIn`
Fade Out	`btnFadeOut`
Fade In Out	`btnFadeInOut`

Existing text property	Value of id property to set
Zoom In	`btnZoomIn`
Zoom Out	`btnZoomOut`
Left Right	`btnLeftRight`
Right Left	`btnRightLeft`
Top Bot	`btnTopBottom`
Bounce	`btnBounce`
Flash	`btnFlash`
Rotate Left	`btnRotateLeft`
Rotate Right	`btnRotateRight`

We will see how to use this newcomer to our UI (`SeekBar`) when we get to coding `MainActivity` in a few sections' time.

Coding the XML Animations

Right-click on the **res** folder and select **New | Android resource directory**. Enter `anim` in the **Directory name:** field and left-click **OK**.

Now right-click on the new **anim** directory and select **New | Animation resource file**. In the **File name:** field, type `fade_in` and then left-click **OK**. Delete the entire contents and add this code to create the animation:

```xml
<?xml version="1.0" encoding="utf-8"?>
<set xmlns:android="http://schemas.android.com/apk/res/android"
android:fillAfter="true" >

    <alpha
                android:fromAlpha="0.0"
                android:interpolator="
                        @android:anim/accelerate_interpolator"

                android:toAlpha="1.0" />
</set>
```

Right-click on the **anim** directory and select **New | Animation resource file**. In the `File name:` field, type `fade_out` and then left-click **OK**. Delete the entire contents and add this code to create the animation:

```xml
<?xml version="1.0" encoding="utf-8"?>
<set xmlns:android="http://schemas.android.com/apk/res/android"
```

```
below "t" of the above set
android:fillAfter="true" >

    <alpha
         android:fromAlpha="1.0"
         android:interpolator="
                  @android:anim/accelerate_interpolator"

         android:toAlpha="0.0" />
</set>
```

Right-click on the **anim** directory and select **New | Animation resource file**. In the `File name:` field, type `fade_in_out` and then left-click **OK**. Delete the entire contents and add this code to create the animation:

```
<?xml version="1.0" encoding="utf-8"?>
<set xmlns:android="http://schemas.android.com/apk/res/android"
        android:fillAfter="true" >

    <alpha
         android:fromAlpha="0.0"
         android:interpolator="
             @android:anim/accelerate_interpolator"

             android:toAlpha="1.0" />

<alpha
    android:fromAlpha="1.0"
    android:interpolator="
        @android:anim/accelerate_interpolator"

    android:toAlpha="0.0" />

</set>
```

Right-click on the **anim** directory and select **New | Animation resource file**. In the `File name:` field, type `zoom_in` and then left-click **OK**. Delete the entire contents and add this code to create the animation:

```
<set xmlns:android="http://schemas.android.com/apk/res/android"
    android:fillAfter="true" >

    <scale
        android:fromXScale="1"
        android:fromYScale="1"
        android:pivotX="50%"
        android:pivotY="50%"
```

```
            android:toXScale="6"
            android:toYScale="6" >
    </scale>

</set>
```

Right-click on the **anim** directory and select **New | Animation resource file**. In the `File name:` field, type `zoom_out` and then left-click **OK**. Delete the entire contents and add this code to create the animation:

```xml
<?xml version="1.0" encoding="utf-8"?>
<set xmlns:android="http://schemas.android.com/apk/res/android">
    <scale
        android:fromXScale="6"
        android:fromYScale="6"
        android:pivotX="50%"
        android:pivotY="50%"
        android:toXScale="1"
        android:toYScale="1" >
    </scale>

</set>
```

Right-click on the **anim** directory and select **New | Animation resource file**. In the `File name:` field, type `left_right` and then left-click **OK**. Delete the entire contents and add this code to create the animation:

```xml
<?xml version="1.0" encoding="utf-8"?>
<set xmlns:android="http://schemas.android.com/apk/res/android">
    <translate

        android:fromXDelta="-500%"
        android:toXDelta="0%"/>
</set>
```

Right-click on the **anim** directory and select **New | Animation resource file**. In the **File name:** field, type `right_left` and then left-click **OK**. Delete the entire contents and add this code to create the animation:

```xml
<?xml version="1.0" encoding="utf-8"?>
<set xmlns:android="http://schemas.android.com/apk/res/android">
    <translate
        android:fillAfter="false"
        android:fromXDelta="500%"
        android:toXDelta="0%"/>
</set>
```

Right-click on the **anim** directory and select **New | Animation resource file**. In the **File name:** field, type top_bot and then left-click **OK**. Delete the entire contents and add this code to create the animation:

```xml
<?xml version="1.0" encoding="utf-8"?>
<set xmlns:android="http://schemas.android.com/apk/res/android">
    <translate
        android:fillAfter="false"
        android:fromYDelta="-100%"
        android:toYDelta="0%"/>
</set>
```

Right-click on the **anim** directory and select **New | Animation resource file**. In the **File name:** field, type flash and then left-click **OK**. Delete the entire contents and add this code to create the animation:

```xml
<?xml version="1.0" encoding="utf-8"?>
<set xmlns:android="http://schemas.android.com/apk/res/android">
    <alpha android:fromAlpha="0.0"
      android:toAlpha="1.0"
      android:interpolator="
        @android:anim/accelerate_interpolator"

      android:repeatMode="reverse"
      android:repeatCount="10"/>
</set>
```

Right-click on the **anim** directory and select **New | Animation resource file**. In the **File name:** field, type bounce and then left-click **OK**. Delete the entire contents and add this code to create the animation:

```xml
<?xml version="1.0" encoding="utf-8"?>
<set xmlns:android="http://schemas.android.com/apk/res/android"
      android:fillAfter="true"
      android:interpolator="
            @android:anim/bounce_interpolator">

    <scale
        android:fromXScale="1.0"
        android:fromYScale="0.0"
        android:toXScale="1.0"
        android:toYScale="1.0" />

</set>
```

Right-click on the **anim** directory and select **New | Animation resource file**. In the **File name:** field, type `rotate_left` and then left-click **OK**. Delete the entire contents and add this code to create the animation. Here we see something new: `pivotX="50%"` and `pivotY="50%"`. This makes the rotate animation central on the widget that will be animated. We can think of this as setting the *pivot* point of the animation:

```xml
<?xml version="1.0" encoding="utf-8"?>
<set xmlns:android="http://schemas.android.com/apk/res/android">
        <rotate android:fromDegrees="360"
                android:toDegrees="0"
                android:pivotX="50%"
                android:pivotY="50%"
                android:interpolator="
                        @android:anim/cycle_interpolator"/>

</set>
```

Right-click on the **anim** directory and select **New | Animation resource file**. In the **File name:** field, type `rotate_right` and then left-click **OK**. Delete the entire contents and add this code to create the animation:

```xml
<?xml version="1.0" encoding="utf-8"?>
<set xmlns:android="http://schemas.android.com/apk/res/android">
        <rotate android:fromDegrees="0"
                android:toDegrees="360"
                android:pivotX="50%"
                android:pivotY="50%"
                android:interpolator="
                        @android:anim/cycle_interpolator"/>

</set>
```

Now we can write the Java code to add our animations to our UI.

Wiring up the Animation Demo app in Java

Open the `MainActivity.java` file. Now following is the class declaration. We can declare the following member variables for animations:

```java
Animation animFadeIn;
Animation animFadeOut;
Animation animFadeInOut;

Animation animZoomIn;
```

```
Animation animZoomOut;

Animation animLeftRight;
Animation animRightLeft;
Animation animTopBottom;

Animation animBounce;
Animation animFlash;

Animation animRotateLeft;
Animation animRotateRight;
```

Now add these member variables for the UI after the previous code:

```
ImageView imageView;
TextView textStatus;

Button btnFadeIn;
Button btnFadeOut;
Button btnFadeInOut;
Button zoomIn;
Button zoomOut;
Button leftRight;
Button rightLeft;
Button topBottom;
Button bounce;
Button flash;
Button rotateLeft;
Button rotateRight;
SeekBar seekBarSpeed;
TextView textSeekerSpeed;
```

> You will need to add the following import statements at this point:
> ```
> import android.view.animation.Animation;
> import android.widget.Button;
> import android.widget.ImageView;
> import android.widget.SeekBar;
> import android.widget.TextView;
> ```

Next we add an `int` member variable, which will be used to track the current value/position of SeekBar:

```
int seekSpeedProgress;
```

```
@Override
protected void onCreate(Bundle savedInstanceState) {
    super.onCreate(savedInstanceState);
    setContentView(R.layout.activity_main);

    loadAnimations();
    loadUI();


}
```

At this point, the two new lines of code will have errors until we implement the two new methods.

Now we will implement the loadAnimations method. Although the code in this method is quite extensive, it is also very straightforward. All we are doing is using the static loadAnimation method of the AnimationUtils class to initialize each of our Animation references with one of our XML animations. Notice also that for the animFadeIn Animation, we also call setAnimationListener on it. We will write the methods to listen for events shortly.

Add the loadAnimations method:

```
private void loadAnimations(){
    animFadeIn = AnimationUtils.loadAnimation(
            this, R.anim.fade_in);
    animFadeIn.setAnimationListener(this);
    animFadeOut = AnimationUtils.loadAnimation(
            this, R.anim.fade_out);
    animFadeInOut = AnimationUtils.loadAnimation(
            this, R.anim.fade_in_out);

    animZoomIn = AnimationUtils.loadAnimation(
            this, R.anim.zoom_in);
    animZoomOut = AnimationUtils.loadAnimation(
            this, R.anim.zoom_out);

    animLeftRight = AnimationUtils.loadAnimation(
            this, R.anim.left_right);
    animRightLeft = AnimationUtils.loadAnimation(
            this, R.anim.right_left);
```

```
animTopBottom = AnimationUtils.loadAnimation(
        this, R.anim.top_bot);


animBounce = AnimationUtils.loadAnimation(
        this, R.anim.bounce);
animFlash = AnimationUtils.loadAnimation(
        this, R.anim.flash);


animRotateLeft = AnimationUtils.loadAnimation(
        this, R.anim.rotate_left);
animRotateRight = AnimationUtils.loadAnimation(
        this, R.anim.rotate_right);
}
```

 You will need to import one new class at this point:
`import android.view.animation.AnimationUtils;`

Implement the `loadUI` method in three sections. First, let's get a reference to the parts of our XML layout in the usual way:

```
private void loadUI(){

    imageView = (ImageView) findViewById(R.id.imageView);
    textStatus = (TextView) findViewById(R.id.textStatus);

    btnFadeIn = (Button) findViewById(R.id.btnFadeIn);
    btnFadeOut = (Button) findViewById(R.id.btnFadeOut);
    btnFadeInOut = (Button) findViewById(R.id.btnFadeInOut);
    zoomIn = (Button) findViewById(R.id.btnZoomIn);
    zoomOut = (Button) findViewById(R.id.btnZoomOut);
    leftRight = (Button) findViewById(R.id.btnLeftRight);
    rightLeft = (Button) findViewById(R.id.btnRightLeft);
    topBottom = (Button) findViewById(R.id.btnTopBottom);
    bounce = (Button) findViewById(R.id.btnBounce);
    flash = (Button) findViewById(R.id.btnFlash);
    rotateLeft = (Button) findViewById(R.id.btnRotateLeft);
    rotateRight = (Button) findViewById(R.id.btnRotateRight);
```

Now we will add a click-listener for each button. Add this code immediately after the last block within the `loadUI` method:

```
btnFadeIn.setOnClickListener(this);
btnFadeOut.setOnClickListener(this);
btnFadeInOut.setOnClickListener(this);
```

```
zoomIn.setOnClickListener(this);
zoomOut.setOnClickListener(this);
leftRight.setOnClickListener(this);
rightLeft.setOnClickListener(this);
topBottom.setOnClickListener(this);
bounce.setOnClickListener(this);
flash.setOnClickListener(this);
rotateLeft.setOnClickListener(this);
rotateRight.setOnClickListener(this);
```

 The code we just added creates errors in all the lines of code. We can ignore them for now, as we will fix them shortly and discuss what happened.

The third and last section of the loadUI method sets up an anonymous class to handle the SeekBar. We could have added this as an interface to MainActivity as we did with listening for button clicks and animation events, but with a single SeekBar like this, it makes sense to handle it directly.

We will override three methods, as it is required by the interface when implementing OnSeekBarChangeListener:

- A method that detects a change in the position of the seek bar called onProgressChanged

- A method that detects the user starting to change the position called onStartTrackingTouch

- A method that detects when the user has finished using the seek bar called onStopTrackingTouch

To achieve our goals, we only need to add code to the onProgressChanged method, but we must still override them all.

All we do in the onProgressChanged method is assign the current value of the seek bar to the seekSpeedProgress member variable so that it can be accessed from elsewhere. Then we use this value along with the maximum possible value of the SeekBar, which is obtained by calling seekBarSpeed.getMax(), and output a message to the textSeekerSpeed TextView.

Add the code we have just discussed into the loadUI method:

```
seekBarSpeed = (SeekBar) findViewById(R.id.seekBarSpeed);
textSeekerSpeed = (TextView) findViewById(R.id.textSeekerSpeed);
```

```
seekBarSpeed.setOnSeekBarChangeListener(new
SeekBar.OnSeekBarChangeListener() {

    @Override
    public void onProgressChanged(SeekBar seekBar,
            int value, boolean fromUser) {

        seekSpeedProgress = value;
        textSeekerSpeed.setText(""
        + seekSpeedProgress
        + " of "
        + seekBarSpeed.getMax());
    }

    @Override
    public void onStartTrackingTouch(SeekBar seekBar) {
    }

    @Override
    public void onStopTrackingTouch(SeekBar seekBar) {

    }

});

}
```

Now we need to alter the `MainActivity` class declaration to implement two interfaces. In this app, we will be listening for clicks and for animation events, so the two interfaces we will be using are `View.OnClickListener` and `Animation.AnimationListener`. Notice that to implement more than one interface, we simply separate the interfaces with a comma.

Alter the `MainActivity` class declaration by adding the highlighted code we have just discussed:

```
public class MainActivity extends AppCompatActivity
    implements View.OnClickListener,
Animation.AnimationListener {
```

At this stage, we can add and implement the required methods for those interfaces. First, the `AnimationListener` methods `onAnimationEnd`, `onAnimationRepeat`, and `onaAnimationStart`. We only need to add a little code to two of these methods. In `onAnimationEnd`, we set the text property of `textStatus` to STOPPED, and in `onAnimationStart`, we set it to RUNNING. This will demonstrate our animation listeners are indeed listening and working:

```java
@Override
public void onAnimationEnd(Animation animation) {
    textStatus.setText("STOPPED");

}

@Override
public void onAnimationRepeat(Animation animation) {


}

@Override
public void onAnimationStart(Animation animation) {
    textStatus.setText("RUNNING");

}
```

The `onClick` method is quite long, but not anything complicated. Each `case` that handles each button from the UI simply sets the duration of an animation based on the current position of the seek bar, sets up the animation so it can be listened to for events, and then starts the animation.

 You will need to use your preferred technique to import the `View` class:
```java
import android.view.View;
```

Add the `onClick` method we have just discussed, and we have then completed this mini app:

```java
@Override
public void onClick(View v) {


    switch(v.getId()){
        case R.id.btnFadeIn:
            animFadeIn.setDuration(seekSpeedProgress);
```

```
        animFadeIn.setAnimationListener(this);
        imageView.startAnimation(animFadeIn);

        break;

    case R.id.btnFadeOut:

        animFadeOut.setDuration(seekSpeedProgress);
        animFadeOut.setAnimationListener(this);
        imageView.startAnimation(animFadeOut);

        break;

    case R.id.btnFadeInOut:

        animFadeInOut.setDuration(seekSpeedProgress);
        animFadeInOut.setAnimationListener(this);
        imageView.startAnimation(animFadeInOut);

        break;

    case R.id.btnZoomIn:
        animZoomIn.setDuration(seekSpeedProgress);
        animZoomIn.setAnimationListener(this);
        imageView.startAnimation(animZoomIn);

        break;

    case R.id.btnZoomOut:
        animZoomOut.setDuration(seekSpeedProgress);
        animZoomOut.setAnimationListener(this);
        imageView.startAnimation(animZoomOut);

        break;



    case R.id.btnLeftRight:
        animLeftRight.setDuration(seekSpeedProgress);
        animLeftRight.setAnimationListener(this);
        imageView.startAnimation(animLeftRight);

        break;
```

```
case R.id.btnRightLeft:
    animRightLeft.setDuration(seekSpeedProgress);
    animRightLeft.setAnimationListener(this);
    imageView.startAnimation(animRightLeft);

    break;

case R.id.btnTopBottom:
    animTopBottom.setDuration(seekSpeedProgress);
    animTopBottom.setAnimationListener(this);
    imageView.startAnimation(animTopBottom);

    break;

case R.id.btnBounce:
    /*
        Divide seekSpeedProgress by 10 because with
        the seekbar having a max value of 5000 it
        will make the animations range between
        almost instant and half a second
        5000 /  10 = 500 milliseconds
    */
    animBounce.setDuration(seekSpeedProgress / 10);
    animBounce.setAnimationListener(this);
    imageView.startAnimation(animBounce);

    break;

case R.id.btnFlash:
    animFlash.setDuration(seekSpeedProgress / 10);
    animFlash.setAnimationListener(this);
    imageView.startAnimation(animFlash);

    break;

case R.id.btnRotateLeft:
    animRotateLeft.setDuration(seekSpeedProgress);
    animRotateLeft.setAnimationListener(this);
    imageView.startAnimation(animRotateLeft);

    break;

case R.id.btnRotateRight:
```

```
animRotateRight.setDuration(seekSpeedProgress);
animRotateRight.setAnimationListener(this);
imageView.startAnimation(animRotateRight);

break;
    }


  }
```

Now run the app. Move the seek bar to roughly the center so the animations run for a reasonable amount of time:

Click the **ZOOM IN** button.

Notice how text on the Android robot changes from **RUNNING** to **STOPPED** at the appropriate time. Now click one of the **ROTATE** buttons:

Most of the other animations don't do themselves justice in a screenshot, so be sure to try them all out for yourself.

Frequently asked questions

Q1) We know how to animate widgets now, but what about shapes or images that I create myself?

A) An `ImageView` can hold any image you like. Just add the image to the `drawable` folder and then set the appropriate `src` attribute on the `ImageView`. You can then animate whatever image is being shown in the `ImageView`.

Q2) But what if I want more flexibility than this, more like a drawing app or even a game?

A) To implement this kind of functionality, we will need to learn another general computing concept, **threads**, as well as some more Android classes such as `Paint`, `Canvas`, and `SurfaceView`. We will learn how to draw anything, from a single pixel to shapes, and then move them around the screen, starting in the next, *Chapter 20, Drawing Graphics*.

Summary

Now we have another app-enhancing trick up our sleeves. In this chapter, we saw that animations in Android are quite straightforward. We design an animation in XML and add the file to the `anim` folder. Next, we get a reference to the animation in XML with an `Animation` object in our Java code.

We can then use a reference to a widget in our UI and set an animation to it using `setAmimation` and passing in the `Animation` object. We commence the animation by calling `startAnimation` on the reference to the widget.

We also saw that we can control the timing of animations, as well as listening for animation events.

In the next chapter, we will learn about drawing graphics in Android. This will be the start of several chapters on graphics in which we will build a kid's-style drawing app.

20
Drawing Graphics

This entire chapter will be about the Android `Canvas` class and some related classes such as `Paint`, `Color`, and Bitmap. These classes combined bring great power when it comes to drawing to the screen. Sometimes, the default UI provided by the Android API isn't what we need. If we want to make a drawing app, draw graphs, or perhaps make a game, we need to take control of every pixel that the Android device has to offer.

In this chapter, we will do the following:

- Talk about understanding the `Canvas` and related classes
- Write a `Canvas`-based demo app
- Look at the Android coordinate system so we know where to do our drawing
- Learn about drawing and manipulating Bitmaps
- Write a Bitmap-based demo app

Let's draw!

Understanding the Canvas class

The `Canvas` class is part of the `android.graphics` package. In the next two chapters, we will be using all the following import statements from the `android.graphics` package, and one more from the now-familiar `View` package. They give us access to some powerful drawing methods from the Android API:

```
import android.graphics.Bitmap;
import android.graphics.Canvas;
import android.graphics.Color;
import android.graphics.Paint;
import android.widget.ImageView;
```

First, let's talk about Bitmap, Canvas, and ImageView, as highlighted in the previous code.

Getting started drawing with Bitmap, Canvas, and ImageView

As Android is designed to run all types of mobile apps, we can't immediately start typing our drawing code and expect it to work. We need to do a bit of preparation (coding) to consider the specific device our app is running on. It is true that some of this preparation can be slightly counterintuitive, but we will go through it a step at a time.

Canvas and Bitmap

Depending on how you use the Canvas class, the term can be slightly misleading. While the Canvas class *is* the class to which you draw your graphics, like a painting canvas, you still need a **surface** to transpose the canvas to.

The surface, in this case (and in our first two demo apps), will be from the Bitmap class. We can think of it like this: We get a Canvas object and a Bitmap object, and then set the Bitmap object as the part of the Canvas to draw upon.

This is slightly counterintuitive if you take the word "canvas" in its literal sense, but once it is all set up, we can forget about it and concentrate on the graphics we want to draw.

 The Canvas class supplies the *ability* to draw. It has all the methods for doing things such as drawing shapes, text, lines, and image files (like other bitmaps), and even supports plotting individual pixels.

The Bitmap class is used by the Canvas class and is the surface that gets drawn upon. You can think of the Bitmap instance as being inside a picture frame on the Canvas instance.

Paint

In addition to Canvas and Bitmap, we will be using the Paint class. This is much more easily understood. Paint is the class used to configure specific properties such as the color that we will draw on the Bitmap (within the Canvas).

There is still another piece of the puzzle before we can get things drawn.

ImageView and Activity

The `ImageView` is the class that the `Activity` class will use to display output to the player. The reason for this third layer of abstraction is that, as we have seen throughout the book, the Activity class needs to pass a `View` to the `setContentView` method to display something to the user. Throughout the book so far, this has been a layout that we created in the visual designer or in XML code.

This time, we don't want a UI; we want to draw lines, pixels, and shapes.

There are multiple types of class extending `View` enabling all different types of app to be made, and they will all be compatible with the `Activity` class, which is the foundation of all regular Android apps (including drawing apps and games).

It is therefore necessary to associate the `Bitmap` that gets drawn on (through its association with `Canvas`) with the `ImageView` once the drawing is done. The last step will be telling the `Activity` that our `ImageView` represents the content for the user to see by passing it to `setContentView`.

Canvas, Bitmap, Paint, and ImageView – quick summary

If the theory of the code structure we need to set up seems like it is not simple, you will breathe a sigh of relief when you see the relatively simple code very shortly.

A quick summary of what we've covered so far:

- Every app needs an `Activity` to interact with the user and the underlying operating system. Therefore, we must conform to the required hierarchy if we want to succeed.

- We will use the `ImageView` class, which is a type of `View` class. The `View` class is what `Activity` needs to display our app to the user.

- The `Canvas` class supplies the *ability* to draw lines, pixels, and other graphics too. It has all the methods for doing things like drawing shapes, text, lines, and image files, and even supports plotting individual pixels.

- The `Bitmap` class will be associated with the `Canvas` class, and it is the surface that gets drawn upon.

- The `Canvas` class uses the `Paint` class to configure details like the color.

- Finally, once the Bitmap has been drawn upon, we must associate it with the ImageView, which in turn is set as the view for the Activity.

- The result will be that what we draw on the Bitmap in the Canvas, which is displayed to the user through the ImageView via the call to setContentView. Phew!

> It doesn't matter if that isn't 100% clear. It is not you that isn't seeing things clearly — it simply isn't a clear relationship. Writing the code and using the techniques over and over will cause things to become clearer. Look at the code, do the demo apps in this chapter and the next, and then re-read this section.

Let's look at how to set up this relationship in code. Don't worry about typing the code, just study it first.

Using the Canvas class

Let's look at the code and the different stages required to get drawing, then we can quickly move on to drawing something for real with the Canvas demo app.

Preparing the instances of the required classes

The first step is to turn the classes we need into real, working things, objects/instances.

First we state the type, which in this case happens to be a class, and then we state the name we would like our working object to have:

```
// Here are all the objects(instances)
// of classes that we need to do some drawing
ImageView myImageView;
Bitmap myBlankBitmap;
Canvas myCanvas;
Paint myPaint;
```

The previous code declares reference type variables of the ImageView, Bitmap, Canvas, and Paint types. They are named myImageView, myBlankBitmap, myCanvas, and myPaint, respectively.

Initializing the objects

Next, we need to initialize our new objects before using them:

```
// Initialize all the objects ready for drawing
// We will do this inside the onCreate method
int widthInPixels = 800;
int heightInPixels = 800;

myBlankBitmap = Bitmap.createBitmap(widthInPixels,
        heightInPixels,
        Bitmap.Config.ARGB_8888);

myCanvas = new Canvas(myBlankBitmap);
myImageView = new ImageView(this);
myPaint = new Paint();
// Do drawing here
```

Notice the comment in the previous code:

```
// Do drawing here
```

This is where we would configure our color and draw stuff. Also, notice at the top of the code that we declare and initialize two `int` variables called `widthInPixels` and `heightInPixels`. When we code the `Canvas` demo app, I will go into greater detail about some of those lines of code.

We are now ready to draw. All we must do is assign the `ImageView` to the `Activity`.

Setting the Activity content

Finally, before we can see our drawing, we tell Android to use our `ImageView`, called `myImageView`, as the content to display to the user:

```
// Associate the drawn upon Bitmap with the ImageView
myImageView.setImageBitmap(myBlankBitmap);

// Tell Android to set our drawing
// as the view for this app
// via the ImageView
setContentView(myImageView);
```

As we have already seen in every app so far, the `setContentView` method is part of the `Activity` class, and we pass in `myImageView` as an argument instead of an XML layout, as we have been doing throughout the book so far. That's it. All we must learn now is how to actually draw on that `Bitmap`.

Before we do some drawing, I thought it would be useful to start a real project, copy and paste the code we have just discussed, a step at a time, into the correct place, and then actually see something drawn to the screen.

Let's do some drawing.

The Canvas Demo app

Create a new project to explore the topic of drawing with Canvas. We will reuse what we just learned, and this time we will also draw to the Bitmap.

Creating a new project

Create a new project and call it Canvas Demo. This time, be sure to choose the **Empty Activity** option on the **Add an Activity to Mobile** screen before clicking **Next**. Also, be sure to uncheck **Generate Layout File** and **Backwards Compatibility (AppCompat)**. Don't worry about naming the Activity; this is just an app to play around with. We will not be returning to it.

Notice that Android Studio has not created an XML layout, and furthermore it has not added a line of code in MainActivity.java that calls setContentView. If you ran the app at this stage, you would get a blank black screen.

In addition, we are using the Vanilla version of Activity class, and MainActivity therefore extends Activity instead of AppCompatActivity, as we have been using previously.

[The complete code for this app can be found in the download bundle in the Chapter 20/Canvas Demo folder.]

Coding the Canvas demo app

To get started, add the highlighted code after the class declaration but before the onCreate method. This is what the code will look like after this step:

```
public class MainActivity extends Activity {

    // Here are all the objects(instances)
    // of classes that we need to do some drawing
    ImageView myImageView;
    Bitmap myBlankBitmap;
    Canvas myCanvas;
```

```
    Paint myPaint;


    @Override
    protected void onCreate(Bundle savedInstanceState) {
        super.onCreate(savedInstanceState);
    }
}
```

Notice in Android Studio that each of the four new classes is underlined in red. This is because we need to add the appropriate `import` statements. You could copy them from the first page of this chapter, but it would be much quicker to place the mouse pointer on each error in turn and then hold the *ALT* key and tap the *Enter* key. If prompted from the pop-up options, select **Import class**.

Once you have done this for each of `ImageView`, `Bitmap`, `Canvas`, and `Paint`, all the errors will be gone and the relevant `import` statements will have been added to the top of the code.

Now that we have declared instances of the required classes, we can initialize them. Add the following code to the `onCreate` method after the call to `super.onCreate...`, as shown in this next code:

```
@Override
protected void onCreate(Bundle savedInstanceState) {
    super.onCreate(savedInstanceState);

    // Initialize all the objects ready for drawing
    // We will do this inside the onCreate method
    int widthInPixels = 800;
    int heightInPixels = 600;

    // Create a new Bitmap
    myBlankBitmap = Bitmap.createBitmap(widthInPixels,
                heightInPixels,
                Bitmap.Config.ARGB_8888);

    // Initialize the Canvas and associate it
    // with the Bitmap to draw on
    myCanvas = new Canvas(myBlankBitmap);

    // Initialize the ImageView and the Paint
    myImageView = new ImageView(this);
    myPaint = new Paint();
}
```

This code is the same as we saw when we were discussing `Canvas` in theory. It is worth exploring the `Bitmap` class initialization, as it is not straightforward.

Exploring the Bitmap initialization

Bitmaps, more typically in graphics-based apps and games, are used to represent objects such as different brushes to paint with, the player, backgrounds, game objects, and so on. Here we are simply using it to draw upon. In the next project, we will use bitmaps to represent the subject of our drawing, not just the surface to draw upon.

The method that needs explaining is the `createBitmap` method. The parameters from left to right are as follows:

- Width (in pixels)
- Height (in pixels)
- The bitmap configuration

Bitmaps can be configured in several different ways. The `ARGB_8888` configuration means that each pixel is represented by 4 bytes of memory.

 There are a few bitmap formats that Android can use. This one is perfect for a good range of color and will ensure that the bitmaps we use and the color we request will be drawn as intended. There are higher and lower configurations, but ARGB_8888 is perfect for both the entirety of this chapter and the Snake game in the penultimate chapter of the book.

Now we can do the actual drawing.

Drawing on the screen

Add this next highlighted code after the initialization of `myPaint` and inside the closing curly brace of the `onCreate` method:

```
myPaint = new Paint();

// Draw on the Bitmap
// Wipe the Bitmap with a blue color
myCanvas.drawColor(Color.argb(255, 0, 0, 255));

// Re-size the text
myPaint.setTextSize(100);
// Change the paint to white
```

```
myPaint.setColor(Color.argb(255, 255, 255, 255));
// Draw some text
myCanvas.drawText("Hello World!",100, 100, myPaint);

// Change the paint to yellow
myPaint.setColor(Color.argb(255, 212, 207, 62));
// Draw a circle
myCanvas.drawCircle(400,250, 100, myPaint);
}
```

The previous code uses `myCanvas.drawColor` to fill the screen with color.

The `myPaint.setTextSize` defines the size of the text that will be drawn next. The `myPaint.setColor` method determines what color any future drawing will be. The `myCanvas.drawText` actually draws the text to the screen.

Analyze the arguments passed into `drawText` and we can see that the text will say "Hello World!" and that it will be drawn 100 pixels from the left and 100 pixels from the top of our `Bitmap` (`myBitmap`).

Next, we use `setColor` again to change the color that will be used for drawing. Finally, we use the `drawCircle` method to draw a circle that is 400 pixels from the left and 100 pixels from the top. The circle will have a radius of 100 pixels.

I reserved explaining the `Color.argb` method until now.

Explaining Color.argb

The `Color` class, unsurprisingly, helps us manipulate and represent color. The `argb` method used previously returns a color constructed using the **alpha** (opacity/transparency), **red**, **green**, and **blue** model. This model uses values ranging from zero (no color) to 255 (full color) for each element. It is important to note — although, on reflection, it might seem obvious — that the colors mixed are intensities of light and are quite different to what happens when we mix paint, for example.

 To devise an argb value and explore this model further, look at this handy website: `https://www.rapidtables.com/web/color/RGB_Color.html`. The site helps you pick the RGB values; you can then experiment with the alpha values.

The values used to clear the drawing surface were 255, 0, 0, 255. These values mean full opacity (solid color), no red, no green, and full blue. This makes a blue color.

The next call to the argb method is in the first call to setColor, where we are setting the required color for the text. The values 255, 255, 255, 255 mean full opacity, full red, full green, full blue. When you combine light with these values, you get white.

The final call to argb is in the final call to setColor, where we are setting the color to draw the circle. 255, 21, 207, 62 makes a sun-yellow color.

The last step before we can run the code is to add the call to the setContentView method, which places our ImageView (myImageView) as the view to be set as the content for this app. Here are the final lines of code highlighted after the code we have already added but before the closing curly brace of onCreate:

```
// Associate the drawn upon Bitmap with the ImageView
myImageView.setImageBitmap(myBlankBitmap);
// Tell Android to set our drawing
// as the view for this app
// via the ImageView
setContentView(myImageView);
```

Finally, we tell the Activity class to use myImageView by calling setContentView.

This is what the Canvas demo looks like when you run it. We can see an 800 by 800-pixel drawing. In the next chapter, we will use more advanced techniques to utilize the entire screen, and we will also learn about threads to make the graphics move in real time:

It would help to understand the result of the coordinates we use in our Canvas drawing methods if you better understood the Android coordinate system.

Android coordinate system

As we will see, drawing a `Bitmap` is trivial. But the coordinate system that we use to draw our graphics onto needs a brief explanation.

Plotting and drawing

When we draw a `Bitmap` object to the screen, we pass in the coordinates we want to draw the object at. The available coordinates of a given Android device depend upon the resolution of its screen.

For example, the Google Pixel phone has a screen resolution of 1920 pixels (across) by 1080 pixels (down) when held in landscape view.

The numbering system of these coordinates starts in the top left-hand corner at 0,0, and proceeds down and to the right until the bottom-right corner is pixel 1919, 1079. The apparent 1-pixel disparity between 1920/ 1919 and 1080/ 1079 is because the numbering starts at 0.

So, when we draw a `Bitmap` or anything else to the screen (such as `Canvas` circles and rectangles), we must specify an *x, y* coordinate.

Furthermore, a Bitmap (or `Canvas` shape), of course, comprises many pixels. So, which pixel of a given Bitmap is drawn at the *x, y* screen coordinate that we will be specifying?

The answer is the top-left pixel of the Bitmap object. Look at the next diagram, which should clarify the screen coordinates using the Google Pixel phone as an example. As a graphical means for explaining the Android coordinate drawing system, I will use a cute spaceship graphic:

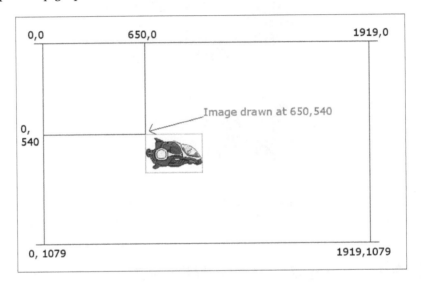

Furthermore, the coordinates are relative to what you draw upon. So, in both the Canvas Demo we just coded and the next demo, the coordinates were relative to the Bitmap (`myBitmap`). In the next chapter, we will use the entire screen, and the previous diagram will be an accurate representation of what is happening.

Let's do some more drawing—this time with Bitmaps. We will use the same starting code as we have seen in this app.

Creating Bitmaps

Let's do a little bit of theory before we dive into the code and consider exactly how we are going to bring images to life on the screen. To draw a bitmap, we will use the `drawBitmap` method of the `Canvas` class.

First, we would need to add a bitmap to the project into the `res/drawable` folder — we will do this for real in the Bitmap demo app coming up shortly. For now, assume the graphics file/bitmap has a name of `myImage.png`.

Next, we would declare an object of the `Bitmap` type, just the same as we did for the `Bitmap` we used for our background in the previous demo:

```
Bitmap mBitmap;
```

Next, we would need to initialize the `mBitmap` using our preferred image, which we previously added to the project's `drawable` folder:

```
mBitmap = BitmapFactory.decodeResource
              (getResources(), R.drawable.myImage);
```

The static `decodeResource` method of the `BitmapFactory` method is used to initialize `mBitmap`. It takes two parameters. The first is a call to `getResources`, which is made available by the `Activity` class. This method, as the name suggests, gives access to the project resources, and the second parameter, `R.drawable.myImage`, points to the `myImage.png` file in the `drawable` folder. The `Bitmap` (`mBitmap`) is now ready to be drawn by the `Canvas` class.

You could then draw the bitmap with the following code:

```
// Draw the bitmap at coordinates 100, 100
mCanvas.drawBitmap(mBitmap,
              100, 100, mPaint);
```

Here is what the spaceship graphic from the previous section looks like when drawn to the screen, just for reference when we talk about rotating bitmaps:

Manipulating Bitmaps

Quite often, however, we need to draw bitmaps in a rotated or otherwise altered state. It would be quite easy to use Photoshop, or whatever your favorite image editing software happens to be, and create more Bitmaps from the original Bitmap to face other directions.

Then, when we come to draw our bitmap, we can simply decide which way and draw the appropriate pre-loaded Bitmap.

However, I thought it would be much more interesting and instructive if we worked with just the one single source image and learned about the class that Android provides to manipulate images in our Java code. You will then be able to add rotating and inverting graphics to your app developer's toolkit.

What is a Bitmap exactly?

A Bitmap is called a Bitmap because that is exactly what it is. A *map of bits*. While there are many Bitmap formats that use different ranges and values to represent colors and transparency, they all amount to the same thing. They are a grid/map of values, and each value represents the color of a single pixel.

Therefore, to rotate, scale, or invert a Bitmap, we must perform the appropriate mathematical calculation upon each pixel/bit of the image/grid/map of the Bitmap. The calculations are not terribly complicated, but they are not especially simple either. If you took math to the end of high school, you will probably understand the math without too much bother.

Unfortunately, understanding the math isn't enough. We would also need to devise efficient code as well as understand the Bitmap format, and then modify our code for each format. This would not be trivial. Fortunately, the Android API has done it all for us. Meet the Matrix class.

The Matrix class

The class is named Matrix because it uses the mathematical concept and rules to perform calculations on a series of values known as matrices — the plural form of matrix.

 The Android Matrix class has nothing to do with the movie series of the same name. However, the author advises that all aspiring app developers take the **red** pill.

You might be familiar with matrices, but don't worry if you're not because the Matrix class hides all the complexity away. Furthermore, the Matrix class not only allows us to perform calculations on a series of values, but it also has some pre-prepared calculations that enable us to do things such as rotate a point around another point by a specific number of degrees. All this without knowing anything about trigonometry.

If you are intrigued by how the math works and want an absolute beginner's guide to the mathematics of rotating game objects, then look at this series of Android tutorials on my website, which ends with a flyable and rotatable spaceship:

`http://gamecodeschool.com/essentials/calculating-heading-in-2d-games-using-trigonometric-functions-part-1/`

`http://gamecodeschool.com/essentials/rotating-graphics-in-2d-games-using-trigonometric-functions-part-2/`

`http://gamecodeschool.com/android/2d-rotation-and-heading-demo/`

This book will stick to using the Android `Matrix` class, but we will do slightly more advanced math when we create a particle system in the next chapter.

Inverting a bitmap to face the opposite direction

First, we need to create an instance of the `Matrix` class. This next line of code does so in a familiar way by calling `new` on the default constructor:

```
Matrix matrix = new Matrix();
```

Note that you don't need to add any of this code to a project right now; it will all be shown again shortly with much more context. I just thought it would be easier to see all the `Matrix`-related code on its own beforehand.

Now we can use one of the many neat methods of the `Matrix` class. The `preScale` method takes two parameters: one for the horizontal change, and one for the vertical change. Look at this line of code:

```
matrix.preScale(-1, 1);
```

What the `preScale` method will do is loop through every pixel position and multiply all the horizontal coordinates by `-1` and all the vertical coordinates by `1`.

The effect of these calculations is that all the vertical coordinates will remain the same, because if you multiply by one then the number doesn't change. However, when you multiply by minus one, the horizontal position of the pixel will be inverted. For example, horizontal positions 0, 1, 2, 3, and 4 would become 0, -1, -2, -3, and -4.

At this stage, we have created a matrix that can perform the necessary calculations on a Bitmap. We haven't actually done anything with the Bitmap yet. To use the Matrix, we call the `createBitmap` method of the `Bitmap` class, as in this line of code:

```
mBitmapLeft = Bitmap
.createBitmap(mBitmap,
         0, 0, 25, 25, matrix, true);
```

The previous code assumes that `mBitmapLeft` is already initialized as well as `mBitmap`. The parameters to the `createBitmap` method are explained here:

- `mBitmapHeadRight` is a `Bitmap` object that has already been created and scaled, and has the image of the snake (facing to the right) loaded into it. This is the image that will be used as the source for creating the new `Bitmap`. The source `Bitmap` will not actually be altered at all.

- `0, 0` is the horizontal and vertical starting position that we want the new `Bitmap` to be mapped in to.

- The `25, 25` parameters are values that set the size that the bitmap is scaled to.

- The next parameter is our pre-prepared `Matrix` instance, `matrix`.

- The final parameter, `true`, instructs the `createBitmap` method that filtering is required to correctly handle the creation of the `Bitmap`.

This is what `mBitmapLeft` will look like when drawn to the screen:

We can also create the bitmap facing up and down using a rotation matrix.

Rotating the bitmap to face up and down

Let's look at rotating a `Bitmap`, and then we can build the demo app. We already have an instance of the `Matrix` class, so all we must do is call the `preRotate` method to create a matrix capable of rotating every pixel by a specified number of degrees in the single argument to `preRotate`. Look at this line of code:

```
// A matrix for rotating
matrix.preRotate(-90);
```

How simple was that? The `matrix` instance is now ready to rotate any series of numbers we pass to it, anti-clockwise (-), by 90 degrees.

This next line of code has exactly the same parameters as the previous call to `createBitmap` that we dissected, except that the new `Bitmap` is assigned to `mBitmapUp` and the effect of `matrix` is to perform the rotate instead of the `preScale`:

```
mBitmapUp = Bitmap
.createBitmap(mBitmap,
        0, 0, ss, ss, matrix, true);
```

This is what the `mBitmapUp` will look like when drawn:

You can also use the same technique but a different value in the argument to `preRotate to face the Bitmap downwards`. Let's get on with the demo app to see all this stuff in action.

Bitmap manipulation demo app

Now we have studied the theory, let's draw and spin some bitmaps. Create a new project and call it Manipulating Bitmaps. This time, be sure to choose the Empty Activity option on the Add an Activity to Mobile screen before clicking Next. Also, be sure to uncheck Generate Layout File and Backwards Compatibility. Don't worry about naming the Activity; this is just an app to play around with we will not be returning to it.

Add the graphic to the project

Right-click and select **Copy** to copy the `bob.png` graphics file from the download bundle in the `Chapter 20/Manipulating Bitmaps/drawable` folder.

In Android Studio, locate the `app/res/drawable` folder in the project explorer window. This next screenshot makes clear where this folder can be located and what it will look like with the `bob.png` image in it:

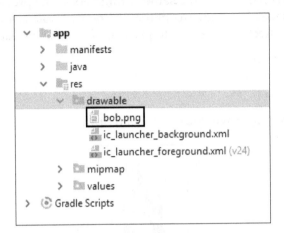

Right-click on the `drawable` folder and select **Paste** to add the `bob.png` file to the project. Click **OK** twice to confirm the default options for importing the file into the project.

Add the required instances as members ready to do some drawing with:

```
// Here are all the objects(instances)
// of classes that we need to do some drawing
ImageView myImageView;
Bitmap myBlankBitmap;
Bitmap bobBitmap;
Canvas myCanvas;
Paint myPaint;
```

Add the following imports:
```
import android.graphics.Bitmap;
import android.graphics.BitmapFactory;
import android.graphics.Canvas;
import android.graphics.Color;
import android.graphics.Matrix;
import android.graphics.Paint;
import android.widget.ImageView;
```

Now we can initialize all the members in `onCreate`:

```
// Initialize all the objects ready for drawing
int widthInPixels = 2000;
int heightInPixels = 1000;

// Create a new Bitmap
myBlankBitmap = Bitmap.createBitmap(widthInPixels,
        heightInPixels,
        Bitmap.Config.ARGB_8888);

// Initialize Bob
bobBitmap = BitmapFactory.decodeResource
        (getResources(), R.drawable.bob);

// Initialize the Canvas and associate it
// with the Bitmap to draw on
myCanvas = new Canvas(myBlankBitmap);

// Initialize the ImageView and the Paint
myImageView = new ImageView(this);
myPaint = new Paint();

// Draw on the Bitmap
// Wipe the Bitmap with a blue color
myCanvas.drawColor(Color.argb(255, 0, 0, 255));
```

Next, we add calls to three methods that we will write soon, and then set our new drawing as the view for the app:

```
// Draw some bitmaps
drawRotatedBitmaps();
drawEnlargedBitmap();
drawShrunkenBitmap();

// Associate the drawn upon Bitmap with the ImageView
myImageView.setImageBitmap(myBlankBitmap);
// Tell Android to set our drawing
// as the view for this app
// via the ImageView
setContentView(myImageView);
```

Now add the `drawRotatedBitmap` method, which does the bitmap manipulation:

```
void drawRotatedBitmaps(){
    float rotation = 0f;
    int horizontalPosition =350;
    int verticalPosition = 25;
    Matrix matrix = new Matrix();

    Bitmap rotatedBitmap = Bitmap.createBitmap(100,
                200,
                Bitmap.Config.ARGB_8888);

    for(rotation = 0; rotation < 360; rotation += 30){
        matrix.reset();
        matrix.preRotate(rotation);
        rotatedBitmap = Bitmap
                    .createBitmap(bobBitmap,
                            0, 0, bobBitmap.getWidth()-1,
                            bobBitmap.getHeight()-1,
                            matrix, true);

        myCanvas.drawBitmap(rotatedBitmap,
                    horizontalPosition,
                    verticalPosition,
                    myPaint);

        horizontalPosition += 120;
        verticalPosition += 70;
    }
}
```

The previous code uses a `for` loop to loop through 360 degrees, 30 degrees at a time. The value, on each pass through the loop, is used in the `Matrix` instance to rotate the image of Bob, and he is then drawn to the screen using the `drawBitmap` method.

Add the final two methods, as shown next:

```
void drawEnlargedBitmap(){
    bobBitmap = Bitmap
                .createScaledBitmap(bobBitmap,
                        300, 400, false);
    myCanvas.drawBitmap(bobBitmap, 25,25, myPaint);


}
```

```
void drawShrunkenBitmap(){
    bobBitmap = Bitmap
                  .createScaledBitmap(bobBitmap,
                          50, 75, false);
    myCanvas.drawBitmap(bobBitmap, 250,25, myPaint);
}
```

The `drawEnlargedBitmap` method uses the `createScaledBitmap` method, which is 300 by 400 pixels. The `drawBitmap` method then draws it to the screen.

The `drawShrunkenBitmap` uses the exact same technique, except it scales and then draws a 50 by 75-pixel image.

Run the app to see Bob grow and then shrink and spin around through 360 degrees at 30 degree intervals, as shown in this next screenshot:

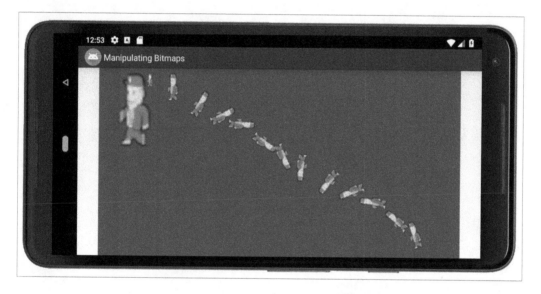

The only thing missing from our drawing repertoire is the ability to watch all this activity as it happens. We will fix this gap in our knowledge next.

Frequently asked question

Q1) I know how to do all this drawing, but I can't see anything move...

A) To see things move, you need to be able to regulate when each part of the drawing occurs. You need to use animation techniques. This is not trivial, but it is not beyond the grasp of a determined beginner, either. We will study the required topics in the next chapter.

Summary

In this chapter, we saw how to draw custom shapes, text, and bitmaps. Now that we know how to draw and manipulate both primitive shapes, text, and bitmaps we can take things up a level.

In the next chapter, we will start our next major app, which is a kid's drawing app that actually comes to life at the press of a button.

21
Threads, and Starting the Live Drawing App

In this chapter, we will get started on our next app. This app will be a kid's drawing app where the user can draw on the screen using their finger. This drawing app will be slightly different, however. The lines that the user draws will be comprised of particle systems that explode into thousands of pieces. We will call the project Live Drawing.

To achieve this, we will do the following.

- Get started with the Live Drawing app
- Learn about real-time interaction, sometimes referred to as a game loop
- Learn about threads
- Code a real-time system that will be ready for us to draw in (in the next chapter)

So, let's get started!

Creating the Live Drawing project

To get started, create a new project in Android Studio and call it `Live Drawing`. Use the **Empty Activity** project and uncheck the box to create the project without a layout file and without backward compatibility support. Name the Activity `LiveDrawingActivity`.

This app consists of Java files only. The Java files with all the code up to the end of this chapter can be found in the `Chapter 21` folder of the download bundle.

Next, we will create empty classes that we will code throughout the project over the next two chapters. Create a new class called LiveDrawingView, a new class called ParticleSystem, and a new class called Particle.

Looking ahead at the Live Drawing app

As this app is more in-depth and needs to respond in real time, it is necessary to use a slightly more in-depth structure. At first, this may seem like a complication, but in the long run, it can even make our code simpler and easier to understand.

We will have four classes in the Live Drawing app:

- LiveDrawingActivity: The Activity class provided by the Android API is the class that interacts with the operating system. We have already seen how the OS interacts with onCreate when the player clicks the app icon to start an app. Rather than have a class called MainActivity that does everything, we will have an Activity-based class that just handles the startup and shutdown of our app, as well as giving some assistance with initialization by getting the screen resolution. It makes sense that this class will be of the Activity type. However, as you will soon see, we will delegate interacting with touches to another class, the same class that will also handle almost every aspect of the app. This will introduce us to some interesting concepts that will be new to us.

- LiveDrawingView: This is the class that will be responsible for doing the drawing and creating the real-time environment that allows the user to interact at the same time as his/her creations are moving and evolving.

- ParticleSystem: This is the class that will manage up to thousands of instances of the Particle class.

- Particle: This class will be the simplest of them all. It will have a location on the screen and a heading. It will update itself around sixty times per second when prompted to by the LiveDrawingView class.

Now, we can start coding.

Coding the LiveDrawingActivity class

Let's get started with coding the Activity-based class. We called this class LiveDrawingActivity, and it was auto-generated for us when we created the project.

Add the first part of the code for the `LiveDrawingActivity` class:

```
import android.app.Activity;
import android.graphics.Point;
import android.os.Bundle;
import android.view.Display;

public class LiveDrawingActivity extends Activity {

    private LiveDrawingView mLiveDrawingView;

    @Override
    protected void onCreate(Bundle savedInstanceState) {
        super.onCreate(savedInstanceState);

        Display display = getWindowManager().getDefaultDisplay();
        Point size = new Point();
        display.getSize(size);

        mLiveDrawingView = new LiveDrawingView(
        this, size.x, size.y);
        setContentView(mLiveDrawingView);
    }

}
```

The preceding code shows a number of errors, and we will talk about them shortly.

The code gets the number of pixels (wide and high) for the device in the following way. Take another look at the first new line of code:

```
Display display = getWindowManager().getDefaultDisplay();
```

Here, we create an object of the `Display` type called `display` and initialize it with the result of calling both the `getWindowManager` and `getDefaultDisplay` methods in turn, which are part of the `Activity` class.

Then, we create a new object called `size` of the `Point` type. We send `size` as an argument to the `display.getSize` method. The `Point` type has an x and y member variable and, therefore, so does the `size` object, which, after the third line of code, now holds the width and height (in pixels) of the display.

Now, we have the screen resolution in the x and y variables hidden away in the `size` object.

The next new thing is that we are declaring an instance of our `LiveDrawingView` class. Currently, this is an empty class:

```
private LiveDrawingView mLiveDrawingView;
```

Next, in `onCreate`, we initialize `mLiveDrawingView` as follows:

```
mLiveDrawingView = new LiveDrawingView(this, size.x, size.y);
```

What we are doing is passing three arguments to the `LiveDrawingView` constructor. We have obviously not coded a constructor yet, and as we already know, the default constructor takes zero arguments. Therefore, this line will cause an error until we fix this.

The arguments passed in are interesting. First, there's `this`, which is a reference to `LiveDrawingActivity`. The `LiveDrawingView` class will need to perform actions (use methods) that it needs this reference for.

The second and third arguments are the horizontal and vertical screen resolution. It makes sense that our app will need these to perform tasks, such as detecting the edge of the screen and scaling the other drawing objects to an appropriate size. We will discuss these arguments further when we code the `LiveDrawingView` constructor.

Next, take a look at the even stranger line that follows:

```
setContentView(mLiveDrawingView);
```

This is where, in the Canvas Demo app, we set the `ImageView` as the content for the app. Remember that the `Activity` class's `setContentView` method must take a `View` object and an `ImageView` is a `View`. This previous line of code seems to be suggesting that we will use our `LiveDrawingView` class as the visible content for the app. However, `LiveDrawingView`, despite its name, isn't a `View`. At least not yet.

We will fix the constructor and the not-a-`View` problem after we add a few more lines of code to `LiveDrawingActivity`.

Reader challenge

Can you guess which OOP concept the solution might be?

Add the following two overridden methods, and then we will talk about them. Add them below the closing curly brace of onCreate, but before the closing curly brace of LiveDrawingActivity:

```
@Override
protected void onResume() {
    super.onResume();

    // More code here later in the chapter
}

@Override
protected void onPause() {
    super.onPause();

    // More code here later in the chapter
}
```

What we have done is overridden two more of the methods in the Activity class. We will see why we need to do this and what we will do inside these methods. The point to note here is that by adding these overridden methods, we are giving the OS the opportunity to notify us of the player's intentions in two more situations, much like we did when saving and loading our data in the Note to Self app.

It makes sense at this point to move on to the LiveDrawingView class, which is the main class of this app. We will come back to LiveDrawingActivity near the end of this chapter.

Coding the LiveDrawingView class

The first thing we will do is solve the problem of our LiveDrawingView class not being of the View type. Update the class declaration as highlighted, as follows:

```
class LiveDrawingView extends SurfaceView {
```

You will be prompted to import the `android.view.SurfaceView` class, as shown in the following screenshot:

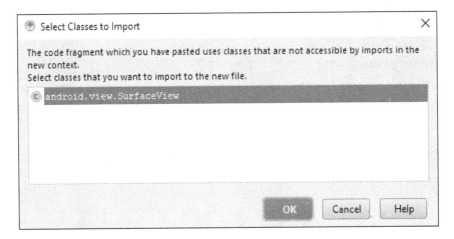

Click **OK** to confirm this.

`SurfaceView` is a descendant of `View` and now `LiveDrawingView` is, by inheritance, also a type of `View`. Look at the `import` statement that has been added. This relationship is made clear, as highlighted in the following code:

```
android.view.SurfaceView
```

> Remember that it is because of polymorphism that we can send descendants of `View` to the `setContentView` method in the `LiveDrawingActivity` class, and that it is because of inheritance that **LiveDrawingView** is now a type of **SurfaceView**.

There are quite a few descendants of `View` that we could have extended to fix this initial problem, but we will see as we continue that `SurfaceView` has some very specific features that are perfect for real-time interactive apps that made this choice the right one for us.

However, we still have errors in both this class and `LiveDrawingActivity`. Both are due to the lack of a suitable constructor method.

Here is screenshot showing the error in the `LiveDrawingView` class since we extended `SurfaceView`:

The error in `LiveDrawingActivity` is more obvious; we are calling a method that doesn't exist. However, the error shown in the previous screenshot is less easily understood. Let's now discuss the error in `LiveDrawingView`.

The `LiveDrawingView` class, now that it is a `SurfaceView`, must be supplied with a constructor because, as mentioned (in a tip) in the OOP chapters, once you have provided your own constructor, the default (no parameter) one ceases to exist. As the `SurfaceView` class implements several different constructors, we must specifically implement one of these or write our own, hence the previous error.

As none of the `SurfaceView` provided constructors are exactly what we need, we will provide our own.

> If you are wondering how on earth to find out what constructors are supplied and any other details you need to find out about an Android class, just Google it. Type in the class name, followed by `API`. Google will almost always supply a link to the relevant page on the Android developer's website as the top result. Here is a direct link to the `SurfaceView` page:
>
> `https://developer.android.com/reference/android/view/SurfaceView.html`.
>
> Look under the **Public constructors** heading, and you will see that some constructors are optionally made available.

The `LiveDrawingActivity` class also requires us to create a constructor that matches the way we try to initialize it in this line of code from `LiveDrawingActivity`:

```
mLiveDrawingView = new LiveDrawingView(this, size.x, size.y);
```

Let's add a constructor that matches the call from LiveDrawingActivity that passes in this and the screen resolution, and solve both problems at once.

Coding the LiveDrawingView class

Remember that LiveDrawingView cannot see the variables in LiveDrawingActivity. By using the constructor, LiveDrawingActivity is providing LiveDrawingView with a reference to itself (this) as well as the screen size in pixels contained in size.x and size.y. Add this constructor to LiveDrawingView. The code must go within the opening and closing curly braces of the class. It is convention, but not mandatory, to place constructors above other methods but after member variable declarations:

```
// The LiveDrawingView constructor
// Called when this line:
// mLiveDrawingView = new LiveDrawingView(this, size.x, size.y);
// is executed from LiveDrawingActivity
public LiveDrawingView(Context context, int x, int y) {
        // Super... calls the parent class
        // constructor of SurfaceView
        // provided by the Android API
        super(context);
}
```

To import the Context class, do the following:

1. Place the mouse pointer on the red colored Context in the new constructor's signature.

2. Hold the *ALT* key and tap the *Enter* key. Choose **Import Class** from the pop-up options.

The previous steps will import the Context class.

Now, we have no errors in our LiveDrawingView class or the LiveDrawingActivity class that initializes it.

At this stage, we could run the app and see that using LiveDrawingView as the View in setContentView has worked and that we have a beautiful blank screen, ready to draw our particle systems on. Try this if you like, but we will be coding the LiveDrawingView class so that it does something, including adding code to the constructor, next.

We will be returning to this class constantly over the course of this project. What we will do right now is get the fundamentals set up ready so that we can add the ParticleSystem instances after we have coded them in the next chapter.

To achieve this, first, we will add a bunch of member variables, and then we will add some code inside the constructor to set the class up when it is instantiated/created by LiveDrawingActivity.

Following on, we get to code the draw method, which will reveal the new steps that we need to take to draw to the screen 60 times per second, and we will also see some familiar code that uses our old friends, Canvas, Paint, and drawText, from the previous chapter.

At this point, we need to discuss some more theory items, such as how we will time the animations of the particles, and how we lock these timings without interfering with the smooth running of Android. These last two topics, the **game loop** and **threads,** will then allow us to add the final code of this chapter and witness our particle system painting app in action, albeit with just a bit of text.

 A game loop is a concept that describes allowing virtual systems to update and draw themselves at the same time as allowing them to be altered/interacted with by the user.

Adding the member variables

Add the variables, as shown in the following code, after the LiveDrawingView declaration, but before the constructor, and then import the necessary extra classes:

```
// Are we debugging?
private final boolean DEBUGGING = true;

// These objects are needed to do the drawing
private SurfaceHolder mOurHolder;
private Canvas mCanvas;
private Paint mPaint;

// How many frames per second did we get?
private long mFPS;
// The number of milliseconds in a second
private final int MILLIS_IN_SECOND = 1000;

// Holds the resolution of the screen
private int mScreenX;
private int mScreenY;
```

```
// How big will the text be?
private int mFontSize;
private int mFontMargin;

// The particle systems will be declared here later

// These will be used to make simple buttons
```

Be sure to study the code, and then we can talk about it.

We are using the naming convention of adding m before the member variable names. As we add local variables to the methods, this will help distinguish them from each other.

Also, notice that all the variables are declared private. You could happily delete all the private access specifiers and the code will still work but, as we have no need to access any of these variables from outside of this class, it is sensible to guarantee that this can never happen by declaring them private.

The first member variable is DEBUGGING. We have declared this as final because we don't want to change its value during the app's execution. Note that declaring it final does not preclude us from switching its value manually when we wish to switch between debugging and not debugging.

The next three classes we declared instances of will handle the drawing on the screen. Observe the new one we have not seen before that I have highlighted:

```
// These objects are needed to do the drawing
private SurfaceHolder mOurHolder;
private Canvas mCanvas;
private Paint mPaint;
```

The SurfaceHolder class is required to enable drawing to take place. It literally is the object that *holds* the drawing surface. We will see the methods it allows us to use to draw to the screen when we code the draw method in a minute.

The next two variables give us a bit of insight into what we will need to achieve our smooth and consistent animation. Here they are again:

```
// How many frames per second did we get?
private long mFPS;
// The number of milliseconds in a second
private final int MILLIS_IN_SECOND = 1000;
```

Both are of the type `long` because they will be holding a huge number. Computers measure time in milliseconds since 1970. More on that when we talk about the game loop, but for now, we need to know that monitoring and measuring the speed of each frame of animation is how we will make sure that the particles move exactly as they should.

The first `mFPS` will be reinitialized every frame of animation, around 60 times per second. It will be passed into each of the particle objects (every frame of animation) so that they know how much time has elapsed and can then calculate how far to move, or not.

The `MILLIS_IN_SECOND` variable is initialized to `1000`. There are indeed `1000` milliseconds in a second. We will use this variable in calculations as it will make our code clearer than if we used the literal value, 1000. It is declared `final` because the number of milliseconds in a second will obviously never change.

The next piece of the code we just added is shown again here for convenience:

```
// Holds the resolution of the screen
private int mScreenX;
private int mScreenY;
// How big will the text be?
private int mFontSize;
private int mFontMargin;
```

The variables `mScreenX` and `mScreenY` will hold the horizontal and vertical resolution of the screen. Remember that they are being passed in from `LiveDrawingActivity` into the constructor.

The next two, `mFontSize` and `mMarginSize`, will be initialized, based on the screen size in pixels, to hold a value in pixels to make formatting of our text neat and more concise than constantly doing calculations for each bit of text.

Just to be clear before we move on, these are the `import` statements that you should currently have at the top of the `LiveDrawingView.java` code file:

```
import android.content.Context;
import android.graphics.Canvas;
import android.graphics.Paint;
import android.view.SurfaceHolder;
import android.view.SurfaceView;
```

Now, we can begin to initialize some of these variables in the constructor.

Coding the LiveDrawingView constructor

Add the following highlighted code to the constructor. Be sure to study the code as well and then we can discuss it:

```
public LiveDrawingView(Context context, int x, int y) {
    // Super... calls the parent class
    // constructor of SurfaceView
    // provided by Android
    super(context);

    // Initialize these two members/fields
    // With the values passed in as parameters
    mScreenX = x;
    mScreenY = y;

    // Font is 5% (1/20th) of screen width
    mFontSize = mScreenX / 20;
    // Margin is 1.5% (1/75th) of screen width
    mFontMargin = mScreenX / 75;

    // getHolder is a method of SurfaceView
     mOurHolder = getHolder();
    mPaint = new Paint();

    // Initialize the two buttons

    // Initialize the particles and their systems
}
```

The code we just added to the constructor begins by using the values passed in as parameters (x and y) to initialize mScreenX and mScreenY. Our entire LiveDrawingView class now has access to the screen resolution whenever it needs it. Here are the two lines again:

```
// Initialize these two members/fields
// With the values passed in as parameters
mScreenX = x;
mScreenY = y;
```

Next, we initialize `mFontSize` and `mFontMargin` as a fraction of the screen width in pixels. These values are a bit arbitrary, but they work, and we will use various multiples of these variables to align text on the screen neatly. Here are the two lines of code I am referring to:

```
// Font is 5% (1/20th) of screen width
mFontSize = mScreenX / 20;
// Margin is 1.5% (1/75th) of screen width
mFontMargin = mScreenX / 75;
```

Moving on, we initialize our `Paint` and `SurfaceHolder` objects. `Paint` uses the default constructor, as we have done previously, but `mHolder` uses the `getHolder` method, which is a method of the `SurfaceView` class. The `getHolder` method returns a reference that is initialized to `mHolder`, so `mHolder` is now that reference. In short, `mHolder` is now ready to be used. We have access to this handy method because `LiveDrawingView` is a `SurfaceView`:

```
// getHolder is a method of SurfaceView
mOurHolder = getHolder();
mPaint = new Paint();
```

We will need to do more preparation in the `draw` method before we can use our `Paint` and `Canvas` classes like we have done before. We will see exactly what this preparation entails very soon. Notice the comments indicating where we will eventually get around to initializing the particle systems, as well as two control buttons.

Let's get ready to draw.

Coding the draw method

Add the `draw` method, which is shown immediately after the constructor method. There will be a couple of errors in the code. We will first deal with them, and then we will go into detail about how the `draw` method will work in relation to `SurfaceView` because there are some completely alien-looking lines of code in there, as well as some familiar ones. This is the code to add:

```
// Draw the particle systems and the HUD
private void draw() {
    if (mOurHolder.getSurface().isValid()) {
        // Lock the canvas (graphics memory) ready to draw
        mCanvas = mOurHolder.lockCanvas();

        // Fill the screen with a solid color
```

```
below //Fill......
            mCanvas.drawColor(Color.argb(255, 0, 0, 0));
            // Choose a color to paint with
            mPaint.setColor(Color.argb(255, 255, 255, 255));

            // Choose the font size
        mPaint.setTextSize(mFontSize);

        // Draw the particle systems

        // Draw the buttons

        // Draw the HUD
        if(DEBUGGING){
                printDebuggingText();
        }


        // Display the drawing on screen
        // unlockCanvasAndPost is a method of SurfaceHolder
        mOurHolder.unlockCanvasAndPost(mCanvas);
    }

}
```

We have two errors. One is that the `Color` class needs importing. You can fix this in the usual way, or add the next line of code manually.

Whichever method you choose, the following extra line needs to be added to the code at the top of the file:

```
import android.graphics.Color;
```

Let's deal with the other error.

Adding the printDebuggingText method

The second error is the call to `printDebuggingText`. This method doesn't exist yet. Let's add that now.

Add the following code after the `draw` method, as follows:

```
private void printDebuggingText(){
    int debugSize = mFontSize / 2;
    int debugStart = 150;
```

```
mPaint.setTextSize(debugSize);
mCanvas.drawText("FPS: " + mFPS ,
        10, debugStart + debugSize, mPaint);

// We will add more code here in the next chapter

}
```

The previous code uses the local variable debugSize to hold a value that is half that of the member variable mFontSize. This means that as mFontSize (which is used for the HUD) is initialized dynamically based on the screen resolution, debugSize will always be half that. The debugSize variable is then used to set the size of the font before we start drawing the text. The debugStart variable is just a guess at a good position vertically to start printing the debugging text.

These two values are then used to position a line of text on the screen that shows the current frames per second. As this method is called from draw, which, in turn, will be called from the game loop, this line of text will be constantly refreshed up to sixty times per second.

 It is possible that on very high or very low resolution screens, you might need to experiment with this value to find something more appropriate for your screen.

Let's explore the new lines of code in the draw method and exactly how we can use SurfaceView, from which our LiveDrawingView class is derived, to handle all of our drawing requirements.

Understanding the draw method and the SurfaceView class

Starting in the middle of the method and working outward for a change, we have a few familiar things, such as the calls to drawColor, setTextSize, and drawText. We can also see the comment that indicates where we will eventually add code to draw the particle systems and the HUD:

- The drawColor code clears the screen with a solid color.

- The setTextSize method sets the size of the text for drawing the HUD.

- We will code the process of drawing the HUD once we have explored particle systems a little more. We will let the player know how many particles and systems their drawing is comprised of.

What is totally new, however, is the code at the very start of the draw method. Here it is again:

```
if (mOurHolder.getSurface().isValid()) {
// Lock the canvas (graphics memory) ready to draw
mCanvas = mOurHolder.lockCanvas();

...

...
```

The if statement contains a call to getSurface and chains it with a call to isValid. If this line returns true, it confirms that if the area of memory that we want to manipulate to represent our frame of drawing is available, the code continues inside the if statement.

What goes on inside those methods (especially the first) is quite complex. They are necessary because all of our drawing and other processing (such as moving the objects) will take place asynchronously with the code that detects the user input and listens to the operating system for messages. This wasn't an issue in the previous project because our code just drew a single frame.

Now that we want to execute the code 60 times a second, we are going to need to confirm that we have access to the memory before we access it.

This raises more questions about how this code runs asynchronously. This will be answered when we discuss threads shortly. For now, just know that the line of code checks whether some other part of our code or Android itself is currently using the required portion of memory. If it is free, then the code inside the if statement executes.

Furthermore, the first line of code to execute inside the if statement calls lockCanvas, so that if another part of the code tries to access the memory while our code is accessing it, it won't be able to.

Then, we do all of our drawing.

Finally, in the draw method, there is this following line (plus comments) right at the end:

```
// Display the drawing on screen
// unlockCanvasAndPost is a method of SurfaceHolder
mOurHolder.unlockCanvasAndPost(mCanvas);
```

The unlockCanvasAndPost method sends our newly decorated Canvas object (mCanvas) for drawing to the screen and releases the lock so that other areas of code can use it again, albeit very briefly before the whole process starts again. This process happens every single frame of animation.

We now understand the code in the `draw` method. However, we still don't have the mechanism that calls the `draw` method over and over. In fact, we don't even call the `draw` method once. Next, we need to talk about game loops and threads.

The game loop

What is a game loop, anyway? Almost every live drawing/graphics/game has a game loop. Even games you might suspect do not, such as turn-based games, still need to synchronize player input with drawing and AI, while following the rules of the underlying operating system.

There is a constant need to update the objects in the app, perhaps by moving them. You need to draw everything in its current position at the same time as responding to user input. A diagram might help:

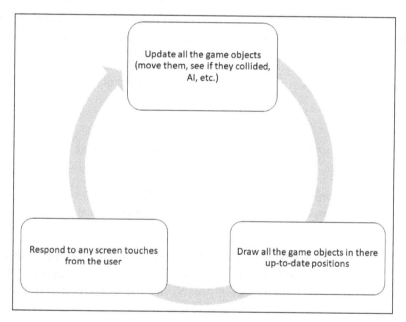

Our game loop is comprised of three main phases:

1. Update all game/drawing objects by moving them, detecting collisions, and processing the artificial intelligence like the particle movements and state changes.

2. Based on the data that has just been updated, draw the frame of animation in its latest state.

3. Respond to screen touches from the user.

We already have a `draw` method for handling that part of the loop. This suggests that we will have a method to do all of the updating as well. We will soon code the outline of an `update` method. In addition, we know that we can respond to screen touches, although we will need to adapt slightly from all of the previous projects because we are no longer working inside an Activity or using conventional UI widgets in a layout.

There is a further issue in that (as I briefly mentioned) all the updating and drawing happens asynchronously to detect screen touches and listen to the operating system.

 Just to be clear, asynchronous means that it does not occur at the same time. Our game code will work by sharing execution time with Android and the user interface. The CPU will very quickly switch back and forth between our code and Android/user input.

But how exactly will these three phases be looped through? How will we code this asynchronous system, within which `update` and `draw` can be called, and how will we make the loop run at the correct speed (frame rate)?

As we can probably guess, writing an efficient game loop is not as simple as a `while` loop.

 Our game loop will, however, also contain a `while` loop.

We need to consider timing, starting, and stopping the loop, as well as not causing the OS to become unresponsive because we are monopolizing the entire CPU within our single loop.

But when and how do we call our `draw` method? How do we measure and keep track of the frame rate? With these things in mind, our finished game loop can probably be better represented by the following diagram. Notice the introduction to the concept of **threads**:

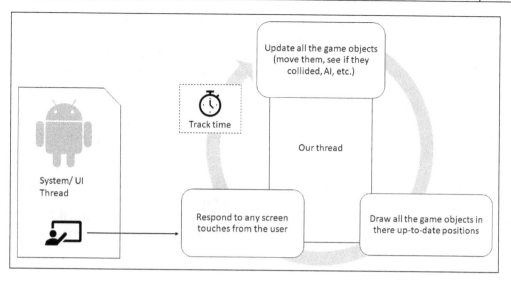

Now that we know what we want to achieve, let's learn about threads.

Threads

So, what is a thread? You can think of threads in programming in the same way you do threads in a story. In one thread of a story, we might have the primary character battling the enemy on the frontline, while in another, the thread shows that the soldier's family are getting by, day to day. Of course, a story doesn't have to have just two threads. We could introduce a third thread. Perhaps the story also tells about the politicians and military commanders making decisions. And these decisions then subtly, or not so subtly, affect what happens in the other threads.

Programming threads is just like this. We create parts/threads in our program that control different aspects for us. In Android, threads are especially useful when we need to ensure that a task does not interfere with the main (UI) thread of the app, or if we have a background task that takes a long time to complete and must not interrupt the main thread of execution. We introduce threads to represent these different aspects for the following reasons:

- They make sense from an organizational point of view
- They are a proven way of structuring a program that works
- The nature of the system we are working on forces us to use them

In Android, we use threads for all three reasons simultaneously. It makes sense, it works, and we have to because the design of the Android system requires it.

Often, we use threads without knowing it. This happens because we use classes that use threads on our behalf. All of the animations we coded in *Chapter 19, Animations and Interpolations,* were all running in threads. Another such example in Android is the `SoundPool` class, which loads sound in a thread. We will see, or rather hear, `SoundPool` in action in *Chapter 23, Supporting Different Versions of Android, Sound Effects, and the Spinner Widget,* and we saw and will see again that our code doesn't have to handle the aspects of threads we are about to learn about because it is all handled internally by the class. In this project, however, we need to get a bit more involved.

In real-time systems, think about a thread that is receiving the player's button taps for moving left and right at the same time as listening for messages from the OS, such as calling `onCreate` (and other methods we will see soon) as one thread, and another thread that draws all the graphics and calculates all the movements.

Problems with threads

Programs with multiple threads can have problems associated with them, like the threads of a story in which, if proper synchronization does not occur, then things can go wrong. What if our soldier went into battle before the battle or even the war existed? Weird.

Consider that we have a variable, `int x`, that represents a key piece of data that, let's say, three threads of our program use. What happens if one thread gets slightly ahead of itself and makes the data "wrong" for the other two. This problem is the problem of **correctness**, and is caused by multiple threads racing to completion obliviously — because, after all, they are just dumb code.

The problem of correctness can be solved by close oversight of the threads and locking. **Locking** means temporarily preventing execution in one thread to be sure things are working in a synchronized manner, kind of like preventing a soldier from boarding a ship to war until the ship has docked and the gangplank has been lowered, thereby avoiding an embarrassing splash.

The other problem with programs with multiple threads is the problem of **deadlock,** where one or more threads become locked waiting for the "right" moment to access `int x`, but that moment never comes and, eventually, the entire program grinds to a halt.

You might have noticed that it was the solution to the first problem (correctness) that is the cause of the second problem (deadlock).

Fortunately, the problem has been solved for us. Just as we use the `Activity` class and override `onCreate` to know when we need to create our app, we can also use other classes to create and manage our threads. Just as with `Activity`, we only need to know how to use them, not how they work exactly.

So, why did I tell you all this stuff about threads when you didn't need to know, you rightly ask. Simply because we will be writing code that looks different and is structured in an unfamiliar manner. If we can do the following:

- Understand the general concept of a thread that is just the same thing as a story thread that happens almost simultaneously, and

- learn the few rules of using a thread,

then we will have no difficulty writing our Java code to create and work within our threads. There are a few different Android classes that handle threads. Different thread classes work best in different situations.

All we need to remember is that we will be writing parts of our program that run at *almost* the same time as each other.

> What do you mean, almost? What is happening is that the CPU switches between threads in turn/asynchronously. However, this happens so fast that we will not be able to perceive anything but simultaneity/synchrony. Of course, in the story thread analogy, people do act entirely synchronously.

Let's take a glimpse of what our thread code will look like. Don't add any code to the project just yet. We can declare an object of the `Thread` type as follows:

```
Thread ourThread;
```

And then initialize and start it like this:

```
ourThread = new Thread(this);
ourThread.start();
```

There is one more conundrum to this thread stuff. Look at the constructor that initializes the thread. Here is the line of code again for your convenience:

```
ourThread = new Thread(this);
```

Look at the highlighted argument that is passed to the constructor. We pass in `this`. Remember that the code is going inside the `LiveDrawingView` class, not `LiveDrawingActivity`. We can, therefore, surmise that `this` is a reference to the `LiveDrawingView` class (which extends `SurfaceView`).

It seems very unlikely that when the nerds at Android HQ wrote the `Thread` class, they would have been aware that one day we would be writing our `LiveDrawingView` class. So, how can this work?

The `Thread` class needs an entirely different type to be passed into its constructor. The `Thread` constructor needs a `Runnable` object.

> You can confirm this fact by looking at the thread class on the Android developer's website here:
>
> `https://developer.android.com/reference/java/lang/`
> `Thread.html#Thread(java.lang.Runnable).`

Do you recall that we talked about interfaces in *Chapter 11, More Object-Oriented Programming*? As a reminder, we can implement an interface by using the `implements` keyword and the interface name after the class declaration, as in the following code:

```
class someClass extends someotherClass implements Runnable{
```

We must then implement the abstract methods of the interface. `Runnable` has just one. It is the `run` method.

> You can confirm this last fact by looking at the `Runnable` interface on the Android developer's website here:
>
> `https://developer.android.com/reference/java/lang/`
> `Runnable.html.`

We can then use the Java `@override` keyword to change what happens when the operating system allows our thread object to run its code:

```
class someClass extends someotherClass implements Runnable{
    @override
    run(){
        // Anything in here executes in a thread
        // No skill needed on our part
        // It is all handled by Android, the Thread class
        // and the Runnable interface
    }
}
```

Within the overridden `run` method, we will call two methods; one that we have started already, `draw`, and the other, which is `update`. The `update` method is where all our calculations and artificial intelligence will go. The code will look a bit like this. Don't add it yet:

```
@override
public void run() {

    // Update the drawing based on
    // user input, physics,
    // collision detection and artificial intelligence
    update();

    // Draw all the particle systems in their updated locations
    draw();

}
```

When appropriate, we can also stop our thread like this:

```
ourThread.join();
```

Now, everything that is in the `run` method is executing in a separate thread, leaving the default or UI thread to listen for touches and system events. We will see how the two threads communicate with each other in the drawing project shortly.

Note that precisely where all these parts of the code will go into our app has not been explained, but it is so much easier to show you in the real project.

Implementing the game loop with a thread

Now that we have learned about the game loop and threads, we can put it all together to implement our game loop in the Living Drawing project.

We will add the entire code for the game loop, including writing two methods in the `LiveDrawingActivity` class, to start and stop the thread that will control the loop.

 Can you guess how the Activity-based class will start and stop the thread in the `LiveDrawingView` class?

Implementing Runnable and providing the run method

Update the class declaration by implementing `Runnable`, just like we discussed previously, and as shown in the following highlighted code:

```
class LiveDrawingView extends SurfaceView implements Runnable{
```

Notice that we have a new error in the code. Hover the mouse pointer over the word `Runnable` and you will see a message informing you that we need to implement the `run` method, again, just as we discussed during the discussion on interfaces and threads in the previous section. Add the empty `run` method, including the @ `override` label, as demonstrated shortly.

It doesn't matter where you add it, provided it is within the `LiveDrawingView` class's curly braces and not inside another method. I added mine right after the constructor method because it is near the top and easy to get to. We will be editing this quite a bit in this chapter. Add the empty `run` method, as shown here:

```
// When we start the thread with:
// mThread.start();
// the run method is continuously called by Android
// because we implemented the Runnable interface
// Calling mThread.join();
// will stop the thread
@Override
public void run() {
}
```

The error is gone and now we can declare and initialize a `Thread` object.

Coding the thread

Declare some variables and instances, shown as follows, underneath all our other members in the `LiveDrawingView` class:

```
// Here is the Thread and two control variables
private Thread mThread = null;
// This volatile variable can be accessed
// from inside and outside the thread
private volatile boolean mDrawing;
private boolean mPaused = true;
```

Now, we can start and stop the thread. Have a think about where we might do this. Remember that the app needs to respond to the operating system starting and stopping the app.

Starting and stopping the thread

Now, we need to start and stop the thread. We have seen the code we need, but when and where should we do it? Let's write two methods, one to start and one to stop, and then we can consider further when and where to call these methods from. Add these two methods inside the `LiveDrawingView` class. If their names sound familiar, it is not by chance:

```java
// This method is called by LiveDrawingActivity
// when the user quits the app
public void pause() {

    // Set mDrawing to false
    // Stopping the thread isn't
    // always instant
    mDrawing = false;
    try {
        // Stop the thread
        mThread.join();
    } catch (InterruptedException e) {
        Log.e("Error:", "joining thread");
    }

}


// This method is called by LiveDrawingActivity
// when the player starts the app
public void resume() {
    mDrawing = true;
    // Initialize the instance of Thread
    mThread = new Thread(this);

    // Start the thread
    mThread.start();
}
```

What is happening is slightly given away by the comments. You did read the comments, right? We now have a `pause` and `resume` method that stop and start the `Thread` object using the same code we discussed previously.

Notice that the new methods are `public` and therefore accessible from outside the class to any other class that has an instance of `LiveDrawingView`.

Remember that `LiveDrawingActivity` has the fully declared and initialized instance of `LiveDrawingView`?

Let's use the Android Activity life cycle to call these two new methods.

Using the Activity lifecycle to start and stop the thread

Update the overridden `onResume` and `onPause` methods in `LiveDrawingActivity`, as shown in the highlighted lines of code:

```
@Override
protected void onResume() {
    super.onResume();

    // More code here later in the chapter
    mLiveDrawingView.resume();
}

@Override
protected void onPause() {
    super.onPause();

    // More code here later in the chapter
    mLiveDrawingView.pause();
}
```

Now, our thread will be started and stopped when the operating system is resuming and pausing our app. Remember that `onResume` is called after `onCreate` the first time an app is created, not just after resuming from a pause. The code inside `onResume` and `onPause` uses the `mLiveDrawingView` object to call its `resume` and `pause` methods, which, in turn, has the code to start and stop the thread. This code then triggers the thread's `run` method to execute. It is in this `run` method (in `LiveDrawingView`) that we will code our game loop. Let's do that now.

Coding the run method

Although our thread is set up and ready to go, nothing happens because the run method is empty. Code the run method, as shown in the following code:

```java
@Override
public void run() {
    // mDrawing gives us finer control
    // rather than just relying on the calls to run
    // mDrawing must be true AND
    // the thread running for the main
    // loop to execute
    while (mDrawing) {

        // What time is it now at the start of the loop?
        long frameStartTime = System.currentTimeMillis();

        // Provided the app isn't paused
        // call the update method
        if(!mPaused){
            update();
            // Now the particles are in
            // their new positions
        }

        // The movement has been handled and now
        // we can draw the scene.
        draw();

        // How long did this frame/loop take?
        // Store the answer in timeThisFrame
        long timeThisFrame =
                System.currentTimeMillis() - frameStartTime;

        // Make sure timeThisFrame is at least 1 millisecond
        // because accidentally dividing
        // by zero crashes the app
        if (timeThisFrame > 0) {
            // Store the current frame rate in mFPS
            // ready to pass to the update methods of
            // of our particles in the next frame/loop
            mFPS = MILLIS_IN_SECOND / timeThisFrame;
        }
    }
}
```

Notice that there are two errors in Android Studio. This is because we have not written the update method yet. Let's quickly add an empty method (with a comment) for it. I added mine after the run method:

```
private void update() {
    // Update the particles


}
```

Now, let's discuss in detail how the code in the run method achieves the aims of our game loop by looking at the whole thing a bit at a time.

This first part initiates a while loop with the mDrawing condition and wraps the rest of the code inside run so that the thread will need to be started (for run to be called) and mDrawing will need to be true for the while loop to execute:

```
@Override
public void run() {
    // mPlaying gives us finer control
    // rather than just relying on the calls to run
    // mPlaying must be true AND
    // the thread running for the main
    // loop to execute
    while (mPlaying) {
```

The first line of code inside the while loop declares and initializes a local variable, frameStartTime, with whatever the current time is. The static method, currentTimeMillis, of the System class returns this value. If we want to measure how long a frame has taken later on, then we need to know what time it started:

```
    // What time is it now at the start of the loop?
    long frameStartTime = System.currentTimeMillis();
```

Next, still inside the while loop, we need to check whether the app is paused, and only if the app is not paused does the following code get executed. If the logic allows execution inside this block, then update is called:

```
    // Provided the app isn't paused
    // call the update method
    if (!mPaused) {
        update();
        // Now the particles are in
        // their new positions


    }
```

Outside of the previous `if` statement, the `draw` method is called to draw all the objects in the just-updated positions. At this point, another local variable is declared and initialized with the length of time it took to complete the entire frame (updating and drawing). This value is calculated by getting the current time, once again with `currentTimeMillis`, and subtracting `frameStartTime` from it, as follows:

```
// The movement has been handled and collisions
// detected now we can draw the scene.
draw();

// How long did this frame/loop take?
// Store the answer in timeThisFrame
long timeThisFrame =
        System.currentTimeMillis() - frameStartTime;
```

The next `if` statement detects whether `timeThisFrame` is greater than zero. It is possible for the value to be zero if the thread runs before objects are initialized. If you look at the code inside the `if` statement, it calculates the frame rate by dividing the elapsed time by `MILLIS_IN_SECOND`. If you divide by zero, the app will crash, which is why we do the check.

Once `mFPS` gets the value assigned to it, we can use it in the next frame to pass to the `update` method all the particles that we will code in the next chapter. They will use the value to make sure that they move by precisely the correct amount based on their target speed and the length of time the frame has taken:

```
// Make sure timeThisFrame is at least 1 millisecond
// because accidentally dividing
// by zero crashes the app
if (timeThisFrame > 0) {
        // Store the current frame rate in mFPS
        // ready to pass to the update methods of
        // the particles in the next frame/loop
        mFPS = MILLIS_IN_SECOND / timeThisFrame;
    }
  }
}
```

The result of the calculation that initializes `mFPS` each frame is that `mFPS` will hold a fraction of 1. As the frame rate fluctuates, `mFPS` will hold a different value and supply the game objects with the appropriate number to calculate each move.

Running the app

Click the play button in Android Studio and the hard work and theory of the last two chapters will spring to life:

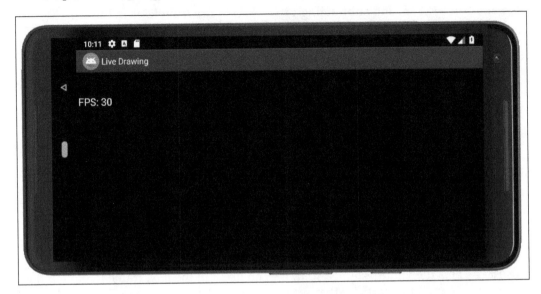

You can see that we now have created a real-time system with our game loop and a thread. If you run this on a real device, you will easily achieve 60 frames per second at this stage.

Summary

This was probably the most technical chapter so far. Threads, game loops, timing, using interfaces along with the Activity lifecycle, and so on... it's an awfully long list of topics to cram in.

If the exact interrelationships between these things are not entirely clear, it is not a problem. All you need to know is that when the user starts and stops drawing with their finger, the LiveDrawingActivity class will handle starting and stopping the thread by calling the LiveDrawingView class's pause and resume methods. It achieves this via the overridden onPause and onResume methods, which are called by the OS.

Once the thread is running, the code inside the run method executes alongside the UI thread that is listening for user input. As we call the update and draw methods from the run method at the same time as keeping track of how long each frame is taking, our app is ready to rock and roll.

We just need to allow the user to add some particles to their artwork, which we can then update in each call to `update`, and draw in each call to `draw`.

In the next chapter, we will be coding, updating, and drawing both the `Particle` and the `ParticleSytem` classes. In addition, we will be writing code so that the user can interact (do some drawing) with the app.

22

Particle Systems and Handling Screen Touches

We already have our real-time system that we implemented in the previous chapter by using a thread. In this chapter, we will create the entities that will exist and evolve in this real-time system as if they have minds of their own and form the appearance of the drawings that the user can achieve.

We will also see how the user implements these entities by learning how to respond to interaction with the screen. This is different to interacting with a widget in a UI layout.

Here is what is coming up in this chapter:

- Adding custom buttons to the screen
- Coding the `Particle` class
- Coding the `ParticleSystem` class
- Handling screen touches

We will start by adding a custom UI to our app.

Adding custom buttons to the screen

We need to let the user control when to start another drawing and clear the screen of their previous work. We need the user to be able to decide if and when to bring the drawing to life. To achieve this, we will add two buttons to the screen, one for each of the tasks.

Add the members highlighted in the `LiveDrawingView` class, as follows:

```
// These will be used to make simple buttons
private RectF mResetButton;
private RectF mTogglePauseButton;
```

We now have two `RectF` instances. These objects hold four floating point coordinates each, one coordinate for each corner of our two proposed buttons.

Initialize the positions in the constructor of `LiveDrawingView` as follows:

```
// Initialize the two buttons
mResetButton = new RectF(0, 0, 100, 100);
mTogglePauseButton = new RectF(0, 150, 100, 250);
```

Now, we have added actual coordinates for the buttons. If you visualize the coordinates on the screen, then you will see that they are in the left-hand top corner, with the pause button just below the reset/clear button.

Now, we can draw the buttons. Add these two lines of code in the `draw` method of the `LiveDrawing`View class:

```
// Draw the buttons
mCanvas.drawRect(mResetButton, mPaint);
mCanvas.drawRect(mTogglePauseButton, mPaint);
```

The new code uses an overridden version of the `drawRect` method and we simply pass our two `RectF` instances straight in, alongside the usual `Paint` instance. Our buttons will now be drawn to the screen.

We will see how we interact with these slightly crude buttons later in this chapter.

Implementing a particle system effect

A particle system is a system that controls particles. In our case, `ParticleSystem` is a class we will write that will spawn instances (lots of instances) of the `Particle` class (also a class we will write) that will create a simple, explosion-like effect.

Here is an image of some particles controlled by a particle system as it may appear by the end of this chapter:

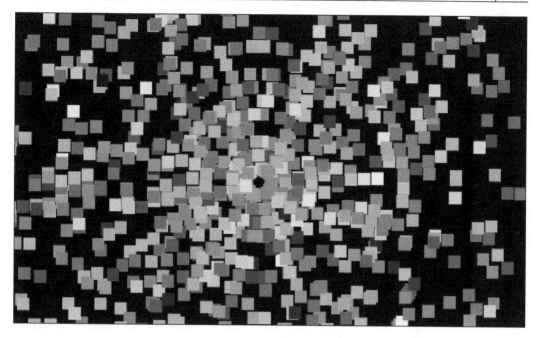

Just for clarification, each of the colored squares is an instance of the Particle class and all the Particle instances are controlled and held by the ParticleSystem class. In addition, the user will create multiple (hundreds of) ParticleSystem instances by drawing with their finger. The particle systems will appear as dots or blocks until the user taps the pause button and they come to life. We will examine the code closely enough so that you will be able to amend in code the size, color, speed, and quantities of Particle and ParticleSystem instances.

 It is left as an exercise for the reader to add additional buttons to the screen to allow the user to change these properties as a feature of the app.

We will start by coding the Particle class.

Coding the Particle class

Add the import statement, the member variables, and the constructor method, as shown in the following code:

```
import android.graphics.PointF;

class Particle {

    PointF mVelocity;
    PointF mPosition;

    Particle(PointF direction)
    {
        mVelocity = new PointF();
        mPosition = new PointF();

        // Determine the direction
        mVelocity.x = direction.x;
        mVelocity.y = direction.y;
    }
}
```

We have two members—one for velocity and one for position. They are both `PointF` objects. `PointF` holds two float values. The position is simple; it is just a horizontal and vertical value. The velocity is worth explaining a little more. Each of the two values in the `PointF` will be a speed, one horizontal and the other vertical. It is the combination of these two speeds that will imply a direction.

In the constructor, the two new `PointF` objects are instantiated and the x and y values of `mVelocity` are initialized with the values passed in by the `PointF` `direction` parameter. Notice the way in which the values are copied from `direction` to `mVelocity`. The `PointF` `mVelocity` is not a reference to the `PointF` passed in as a parameter. Each and every `Particle` instance will certainly copy the values from `direction` (and they will be different for each instance), but `mVelocity` has no lasting connection to `direction`.

Next, add these three methods, and then we can talk about them:

```
void update(float fps)
{
    // Move the particle
    mPosition.x += mVelocity.x;
```

```
        mPosition.y += mVelocity.y;
    }

    void setPosition(PointF position)
    {
        mPosition.x = position.x;
        mPosition.y = position.y;
    }

    PointF getPosition()
    {
        return mPosition;
    }
```

Perhaps unsurprisingly, there is an update method. Each Particle instance's update method will be called each frame of the app by the ParticleSystem's update method, which, in turn, will be called by the LiveDrawingView class (again, in the update method), which we will code later in this chapter.

Inside the update method, the horizontal and vertical values of mPosition are updated using the corresponding values of mVelocity.

Notice that we don't bother using the current frame rate in the update. You could amend this if you want to be certain that your particles all fly at the exactly correct speed, but all of the speeds are going to be random anyway. There is not much to gain from adding this extra calculation (for every particle). As we will soon see, however, the ParticleSystem class will need to take account of the current frames per second to measure how long it should run for.

Next, we coded the setPosition method. Notice that the method receives a PointF, which is used to set the initial position. The ParticleSystem class will pass this position in when the effect is triggered.

Finally, we have the getPosition method. We need this method so that the ParticleSystem class can draw all the particles in the correct position. We could have added a draw method to the Particle class instead of the getPosition method and had the Particle class draw itself. In this implementation, there is no particular benefit to either option.

Now, we can move on to the ParticleSysytem class.

Coding the ParticleSystem class

The `ParticleSystem` class has a few more details than the `Particle` class, but it is still reasonably straightforward. Remember what we need to achieve with this class:

Hold, spawn, update, and draw a bunch (quite a big bunch) of `Particle` instances.

Add the following members and import statements:

```
import android.graphics.Canvas;
import android.graphics.Color;
import android.graphics.Paint;
import android.graphics.PointF;

import java.util.ArrayList;
import java.util.Random;

class ParticleSystem {

    private float mDuration;

    private ArrayList<Particle> mParticles;
    private Random random = new Random();
    boolean mIsRunning = false;

}
```

We have four member variables: first, a `float` called `mDuration` that will be initialized to the number of seconds we want the effect to run for; second, we have the `ArrayList`, called `mParticles` holds `Particle` instances, and will hold all the `Particle` objects we instantiate.

The `Random` instance called `random` is created as a member because we need to generate so many random values that creating a new object each time would be sure to slow us down a bit.

Finally, the `boolean mIsRunning` will track whether the particle system is currently being shown (updating and drawing).

Now, we can code the `init` method. This method will be called each time we want a new `ParticleSystem`. Notice that the one and only parameter is an `int` called `numParticles`.

When we call `init`, we can have some fun initializing crazy amounts of particles. Add the `init` method and then we will look more closely at the code:

```
void init(int numParticles){

    mParticles = new ArrayList<>();
    // Create the particles

    for (int i = 0; i < numParticles; i++){
            float angle = (random.nextInt(360)) ;
            angle = angle * 3.14f / 180.f;

            // Option 1 - Slow particles
            //float speed = (random.nextFloat()/10);

            // Option 2 - Fast particles
            float speed = (random.nextInt(10)+1);

            PointF direction;

            direction = new PointF((float)Math.cos(angle) * speed,
                            (float)Math.sin(angle) * speed);

            mParticles.add(new Particle(direction));
    }
}
```

The `init` method consists of just one `for` loop that does all the work. The `for` loop runs from zero to `numParticles` -1.

First, a random number between zero and 359 is generated and stored in the `float` angle. Next, there is a little bit of math, and we multiply `angle` by `3.14/180`. This turns the angle in degrees to radian measurements, which is required by the `Math` class that we will use in a moment.

Then, we generate another random number between 1 and 10 and assign the result to a `float` variable called `speed`.

 Observe that I have added comments to suggest different options for values in this part of the code. I do this in several places in the `ParticleSystem` class and, when we get to the end of this chapter, we will have some fun altering these values and see what effect it has on the drawing app.

Now that we have a random angle and speed, we can convert and combine them into a vector that can be used inside the update method each frame.

 A vector is a value that determines both direction and speed. Our vector is stored in the direction object until it is passed into the Particle constructor. Vectors can be of many dimensions. Ours is two dimensions and therefore defines a heading between zero and 359 degrees, and a speed between 1 and 10. You can read more about vectors, headings, sine, and cosine on my website here: http://gamecodeschool.com/essentials/calculating-heading-in-2d-games-using-trigonometric-functions-part-1/.

The single line of code that uses Math.sin and Math.cos to create a vector I have decided not to explain in full because the magic occurs partly in the following formulas:

- Cosine of an angle * speed
- Sine of an angle * speed

And the other part of the magic takes place in the hidden calculations within the cosine and sine functions provided by the Math class. If you want to know their full details, then see the previous tip.

Finally, a new Particle is created and then added to the mParticles ArrayList.

Next, we will code the update method. Notice that the update method needs the current frame rate as a parameter. Code the update method as follows:

```
void update(long fps){
    mDuration -= (1f/fps);

    for(Particle p : mParticles){
        p.update(fps);
    }

    if (mDuration < 0)
    {
        mIsRunning = false;
    }
}
```

The first thing that happens inside the update method is that the elapsed time is taken off mDuration. Remember that fps is frames per second, so 1/fps gives a value as a fraction of a second.

Next, there is an enhanced `for` loop, which calls the `update` method for every `Particle` instance in the `mParticles` ArrayList.

Finally, the code checks to see whether the particle effect has run its course with `if(mDuration < 0)` and whether it sets `mIsRunning` to `false`.

Now, we can code the `emitParticles` method, which will set each `Particle` instance running. This is not to be confused with `init`, which creates all the new particles and gives them their velocities. The `init` method will be called once before the user gets to interact, while the `emitParticles` method will be called each time the effect needs to be started as the user draws on the screen.

Add the `emitParticles` method:

```
void emitParticles(PointF startPosition){
    mIsRunning = true;

    // Option 1 - Sysstem lasts for half a minute
    //mDuration = 30f;

    // Option 2 - System lasts for 2 seconds
    mDuration = 3f;

    for(Particle p : mParticles){
        p.setPosition(startPosition);
    }

}
```

First, notice that a `PointF` where all the particles will start is passed in as a parameter. All the particles will start at exactly the same position and then fan out every frame, based on their individual velocities.

The `mIsRunning` boolean is set to `true` and `mDuration` is set to `1f` so that the effect will run for one second. The enhanced `for` loop calls the `setPosition` of every particle to move them to their starting coordinates.

The final method for our `ParticleSysytem` is the `draw` method, which will reveal the effect in all its glory. The method receives a reference to `Canvas` and `Paint`, so it can draw to the same canvas that `LiveDrawingView` has just locked in its `draw` method.

Add the draw method:

```
void draw(Canvas canvas, Paint paint){

    for (Particle p : mParticles) {

            // Option 1 - Coloured particles
            //paint.setARGB(255, random.nextInt(256),
                    //random.nextInt(256),
                    //random.nextInt(256));

            // Option 2 - White particles
            paint.setColor(Color.argb(255,255,255,255));


            // How big is each particle?
            float sizeX = 0;
            float sizeY = 0;

            // Option 1 - Big particles
            //sizeX = 25;
            //sizeY = 25;

            // Option 2 - Medium particles
            sizeX = 10;
            sizeY = 10;

            // Option 3 - Tiny particles
            //sizeX = 1;
            //sizeY = 1;

            // Draw the particle
            // Option 1 - Square particles
            //canvas.drawRect(p.getPosition().x,
                    //p.getPosition().y,
                    //p.getPosition().x + sizeX,
                    //p.getPosition().y + sizeY,
                    //paint);

            // Option 2 - Circle particles
            canvas.drawCircle(p.getPosition().x,
                    p.getPosition().y,
                    sizeX, paint);
    }
}
```

An enhanced `for` loop steps through each of the `Particle` instances in `mParticles`. Each `Particle`, in turn, is drawn using `drawRect` and the `getPosition` method. Notice the call to `paint.setARGB`. You will see that we generate each of the color channels randomly.

 Notice again how I have suggested different options for code changes so that we can have some fun when we have finished coding.

We can now start to put the particle system to work.

Spawning particle systems in the LiveDrawingView class

Add an ArrayList full of systems and some more members to keep track of things. Add the highlighted code in the positions indicated by the existing comments:

```
// The particle systems will be declared here later
private ArrayList<ParticleSystem>
        mParticleSystems = new ArrayList<>();

private int mNextSystem = 0;
private final int MAX_SYSTEMS = 1000;
private int mParticlesPerSystem = 100;
```

We can now keep track of up to 1,000 particle systems with 100 particles in each. Feel free to play with these numbers. On a modern device, you can run particles into the millions without any trouble, but on the emulator, it will struggle with hundreds of thousands.

Initialize the systems in the constructor by adding the following highlighted code:

```
// Initialize the particles and their systems
for (int i = 0; i < MAX_SYSTEMS; i++) {
   mParticleSystems.add(new ParticleSystem());
   mParticleSystems.get(i).init(mParticlesPerSystem);
}
```

The code loops through the `ArrayList`, calling the constructor followed by `init` on each of the `ParticleSystem` instances.

Update the systems on each frame of the loop by adding the following highlighted code in the `update` method:

```
private void update() {
    // Update the particles
    for (int i = 0; i < mParticleSystems.size(); i++) {
        if (mParticleSystems.get(i).mIsRunning) {
            mParticleSystems.get(i).update(mFPS);
        }
    }
}
```

The previous code loops through each of the `ParticleSystem` instances, first checking whether they are active and then calling `update` and passing in the current frames per second.

Draw the systems each frame of the loop by adding the following highlighted code to the `draw` method:

```
// Choose a color to paint with
mPaint.setColor(Color.argb(255, 255, 255, 255));

// Choose the font size
mPaint.setTextSize(mFontSize);

// Draw the particle systems
for (int i = 0; i < mNextSystem; i++) {

    mParticleSystems.get(i).draw(mCanvas, mPaint);

}

// Draw the buttons
mCanvas.drawRect(mResetButton, mPaint);
mCanvas.drawRect(mTogglePauseButton, mPaint);
```

The previous code loops through `mParticleSystems`, calling the `draw` method on each. Of course, we haven't actually spawned any instances yet. For that, we will need to learn how to respond to screen interactions.

Handling touches

To get started with this conversation, add the `OnTouchEvent` method to the `LiveDrawingView` class:

```
@Override
public boolean onTouchEvent(MotionEvent motionEvent) {



    return true;
}
```

This is an overridden method and it is called by Android every time the user interacts with the screen. Look at the one and only parameter of `onTouchEvent`.

It turns out that `motionEvent` has a whole bunch of data tucked away inside of it, and this data contains the details of the touch that just occurred. The operating system sent it to us because it knows we will probably need some of it.

Notice that I said *some* of it. The `MotionEvent` class is quite extensive. It contains within it dozens of methods and variables.

 Over the course of this book, we will uncover quite a lot of them, but nowhere near all of them. You can explore the `MotionEvent` class here: `https://stuff.mit.edu/afs/sipb/project/android/docs/reference/android/view/MotionEvent.html`.

Note that it is not necessary to do further research to complete this book.

For now, all we need to know is the screen coordinates at the precise moment when the player's finger was moved, touched the screen, or removed.

Some of the variables and methods contained within `motionEvent` that we will use include the following:

- The `getAction` method, which, unsurprisingly, "gets" the action that was performed. Unfortunately, it supplies this information in a slightly encoded format, which explains the need for some of these other variables.

- The `ACTION_MASK` variable, which provides a value known as a mask, which, with the help of a little bit more Java trickery, can be used to filter the data from `getAction`.

- The `ACTION_UP` variable, which we can use to compare to see whether the action performed is the one (removing a finger) we want to respond to.

- The ACTION_DOWN variable, which we can use to compare to see whether the action performed is the one we want to respond to.

- The ACTION_MOVE variable, which we can use to compare to see whether the action performed is a move/drag.

- The getX method notifies us of a horizontal floating point coordinate where the event happened.

- The getY method notifies us of a vertical floating-point coordinate where the event happened.

As a specific example, say we need to filter the data returned by getAction using ACTION_MASK and see whether the result is the same as ACTION_UP. If it is, then we know that the user has just removed their finger from the screen; perhaps because they just tapped a button. Once we are sure that the event is of the correct type, we will need to find out where it happened using getX and getY.

There is one final complication. The Java trickery I referred to is the & bitwise operator, which is not to be confused with the logical && operator we have been using in conjunction with the if keyword.

The & bitwise operator checks to see whether each corresponding part in two values is true. This is the filter that is required when using ACTION_MASK with getAction.

Sanity check. I was hesitant to go into detail about MotionEvent and bitwise operators. It is possible to complete this entire book and even a professional quality interactive app without ever needing to fully understand them. If you know that the line of code we write in the next section determines the event type the player has just triggered, that is all you need to know. I just guessed that a discerning reader such as yourself would like to know the ins and outs. In summary, if you understand bitwise operators, great, you are good to go. If you don't, it doesn't matter; you are still good to go. If you are curious about bitwise operators (there are quite a few), you can read more about them here: https://en.wikipedia.org/wiki/Bitwise_operation.

Now, we can code the onTouchEvent method and see all the MotionEvent stuff in action.

Coding the onTouchEvent method

You can handle the user moving their finger on the screen by adding the following highlighted code inside the onTouchEvent method to the code we already have:

```
// User moved a finger while touching screen
    if ((motionEvent.getAction() &
                MotionEvent.ACTION_MASK)
            == MotionEvent.ACTION_MOVE) {

        mParticleSystems.get(mNextSystem).emitParticles(
                new PointF(motionEvent.getX(),
                        motionEvent.getY()));

        mNextSystem++;
        if (mNextSystem == MAX_SYSTEMS) {
            mNextSystem = 0;
        }
    }

    return true;
```

The if condition checks to see whether the type of event was the user moving their finger. If it was, then the next particle system in mParticleSystems has its emitParticles method called. Afterward, the mNextSystem variable is incremented and a test is performed to see whether it was the last particle system. If it was, then mNextSystem is set to zero ready to start reusing existing particle systems the next time one is required.

You can handle the user pressing one of the buttons by adding the following highlighted code right after the previous code we have just discussed, and before the return statement we have already coded:

```
// Did the user touch the screen
    if ((motionEvent.getAction() &
                MotionEvent.ACTION_MASK)
            == MotionEvent.ACTION_DOWN) {

        // User pressed the screen see if it was in a button
        if (mResetButton.contains(motionEvent.getX(),
                motionEvent.getY())) {
            // Clear the screen of all particles
```

```
                            mNextSystem = 0;
              }

              // User pressed the screen see if it was in a button
              if (mTogglePauseButton.contains(motionEvent.getX(),
                      motionEvent.getY())) {
                  mPaused = !mPaused;
              }
       }

       return true;
```

The condition of the `if` statement checks to see whether the user has tapped the screen. If they have, then the `contains` method of the `RectF` class is used in conjunction with `getX` and `getY` to see whether that press was inside one of our custom buttons. If the reset button was pressed, all the particles will disappear when `mNextSystem` is set to zero. If the paused button is pressed, then the value of `mPaused` is toggled, causing the `update` method to stop/start being called in the thread.

Finishing the HUD

Add the following highlighted code to the `printDebuggingText` method:

```
       // We will add more code here in the next chapter
       mCanvas.drawText("Systems: " + mNextSystem,
               10, mFontMargin + debugStart + debugSize * 2, mPaint);

       mCanvas.drawText("Particles: " + mNextSystem * mParticlesPerSystem,
               10, mFontMargin + debugStart + debugSize * 3, mPaint);
```

This code will just print some interesting statistics to the screen to tell us how many particles and systems are currently being drawn.

Running the app

Now, we get to see the live drawing app in action and play with some of the different options we commented out in the code.

Run the app with small, round, colorful, fast particles. Just tap the screen in a number of places, as demonstrated in the following image:

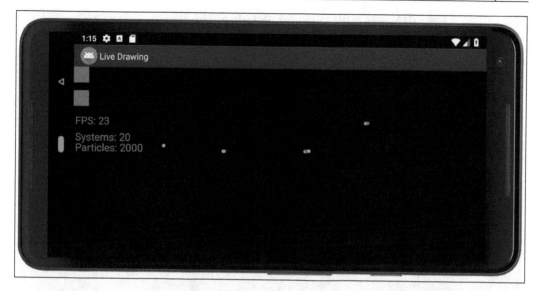

Then, resume the drawing, as follows:

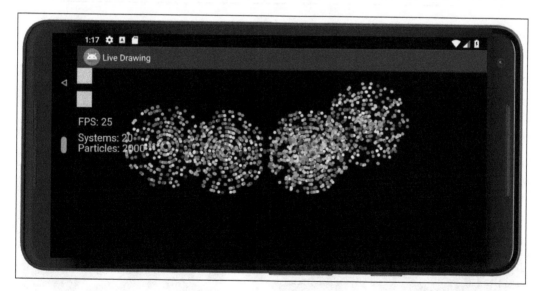

You can do a kid's drawing with particles that are small, white, square, slow, and of long duration, as follows:

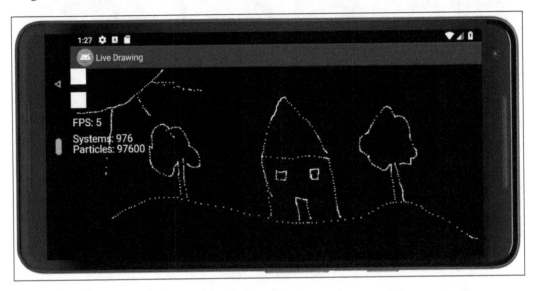

Then, resume the drawing and wait for 20 seconds while the drawing comes to life and changes:

Summary

In this chapter, we saw how we can add thousands of self-contained entities to our real-time system. The entities were controlled by the `ParticleSystem` class, which, in turn, interacted with, and was controlled by, the game loop. As the game loop was running in a thread, we saw that the user can still interact seamlessly with the screen, and the operating system sends us the details of these interactions via the `onTouchEvent` method.

In the next chapter, our apps will finally get a bit noisier when we explore how to play sound effects at the same time as we learn how to detect different versions of Android.

23
Supporting Different Versions of Android, Sound Effects, and the Spinner Widget

In this chapter, we will learn about how we can detect and handle different versions of Android. We will then be able to study the `SoundPool` class and the different ways we can use it depending on the Android version the app is running on. At this point, we can then put everything we have learned into producing cool sound demo apps, which will also introduce us to a new UI widget – the **Spinner**.

In summary, in this chapter, we will cover the following topics:

- How to handle different versions of Android
- How to use the Android `SoundPool` class
- Coding a sound-based app by using `SpinnerView`

Let's get started.

Handling different versions of Android

Most of the time throughout this book, we haven't paid any attention to supporting older Android devices, the main reason being that all the up-to-date parts of the API we have been using work on such a high percentage of devices (in excess of 95%) that it has not seemed worthwhile. Unless you intend to carve out a niche in apps for ancient Android relics, this seems like a sensible approach. In regard to playing of sounds, however, there have been some relatively recent modifications to the Android API.

Actually, this isn't immediately a big deal because devices that are newer than this can still use the old parts of the API. But it is good practice to specifically handle these differences in compatibility, because eventually, one day, the older parts might not work on newer versions of Android.

The main reason for discussing this here and now is that the slight differences in pre- and post-Android Lollipop sound handling gives us a good excuse to see how we can deal with things like this in our code.

We will see how we can make our app compatible with the very latest devices and the pre-Lollipop devices as well.

The class we will be using to make some noise is the SoundPool class. First, let's look at some simple code for detecting the current Android version.

Detecting the current Android version

We can determine the current version of Android by using the static variables of the Build.Version class, SDK_INT, and we can determine whether it is newer than a specific version by comparing it to that version's appropriate Build.VERSION_CODES variable. If that explanation was a bit of a mouthful, just look at how we determine whether the current version is equal to or newer (greater) than Lollipop:

```
if (Build.VERSION.SDK_INT >= Build.VERSION_CODES.LOLLIPOP) {

    // Lollipop or newer code goes here

} else {

    // Code for devices older than lollipop here

}
```

Now, let's see how to make a noise with Android devices that are newer, and then older, than Lollipop.

The Soundpool class

The SoundPool class allows us to hold and manipulate a collection of sound FX; literally, a pool of sounds. The class handles everything from decompressing a sound file such as a .wav or a .ogg, keeping an identifying reference to it via an integer id and, of course, playing the sound. When the sound is played, it is done so in a non-blocking manner (using a thread behind the scenes) that does not interfere with the smooth running of our app or our user's interaction with it.

The first thing we need to do is add the sound effects to a folder called `assets` in the `main` folder of the game project. We will do this for real shortly.

Next, in our Java code, declare an object of the `SoundPool` type and an `int` identifier for each and every sound effect we intend to use. We also need to declare another `int` called `nowPlaying`, which we can use to track which sound is currently playing. We will see how we do this shortly:

```
// create an identifier
SoundPool sp;
int nowPlaying =-1;
int idFX1 = -1;
float volume = 1;// Volumes rage from 0 through 1
```

Now, we will look at the two different ways we initialize a `SoundPool`, depending upon the version of Android the device is using. This is the perfect opportunity to use our method of writing different code for different versions of Android.

Initializing SoundPool the new way

The new way of initializing SoundPool involves us using an `AudioAttributes` object to set the attributes of the pool of sound we want.

The first block of code uses chaining and calls four separate methods on one object that initializes our `AudioAttributes` object (`audioAttributes`). Also note that it is fine to have comments in-between parts of the chained method calls as these are ignored entirely by the compiler:

```
// Instantiate a SoundPool dependent on Android version
if (Build.VERSION.SDK_INT >= Build.VERSION_CODES.LOLLIPOP) {

    // The new way
    // Build an AudioAttributes object
    AudioAttributes audioAttributes =
            // First method call
        new AudioAttributes.Builder()
            // Second method call
            .setUsage
            (AudioAttributes.USAGE_ASSISTANCE_SONIFICATION)
            // Third method call
            .setContentType
            (AudioAttributes.CONTENT_TYPE_SONIFICATION)
            // Fourth method call
```

```
            .build();// Yay! A semicolon

    // Initialize the SoundPool
    sp = new SoundPool.Builder()
              .setMaxStreams(5)
              .setAudioAttributes(audioAttributes)
              .build();
}
```

In the preceding code, we used chaining and the `Builder` method of this class to initialize an `AudioAttributes` object to let it know that it will be used for user interface interaction with `USAGE_ASSISTANCE_SONIFICATION`.

We also used `CONTENT_TYPE_SONIFICATION`, which lets the class know it is for responsive sounds, for example, button clicks, a collision, or similar.

Now, we can initialize the `SoundPool` (`sp`) itself by passing in the `AudioAttributes` object (`audioAttributes`) and the maximum number of simultaneous sounds we are likely to want to play.

The second block of code chains another four methods to initialize `sp`, including a call to `setAudioAttributes` that uses the `audioAttributes` object that we initialized in the earlier block of chained methods.

Now, we can write an `else` block of code that will, of course, have the code for the old way of doing things.

Initializing SoundPool the old way

There is no need for an `AudioAttributes` object. Simply initialize the `SoundPool` (`sp`) by passing in the number of simultaneous sounds. The final parameter is for sound quality, and passing zero is all we need to do. This is much simpler than the new way, but also less flexible regarding the choices we can make:

```
    else {
        // The old way
        sp = new SoundPool(5, AudioManager.STREAM_MUSIC, 0);
    }
```

We could use the old way, and the newer versions of Android would handle this. However, we get a warning about using deprecated methods. This is what the official documentation says about it:

> ## SoundPool
>
> ```
> SoundPool (int maxStreams,
>            int streamType,
>            int srcQuality)
> ```
>
> **This constructor was deprecated in API level 21.**
>
> use SoundPool.Builder instead to create and configure a SoundPool instance

Furthermore, the new way gives access to more features, as we saw previously. And anyway, it's a good excuse to look at some simple code to handle different versions of Android.

Now, we can go ahead and load up (decompress) the sound files into our SoundPool.

Loading sound files into memory

As with our thread control, we are required to wrap our code in try-catch blocks. This makes sense because reading a file can fail for reasons beyond our control, but also because we are forced to because the method that we use throws an exception and the code we write will not compile otherwise.

Inside the try block, we declare and initialize objects of the AssetManager and AssetFileDescriptor types.

The AssetFileDescriptor is initialized by using the openFd method of the AssetManager object that actually decompresses the sound file. We then initialize our id (idFX1) at the same time as we load the contents of the AssetFileDescriptor into our SoundPool.

The catch block simply outputs a message to the console to let us know whether something has gone wrong. Note that this code is the same, regardless of the Android version:

```
try{

    // Create objects of the 2 required classes
    AssetManager assetManager = this.getAssets();
```

```
        AssetFileDescriptor descriptor;

        // Load our fx in memory ready for use
        descriptor = assetManager.openFd("fx1.ogg");
        idFX1 = sp.load(descriptor, 0);
}catch(IOException e){

        // Print an error message to the console
        Log.d("error", "failed to load sound files");

}
```

We are ready to make some noise.

Playing a sound

At this point, there is a sound effect in our SoundPool, and we have an id by which we can refer to it.

This code is the same regardless of how we built the SoundPool object, and this is how we play the sound. Notice in the following line of code that we initialize the nowPlaying variable with the return value from the same method that actually plays the sound.

The following code therefore simultaneously plays a sound and loads the value of the id that is being played into nowPlaying:

```
nowPlaying = sp.play(idFX1, volume, volume, 0, repeats, 1);
```

 It is not necessary to store the id in nowPlaying in order to play a sound, but it has its uses, as we will now see.

The parameters of the play method are as follows:

- The id of the sound effect
- The left and right speaker volumes
- The priority over other sounds
- The number of times the sound is repeated
- The rate/speed it is played at (1 being the normal rate)

There's just one more thing we need to do before we make the sound demo app.

Stopping a sound

It is also very trivial to stop a sound when it is still playing with the `stop` method. Note that there might be more than one sound effect playing at any given time, so the `stop` method needs the ID of the sound effect to stop:

```
sp.stop(nowPlaying);
```

When you call `play`, you only need to store the ID of the currently playing sound if you want to track it so that you can interact with it at a later time.

Now, we can make the Sound Demo app.

Sound demo app introducing Spinner widget

Of course, with all this talk of sound FX, we need some actual sound files. You can make you own with BFXR (explained next) or use the ones supplied. The sound effects for this app are in the download bundle and can be found in the `assets` folder of the `Chapter 23/Sound Demo` folder. However, you might want to make your own.

Making sound FX

There is an open source app called BFXR that allows us to make our own sound FX. Here is a very fast guide to making your own sound FX using BFXR. Grab a free copy from `www.bfxr.net`.

> Note that the sound effects for the Sound demo app are supplied to you in the `Chapter 23/assets` folder. You don't have to create your own sound effects unless you want to, but it is still worth getting this free software and learning how to use it.

Follow the simple instructions on the website to set it up. Try out a few of these things to make cool sound FX:

> This is a seriously condensed tutorial. You can do so much with BFXR. To learn more, read the tips on the website at the previous URL.

1. Run bfxr:

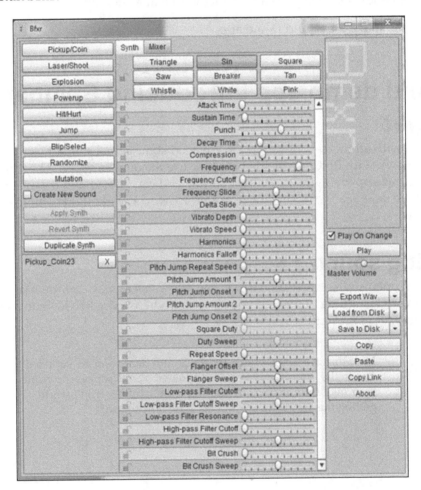

2. Try out all the preset types that generate a random sound of that type. When you have a sound that is close to what you want, move to the next step:

3.   Use the sliders to fine-tune the pitch, duration, and other aspects of your new sound:

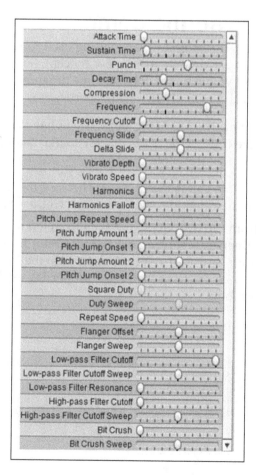

4. Save your sound by clicking the **Export Wav** button. Despite the text of this button, as we will see, we can save in formats other than .wav, too:

5. Android works very well with sounds in the OGG format, so when asked to name your file, use the .ogg extension on the end of the filename.

6. Repeat steps 2 to 5 to create three cool sound FX. Name them fx1.ogg, fx2. ogg, and fx3.ogg. We use the .ogg file format as it is more compressed than formats like WAV.

When you have your sound files ready, we can proceed with the app.

Laying out the sound demo

I will describe the parts of the project we are getting used to a little more tersely than previous projects. Every time there is a new concept, however, I will be sure to explain it in full. I guess by now you will be just fine dragging a few widgets onto a ConstraintLayout and changing their text properties.

With this in mind, complete the following steps. If you have any problems at all, you can copy or view the code in the Chapter 23/Sound Demo folder of the download bundle:

1. Create a new project, call it Sound Demo, choose a **Basic Activity**, leave all the other settings at their defaults, and delete the **Hello world!** TextView.

2. In this order, from top to bottom, and then from left to right, drag a **Spinner** from the **Containers** category, a **SeekBar (discrete)** from the **Widgets** category, and four **Buttons** from the palette onto the layout while arranging and resizing them and setting their text properties, as shown in the following screenshot:

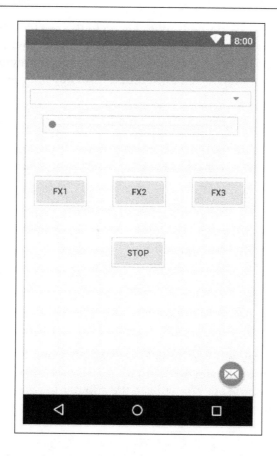

3. Click the **Infer Constraints** button.

4. Use the following table to set the properties that we will need in our Java code:

Widget	Property to change	Value to set
Spinner	id	spinner
Spinner	spinnerMode	dropdown
Spinner	entries	@array/spinner_options
SeekBar	id	seekBar
SeekBar	max	10
Button (**FX 1**)	id	btnFX1
Button (**FX 2**)	id	btnFX2
Button (**FX 3**)	id	btnFX3
Button (**STOP**)	id	btnStop

5. Next, add the following highlighted code to the `strings.xml` file in the `values` folder. We used this array of string resources, which is named `spinner_options`, for the `options` property in the previous step. It will represent the options that can be chosen from our Spinner:

```
<resources>
    <string name="app_name">Sound Demo</string>

    <string name="hello_world">Hello world!</string>
    <string name="action_settings">Settings</string>

    <string-array name="spinner_options">
      <item>0</item>
      <item>1</item>
      <item>3</item>
      <item>5</item>
      <item>10</item>
    </string-array>

</resources>
```

Run the app now and you will not initially see anything that we haven't seen before. If you click on the spinner, however, then you will see the options from our string array called `spinner_options`. We will use the spinner to control the number of times a sound effect repeats itself when played, which is demonstrated as follows:

Let's write the Java code to make this app work, including how we interact with our spinner.

Using your operating system's file browser, go to the `app\src\main` folder of the project and add a new folder called `assets`.

There are three sound files that have been made for you in the `Chapter 23/ SoundDemo/assets` folder of the download bundle. Place these three files into the `assets` directory you just created, or use the ones you created yourself. The important thing is that their filenames must be `fx1.ogg`, `fx2.ogg`, and `fx3.ogg`.

Coding the Sound demo

First, we will change the class declaration so that we can handle interaction with all our widgets efficiently. Edit the declaration to implement `View.OnClickListener,` as highlighted in the following code:

```
public class MainActivity extends AppCompatActivity
implements View.OnClickListener {
```

We will add the required `onClick` method shortly.

Now, we will add some member variables for our `SoundPool`, sound FX IDs, and a `nowPlaying` int, as we discussed previously, and we will also add a `float` to hold a value for volume between 0 (silent) and 1 (full volume based on the current volume of the device). We will also add an `int` called `repeats`, which, unsurprisingly, holds the value of the number of times we will repeat a given sound FX:

```
SoundPool sp;

int idFX1 = -1;
int idFX2 = -1;
int idFX3 = -1;
int nowPlaying = -1;

float volume = .1f;
int repeats = 2;
```

Now, in `onCreate`, we can get a reference and set a click listener for our buttons in the usual way:

```
Button buttonFX1 = (Button) findViewById(R.id.btnFX1);
buttonFX1.setOnClickListener(this);

Button buttonFX2 = (Button) findViewById(R.id.btnFX2);
```

```
buttonFX2.setOnClickListener(this);

Button buttonFX3 = (Button) findViewById(R.id.btnFX3);
buttonFX3.setOnClickListener(this);

Button buttonStop = (Button) findViewById(R.id.btnStop);
buttonStop.setOnClickListener(this);
```

Still in onCreate, we can initialize our SoundPool (sp) based on the version of Android that the device is using:

```
// Instantiate our SoundPool based on the version of Android
if (Build.VERSION.SDK_INT >= Build.VERSION_CODES.LOLLIPOP) {
    AudioAttributes audioAttributes =
        new AudioAttributes.Builder()
    .setUsage(AudioAttributes. USAGE_ASSISTANCE_SONIFICATION)

    .setContentType(AudioAttributes.CONTENT_TYPE_SONIFICATION)
                .build();

    sp = new SoundPool.Builder()
                .setMaxStreams(5)
                .setAudioAttributes(audioAttributes)
                .build();
} else {
    sp = new SoundPool(5, AudioManager.STREAM_MUSIC, 0);
}
```

Add the following import statements for the previous code using your preferred method:

```
import android.media.AudioAttributes;
import android.media.AudioManager;
import android.media.SoundPool;
import android.os.Build;

import android.view.View;
import android.widget.Button;
```

Next, we load each of our sound FX in turn and initialize our ids with a value that points to the related sound FX that we loaded into the `SoundPool`. The whole thing is wrapped in a try-catch block as required:

```
try{
    // Create objects of the 2 required classes
    AssetManager assetManager = this.getAssets();
    AssetFileDescriptor descriptor;

    // Load our fx in memory ready for use
    descriptor = assetManager.openFd("fx1.ogg");
    idFX1 = sp.load(descriptor, 0);

    descriptor = assetManager.openFd("fx2.ogg");
    idFX2 = sp.load(descriptor, 0);

    descriptor = assetManager.openFd("fx3.ogg");
    idFX3 = sp.load(descriptor, 0);


}catch(IOException e){
    // Print an error message to the console
    Log.e("error", "failed to load sound files");
}
```

Add the following import statements for the previous code using your preferred method:

```
import android.content.res.AssetFileDescriptor;
import android.content.res.AssetManager;
import android.util.Log;
import java.io.IOException;
```

Now, we will look at how we are going to handle the `SeekBar`. As we have probably come to expect, we use an anonymous class for this. We use `OnSeekBarChangeListener` and override the `onProgressChanged`, `onStartTrackingTouch`, and `onStopTrackingTouch` methods.

We only need to add code to the onProgressChanged method. Within this method, we simply change the value of our volume variable and then use the setVolume method on our SoundPool object, passing in the currently playing sound FX and the volume of the left and right channels of sound:

```
// Now setup the seekbar
SeekBar seekBar = (SeekBar) findViewById(R.id.seekBar);


seekBar.setOnSeekBarChangeListener(new
SeekBar.OnSeekBarChangeListener() {

        @Override
        public void onProgressChanged(SeekBar seekBar,
                    int value,
                    boolean fromUser) {

                volume = value / 10f;
                sp.setVolume(nowPlaying, volume, volume);
    }

    @Override
    public void onStartTrackingTouch(SeekBar seekBar) {
    }

    @Override
    public void onStopTrackingTouch(SeekBar seekBar) {

    }
});
```

 Add the following import statements for the previous code using your preferred method:

```
import android.widget.SeekBar;
```

After the SeekBar comes the Spinner, and another anonymous class to handle user interaction. We use AdapterView.OnItemSelectedListener to override the onItemSelected and onNothingSelected methods.

All our code goes in the `onItemSelected` method, which creates a temporary `String` named `temp`, and then uses the `Integer.ValueOf` method to convert the `String` to an `int` that we can use to initialize the repeats variable:

```
// Now for the spinner
Final Spinner spinner = (Spinner) findViewById(R.id.spinner);
spinner.setOnItemSelectedListener(
new AdapterView.OnItemSelectedListener() {

        @Override
        public void onItemSelected(AdapterView<?>
                parentView,
                View selectedItemView,
                int position,
                long id) {

                String temp = String.valueOf(
                        spinner.getSelectedItem());

                repeats = Integer.valueOf(temp);
    }

    @Override
    public void onNothingSelected(AdapterView<?> parentView) {

    }

});
```

 Add the following import statements for the previous code using your preferred method:
```
import android.widget.AdapterView;
import android.widget.Spinner;
```

That's everything from `onCreate`.

Now, implement the `onClick` method, which is required because this class implements the `View.OnClickListener` interface. Quite simply, there is a `case` statement for each button. In each `case`, notice that the return value for each call to `play` is stored in `nowPlaying`. When the user presses the **STOP** button, we simply call `stop` with the current value of `nowPlaying`, which causes the most recently started sound FX to stop:

```
@Override
public void onClick(View v) {
    switch (v.getId()){
        case R.id.btnFX1:
                sp.stop(nowPlaying);
                nowPlaying = sp.play(idFX1, volume,
                    volume, 0, repeats, 1);
                break;

        case R.id.btnFX2:
                sp.stop(nowPlaying);
                nowPlaying = sp.play(idFX2,
                    volume, volume, 0, repeats, 1);
                break;

        case R.id.btnFX3:
                sp.stop(nowPlaying);
                nowPlaying = sp.play(idFX3,
                    volume, volume, 0, repeats, 1);
                break;

        case R.id.btnStop:
                sp.stop(nowPlaying);
                break;
    }
}
```

We can now run the app. Make sure that the volume on your device is turned up if you can't hear anything.

Click the appropriate button for the sound FX you want to play. Change the volume and the number of times it is repeated and, of course, try stopping it with the **STOP** button.

Also note that you can repeatedly tap multiple play buttons when a sound FX is already playing, and the sounds will be played simultaneously up to the maximum number of streams (5) that we set.

Summary

In this chapter, we looked closely at `SoundPool`, including how we can detect which version of Android the player has and varied our code accordingly. Finally, we used all of this knowledge to complete the Sound Demo app.

In the next chapter, we will learn about how to make our apps work with multiple different layouts.

24

Design Patterns, Multiple Layouts, and Fragments

We have come a long way since the start when we were just setting up Android Studio. Back then, we went through everything step by step, but as we have proceeded we have tried to show not just how to add x to y, or feature a to app b, but to enable you to use what you have learned in your own way in order to bring your own ideas to life.

This chapter is more about your future apps than anything in the book so far. We will look at a few aspects of Java and Android that you can use as a framework or template for making ever more exciting and complex apps at the same time as keeping the code manageable. Furthermore, I will suggest areas of further study that are barely touched on in this book given its limited scope.

In this chapter, we will learn about the following:

- Patterns and the model-view-controller
- Android design guidelines
- Getting started with real-world designs and handling multiple different devices
- An introduction to Fragments

Let's get started.

Introducing the model-view-controller pattern

Model View Controller is the separation of different aspects of our app into distinct parts called **layers**. Android apps commonly use the model-view-controller **pattern**. A pattern is simply a recognized way to structure our code and other application resources, such as layout files, images, and databases.

Patterns are useful to us because, by conforming to a pattern, we can be more confident we are doing things right and are less likely to have to undo lots of hard work because we have coded ourselves into an awkward situation.

There are many patterns in computer science, but an understanding of MVC will be enough to create some professionally built Android apps.

We have been partly using MVC already, so let's look at each of the three layers in turn.

Model

The model refers to the data that drives our app and any logic/code that specifically manages it and makes it available to the other layers. For example, in our Note to Self app, the Note class, along with its getters, setters and JSON code, was the data and logic.

View

The view of the Note to Self app was all the widgets in all the different layouts. Anything the user can see or interact with on the screen is typically part of the view. And you probably remember that the widgets came from the View class hierarchy of the Android API.

Controller

The controller is the bit in-between the view and the model. It interacts with both and keeps them separate. It contains what is known in geek speak as the **application logic**. If a user taps a button, the application layer decides what to do about it. When the user clicks **OK** to add a new note, the application layer was listening for the interaction on the view layer. It captures the data contained in the view and passes it to the model layer. Well almost ...

Design patterns are a huge topic. There are many different design patterns and if you want a beginner-friendly introduction to the topic in general, I would recommend Head first design patterns. If you want to really dive into the world of design patterns, then you can try Design Patterns: Elements of Reusable Object-Oriented Software, which is recognized as a kind of design pattern oracle but is a much harder read.

As the book progresses, we will also begin to utilize more of the object-oriented programming aspects we have discussed but not fully benefited from so far. We will do so step by step.

Android design guidelines

App design is a vast topic. It is a topic that could only begin to be taught in a book of its own. Also, like programming, you can only start to get good at app design with constant practice, review, and improvement.

So, what exactly do I mean by design? I am talking about where you put the widgets on the screen, which widgets, what color should they be, how big should they be, how to transition between screens, the best way to scroll a page, when and which animation interpolators to use, what screens should your app be divided into, and much more besides.

This book will hopefully leave you well qualified to be able to *implement* all your choices relating to the preceding questions and many more besides. Unfortunately, it does not have the space, and the author probably doesn't have the skill to teach you how to *make* those choices.

You might be wondering "What should I do?" Keep making apps and don't let a lack of design experience and knowledge stop you! Even release your apps to the App Store. Keep in mind, however, that there is a whole other topic, design, that needs some attention if your apps are going to truly be world class.

In even medium-sized development companies, the designer is rarely also the programmer, and even very small companies will often outsource the design of their app (or designers might outsource the coding).

Designing is both art and science, and Google has demonstrated that it recognizes this with high-quality support for both existing and aspiring designers.

I highly recommend you visit and bookmark this web page: https://developer.android.com/design/. It is quite detailed and comprehensive, is totally Android focused, and has a digital ton of resources in the form of images, color palettes, and guidelines.

Make understanding design principles a short-term goal. Make improving your actual design skills an ongoing task. Visit and read design-focused websites and try and implement the ideas that you find exciting.

Most important of all, however: don't wait until you are a design expert to make apps. Keep bringing your ideas to life and publishing them. Make a point of making the design of each app a little better than the last.

We will see in the coming chapters, and have seen to a certain extent already, that the Android API makes available to us a whole bunch of super-stylish UIs that we can take advantage of with very little code or design skill. These go a long way to making your apps look like they have been designed by a professional.

Real-world apps

So far, we have built a dozen or more apps of various complexity. Most were designed and tested on a phone.

Of course, in the real world, our apps need to work well on any device and must be able to handle what happens when in either portrait or landscape view (on all devices).

Furthermore, it is often not enough for our apps to just work and look OK on different devices. Often, our apps will need to behave differently and appear with significantly different UI based on whether the device is a phone, a tablet, or landscape/portrait orientation.

Android supports apps for large screen TVs, smart watches via the Wear API, virtual and augmented reality, as well as "things" for the Internet of Things. We will not be covering the latter two aspects in this book but, by the end of it, it is the author's guess that you will be sufficiently prepared to venture into these topics should you choose to.

Look at this screenshot of the BBC news app running on an Android phone in portrait orientation. Look at the basic layout, but also notice that the categories of news (**Top Stories, World, UK**) are all visible and allow the user to scroll to see more categories, or to swipe left and right between the stories within each category:

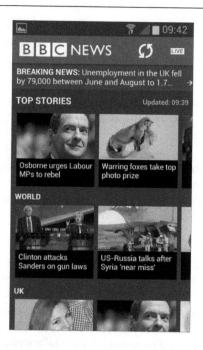

We will see how we can implement a swiping/paging UI using `ImagePager` and `FragmentPager` classes in the next chapter, but before we can do that, we need to understand some more fundamentals that we explore in this chapter. For now, the purpose of the previous image is not so much to show you the specific UI features, but to allow you to compare it with the next image. Look at the exact same app running on a tablet in landscape orientation:

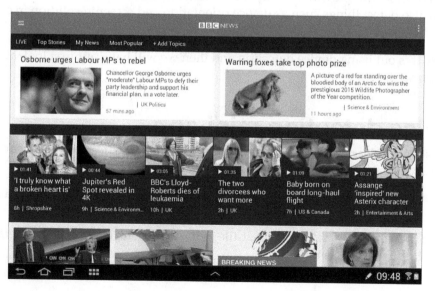

Notice that the stories (data layer) are identical, but that the layout (view layer) is very different. The user is not only given the option to select categories from a menu of tabs at the top of the app; they are also invited to add their own tabs through the **Add Topics** option.

The point of this image again is not so much the specific UI, or even how we might implement one like it, but more that they are so different they could easily be mistaken for totally different apps.

Android allows us to design real-world apps like this where not only is the layout different for varying device types/orientations/sizes, but so is the behavior, the application layer. Android's secret weapon that makes this possible is Fragments.

Google says

"A Fragment represents a behavior or a portion of user interface in an Activity. You can combine multiple fragments in a single activity to build a multi-pane UI and reuse a fragment in multiple activities.

You can think of a fragment as a modular section of an activity, which has its own lifecycle, receives its own input events, and which you can add or remove while the activity is running (sort of like a "sub activity" that you can reuse in different activities).

A fragment must always be embedded in an activity, and the fragment's lifecycle is directly affected by the host activity's lifecycle."

We can design multiple different layouts in different XML files, and will do so soon. We can also detect things such as device orientation and screen resolution in code, so we can then make decisions about layout, dynamically.

Let's try this out using device detection and then we will have our first look at Fragments.

Device detection mini-app

The best way to learn about detecting and responding to devices and their varying attributes (screens, orientations, and so on) is to make a simple app:

1. Create a new Basic Activity project and call it Device Detection. Leave all the other settings at their defaults.

2. Open the activity_main.xml file in the design tab and delete the default **Hello world!** TextView.

3. Drag a **Button** onto the top of the screen and set its **onClick** property to `detectDevice`. We will code this method in a minute.

4. Drag two **TextView** widgets onto the layout, one below the other, and set their **id** properties to `txtOrientation` and `txtResolution` respectively.

5. Check you have a layout that looks something like the following screenshot:

 I have stretched my widgets (mainly horizontally) and increased the `textSize` attributes to `24 sp` to make them clearer on the screen, but this is not required for the app to work correctly.

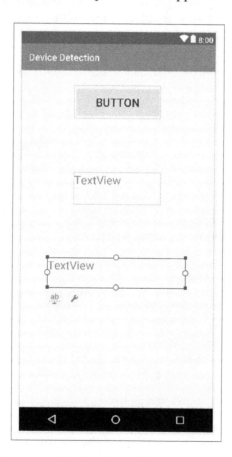

6. Click the **Infer Constraints** button to secure the positions of the UI elements.

Now we will do something new. We will build a layout specifically for landscape orientation.

In Android Studio, make sure the `activity_main.xml` file is selected in the editor and locate the **Orientation for preview** button, as shown in the following screenshot:

Click it and then select **Create landscape variation**.

You now have a new layout XML file with the same name, but orientated in landscape mode. The layout appears blank in the editor but, as we will see, this is not the case. Look at the `layout` folder in the project explorer and notice that there are indeed two files named `activity_main` and one of them (the new one we just created) is postfixed with **land**. This is shown in the following screenshot:

Select this new file (the one postfixed with **land**) and now look at the component tree. It is depicted in the following screenshot:

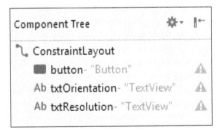

It would appear that the layout already contains all our widgets — we just cannot see them in the design view. The reason for this anomaly is that when we created the landscape layout, Android Studio copied the portrait layout, including all the constraints. The portrait constraints rarely match the landscape constraints.

To solve the problem, click the **Remove all constraints** button; it's the button to the left of the **Infer constraints** button. The UI is now unconstrained. This is what mine looks like:

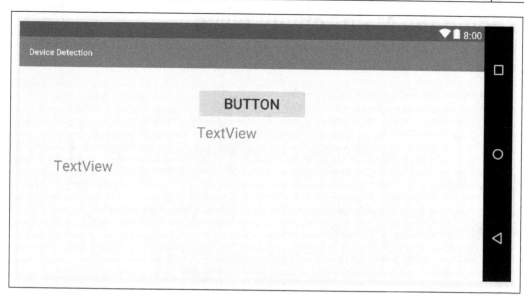

The layout is a bit jumbled up, but at least we can see it now. Rearrange it to make it look neat and tidy. This is how I rearranged mine:

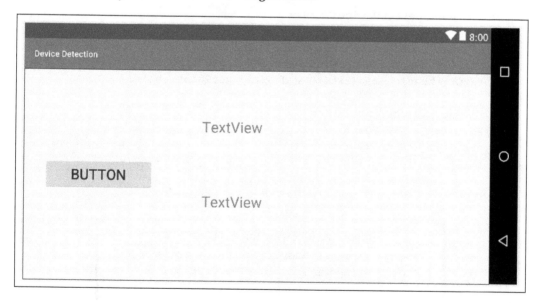

Click the **Infer constraints** button to lock the layout in the new positions.

Now that we have a basic layout for two different orientations, we can turn our attention to Java.

Coding the MainActivity class

Add the following members just after the `MainActivity` class declaration in order to hold references to our two `TextView` widgets:

```
private TextView txtOrientation;
private TextView txtResolution;
```

Import the `TextView` class at this point, as follows:
```
import android.widget.TextView;
```

Now, in the `onCreate` method of `MainActivity`, just after the call to `setContentView`, add this code:

```
// Get a reference to our TextView widgets
txtOrientation = (TextView) findViewById(R.id.txtOrientation);
txtResolution = (TextView) findViewById(R.id.txtResolution);
```

After `onCreate`, add the method that handles our button click and runs our detection code:

```
public void detectDevice(View v){

    // What is the orientation?
    Display display = getWindowManager().getDefaultDisplay();
    txtOrientation.setText("" + display.getRotation());

    // What is the resolution?
    Point xy = new Point();
    display.getSize(xy);
    txtResolution.setText("x = " + xy.x + " y = " + xy.y);

}
```

Import the following three classes:
```
import android.graphics.Point;
import android.view.Display;
import android.view.View;
```

This code works by declaring and initializing an object of the `Display` type called `display`. This object (`display`) now holds a whole bunch of data about the specific display properties of the device.

The result of the `getRotation` method is output into the top `TextView`.

The code then initializes an object of the `Point` type called `xy`. The `getSize` method then loads up the screen resolution into `xy`. The `setText` method is then used to output the horizontal (`xy.x`) and vertical (`xy.y`) resolution into the `TextView`.

Each time the button is clicked, the two `TextView` widgets will be updated.

Unlocking the screen orientation

Before we run the app, we want to make sure the device isn't locked in portrait mode (most new phones are by default). From the app drawer of the emulator (or the device you will be using), tap the **Settings** app and choose **Display,** and then use the switch to set **Auto-rotate screen** to on. I have shown this setting in the following screenshot:

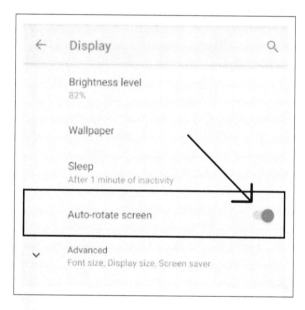

Running the app

Now you can run the app and click the button:

Rotate the device, using one of the rotate buttons on the emulator control panel, to landscape:

[On some computers, the emulator is prone to crashing when it is rotated. If necessary, test this on an actual device.]

[You can also use *CTRL + F11* on a PC, or *CTRL + FN + F11* on a macOS device.]

Now click the button again and you will see the landscape layout in action:

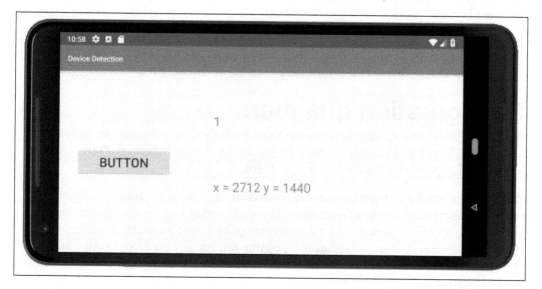

The first thing you will probably notice is that when you rotate the screen, it briefly goes blank. This is the Activity restarting and going through `onCreate` again. Just what we need. It calls `setContentView` on the landscape version of the layout and the code in `MainActivity` refers to widgets with the same ID, so the exact same code works.

 Just for a moment, consider how we might handle things if we needed different behavior as well as layout between the two orientations. Don't spend too long pondering this because we will discuss it later in the chapter.

If the 0 and 1 results are less than obvious regarding device orientation, they refer to `public static final` variables of the `Surface` class, where `Surface.ROTATION_0` equals zero and `Surface.ROTATION_180` equals one.

 Note that if you rotated the screen to the left, then your value will be 1, the same as mine, but if you rotated it to the right, you would have seen the value 3. If you rotate the device to portrait mode upside down, you will get the value 4.

And we could `switch` based on the results of these detection tests and load up different layouts.

But, as we have just seen, Android makes this simpler than this for us by allowing us to add specific layouts into folders with configuration qualifiers, such as **land**.

Configuration qualifiers

We have already met configuration qualifiers, such as `layout-large` or `layout-xhdpi`, in *Chapter 3, Exploring Android Studio and the Project Structure*. Here, we will refresh and expand our understanding of them.

We can begin to alleviate our reliance on the controller layer to influence app layout by using configuration qualifiers. There are configuration qualifiers for size, orientation, and pixel density. To take advantage of a configuration qualifier, we simply design a layout in the usual way, optimized for our preferred configuration, and then place that layout in a folder with a name that Android recognizes as being for that particular configuration.

For example, in the previous app, putting a layout in the `land` folder tells Android to use that layout when the device is in the landscape orientation.

It is likely that the above statement seems slightly ambiguous. This is because the Android Studio project explorer window shows us a file and folder structure that doesn't exactly correspond to reality—it is trying to simplify things and "help" us. If you select the **Project Files** option from the drop-down list at the top of the project explorer window and then examine the project contents, you will indeed see that there is a layout and `layout-land` folder, as shown in the following screenshot:

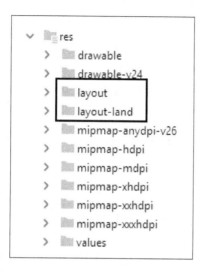

Switch back to the **Android** layout, or leave it on the **Project Files** view, whichever you prefer.

So, if we want to have a different layout for landscape and portrait, we would create a folder called `layout-land` in the `res` folder (or use the shortcut we used in the previous app) and place our specially designed layout within it.

When the device is in portrait orientation, the regular layout from the `layout` folder would be used, and when it is in landscape orientation, the layout from the `layout-land` folder would be used.

If we are designing for different sizes of screen, we place layouts into folders with the following names:

- `layout-small`
- `layout-normal`
- `layout-large`
- `layout-xlarge`

If we are designing for screens with different pixel densities, we can place XML layouts into folders with names such as these:

- `layout-ldpi` for low DPI devices
- `layout-mdpi` for medium DPI devices
- `layout-hdpi` for high DPI devices
- `layout-xhdpi` for extra high DPI devices
- `layout-xxhdpi` for extra, extra high DPI devices
- `layout-xxxhdpi` for extra, extra, extra high DPI devices
- `layout-nodpi` for devices with a DPI you have not otherwise catered for
- `layout-tvdpi` for TVs

What exactly qualifies as low, high, or extra high DPI and so on can be researched at the link in the next info box. The point here is the principle.

It is worth pointing out that what we have just discussed is a long way from the whole story regarding configuration qualifiers and, as with design, it is worth putting this on your list of things to study further.

 As so often, the Android developer site has lots of detailed information on handling layouts for different devices. Try this link for more information: `https://developer.android.com/guide/practices/screens_support`.

The limitation of configuration qualifiers

What the previous app and our discussion on configuration qualifiers have shown us is certainly very useful in a number of situations. Unfortunately, however, configuration qualifiers and detecting attributes in code only solves the problem in the view layer of our MVC pattern.

As discussed, our apps sometimes need to have different *behavior* as well as layout. This perhaps implies multiple branches of our Java code in the controller layer (`MainActivity` in our previous app) and perhaps summons nightmarish visions of having huge great `if` or `switch` blocks with different code for each different scenario.

Fortunately, this is not how it's done. For such situations, in fact for most apps, Android has **fragments**.

Fragments

Fragments will likely become a staple of almost every app you make. They are so useful, there are so many reasons to use them, and once you get used to them, they are so simple, there is almost no reason not to use them.

Fragments are reusable elements of an app just like any class, but, as mentioned previously, they have special features, such as the ability to load their own view/ layout as well as their very own lifecycle methods, which make them perfect for achieving the goals we discussed in the *Real world apps* section.

Let's dig a bit deeper into fragments one feature at a time.

Fragments have a lifecycle too

We can set up and control fragments, very much like we do Activities, by overriding the appropriate lifecycle methods.

onCreate

In the onCreate method, we can initialize variables and do almost all the things we would typically have done in the Activity onCreate method. The big exception to this is initializing our UI.

onCreateView

In this method, we will, as the name suggests, get a reference to any of our UI widgets, set up anonymous classes to listen for clicks, and more besides, as we will soon see.

onAttach and onDetach

These methods are called just before the Fragment is put into use/taken out of use.

onStart, onPause, and onStop

In these methods, we can take certain actions, such as creating or deleting objects or saving data, just like we have done with their Activity-based counterparts.

There are other Fragment lifecycle methods as well, but we know enough to start using Fragments already. If you want to study the details of the Fragment lifecycle, you can do so on the Android developer website at this link: https://developer.android.com/guide/components/fragments.

This is all fine, but we need a way to create our fragments in the first place and be able to call these methods at the right time.

Managing Fragments with FragmentManager

The FragmentManager class is part of the Activity. We use it to initialize a Fragment, add Fragments to the Activities layout, and to end a Fragment. We briefly saw FragmentManager before when we initialized our FragmentDialogs.

It is very hard to learn much about Android without bumping in to the Fragment class, just as it is tough to learn much about Java without constantly bumping in to OOP/classes, and so on.

The following highlighted code shows how we used the FragmentManager (which is already a part of the Activity) being passed in as an argument to create the pop-up dialog:

```java
button.setOnClickListener(new View.OnClickListener() {
    @Override
    public void onClick(View v) {

        // Create a new DialogShowNote called dialog
        DialogShowNote dialog = new DialogShowNote();

        // Send the note via the sendNoteSelected method
        dialog.sendNoteSelected(mTempNote);

        // Create the dialog
        dialog.show(getFragmentManager(), "123");
    }
});
```

At the time, I asked you not to concern yourself with the arguments of the method call. The second argument of the method call is an id for the Fragment. We will see how we use FragmentManager more extensively, as well as use the Fragment id as well.

`FragmentManager` does exactly what its name suggests. What is important here is that an `Activity` only has one `FragmentManager`, but it can take care of many fragments. This is just what we need to have multiple behaviors and layouts within a single app.

`FragmentManager` also calls the various lifecycle methods of the fragments it is responsible for. This is distinct from the `Activity` lifecycle methods, which are called by Android, yet closely related because the `FragmentManager` calls many of the `Fragment` lifecycle methods *in response to* the `Activity` lifecycle methods being called. As usual, we don't need to worry too much about when and how, provided we respond appropriately in each situation.

Fragments are going to be a fundamental part of many, if not all, of our future apps. As we did with naming conventions, string resources, and encapsulation, however, we will not use fragments for simple learning purposes or very small apps when they would be overkill. The exception to this will, of course, be when we are learning about or making apps to specifically demonstrate fragments.

Our first Fragment app

Let's build a `Fragment` in its simplest possible form so we can understand what is going on, before in later chapters we start producing Fragments all over the place that are of genuine use.

I urge all readers to go through and build this project. There is a lot of jumping around from file to file, and just reading alone can make it seem more complex than it really is. Certainly, you can copy and paste the code from the download bundle, but please also follow the steps, and create your own projects and classes. Fragments are not too tough, but their implementation, like their name suggests, is a little fragmented.

Create a new project called `Simple Fragment` using the Basic Activity template and leaving the rest of the settings at their defaults.

Note that there is the option to create a project with a `Fragment`, but we will learn more doing things ourselves from scratch.

Switch to `activity_main.xml` and delete the default **Hello world!** `TextView`.

Now make sure the root ConstraintLayout is selected by left-clicking it in the **Component tree** window, and then change its **id** property to fragmentHolder. We will now be able to get a reference to this layout in our Java code and, as the id property implies, we will be adding a Fragment to it.

Now we will create a layout that will define our fragment's appearance. Right-click the **layout** folder and choose **New | Layout resource file**. In the **File name** field, type fragment_layout, and left-click **OK**. We have just created a new layout of the LinearLayout type.

Add a single **Button** widget anywhere on the layout and make its **id** property button.

Now that we have a simple layout for our fragment to use, let's write some Java code to make the actual fragment.

Note that you can create a Fragment by simply dragging and dropping one from the palette, but doing things this way is much less flexible and controllable, and flexibility and control are the big benefits to fragments, as we will see throughout the next chapter. By creating a class that extends Fragment, we can make as many fragments from it as we like.

In the project explorer, right-click the folder that contains the MainActivity file. From the context menu, choose **New | Java class**. In the **Name** field, type SimpleFragment and left-click OK.

Note that there are options to create Fragment classes in various pre-coded states to enable you to implement a Fragment more quickly, but these will slightly cloud the learning objectives of this app.

In our new SimpleFragment class, change the code to extend Fragment. As you type the code, you will be asked to choose the specific Fragment class to import, as shown in the following screenshot:

```
public class SimpleFragment extends Frag|
}
       © b  Fragment (android.app)
       © b  FragmentManager (android.app)
       © b  Fragment (android.support.v4.app)
       © b  FragmentTransaction (android.app)
       © b  FragmentActivity (android.support.v4.app)
       © b  FragmentManager (android.support.v4.app)
       © b  FragmentPagerAdapter (android.support.v4.app)
       © b  FragmentStatePagerAdapter (android.support.v4.app)
       © b  FragmentTabHost (android.support.v4.app)
       © b  FragmentTransaction (android.support.v4.app)
       Press Ctrl+Space to see non-imported classes >>
```

Choose the top option (as shown in the previous screenshot), which is the regular
`Fragment` class.

> We will need all of the following import statements in this class:
>
> ```
> import android.app.Fragment;
> import android.os.Bundle;
> import android.view.LayoutInflater;
> import android.view.View;
> import android.view.ViewGroup;
> import android.widget.Button;
> import android.widget.Toast;
> ```

Now add a single `String` variable called `myString`, and a `Button` variable called
`myButton`, as members.

Now override the `onCreate` method. Inside the `onCreate` method, initialize
`myString` to `Hello from SimpleFragment`. Our code so far (excluding the package
declaration and import statements) will look exactly like this next code:

```
public class SimpleFragment extends Fragment {

    // member variables accessible from anywhere in this fragment
    String myString;
    Button myButton;

    @Override
    public void onCreate(Bundle savedInstanceState){
        super.onCreate(savedInstanceState);

        myString = "Hello from SimpleFragment";
    }
}
```

In the previous code, we created a member variable called `myString`, and then, in the `onCreate` method, we initialized it. This is very much like we do for our previous apps when only using `Activity`.

The difference, however, is that we did not set the view or attempt to get a reference to our `Button` member variable, `myButton`.

When using `Fragment`, we need to do this in the `onCreateView` method. Let's override that now and see how we set the view and get a reference to our `Button`.

Add this code to the `SimpleFragment` class after the `onCreate` method:

```
@Override
public View onCreateView(LayoutInflater inflater, ViewGroup
container, Bundle savedInstanceState) {

    View view = inflater.inflate(R.layout.fragment_layout,
        container, false);

    myButton = (Button) view.findViewById(R.id.button);

    return view;
}
```

To understand the previous block of code, we must first look at the `onCreateView` method signature. Observe in the first instance that the start of the method states that it must return an object of the `View` type:

```
public View onCreateView...
```

Next, we have the three arguments. Let's look at the first two:

```
(LayoutInflater inflater, ViewGroup container,...
```

We need `LayoutInflater` as we cannot call `setContentView` because `Fragment` provides no such method. In the body of `onCreateView`, we use the `inflate` method of `inflater` to inflate our layout contained in `fragment_layout.xml` and initialize `view` (an object of the `View` type) with the result.

We use `container`, which was passed in to `onCreateView`, as an argument in the `inflate` method as well. The `container` variable is a reference to the layout in `activity_main.xml`.

It might seem obvious that `activity_main.xml` is the containing layout, but, as we will see later in the chapter, the `ViewGroup container` argument allows *any* `Activity` with *any* layout to be the container for our fragment. This is exceptionally flexible and makes our `Fragment` code reusable to a significant extent.

The third argument we pass in to `inflate` is `false`, which means that we don't want our layout added immediately to the containing layout. We will do this ourselves soon from another part of the code.

The third argument of `onCreateView` is `Bundle savedInstanceState`, which is there to help us maintain the data that our fragments hold.

Now that we have an inflated layout contained in `view`, we can use this to get a reference to our `Button` as follows:

```
myButton = (Button) view.findViewById(R.id.button);
```

And use it as the `return` value to the calling code, as required:

```
return view;
```

Now we can add an anonymous class to listen for clicks on our button in the usual manner. In the `onClick` method, we display a pop up `Toast` message to demonstrate that everything is working as expected.

Add this code just before the `return` statement in `onCreateView`, as highlighted in the following code:

```
@Override
public View onCreateView(LayoutInflater inflater,
        ViewGroup container,
        Bundle savedInstanceState) {

    View view = inflater.inflate(R.layout.fragment_layout,
    container, false);

    myButton = (Button) view.findViewById(R.id.button);

    myButton.setOnClickListener(
            new View.OnClickListener() {

                @Override
                public void onClick(View v) {

                    Toast.makeText(getActivity(),
                            myString ,
                        Toast.LENGTH_SHORT).
                        show();
                }
            });

    return view;
}
```

As a reminder, the getActivity() call used as an argument in makeText gets a reference to the Activity that contains the Fragment. This is required to display a Toast message. We also used getActivity in our FragmentDialog-based classes in the Note to self app.

We can't run our app just yet; it will not work because there is one more step required. We need to create an instance of SimpleFragment and initialize it appropriately. This is where FragmentManager will get introduced.

This next code creates a new FragmentManager by calling getFragmentManager. It creates a new Fragment, based on our SimpleFragment class using the FragmentManager, and passing in the id of the layout (within the Activity) that will hold it.

Add this code to the onCreate method of MainActivity.java just after the call to setContentView:

```java
// Get a fragment manager
FragmentManager fManager = getFragmentManager();

// Create a new fragment using the manager
// Passing in the id of the layout to hold it
Fragment frag = fManager.findFragmentById(R.id.fragmentHolder);

// Check the fragment has not already been initialized
if(frag == null){

    // Initialize the fragment based on our SimpleFragment
    frag = new SimpleFragment();
    fManager.beginTransaction()
            .add(R.id.fragmentHolder, frag)
            .commit();

}
```

You will need to add the following import statements to the MainActivity class:

```java
import android.app.Fragment;
import android.app.FragmentManager;
```

Now run the app and gaze in wonder at our clickable button that displays a message with the `Toast` class, and which took two layouts and two whole classes to create:

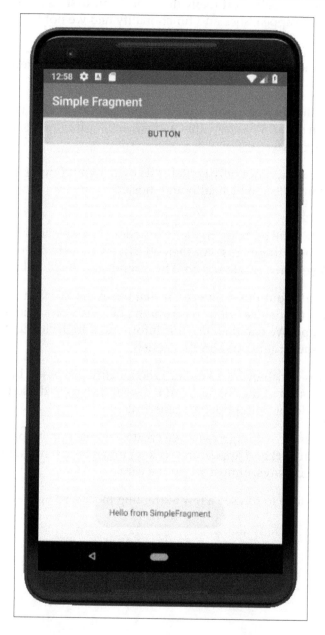

If you remember doing that way back in *Chapter 2, First Contact: Java, XML and the UI Designer*, and with far less code, then it is clear that we need a fragment reality check to answer a question; like, WHY!

Fragment reality check

So, what does this `Fragment` stuff really do for us? Our first `Fragment` mini-app would have the same appearance and functionality had we not bothered with the `Fragment` at all.

In fact, using `Fragment` has made the whole thing more complicated! Why would we want to do this?

We kind of know the answer to this already; it just isn't especially clear based on what we have seen so far. We know that a `Fragment`, or fragments, can be added to the layout of an `Activity`.

We know that a `Fragment` not only contains its own layout (view), but also its very own code (controller), which, although hosted by an `Activity`, is virtually independent.

Our quick app only showed one `Fragment` in action, but we could have an `Activity` that hosts two or more fragments. We then effectively have two almost independent controllers displayed on a single screen. This sounds like it could be useful.

What is most useful about this, however, is that when the `Activity` starts, we can detect attributes of the device our app is running on, perhaps a phone or tablet, portrait or landscape. We can then use this information to decide to display either just one or two of our fragments simultaneously.

This not only helps us achieve the kind of functionality discussed in the *Real- world apps* section, at the start of the chapter, but it also allows us to do so using the exact same `Fragment` code for both possible scenarios!

This really is the essence of fragments. We create a whole app by pairing up both functionality (controller) and appearance (view) into a bunch of fragments that we can reuse in different ways, almost without a care.

It is, of course, possible to foresee a few stumbling blocks, so take a look at this FAQ.

Frequently asked question

Q) The missing link is that if all these fragments are fully-functioning, independent controllers, then we need to learn a bit more about how we would implement our model layer. If we simply have an `ArrayList`, like with Note to Self, where will it go? How would we share it between fragments (assuming both/all fragments need access to the same data)?

A) There is an entirely more elegant solution we can use to create a model layer (both data itself and the code to maintain the data). We will see this when we explore `NavigationView` in *Chapter 26, Advanced UI with Navigation Drawer and Fragment,* and Android databases in *Chapter 27, Android Databases.*

Summary

Now we have a broad understanding of what Fragments are meant for, and how we can begin to use them, we can start to go deeper into how they are used. In the next chapter, we will complete a couple of apps that use multiple Fragments in different ways.

25
Advanced UI with Paging and Swiping

Paging is the act of moving from page to page, and, on Android, we do this by swiping a finger across the screen. The current page transitions in a direction and speed to match the finger movement. It is a useful and practical way to navigate around an app, but perhaps even more than this, it is an extremely satisfying visual effect for the user. Also, as with `RecyclerView`, we can selectively load just the data required for the current page and perhaps the data for the previous and next pages.

The Android API, as you would have come to expect, has a number of solutions for achieving paging in a quite simple manner.

In this chapter, we will learn to do the following:

*   Achieve paging and swiping with images like you might find in a photo gallery app.
*   Implement paging and swiping with fragments, giving the potential to offer our users the ability to swipe their way through a selection of entire user interfaces, thereby giving our apps enormous potential.

First, let's look at a swiping example.

Angry birds classic swipe menu

Here, we can see the famous Angry Birds level selection menu showing swiping/paging in action:

Let's build two paging apps, one with images, and one with fragments.

Building an image gallery/slider app

Create a new project in Android Studio called `Image Pager`. Use the Basic Activity template and leave the remainder of the settings at their defaults.

The images are located in the download bundle in the `Chapter 25/Image Pager/ drawable` folder. The following diagram shows them in Windows Explorer:

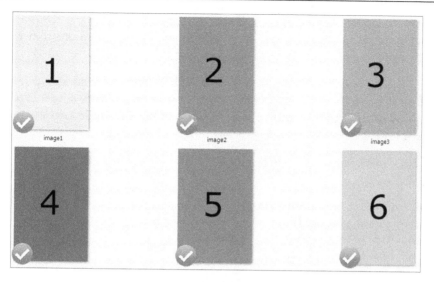

Add the images to the `drawable` folder in the project explorer or, of course, you could add more interesting images, perhaps some photos you have taken.

Implementing the layout

For a simple image paging app, we use the `PagerAdapter` class. We can think of this as being like `RecyclerApater`, but for images, as it will handle the display of an array of images in a `ViewPager` widget. This is much like how `RecyclerAdapter` handles the display of the content of an `ArrayList` in a `ListView`. All we need to do is override the appropriate methods.

To implement an image gallery with `PagerAdapter`, we first need a `ViewPager` in our main layout. So you can see precisely what is required here is the actual XML code for `activity_main.xml`. Edit `layout_main.xml` to look exactly like this:

```
<RelativeLayout xmlns:android=
    "http://schemas.android.com/apk/res/android"
    android:layout_width="fill_parent"
    android:layout_height="fill_parent" >

    <androidx.viewpager.widget.ViewPager
        android:id="@+id/pager"
        android:layout_width="wrap_content"
        android:layout_height="wrap_content" />

</RelativeLayout>
```

The slightly unusually named class, androidx.ViewPager.widget.ViewPager, is the class that makes this functionality available in Android versions that were released prior to ViewPager.

Next, a bit like we needed a layout to represent a list item, we need a layout to represent an item, in this case an image, in our ViewPager. Create a new layout file in the usual way, and call it pager_item.xml. It will have a single ImageView with an id of imageView.

Use the visual designer to achieve this or copy the following XML into pager_item.xml:

```
<RelativeLayout xmlns:android=
    "http://schemas.android.com/apk/res/android"
     android:layout_width="fill_parent"
     android:layout_height="fill_parent" >

    <androidx.viewpager.widget.ViewPager
        android:id="@+id/pager"
        android:layout_width="wrap_content"
        android:layout_height="wrap_content" />

</RelativeLayout>
```

Now we can make a start on our PagerAdapter.

Coding the PagerAdapter class

Next, we need to extend PagerAdapter to handle images. Create a new class called ImagePagerAdapter and make it extend PagerAdapter.

Add the following imports to the top of the ImagePagerAdapter class. We normally rely on using the shortcut *Alt + Enter* to add imports. We are doing things slightly differently this time because there are some very similarly named classes that will not suit our objectives.

Add the following imports to the ImagePagerAdapter class:

```
import android.content.Context;
import android.view.LayoutInflater;
import android.view.View;
import android.view.ViewGroup;
import android.widget.ImageView;
```

```
import android.widget.RelativeLayout;

import androidx.viewpager.widget.PagerAdapter;
import androidx.viewpager.widget.ViewPager;
```

Here is the class declaration with the extends... code added, as well as a couple of member variables. These variables are a Context object that we will use shortly and an int array called images. The reason for having an int array for images is because we will store int identifiers for images. We will see how this works in a few code blocks time. The last member variable is a LayoutInflater, which you can probably guess will be used to inflate each of the instances of pager_item.xml.

Extend PagerAdapter and add the member variables we have just discussed:

```
public class ImagePagerAdapter extends PagerAdapter {

    Context context;

    int[] images;
    LayoutInflater inflater;
}
```

Now we need a constructor that sets up ImagerPagerAdapter by receiving the Context from MainActivity, as well as the int array for the images, and initializing the member variables with them.

Add the highlighted constructor method to the ImagePagerAdapter class;

```
public ImagePagerAdapter(
    Context context,  int[] images) {

    this.context = context;
    this.images = images;
}
```

Now, we must override the required methods of PagerAdapter. Immediately after the previous code, add the overridden getCount method, which simply returns the number of image IDs in the array. This method is used internally by the class:

```
@Override
public int getCount() {

    return images.length;
}
```

Now we must override the `isViewFromObject` method that just returns a `Boolean`, dependent upon whether the current `View` is the same or associated with the current `Object` as passed in as a parameter. Again, this is a method that is used internally by the class. Immediately after the previous code, add this overridden method:

```
@Override
public boolean isViewFromObject(View view, Object object) {
    return view == object;
}
```

Now we must override the `instantiateItem` method and this is where we do most of the work that concerns us. First, we declare a new `ImageView` object, and then we initialize our `LayoutInflater` member. Next, we use the `LayoutInflater` to declare and initialize a new `View` from our `pager_item.xml` layout file.

After this, we get a reference to the `ImageView` inside the `pager_item.xml` layout. We can now add the appropriate image as the content of the `ImageView` based on the position parameter of the `instantiateItem` method and the appropriate ID from the images array.

Finally, we add the layout to the `PagerAdapter` with `addView` and return from the method.

Now add the method we have just discussed:

```
@Override
public Object instantiateItem(
    ViewGroup container, int position) {

    ImageView image;

    Inflater = (LayoutInflater)
            context.getSystemService(
            Context.LAYOUT_INFLATER_SERVICE);

    View itemView = inflater.inflate(
            R.layout.pager_item, container,false);

    // get reference to imageView in pager_item layout
    image = (ImageView)
            itemView.findViewById(R.id.imageView);

    // Set an image to the ImageView
    image.setImageResource(images[position]);

    // Add pager_item layout as the current page to the ViewPager
```

```
((ViewPager) container).addView(itemView);

    return itemView;
}
```

The last method we must override is destroyItem, which the class can call when it needs to remove an appropriate item based on the value of the position parameter.

Add the destroyItem method after the previous code and before the closing curly brace of the ImagePagerAdapter class:

```
@Override
public void destroyItem(ViewGroup container,
    int position,
    Object object) {

    // Remove pager_item layout from ViewPager
    ((ViewPager) container)
        .removeView((RelativeLayout) object);
}
```

As we saw when coding ImagePagerAdapter, there is very little to it. It is just a case of properly implementing the overridden methods that the ImagePagerAdapter class uses to help make things work smoothly behind the scenes.

Now we can code the MainActivity class that will use the ImagePagerAdapter.

Coding the MainActivity class

Finally, we can code our MainActivity class. As with the ImagePagerAdapter class, for clarity, add the following import statements manually to the MainActivity.java class before the class declaration as shown in the following snippet:

```
import androidx.appcompat.app.AppCompatActivity;
import androidx.viewpager.widget.PagerAdapter;
import androidx.viewpager.widget.ViewPager;
```

We need a few member variables. Unsurprisingly, we need a ViewPager, which will be used to get a reference to the ViewPager in our layout, as well as an ImagePagerAdapter reference for the class we have just coded. We also need an int array to hold an array of image ids.

Adapt the `MainActivity` class to be as follows:

```
public class MainActivity extends AppCompatActivity {

    ViewPager viewPager;
    PagerAdapter adapter;

    int[] images;

    @Override
    public void onCreate(Bundle savedInstanceState) {
        super.onCreate(savedInstanceState);
        . . .
```

All the rest of the code goes in onCreate. We initialize our `int` array with each of the images that we added to the `drawable-xhdpi` folder.

We initialize the `ViewPager` in the usual way with the `findViewByID` method. We also initialize our `ImagePagerAdapter` by passing in a reference of `MainActivity` and the `images` array, as required by the constructor that we coded previously. Finally, we bind the adapter to the pager with `setAdapter`.

Code `onCreate` to look just like this following code:

```
@Override
public void onCreate(Bundle savedInstanceState) {
    super.onCreate(savedInstanceState);

    setContentView(R.layout.activity_main);

    // Grab all the images and stuff them in our array
    images = new int[] { R.drawable.image1,
                R.drawable.image2,
                R.drawable.image3,
                R.drawable.image4,
                R.drawable.image5,
                R.drawable.image6 };

    // get a reference to the ViewPager in the layout
    viewPager = (ViewPager) findViewById(R.id.pager);

    // Initialize our adapter
    adapter = new
```

```
        ImagePagerAdapter(MainActivity.this, images);

    // Binds the Adapter to the ViewPager
    viewPager.setAdapter(adapter);

}
```

Now we are ready to run the app.

Running the gallery app

Here we can see the first image from our int array:

Swipe a little right and left to see the pleasing manner in which the images transition smoothly:

Now we will build an app with almost identical functionality, except that each page in the pager will be a Fragment, which could have any or all of the functionality a regular Fragment can have because they are regular Fragments.

Building a Fragment Pager/slider app

We can put whole fragments as pages in a `PagerAdapter`. This is quite powerful because, as we know, a `Fragment` can have a large amount of functionality, even a fully-fledged UI.

To keep the code short and straightforward, we will add a single `TextView` to each `Fragment` layout, just to demonstrate that the pager is working. When we see how easy it is to get a reference to the `TextView`, however, it should be obvious how we could easily add any layout we have learned so far and then let the user interact with it.

 In the next project, we will see yet another way to display multiple `Fragment` instances, `NavigationView`, and we will actually implement multiple coded `Fragment` instances.

The first thing we will do is build the content for the slider. In this case, of course, the content is `Fragment`s. We will build one simple class called `SimpleFragment`, and one simple layout called `fragment_layout`.

You might think this implies that each slide will be identical in appearance, but we will use the **Fragment** id passed in by the `FragmentManager` at instantiation as the text for the one and only `TextView`. This way, when we flip/swipe through the `Fragment`s, it will be clear that each is a new distinct instance.

When we see the code that loads Fragments from a list, it will be easy to design completely different `Fragment` classes, as we have done before, and use these different classes for some or all the slides. Each of these classes could, of course, also use a different layout as well.

Coding the SimpleFragment class

As with the Image Pager app, it is not exactly straightforward which classes need to be auto-imported by Android Studio. We use the classes that we do because they are all compatible with each other and it is possible that if you let Android Studio suggest which classes to import, it will get it wrong. The project files are located in the `Chapter 25/Fragment Pager` folder.

Create a new project called `Fragment Slider` using the Simple Activity template and leave all the settings at the defaults.

Now create a new class called `SimpleFragment`, extend `Fragment`, and add the import statements and one member variable as shown in the following:

```
import android.os.Bundle;
import android.view.LayoutInflater;
import android.view.View;
import android.view.ViewGroup;
import android.widget.TextView;

import androidx.fragment.app.Fragment;

public class SimpleFragment extends Fragment {

// Holds the fragment id passed in when created
public static final String MESSAGE = "";


}
```

We have to add two methods, the first of which is `newInstance`, which we will call from `MainActivity` to set up and return a reference to the `Fragment`. The next code does just as we have seen previously. It creates a new instance of the class, but it also puts a `String` into the `Bundle` object that will eventually be read from the `onCreate` method. The `String` that is added to the `Bundle` is the one that is passed in the one and only parameter of this `newInstance` method.

Add the `newInstance` method to the `SimpleFragment` class, as follows:

```
// Our newInstance method which we
// call to make a new Fragment
public static SimpleFragment newInstance(String message)
{
    // Create the fragment
    SimpleFragment fragment = new SimpleFragment();

    // Create a bundle for our message/id
    Bundle bundle = new Bundle(1);
    // Load up the Bundle
    bundle.putString(MESSAGE, message);
    // Call setArguments ready for
    // when onCreate is called
    fragment.setArguments(bundle);
    return fragment;
}
```

The final method for our `SimpleFragment` class needs to override `onCreateView` where, as usual, we will get a reference to the layout passed in and load up our `fragment_layout` as the layout.

Then, the first line of code unpacks the `String` from the `Bundle` using `getArguments.getString` and the `MESSAGE` identifier of the key-value pair.

Add the `onCreateView` method we have just discussed:

```
@Override
public View onCreateView(LayoutInflater inflater,
                ViewGroup container,
                Bundle savedInstanceState) {

    // Get the id from the Bundle
    String message = getArguments().getString(MESSAGE);

    // Inflate the view as normal
    View view = inflater.inflate(
            R.layout.fragment_layout, container, false);

    // Get a reference to textView
    TextView messageTextView = (TextView)
            view.findViewById(R.id.textView);

    // Display the id in the TextView
    messageTextView.setText(message);

    // We could also handle any UI
    // of any complexity in the usual way
    // And we will over the next two chapters
    // ..
    // ..

    return view;
}
```

Let's also make a super-simple layout for the `Fragment`, which will, of course, contain the `TextView` we have just been using.

The fragment_layout

The `fragment_layout` is the simplest layout we have ever made. Right-click on the **layout** folder and choose **New | Resource layout file**. Name the file `fragment_layout`, and left-click **OK**. Now add a single `TextView` and set its `id` property to `textView`.

We can now code the `MainActivity` class that handles the `FragmentPager` and brings our `SimpleFragment` instances to life.

Coding the MainActivity class

This class consists of two main parts. First, the changes we will make to the overridden `onCreate` method, and second, the implementation of our inner class and its overridden methods of `FragmentPagerAdapter`.

First, add the following imports and a single member variable that will be our instance of our implementation of a `FragmentPagerAdapter`, and `SimpleFragmentPagerAdapter`:

```
import android.os.Bundle;
import java.util.ArrayList;
import java.util.List;

import androidx.appcompat.app.AppCompatActivity;
import androidx.fragment.app.Fragment;
import androidx.fragment.app.FragmentManager;
import androidx.fragment.app.FragmentPagerAdapter;
import androidx.viewpager.widget.ViewPager;

public class MainActivity extends AppCompatActivity {

    SimpleFragmentPagerAdapter pageAdapter;
```

Next, in the `onCreate` method, we create a `List` for Fragments, and then create and add three instances of `SimpleFragment`, passing in a numerical identifier to be packed away in the `Bundle`.

We then initialize `SimpleFragmentPagerAdapter` (which we will code soon), passing in our list of fragments.

We get a reference to the `ViewPager` with `findViewByID` and bind our adapter to it with `setAdapter`.

Then add code to the onCreate method of MainActivity:

```
@Override
public void onCreate(Bundle savedInstanceState) {
    super.onCreate(savedInstanceState);
    setContentView(R.layout.activity_main);

    // Initialize a list of three fragments
    List<Fragment> fragmentList =
                new ArrayList<Fragment>();

    // Add three new Fragments to the list
    fragmentList.add(SimpleFragment.newInstance("1"));
    fragmentList.add(SimpleFragment.newInstance("2"));
    fragmentList.add(SimpleFragment.newInstance("3"));

    pageAdapter = new SimpleFragmentPagerAdapter(
                getSupportFragmentManager(), fragmentList);

    ViewPager pager = (ViewPager)findViewById(R.id.pager);
    pager.setAdapter(pageAdapter);

}
```

Now, we will add our inner class, SimpleFragmentPagerAdapter. All we do is add a List for Fragments as a member variable and a constructor that initializes it with the passed-in list.

Then we override the getItem and getCount methods, which are used internally, in the same way we did in the last project, except this time we use the methods of List instead of the size of the array.

Add the following inner class that we have just discussed to the MainActivity class:

```
private class SimpleFragmentPagerAdapter
    extends FragmentPagerAdapter {

    // A List to hold our fragments
    private List<Fragment> fragments;

    // A constructor to receive a
    // fragment manager and a List
    public SimpleFragmentPagerAdapter(
            FragmentManager fm,
```

```
            List<Fragment> fragments) {

        super(fm);
        this.fragments = fragments;
    }


    // Just two methods to override to get
    // the current position of the adapter
    // and the size of the List
    @Override
    public Fragment getItem(int position) {
            return this.fragments.get(position);
    }


    @Override
    public int getCount() {
            return this.fragments.size();
    }
}
```

The last thing we need to do is add the layout for MainActivity.

The activity_main layout

Implement the activity_main layout by copying the following code. It contains a single widget, a ViewPager, and it is important that it is from the correct hierarchy so that it is compatible with the other classes that we use in this project.

Amend the code in the layout_main.xml file that we have just discussed:

```
<RelativeLayout xmlns:android=
        "http://schemas.android.com/apk/res/android"
        xmlns:tools="http://schemas.android.com/tools"
        android:layout_width="match_parent"
        android:layout_height="match_parent"
        tools:context=".MainActivity">

        <androidx.viewpager.widget.ViewPager
        android:id="@+id/pager"
        android:layout_width="wrap_content"
        android:layout_height="wrap_content" />


    </RelativeLayout>
```

Let's see our Fragment slider in action.

Running the fragment slider app

Run the app and you can swipe your way, left or right, through the fragments in the slider. The following screenshot shows the visual effect produced by `FragmentPagerAdapter` when the user tries to swipe beyond the final `Fragment` in the `List`:

Summary

In this chapter, we saw that we can use pagers for simple image galleries or for swiping through complex pages of an entire UI, although we demonstrated this by means of a very simple TextView.

In the next chapter, we will look at another really cool UI element that is used in many of the latest Android apps, probably because it looks great and is a real pleasure, as well as extremely practical, to use. Let's take a look at NavigationView.

26
Advanced UI with Navigation Drawer and Fragment

In this chapter, we will see what is (arguably) the most advanced UI. The `NavigationView`, or navigation drawer because of the way it slides out its content, can be created simply by choosing it as a template when you create a new project. We will do just that, and then we will examine the auto-generated code and learn how to interact with it. We will then use everything we know about `Fragment` to populate each of the "drawers" with different behaviors and views. Then, in the next chapter, we will learn about databases to add some new functionality to each `Fragment`.

In this chapter, the following topics will be covered:

- Introducing `NavigationView`
- Getting started with the simple database app
- Implementing a `NavigationView` using the project template
- Adding multiple Fragments and layouts to `NavigationView`

Let's take a look at this extremely cool UI pattern.

Introducing the NavigationView

What's so great about `NavigationView`? Well the first thing that might catch your eye is that it can be made to look extremely stylish. Take a look at this following screenshot, which shows off `NavigationView` in action in the Google Play app:

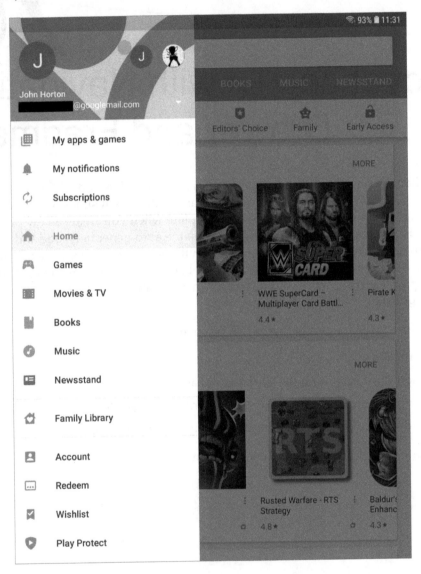

To be honest right from the outset, ours is not going to be as fancy as the one in the Google Play app. However, the same functionality will be present in our app.

What else is neat about this UI is the way that it slides to hide/reveal itself when required. It is because of this behavior that it can be a significant size, making it extremely flexible with regard to the options that can be put on it and, when the user is finished with it, completely disappears, like a drawer.

I suggest trying the Google Play app now and seeing how it works if you haven't already.

You can slide your thumb/finger from the left-hand edge of the screen and the drawer will slowly slide out. You can, of course, slide it away again in the opposite direction.

While the navigation drawer is open, the rest of the screen is slightly dimmed (as seen in the previous screenshot), helping the user to focus on the navigation options offered.

You can also tap anywhere off the Navigation Drawer while it is open, and it will slide itself away, leaving the entire screen clear for the rest of the app.

The drawer can also be opened by tapping on the menu icon in the top-left corner.

We can also tweak and refine the behavior of the navigation drawer, as we will see toward the end of the chapter.

Examining the Simple Database app

In this chapter, we will focus on creating the NavigationView and populating it with four Fragment classes and their respective layouts. In the next chapter, we will learn about, and implement, the database functionality.

The screens of the database app are as follows. Here is what our NavigationView looks like in all its glory. Note that many of the options, and most of the appearance and decoration, is provided by default when using the NavigationView Activity template:

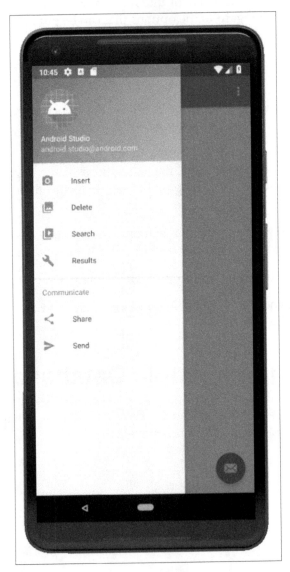

The four main options are what we will add to the UI. They are **Insert**, **Delete**, **Search**, and **List**. The layouts are shown, and their purposes described as follows:

Insert

The first screen allows the user to insert a person's name and their associated age into the database:

This simple layout has two EditText widgets and a button. The user will enter a name and an age, and then click the **INSERT** button to add them to the database.

Delete

This screen is even simpler. The user will enter a name in the EditText and click the button:

If the name entered is present in the database, then the entry (name and age) will be deleted.

Search

This layout is much the same as the previous layout, but has a different purpose:

The user will enter a name into the EditText and then click the button. If the name is present in the database, then it will be displayed along with the matching age.

Results

This screen shows all the entries in the entire database:

Let's get started with the Navigation Drawer.

Starting the Simple Database project

Create a new project in Android Studio. Call it `Age Database`, use the **Navigation Drawer Activity** template, and leave all the Activity and layout names at their defaults. Before we do anything else, it is well worth running the app on an emulator to see how much has been auto-generated as part of this template, as can be seen in the following screenshot:

At first glance, it is just a plain old layout with a `TextView`. But swipe from the left edge, or press the menu button, and the Navigation Drawer reveals itself:

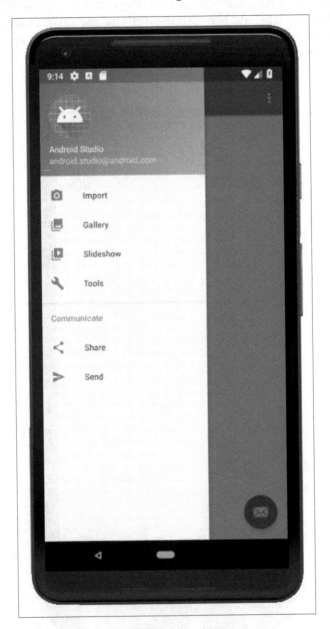

Now we can modify the options and insert a `Fragment` (with layout) for each option. To understand how it works, let's examine the auto-generated code.

Exploring the auto-generated code and assets

In the `drawable` folder, there are a number of icons, as shown in the following screenshot:

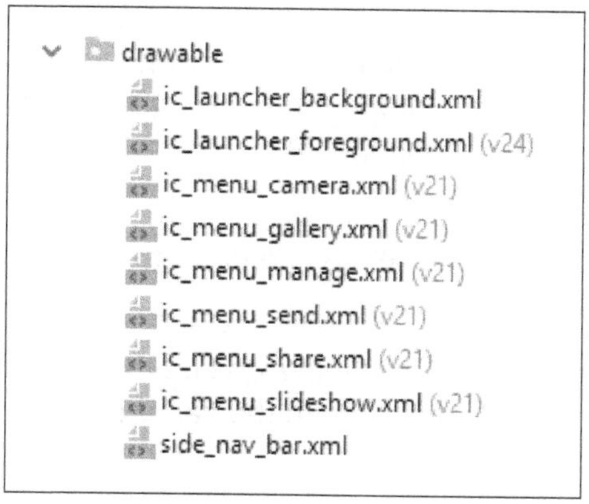

These are the usual icons but also the ones that appear in the menu of the navigation drawer. We will not take the trouble to change these, but if you want to personalize the icons in your app, it should be plain by the end of this exploration how to do so.

Next, open the `res/menu` folder. Notice that there is an extra file titled `activity_main_drawer.xml`. This next code is an excerpt from this file, so we can discuss its contents:

```
<group android:checkableBehavior="single">
    <item
        android:id="@+id/nav_camera"
        android:icon="@drawable/ic_menu_camera"
        android:title="Import" />
    <item
        android:id="@+id/nav_gallery"
        android:icon="@drawable/ic_menu_gallery"
        android:title="Gallery" />
    <item
        android:id="@+id/nav_slideshow"
        android:icon="@drawable/ic_menu_slideshow"
        android:title="Slideshow" />
```

```
    <item
        android:id="@+id/nav_manage"
        android:icon="@drawable/ic_menu_manage"
        android:title="Tools" />
</group>
```

Notice there are four `item` tags within a `group` tag. Now notice how the `title` tags from top to bottom (`Import`, `Gallery`, `Slideshow`, and `Tools`) exactly correspond to the first four text options in the menu of the auto-generated navigation drawer. Also notice that within each `item` tag that there is an `id` tag, so we can refer to them in our Java code, as well as an `icon` tag, which corresponds to one of the icons in the `drawable` folder we have just seen.

Also look in the `layout` folder at the `nav_header_main.xml` file, which contains the layout for the header of the drawer.

The rest of the files are as we have come to expect, but there are a few more key points to note in the Java code. These are in the `MainActivity.java` file. Open it up now and we will look at them.

The first is the extra code in the `onCreate` method that handles aspects of our UI. Take a look at this additional code and then we can discuss it. Note that I have reformatted it slightly to present it tidily in this book:

```java
DrawerLayout drawer = (DrawerLayout)
    findViewById(R.id.drawer_layout);

ActionBarDrawerToggle toggle = new ActionBarDrawerToggle(
        this, drawer, toolbar, R.string.navigation_drawer_open,
        R.string.navigation_drawer_close);

drawer.addDrawerListener(toggle);
toggle.syncState();

NavigationView navigationView =
    (NavigationView) findViewById(R.id.nav_view);

navigationView.setNavigationItemSelectedListener(this);
```

The code gets a reference to a `DrawerLayout`, which corresponds to the layout we have just seen. The code also creates a new instance of an `ActionBarDrawerToggle`, which allows the controlling/toggling of the drawers. Next, a reference is captured to the layout file itself (`nav_view`), and the final line of code sets a listener on the `NavigationView`. Now, Android will call a special method every time the user interacts with the Navigation Drawer. This special method I refer to is `onNavigationItemSelected`. We will see this auto-generated method in a minute.

Next, look at the `onBackPressed` method:

```
@Override
public void onBackPressed() {
    DrawerLayout drawer = (DrawerLayout)
            findViewById(R.id.drawer_layout);

    if (drawer.isDrawerOpen(GravityCompat.START)) {
            drawer.closeDrawer(GravityCompat.START);
    } else {
            super.onBackPressed();
    }
}
```

This is an overridden method of Activity and it handles what happens when the user presses the back button on their device. The code closes the drawer if it is open and, if it is not, simply calls `super.onBackPressed`. This means that the back button will close the drawer if it is open or use the default behavior if it was already closed.

Now look at the `onNavigationItemSelected` method, which is key to the functionality of this app:

```
@SuppressWarnings("StatementWithEmptyBody")
@Override
public boolean onNavigationItemSelected(MenuItem item) {
    // Handle navigation view item clicks here.
    int id = item.getItemId();

    if (id == R.id.nav_camera) {
            // Handle the camera action
    } else if (id == R.id.nav_gallery) {

    } else if (id == R.id.nav_slideshow) {

    } else if (id == R.id.nav_manage) {
```

```
    } else if (id == R.id.nav_share) {

    } else if (id == R.id.nav_send) {

    }

    DrawerLayout drawer = (DrawerLayout)
        findViewById(R.id.drawer_layout);

    drawer.closeDrawer(GravityCompat.START);
    return true;
}
```

Notice that the if and else - if statements correspond to the id contained in the activity_main_drawer.xml file. This is where we will respond to the user selecting options in our navigation drawer menu. At the moment, the if and else - if code does nothing. We will change it to load a specific Fragment, along with its related layout, into the main view. This will mean that our app will have entirely separate functionality and a separate UI, depending on the user's choice from the menu.

Let's code the Fragment classes and their layouts, and then we can come back and write the code to use them in the onNavigationItemSelected method.

Coding the Fragment classes and their layouts

We will create the four classes, including the code that loads the layout as well as the actual layouts as well, but we won't put any of the database functionality into the Java code until we have learned about Android databases in the next chapter.

Once we have our four classes and their layouts, we will see how to load them from the Navigation Drawer menu. By the end of the chapter, we will have a fully working Navigation Drawer that lets the user swap between fragments, but the fragments won't actually do anything until the next chapter.

Creating the empty files for the classes and layouts

Create four layout files with vertical LinearLayout as their parent view by right-clicking on the layout folder and selecting **New | Layout resource file**. Name the first file content_insert, the second content_delete, the third content_search, and the fourth content_results. All the options can be left at their defaults.

You should now have four new layout files containing `LinearLayout` parents, as shown in the following screenshot:

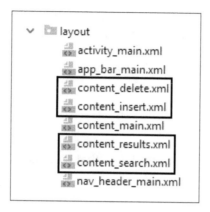

Let's code the Java classes.

Coding the classes

Create four new classes by right-clicking the folder that contains the `MainActivity.java` file and selecting **New | Java class**. Name them `InsertFragment`, `DeleteFragment`, `SearchFragment`, and `ResultsFragment`. It should be plain from the names which fragments will show which layouts.

Just to make it clear, let's add some code to each class to make the classes extend `Fragment` and load their associated layout.

Open `InsertFragment.java` and edit it to contain the following code:

```java
import android.os.Bundle;
import android.view.LayoutInflater;
import android.view.View;
import android.view.ViewGroup;

import androidx.fragment.app.Fragment;

public class InsertFragment extends Fragment {

    @Override
    public View onCreateView(
            LayoutInflater inflater,
            ViewGroup container,
```

```
                        Bundle savedInstanceState) {

            View v = inflater.inflate(
                        R.layout.content_insert,
                        container, false);

            // Database and UI code goes here in next chapter

            return v;
        }
    }
```

Open `DeleteFragment.java` and edit it so that it contains the following code:

```
    import android.os.Bundle;
    import android.view.LayoutInflater;
    import android.view.View;
    import android.view.ViewGroup;

    import androidx.fragment.app.Fragment;

    public class DeleteFragment extends Fragment {

        @Override
        public View onCreateView(
                    LayoutInflater inflater,
                    ViewGroup container,
                    Bundle savedInstanceState) {

            View v = inflater.inflate(
                        R.layout.content_delete,
                        container, false);

            // Database and UI code goes here in next chapter

            return v;
        }
    }
```

Open `SearchFragment.java` and edit it so that it contains the following code:

```
    import android.os.Bundle;
    import android.view.LayoutInflater;
    import android.view.View;
```

```
import android.view.ViewGroup;

import androidx.fragment.app.Fragment;

public class SearchFragment extends Fragment{

    @Override
     public View onCreateView(
                LayoutInflater inflater,
                ViewGroup container,
                Bundle savedInstanceState) {

            View v = inflater.inflate(
                    R.layout.content_search,
                    container, false);

            // Database and UI code goes here in next chapter

            return v;
        }
    }
}
```

Open `ResultsFragment.java` and edit it so that it contains the following code:

```
import android.os.Bundle;
import android.view.LayoutInflater;
import android.view.View;
import android.view.ViewGroup;

import androidx.fragment.app.Fragment;

public class ResultsFragment extends Fragment {

    @Override
    public View onCreateView(
                LayoutInflater inflater,
                ViewGroup container,
                Bundle savedInstanceState) {

        View v = inflater.inflate(
                    R.layout.content_results,
                    container, false);
```

```
            // Database and UI code goes here in next chapter

            return v;
        }
    }
```

Each class is completely devoid of functionality, except that in the `onCreateView` method, the appropriate layout is loaded from the associated layout file.

Let's add the UI to the layout files we created earlier.

Designing the layouts

As we saw at the start of the chapter, all the layouts are simple. Getting your layouts identical to mine is not essential but, as always, the id values must be the same or the Java code we write in the next chapter won't work.

Designing content_insert.xml

Drag two **Plain Text** widgets from the **Text** category of the palette onto the layout. Remember that **Plain Text** widgets are `EditText` instances. Now drag a **Button** onto the layout after the two EditText/Plain Text.

Configure the widgets according to this table:

Widget	Attribute and value
Top edit text	id = editName
Top edit text	text = Name
Second edit text	id = editAge
Second edit text	text = Age
Button	id = btnInsert
Button	text = Insert

This is what your layout should look like in the design view in Android Studio:

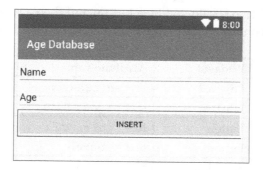

Designing content_delete.xml

Drag a Plain Text/EditText onto the layout with a Button below it. Configure the widgets according to the following table:

Widget	Attribute value
EditText	id = editDelete
EditText	text = Name
Button	id = btnDelete
Button	text = Delete

This is what your layout should look like in the design view in Android Studio:

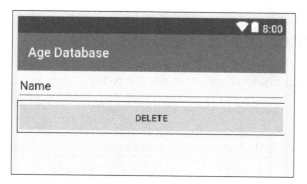

Designing content_search.xml

Drag a Plain Text/EditText, followed by a button and then a regular TextView, onto the layout, and then configure the widgets according to the following table:

Widget	Attribute value
EditText	id = editSearch
EditText	text = Name
Button	id = btnSearch
Button	text = Search
TextView	id = textResult

This is what your layout should look like in the design view in Android Studio:

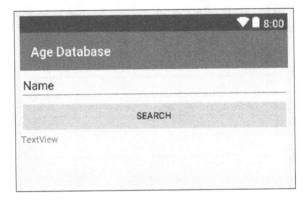

Designing content_results.xml

Drag a single TextView (not Plain Text/EditText this time) onto the layout. We will see in the next chapter how to add an entire list to this single TextView.

Configure the widget according to the following table:

Widget	Attribute value
TextView	id = textResults

This is what your layout should look like in the design view in Android Studio:

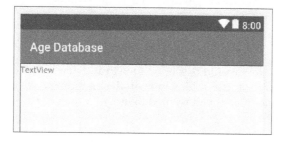

Now we can use the `Fragment`-based classes and their layouts.

Using the Fragment classes and their layouts

This stage has three steps. First, we need to edit the menu of the Navigation Drawer to reflect the options the user has. Next, we need a View in the layout to hold whatever the active `Fragment` instance is, and finally, we need to add code to `MainActivity.java` to switch between the different `Fragment` instances when the user taps on the menu.

Editing the Navigation Drawer menu

Open the `activity_main_drawer.xml` file in the `res/menu` folder of the project explorer. Edit the code within the `group` tags that we saw earlier to reflect our menu options of Insert, Delete, Search, and Results:

```
<group android:checkableBehavior="single">
    <item
        android:id="@+id/nav_insert"
        android:icon="@drawable/ic_menu_camera"
        android:title="Insert" />
    <item
        android:id="@+id/nav_delete"
        android:icon="@drawable/ic_menu_gallery"
        android:title="Delete" />
    <item
        android:id="@+id/nav_search"
        android:icon="@drawable/ic_menu_slideshow"
        android:title="Search" />
    <item
```

```
        android:id="@+id/nav_results"
        android:icon="@drawable/ic_menu_manage"
        android:title="Results" />
</group>
```

[💡 Now would be a good time to add new icons to the drawable folder and edit the preceding code to refer to them if you wanted to use your own icons.]

Adding a holder to the main layout

Open the content_main.xml file in the layout folder and add this highlighted XML code just before the closing tag of the ConstraintLayout:

```
<FrameLayout
    android:id="@+id/fragmentHolder"
    android:layout_width="368dp"
    android:layout_height="495dp"
    tools:layout_editor_absoluteX="8dp"
    tools:layout_editor_absoluteY="8dp">
</FrameLayout>

</androidx.constraintlayout.widget.ConstraintLayout>
```

Now we have a FrameapplyLayout with an id attribute of fragmentHolder that we can get a reference to and load all our Fragment instance layouts into.

Coding the MainActivity.java

Open the MainActivity file and edit the onNavigationItemSelected method to handle all the different menu options the user can choose from:

```
@SuppressWarnings("StatementWithEmptyBody")
@Override
public boolean onNavigationItemSelected(MenuItem item) {
    // Handle navigation view item clicks here.

    // Create a transaction
    FragmentTransaction transaction
            = getSupportFragmentManager().beginTransaction();

    int id = item.getItemId();

    if (id == R.id.nav_insert) {
```

```
        // Create a new fragment of the appropriate type
        InsertFragment fragment = new InsertFragment();
        // What to do and where to do it
        transaction.replace(R.id.fragmentHolder, fragment);

    } else if (id == R.id.nav_search) {
        SearchFragment fragment = new SearchFragment();
        transaction.replace(R.id.fragmentHolder, fragment);

    } else if (id == R.id.nav_delete) {
        DeleteFragment fragment = new DeleteFragment();
        transaction.replace(R.id.fragmentHolder, fragment);

    }  else if (id == R.id.nav_results) {
        ResultsFragment fragment = new ResultsFragment();
        transaction.replace(R.id.fragmentHolder, fragment);
    }

    // Ask Android to remember which
    // menu options the user has chosen
    transaction.addToBackStack(null);

    // Implement the change
    transaction.commit();

    DrawerLayout drawer = (DrawerLayout)
        findViewById(R.id.drawer_layout);

    drawer.closeDrawer(GravityCompat.START);

    return true;
}
```

Let's go through the code we just added. Most of the code should look familiar. For each of our menu options, we create a new `Fragment` of the appropriate type and insert it into our `RelativeLayout` with an id of `fragmentHolder`.

The `transaction.addToBackStack` method means that the chosen `Fragment` will be remembered in order with any others. The result of this is that if the user chooses the insert fragment, then the results fragment taps the back button, and then the app will return the user to the insert fragment.

You can now run the app and use the Navigation Drawer menu to flip between all our different `Fragment` instances. They will look just as they did in the images at the start of this chapter, but they don't have any functionality yet.

Summary

In this chapter, we saw how straightforward it is to have attractive and pleasing UI and, although our Fragment instances don't have any functionality yet, they are set up ready to go once we have learned about databases.

In the next chapter, we will learn about databases in general, and the specific database that Android apps can use, and we will then add the functionality to our Fragment classes.

27
Android Databases

If we are going to make apps that offer our users significant features, then almost certainly we are going to need a way to manage, store, and filter significant amounts of data.

It is possible to efficiently store very large amounts of data with JSON, but when we need to use that data selectively rather than simply restricting ourselves to the options of "save everything" and "load everything" we need to think about which other options are available.

A good computer science course would probably teach the algorithms necessary to handle sorting and filtering our data, but the effort involved would be quite extensive and what are the chances of us coming up with a solution that is as good as the people who provide us with the Android API?

As so often it makes sense to use the solutions provided in the Android API. As we have seen, JSON and SharedPreferences classes have their place but at some point, we need to move on to using real databases for real-world solutions. Android uses the SQLite database management system and as you would expect there is an API to make it as easy as possible.

In this chapter, we will do the following:

- Find out exactly what a database is
- Learn what SQL and SQLite are
- Learn the basics of the SQL language
- Take a look at the Android SQLite API
- Code the Age Database app that we started in the previous chapter

Database 101

Let's answer a whole bunch of those database-related questions and then we can get started making apps that use SQLite.

So, what is a database?

What is a database

A **database** is both a place of storage and the means to retrieve, store, and manipulate data. It helps to be able to visualize a database before learning how to use it. The actual structure of the internals of a database varies greatly depending upon the database in question. SQLite actually stores all its data in a single file.

It will aid our comprehension greatly however if we visualize our data as if it were in a spreadsheet or sometimes, multiple spreadsheets. Our database, like a spreadsheet, will be divided into multiple columns that represent different types of data and rows which represent entries into the database.

Think about a database with names and exam scores. Take a look at this visual representation of this data how we could imagine it in a database.

_ID	name	score
1	Bart	23
2	Lisa	100
3	Jim	66

Notice, however, that there is an extra column of data – an **ID** column. We will talk more about this as we proceed. This single spreadsheet-like structure is called a **table**. As mentioned before, there might be, and often is, multiple tables in a database. Each column of the table will have a name that can be referred to when speaking to the database.

What is SQL

SQL stands for **Structured Query Language**. It is the syntax that is used to get things done with the database.

What is SQLite

SQLite is the name of the entire database system that is favored by Android and it has its own version of SQL. The reason the SQLite version of SQL needs to be slightly different to some other versions is because the database has different features.

The SQL syntax primer that follows will focus on the SQLite version.

SQL syntax primer

Before we can learn how to use SQLite with Android, we need to first learn the basics of how to use SQLite in general, in a platform neutral context.

Let's look at some example SQL code that could be used on an SQLite database directly, without any Java or Android classes, and then we can more easily understand what our Java code is doing later on.

SQLite example code

SQL has keywords, much like Java, that cause things to happen. Here is a flavor of some of the SQL keywords we will soon be using:

- INSERT: Allows us to add data to the database
- DELETE: Allows us to remove data from the database
- SELECT: Allows us to read data from the database
- WHERE: Allows us to specify the parts of the database that match a specific criteria we want to INSERT, DELETE, or SELECT from
- FROM: Used for specifying a table or column name in a database

There are many more SQLite keywords than this and, for a comprehensive list, take a look at this link: https://sqlite.org/lang_keywords.html.

In addition to keywords, SQL has **types**. Some examples of SQL types are as follows:

- **integer**: Just what we need for storing whole numbers
- **text**: Perfect for storing a simple name or address
- **real**: For large floating point numbers

There are many more SQLite types than this and, for a comprehensive list, take a look at this link: https://www.sqlite.org/datatype3.html.

Let's look at how we can combine those types with keywords to create tables, and add, remove, modify, and read data, using full SQLite statements.

Creating a table

It would be a perfectly decent question to ask why we don't first create a new database. The reason for this is that every app has access to a SQLite database by default. The database is private to that app. Here is the statement we would use to create a table within that database. I have highlighted a few parts to make the statement clearer:

```
create table StudentsAndGrades
    _ID integer primary key autoincrement not null,
    name text not null,
    score int;
```

The previous code creates a table called StudentsAndGrades with an **integer** row **id** that will be automatically increased (incremented) each time a row of data is added.

The table will also have a name column that will be of the text type and cannot be blank (not null).

It will also have a score column that will be of the int type. Also notice that the statement is completed by a semicolon.

Inserting data into the database

Here is how we might insert a new row of data into that database:

```
INSERT INTO StudentsAndGrades
    (name, score)
    VALUES
    ("Bart", 23);
```

The previous code added a row to the database. After the preceding statement, the database will have one entry with the values (1, "Bart", 23) for the columns (_ID, name, and score).

Here is how we might insert another new row of data into that database:

```
INSERT INTO StudentsAndGrades
    (name, score)
    VALUES
    ("Lisa", 100);
```

The previous code added a new row of data with the values (2, "Lisa", 100) for the columns (_ID, name, and score).

Our spreadsheet-like structure would now look like the following diagram:

_ID	name	score
1	Bart	23
2	Lisa	100

Retrieving data from the database

Here is how we would access all the rows and columns from our database;

```
SELECT * FROM StudentsAndGrades;
```

The previous code asks for every row and column. The * symbol can be read as **all**.

We can also be a little more selective, as the following code demonstrates:

```
SELECT score FROM StudentsAndGrades
    where name = "Lisa";
```

The previous code would only return 100, which, of course, is the score associated with the name Lisa.

Updating the database structure

We can even add new columns after the table has been created and the data added. This is simple as far as the SQL is concerned, but can cause some issues with regard to a user's data on already published apps. The next statement adds a new column called age that is of the int type:

```
ALTER TABLE StudentsAndGrades
    ADD
    age int;
```

There are many more data types, keywords, and ways to use them than we have seen so far. Next, let's look at the Android SQLite API and we will begin to see how we can use our new SQLite skills.

Android SQLite API

There are a number of different ways in which the Android API makes it fairly easy to use our app's database. The first class we need to get familiar with is SQLiteOpenHelper.

SQLiteOpenHelper and SQLiteDatabase

The `SQLiteDatabase` class is the class that represents the actual database. The `SQLiteOpenHelper` class, however, is where most of the action takes place. This class will enable us to get access to a database and initialize an instance of `SQLiteDatabase`.

In addition, the `SQLiteOpenHelper`, which we will extend in our Age Database app, has two methods to override. First, it has an `onCreate` method, which is called the first time a database is used, and it therefore makes sense that we would incorporate our SQL in which to create our table structure.

The other method we must override is `onUpgrade`, which, you can probably guess, is called when we upgrade our database (`ALTER` its structure).

Building and executing queries

As our database structures become more complex and as our SQL knowledge grows, our SQL statements will get quite long and awkward. The potential for errors is high.

The way we will help overcome the problem of complexity is to build our queries from parts into a String. We can then pass that String to the method (we will see this soon) that will execute the query for us.

Furthermore, we will use `final` strings to represent things such as table and column names, so we can't get in a muddle with them.

For example, we could declare the following members, which would represent the table name and column names from the fictitious example from earlier. Note that we will also give the database itself a name and have a string for that too:

```
private static final String DB_NAME = "MyCollegeDB";
private static final String TABLE_S_AND_G = " StudentsAndGrades";

public static final String TABLE_ROW_ID = "_id";
public static final String TABLE_ROW_NAME = "name";
public static final String TABLE_ROW_SCORE = "score";
```

Notice that in the preceding code, where we will benefit from accessing the String outside the class as well, we declare it `public`.

We could then build a query like this in the next example. The following example adds a new entry to our hypothetical database and incorporates Java variables into the SQL statement:

```
String name = "Onkar";
int score = 95;

// Add all the details to the table
String query = "INSERT INTO " + TABLE_S_AND_G + " (" +
        TABLE_ROW_NAME + ", " +
        TABLE_ROW_SCORE +
        ") " +
        "VALUES (" +
        "'" + name + "'" + ", " +
        score +
        ");";
```

Notice that in the previous code, the regular Java variables, `name` and `score`, are highlighted. The previous String called `query` is now the SQL statement, exactly equivalent to this:

```
INSERT INTO StudentsAndGrades (
    name, score)
    VALUES ('Onkar',95);
```

> It is not essential to completely grasp the previous two blocks of code in order to proceed with learning Android programming. But if you want to build your own apps and construct SQL statements that do exactly what you need, it *will* help to do so. Why not study the previous two blocks of code in order to discern the difference between the pairs of double quote marks " that are the parts of the String joined together with +, the pairs of single quote marks ' that are part of the SQL syntax, the regular Java variables, and the distinct semicolons from the SQL statement in the String and Java.

Throughout the typing of the query, Android Studio prompts us as to the names of our variables, making the chances of an error much less likely, even though it is more verbose than simply typing the query.

Now we can use the classes we introduced previously to execute the query:

```
// This is the actual database
private SQLiteDatabase db;

// Create an instance of our internal CustomSQLiteOpenHelper class
CustomSQLiteOpenHelper helper = new
```

```
        CustomSQLiteOpenHelper(context);

   // Get a writable database
   db = helper.getWritableDatabase();

   // Run the query
   db.execSQL(query);
```

When adding data to the database, we will use `execSQL`, as in the previous code, and when getting data from the database, we will use the `rawQuery` method, demonstrated as follows:

```
   Cursor c = db.rawQuery(query, null);
```

Notice that the `rawQuery` method returns an object of type `Cursor`.

There are several different ways in which we can interact with SQLite, and they each have their advantages and disadvantages. We have chosen to use raw SQL statements as it is entirely transparent as to what we are doing, at the same time as reinforcing our knowledge of the SQL language. Refer to the next tip if you want to know more.

Database cursors

In addition to the classes that give us access to the database, and the methods that allow us to execute our queries, there is the issue of exactly how the results we get back from our queries are formatted.

Fortunately, there is the `Cursor` class. All our database queries will return objects of the `Cursor` type. We can use the methods of the `Cursor` class to selectively access the data returned from the queries, as in the following code:

```
   Log.i(c.getString(1), c.getString(2));
```

The previous code would output to logcat the two values stored in the first two columns of the result that the query returned. It is the `Cursor` object itself that determines which row of our returned data we are currently reading.

We can access a number of methods of the `Cursor` object, including the `moveToNext` method, which, unsurprisingly, would move the `Cursor` to the next row ready for reading:

```
   c.moveToNext();

   /*
       This same code now outputs the data in the
```

```
    first and second column of the returned
    data but from the SECOND row.
*/
```

```
Log.i(c.getString(1), c.getString(2));
```

On certain occasions, we will be able to bind a `Cursor` to a part of our UI (like `RecyclerView`), as we did with an `ArrayList` in the Note to Self app, and just leave everything to the Android API.

There are many more useful methods in the `Cursor` class, some of which we will see soon.

> This introduction to the Android SQLite API really only scratches the surface of its capabilities. We will bump into a few more methods and classes as we proceed further. It is, however, worth studying further if your app idea requires complex data management.

Now we can see how all this theory comes together and how we will structure our database code in the Age Database app.

Coding the database class

Here, we will put into practice everything we have learned so far and finish coding the Age Database app. Before our `Fragment` classes from the previous section can interact with a shared database, we need a class to handle interaction with, and creation of, the database.

We will create a class that manages our database by implementing `SQLiteOpenHHelper`. It will also define some `final` `Strings` to represent the names of the table and its columns. Furthermore, it will supply a bunch of helper methods we can call to perform all the necessary queries. Where necessary, these helper methods will return a `Cursor` object that we can use to show the data we have retrieved. It would be trivial then to add new helper methods should our app need to evolve:

Create a new class called `DataManager` and add the following member variables:

```
public class DataManager {

    // This is the actual database
    private SQLiteDatabase db;

    /*
```

```
        Next we have a public static final string for
        each row/table that we need to refer to both
        inside and outside this class
*/

public static final String TABLE_ROW_ID = "_id";
public static final String TABLE_ROW_NAME = "name";
public static final String TABLE_ROW_AGE = "age";

/*
    Next we have a private static final strings for
    each row/table that we need to refer to just
    inside this class
*/

private static final String DB_NAME = "name_age_db";
private static final int DB_VERSION = 1;
private static final String TABLE_N_AND_A =
                            "name_and_age";

}
```

Next, we add the constructor that will create an instance of our custom version of
SQLiteOpenHelper. We will actually implement this class as an inner class soon. The
constructor also initializes the db member, which is our SQLiteDatabase reference.

Add the following constructor that we have just discussed to the DataManager class
as follows:

```
public DataManager(Context context) {
    // Create an instance of our internal CustomSQLiteOpenHelper

    CustomSQLiteOpenHelper helper = new
        CustomSQLiteOpenHelper(context);

    // Get a writable database
    db = helper.getWritableDatabase();
}
```

Now we can add the helper methods we will access from our Fragment classes; first,
the insert method, which executes an INSERT SQL query based on the name and
age parameters passed into the method.

Add the `insert` method to the `DataManager` class:

```
// Here are all our helper methods

// Insert a record
public void insert(String name, String age){

    // Add all the details to the table
    String query = "INSERT INTO " + TABLE_N_AND_A + " (" +
                TABLE_ROW_NAME + ", " +
                TABLE_ROW_AGE +
                ") " +
                "VALUES (" +
                "'" + name + "'" + ", " +
                "'" + age + "'" +
                ");";

    Log.i("insert() = ", query);

    db.execSQL(query);

}
```

This next method, called `delete`, will delete a record from the database if it has a matching value in the name column to that of the passed-in `name` parameter. It achieves this using the SQL `DELETE` keyword.

Add the `delete` method to the `DataManager` class:

```
// Delete a record
public void delete(String name){

    // Delete the details from the table if already exists
    String query = "DELETE FROM " + TABLE_N_AND_A +
                " WHERE " + TABLE_ROW_NAME +
                " = '" + name + "';";

    Log.i("delete() = ", query);

    db.execSQL(query);

}
```

Next, we have the `selectAll` method, which also does as the name suggests. It achieves this with a SELECT query using the * parameter, which is equivalent to specifying all the columns individually. Also note that the method returns a `Cursor`, which we will use in some of the Fragment classes.

Add the `selectAll` method to the `DataManager` class as follows:

```
// Get all the records
public Cursor selectAll() {
    Cursor c = db.rawQuery("SELECT *" +" from " +
                TABLE_N_AND_A, null);

    return c;
}
```

Now we add a `searchName` method, which has a String parameter for the name the user wants to search for. It also returns a `Cursor`, which will contain all the entries that were found. Notice that the SQL statement uses SELECT, FROM, and WHERE to achieve this:

```
// Find a specific record
public Cursor searchName(String name) {
    String query = "SELECT " +
                TABLE_ROW_ID + ", " +
                TABLE_ROW_NAME +
                ", " + TABLE_ROW_AGE +
                " from " +
                TABLE_N_AND_A + " WHERE " +
                TABLE_ROW_NAME + " = '" + name + "';";

    Log.i("searchName() = ", query);

    Cursor c = db.rawQuery(query, null);

    return c;
}
```

Finally, for the `DataManager` class, we create an inner class that will be our implementation of `SQLiteOpenHelper`. It is a barebones implementation.

We have a constructor that receives a `Context` object, the database name, and the database version.

We also override the `onCreate` method, which has the SQL statement that creates our database table with _ID, name, and age columns.

The onUpgrade method is left intentionally blank for this app.

Add the inner CustomSQLiteOpenHelper class to the DataManager class:

```
// This class is created when our DataManager is initialized
private class CustomSQLiteOpenHelper extends SQLiteOpenHelper {
    public CustomSQLiteOpenHelper(Context context) {
        super(context, DB_NAME, null, DB_VERSION);
    }

    // This runs the first time the database is created
    @Override
    public void onCreate(SQLiteDatabase db) {

        // Create a table for photos and all their details
        String newTableQueryString = "create table "
                        + TABLE_N_AND_A + " ("
                        + TABLE_ROW_ID
                        + " integer primary key
                                autoincrement not null,"
                        + TABLE_ROW_NAME
                        + " text not null,"
                        + TABLE_ROW_AGE
                        + " text not null);";


        db.execSQL(newTableQueryString);

    }

    // This method only runs when we increment DB_VERSION
    @Override
    public void onUpgrade(SQLiteDatabase db,
            int oldVersion, int newVersion) {
            // Not needed in this app
            // but we must still override it

        }

    }
```

Now we can add code to our Fragment classes to use our new DataManager.

Coding the Fragment classes to use the DataManager

Add this highlighted code to the `InsertFragment` class to update the `onCreateView` method as follows:

```
View v = inflater.inflate(R.layout.content_insert,
    container, false);

final DataManager dm =
    new DataManager(getActivity());

Button btnInsert = (Button)
    v.findViewById(R.id.btnInsert);

final EditText editName = (EditText)
    v.findViewById(R.id.editName);

final EditText editAge = (EditText)
    v.findViewById(R.id.editAge);

btnInsert.setOnClickListener(new View.OnClickListener() {
    @Override
    public void onClick(View v) {
            dm.insert(editName.getText().toString(),
                        editAge.getText().toString());

    }
});


    return v;
```

In the code, we get an instance of our `DataManager` class and a reference to each of our UI widgets. Then, in the `onClick` method of the button, we use the insert method to add a new name and age to the database. The values to insert are taken from the two `EditText` widgets.

Add this highlighted code to the `DeleteFragment` class to update the `onCreateView`:

```
View v = inflater.inflate(R.layout.content_delete,
    container, false);

final DataManager dm =
```

```
   new DataManager(getActivity());

Button btnDelete = (Button)
   v.findViewById(R.id.btnDelete);

final EditText editDelete = (EditText)
   v.findViewById(R.id.editDelete);

btnDelete.setOnClickListener(new View.OnClickListener() {
   @Override
   public void onClick(View v) {
         dm.delete(editDelete.getText().toString());
   }
});

   return v;
```

In the `DeleteFragment` class, we create an instance of our `DataManager` class and then get a reference to the `EditText` and the `Button` from our layout. When the button is clicked, the `delete` method is called, passing in the value of any text from the `EditText`. The delete method searches our database for a match and, if one is found, it deletes it.

Add this highlighted code to the `SearchFragment` class to update `onCreateView`:

```
View v = inflater.inflate(R.layout.content_search,
   container,false);

Button btnSearch = (Button)
   v.findViewById(R.id.btnSearch);

final EditText editSearch = (EditText)
   v.findViewById(R.id.editSearch);

final TextView textResult = (TextView)
   v.findViewById(R.id.textResult);

// This is our DataManager instance
final DataManager dm =
   new DataManager(getActivity());

btnSearch.setOnClickListener(new View.OnClickListener() {
   @Override
```

```
        public void onClick(View v) {

                Cursor c = dm.searchName(
                        editSearch.getText().toString());

                // Make sure a result was found before using the Cursor
                if(c.getCount() > 0) {
                        c.moveToNext();
                        textResult.setText("Result = " +
                                c.getString(1) + " - " + c.getString(2));
                }

        }
});

    return v;
```

As we do for all our different `Fragment` classes, we create an instance of `DataManager` and get a reference to all the different UI widgets in the layout. In the `onClick` method of the button, the `searchName` method is used, passing in the value from the `EditText`. If the database returns a result in the `Cursor`, then the `TextView` uses its `setText` method to output the results.

Add this highlighted code to the `ResultsFragment` class to update the `onCreateView`:

```
View v = inflater.inflate(R.layout.content_results,
    container, false);

// Create an instance of our DataManager
DataManager dm =
    new DataManager(getActivity());

// Get a reference to the TextView to show the results
TextView textResults = (TextView)
    v.findViewById(R.id.textResults);

// Create and initialize a Cursor with all the results
Cursor c = dm.selectAll();

// A String to hold all the text
String list = "";

// Loop through the results in the Cursor
while (c.moveToNext()){
```

```
        // Add the results to the String
        // with a little formatting
        list+=(c.getString(1) + " - " + c.getString(2) + "\n");
    }


    // Display the String in the TextView
    textResults.setText(list);



    return v;
```

In this class, the `Cursor` is loaded up with data using the `selectAll` method before any interactions take place. The contents of the `Cursor` are then output into the `TextView` by concatenating the results. The `\n` in the concatenation is what creates a new line between each result in the `Cursor`.

Running the Age Database app

Let's run through some of the functions of our app to make sure it is working as expected.

First, I added a new name to the database using the **Insert** menu option:

And then I confirmed it was there by viewing the **Results** option:

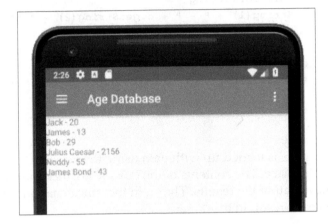

Then I used the **Delete** menu option and looked at the **Results** option again to check that my chosen name was, in fact, removed:

Next, I searched for a name that I knew existed to test the **Search** function:

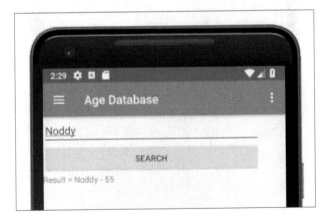

Let's review what we have done in this chapter.

Summary

We have covered a lot in this chapter. We have learned about databases and, in particular, the database of Android apps, SQLite. We have practiced the basics of communicating with a database using the SQL language.

We have seen how the Android API helps us use a SQLite database, and have implemented our first working app with a database.

In the next chapter, we will start to build an app from the most popular category on Google Play—a game.

28

Coding a Snake Game Using Everything We Have Learned So Far

In this bonus and final project, we will use a bit of everything we have leaned throughout the book: interfaces, creating classes, graphics, sound, threads, screen touches, and more.

The history of the Snake game goes back to the 1970s. However, it was the 1980s when the game took on the look that we will be using in this chapter. It was sold under numerous names and on many platforms, but probably gained widespread recognition when it was shipped as standard on Nokia mobile phones in the late 1990s.

Here is what we are going to do in this chapter:

- Look more closely at the finished game
- Set up the screen and code the outline of the project
- Code the `Activity` class
- Code the game engine
- Code the apple

Let's get started.

How to play

The game involves controlling a single block or snake head by turning only left or right by ninety degrees until you manage to eat an apple. When you get the apple, the Snake grows an extra block or body segment.

If, or rather when, the snake bumps into the edge of the screen, or accidentally eats himself, the game is over. The more apples the snake eats, the higher the score and the longer and more unwieldy the snake.

> You can learn more about the history of Snake here:
> `https://en.wikipedia.org/wiki/Snake_(video_game_genre)`.

The game starts with a message to get the game started:

When the player taps the screen, the game begins, and they must guide the tiny snake head to get the first apple:

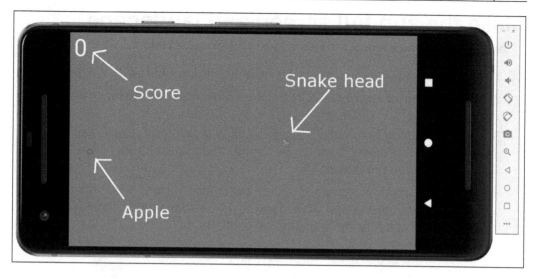

Note that the snake is always moving in the direction it is facing. It never stops.

If the player is skilled and a little bit lucky, then enormous snakes and scores can be achieved.

Getting started with the Snake game

To get started, make a new project called Snake. This time, we will use the Empty Activity template as we will not be creating any UI whatsoever.

- Rename the **Activity Name** to SnakeActivity.

- Uncheck the **Generate Layout File** option — we do not want a layout generated as we will be laying out every pixel ourselves.

- Uncheck **Backwards Compatibility (AppCompat)** — we won't need it for our game and it will still run on almost every phone and tablet. We will be working with the plain vanilla Activity class in this final project.

All the code and assets for this project are in the Chapter 28 folder of the download bundle. Note that for this project, the completed game, as it will be by completing the steps up to the end of *Chapter 29, Enumerations and Finishing the Snake Game*, is in the Chapter 28 folder. There is no separate code bundle for *Chapter 29, Enumerations and Finishing the Snake Game*.

Now, we will take an additional step to stop the screen from rotating and locking it in the landscape position.

Make the app full screen and landscape

Here is how to edit the `AndroidManifest.xml` file to achieve this:

1. Open the `AndroidManifest.xml` file in the editor window.

2. In the `AndroidManifest.xml` file, locate the following line of code:
   `android:name=".SnakeActivity">`

3. Place the cursor before the closing > symbol shown previously. Tap the *Enter* key a couple of times to move the > symbol a couple of lines below the rest of the line shown previously.

4. Immediately below `SnakeActivity`, but before the newly positioned > symbol, type or copy and paste these two lines to make the game run full screen and lock it in the landscape orientation:
   ```
   android:theme="@android:style/Theme.NoTitleBar.Fullscreen"
   android:screenOrientation="landscape"
   ```

[For more context/details, refer to the `AndroidManifest.xml` file in the download bundle.]

Adding some empty classes

We will also make some empty classes ready for us to add code as we proceed through the project. This will mean there are fewer errors as we proceed.

As we have done in previous projects, you can create a new class by selecting **File | New | Java Class**. Create three empty classes called `Snake`, `Apple`, and `SnakeGame`.

Coding SnakeActivity

Now we are getting comfortable with OOP, we will save a couple of lines of code and pass `point` straight into the `SnakeGame` constructor instead of dissecting it into separate horizontal and vertical `int` variables, as we did in the Live Drawing project. Add all of the following code.

Here is the entire `SnakeActivity` code:

```
import android.app.Activity;
import android.graphics.Point;
import android.os.Bundle;
```

```java
import android.view.Display;

public class SnakeActivity extends Activity {

    // Declare an instance of SnakeGame
    SnakeGame mSnakeGame;

    // Set the game up
    @Override
    protected void onCreate(Bundle savedInstanceState) {

        super.onCreate(savedInstanceState);

        // Get the pixel dimensions of the screen
        Display display = getWindowManager()
                .getDefaultDisplay();

        // Initialize the result into a Point object
        Point size = new Point();
        display.getSize(size);

        // Create a new instance of the SnakeEngine class
        mSnakeGame = new SnakeGame(this, size);

        // Make snakeEngine the view of the Activity
        setContentView(mSnakeGame);
    }

    // Start the thread in snakeEngine
    @Override
    protected void onResume() {
        super.onResume();
        mSnakeGame.resume();
    }

    // Stop the thread in snakeEngine
    @Override
    protected void onPause() {
        super.onPause();
        mSnakeGame.pause();
    }
}
```

The previous code should look very familiar.

As mentioned previously, we don't bother reading the x and y values from `size`; we just pass it straight into the `SnakeGame` constructor.

The rest of the code for the `SnakeActivity` is identical in function to the Live Drawing project. Obviously, we are using a new variable name, `mSnakeGame`.

Adding the sound effects

Grab the sound files for this project; they are in the `Chapter 28` folder of the download bundle. Copy the `assets` folder, and then navigate to `Snake/app/src/main` using your operating system's file browser and paste the `assets` folder along with all its contents.

The sound files are now available for the project.

Coding the game engine

Let's get started with the most significant class of this project—`SnakeGame`. This will be the game engine for the Snake game.

Coding the members

In the `SnakeGame` class that you created previously, add the following `import` statements along with all the member variables shown next. Study the names and types of the variables as you add them because they will give a good insight into what we will be coding in this class:

```
import android.content.Context;
import android.content.res.AssetFileDescriptor;
import android.content.res.AssetManager;
import android.graphics.Canvas;
import android.graphics.Color;
import android.graphics.Paint;
import android.graphics.Point;
import android.media.AudioAttributes;
import android.media.AudioManager;
import android.media.SoundPool;
import android.os.Build;
import android.view.MotionEvent;
import android.view.SurfaceHolder;
```

```java
import android.view.SurfaceView;
import java.io.IOException;

class SnakeGame extends SurfaceView implements Runnable{

    // Objects for the game loop/thread
    private Thread mThread = null;
    // Control pausing between updates
    private long mNextFrameTime;
    // Is the game currently playing and or paused?
    private volatile boolean mPlaying = false;
    private volatile boolean mPaused = true;

    // for playing sound effects
    private SoundPoolmSP;
    private intmEat_ID = -1;
    private intmCrashID = -1;

    // The size in segments of the playable area
    private final int NUM_BLOCKS_WIDE = 40;
    private intmNumBlocksHigh;

    // How many points does the player have
    private intmScore;

    // Objects for drawing
    private Canvas mCanvas;
    private SurfaceHoldermSurfaceHolder;
    private Paint mPaint;

    // A snake ssss
    private Snake mSnake;
    // And an apple
    private Apple mApple;
}
```

Let's run through those variables. Many of them will be familiar. We have
mThread, which is our `Thread` object, but we also have a new `long` variable called
mNextFrameTime. We will use this variable to keep track of when we want to call the
update method. This is a little different to the Live Drawing project because there,
we just looped around update and draw as quickly as we could and, depending on
how long the frame took, updated the particles accordingly.

What we will do in this app is only call update at specific intervals to make the snake move one block at a time rather than smoothly glide. How this works will become clear soon.

We have two boolean variables, mPlaying and mPaused, which will be used to control the thread and when we call the update method, so we can start and stop the gameplay.

Next, we have a SoundPool and a couple of int variables for the related sound effects.

Following on, we have a final int (which can't be changed during execution) called NUM_BLOCKS_WIDE. This variable has been assigned the value 40. We will use this variable in conjunction with others (most notably the screen resolution) to map out the grid onto which we will draw the game objects. Notice that after NUM_BLOCKS_WIDE, there is mNumBlocksHigh, which will be assigned a value dynamically in the constructor.

The member mScore is an int that will keep track of the player's current score.

The next three variables—mCanvas, mSurfaceHolder and mPaint—are used in exactly the same way as they were in the Live Drawing project and are the classes of the Android API that enable us to do our drawing.

Finally, we declare an instance of a Snake called mSnake and an Apple called mApple. Clearly, we haven't coded these classes yet, but we did create empty classes to avoid this code showing an error at this stage.

Coding the constructor

We will use the constructor method to set up the game engine. Much of the code that follows will be familiar to you from the Live Drawing project, like the fact that the signature allows for a Context object and the screen resolution to be passed in.

Also familiar will be the way that we set up the SoundPool and load all the sound effects. Furthermore, we will initialize our Paint and SurfaceHolder methods, just as we have done before. There is some new code, however, at the start of the constructor method. Be sure to read the comments and examine the code as you add it.

Add the constructor to the `SnakeGame` class and we will then examine the two lines of new code:

```
// This is the constructor method that gets called
// from SnakeActivity
public SnakeGame(Context context, Point size) {
    super(context);

    // Work out how many pixels each block is
    intblockSize = size.x / NUM_BLOCKS_WIDE;
    // How many blocks of the same size will fit into the height
    mNumBlocksHigh = size.y / blockSize;

    // Initialize the SoundPool
    if (Build.VERSION.SDK_INT>= Build.VERSION_CODES.LOLLIPOP) {
        AudioAttributesaudioAttributes =
                new AudioAttributes.Builder()
                .setUsage(AudioAttributes.USAGE_MEDIA)
                .setContentType(AudioAttributes
                .CONTENT_TYPE_SONIFICATION)
                .build();

        mSP = new SoundPool.Builder()
                .setMaxStreams(5)
                .setAudioAttributes(audioAttributes)
                .build();
    } else {
        mSP = new SoundPool(5, AudioManager.STREAM_MUSIC, 0);
    }
    try {
        AssetManager assetManager = context.getAssets();
        AssetFileDescriptor descriptor;

        // Prepare the sounds in memory
        descriptor = assetManager.openFd("get_apple.ogg");
        mEat_ID = mSP.load(descriptor, 0);

        descriptor = assetManager.openFd("snake_death.ogg");
        mCrashID = mSP.load(descriptor, 0);

    } catch (IOException e) {
```

```
        // Error
    }
    // Initialize the drawing objects
    mSurfaceHolder = getHolder();
    mPaint = new Paint();

    // Call the constructors of our two game objects


}
```

Here are those two new lines again for your convenience:

```
// Work out how many pixels each block is
intblockSize = size.x / NUM_BLOCKS_WIDE;
// How many blocks of the same size will fit into the height
mNumBlocksHigh = size.y / blockSize;
```

A new, local (on the Stack) int called `blockSize` is declared and then initialized by dividing the width of the screen in pixels by NUM_BLOCKS_WIDE. The `blockSize` variable now represents the number of pixels that one position (block) of the grid uses to draw the game. For example, a snake segment and an apple will be scaled using this value.

Now we have the size of a block, we can initialize `mNumBlocksHigh` by dividing the number of pixels vertically by the variable we just initialized. It would have been possible to initialize `mNumBlocksHigh` without using `blockSize` in just a single line of code but doing it as we did makes our intentions, and the concept of a grid made of blocks, much clearer.

Coding the newGame method

This method only has two lines of code in it for now, but we will add more as the project proceeds. Add the `newGame` method to the `SnakeGame` class:

```
// Called to start a new game
public void newGame() {

    // reset the snake

    // Get the apple ready for dinner

    // Reset the mScore
```

```
    mScore = 0;

    // Setup mNextFrameTime so an update can triggered
    mNextFrameTime = System.currentTimeMillis();
}
```

As the name suggests, this method will be called each time the player starts
a new game. For now, all that happens is that the score is set to zero and the
mNextFrameTime variable is set to the current time. Next, we will see how we can
use mNextFrameTime to create the blocky/juddering updates that this game needs in
order to look authentic. In fact, by setting mNextFrameTime to the current time, we
are setting things up for an update to be triggered at once.

Coding the run method

This method has some differences to the way we handled the run method in the Live
Drawing project. Add the method, examine the code, and then we will discuss it:

```
// Handles the game loop
@Override
public void run() {
    while (mPlaying) {
        if (!mPaused) {
            // Update 10 times a second
            if (updateRequired()) {
                update();
            }
        }

        draw();
    }
}
```

Inside the run method, which is called by Android repeatedly while the thread is
running, we first check whether mPlaying is true. If it is, we next check to make
sure the game is not paused. Finally, nested inside both these checks, we call
if (updateRequired()). If this method (that we code next) returns true, only then
does the update method get called.

Note the position of the call to the draw method. This position means it will be
constantly called all the time that mPlaying is true.

Also, in the newGame method, you can see a number of comments that hint at some
more code we will be adding later in the project.

Coding the updateRequired method

The `updateRequired` method is what makes the actual `update` method execute only ten times per second and creates the block by block movement of the snake. Add the `updateRequired` method:

```
// Check to see if it is time for an update
public boolean updateRequired() {

    // Run at 10 frames per second
    final long TARGET_FPS = 10;
    // There are 1000 milliseconds in a second
    final long MILLIS_PER_SECOND = 1000;

    // Are we due to update the frame
    if(mNextFrameTime<= System.currentTimeMillis()){
            // Tenth of a second has passed

            // Setup when the next update will be triggered
            mNextFrameTime =System.currentTimeMillis()
                        + MILLIS_PER_SECOND / TARGET_FPS;

            // Return true so that the update and draw
            // methods are executed
            return true;
    }

    return false;
}
```

The `updateRequired` method declares a new `final` variable called `TARGET_FPS` and initializes it to 10. This is the frame rate we are aiming for. The next line of code is a variable created for the sake of clarity. `MILLIS_PER_SECOND` is initialized to `1000` because there are one thousand milliseconds in a second.

The `if` statement that follows is where the method gets its work done. It checks whether `mNextFrameTime` is less than or equal to the current time. If it is, the code inside the `if` statement executes. Inside the `if` statement, `mNextFrameTime` is updated by adding `MILLIS_PER_SECOND`, divided by `TARGET_FPS`, onto the current time.

Next, `mNextFrameTime` is set to one-tenth of a second ahead of the current time ready to trigger the next update. Finally, inside the `if` statement, `return true` will trigger the code in the `run` method to call the `update` method.

Note that had the `if` statement not executed, then `mNextFrameTime` would have been left at its original value, and `return false` would have meant the `run` method would not call the `update` method—yet.

Coding the update method

Code the empty `update` method and look at the comments to see what we will soon be coding inside this method:

```
// Update all the game objects
public void update() {

    // Move the snake

    // Did the head of the snake eat the apple?

    // Did the snake die?

}
```

The `update` method is empty, but the comments give a hint as to what we will be doing later in the project. Make a mental note that it is only called when the thread is running, the game is playing, it is not paused, and when `updateRequired` returns true.

Coding the draw method

Code and examine the `draw` method. Remember that the `draw` method is called whenever the thread is running, and the game is playing even when `update` does not get called:

```
// Do all the drawing
public void draw() {
    // Get a lock on the mCanvas
    if (mSurfaceHolder.getSurface().isValid()) {
        mCanvas = mSurfaceHolder.lockCanvas();

        // Fill the screen with a color
        mCanvas.drawColor(Color.argb(255, 26, 128, 182));

        // Set the size and color of the mPaint for the text
        mPaint.setColor(Color.argb(255, 255, 255, 255));
```

```
mPaint.setTextSize(120);

// Draw the score
mCanvas.drawText("" + mScore, 20, 120, mPaint);

// Draw the apple and the snake

// Draw some text while paused
if(mPaused){

        // Set the size and color of mPaint for the text
        mPaint.setColor(Color.argb(255, 255, 255, 255));
        mPaint.setTextSize(250);

        // Draw the message
        // We will give this an international upgrade soon
        mCanvas.drawText(
                "Tap to Play!", 200, 700, mPaint);
}


        // Unlock the Canvas to show graphics for this frame
        mSurfaceHolder.unlockCanvasAndPost(mCanvas);
    }
}
```

The draw method is mostly just as we have come to expect from the Live Drawing project:

- Check whether the Surface is valid
- Lock the Canvas
- Fill the screen with a color
- Do the drawing
- Unlock the Canvas and reveal our glorious drawings

In the "Do the drawing" phase mentioned in the list, we scale the text size with setTextSize and then draw the score in the top-left corner of the screen. Next, in this phase, we check whether the game is paused and, if it is, draw a message to the center of the screen, **Tap to Play!**. We can almost run the game. Just a few more short methods.

Coding onTouchEvent

Next on our to-do list is `onTouchEvent`, which is called by Android every time the player interacts with the screen. We will add more code here as we progress. For now, add the following code which, if mPaused is true, sets mPaused to false and calls the `newGame` method:

```
@Override
public boolean onTouchEvent(MotionEventmotionEvent) {
    switch (motionEvent.getAction() &MotionEvent.ACTION_MASK) {
        case MotionEvent.ACTION_UP:
            if (mPaused) {
                mPaused = false;
                newGame();

                // Don't want to process snake
                // direction for this tap
                            return true;
            }

            // Let the Snake class handle the input

            break;

        default:
            break;

    }
    return true;
}
```

The preceding code has the effect of toggling the game between paused and not paused with each screen interaction.

Coding pause and resume

Add the `pause` and `resume` methods. Remember that nothing happens if the thread has not been started. When our game is run by the player, the Activity (`SnakeActivity`) will call this `resume` method and start the thread. When the player quits the game, the Activity will call `pause`, which stops the thread:

```
// Stop the thread
public void pause() {
    mPlaying = false;
```

```
        try {
                mThread.join();
        } catch (InterruptedException e) {
                // Error
        }
}


// Start the thread
public void resume() {
    mPlaying = true;
    mThread = new Thread(this);
    mThread.start();
}
```

We can now test our code so far.

Running the game

Run the game and you will see a blank blue screen with the current score and the message **Tap To Play!**:

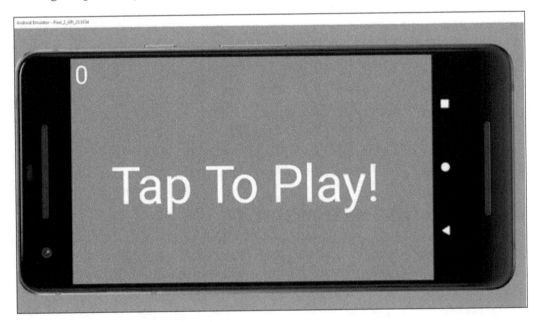

Tap the screen, the text disappears, and the `update` method gets called ten times per second.

We have made a good start with the Snake game, though most of the code we wrote was like the Live Drawing project. The exception was the way in which we selectively call the `update` method only when one-tenth of a second has elapsed since the previous call to `update`.

Adding the graphics

Grab the project's graphics from the download bundle; they are in the `Chapter 28/ drawable` folder. Highlight the contents of this folder and copy them. Now right-click the `drawable` folder in the Android Studio explorer and select **Paste**. These files are the snake head and body segments, as well as the apple. We will look closely at each of the graphics as we use them.

Coding the apple

Let's start with the `Apple` class by adding the required `import` statements and the member variables. Add the code and study it, and then we will discuss it:

```
import android.content.Context;
import android.graphics.Bitmap;
import android.graphics.BitmapFactory;
import android.graphics.Canvas;
import android.graphics.Paint;
import android.graphics.Point;
import java.util.Random;

class Apple {

    // The location of the apple on the grid
    // Not in pixels
    private Point mLocation = new Point();

    // The range of values we can choose from
    // to spawn an apple
    private Point mSpawnRange;
    private int mSize;

    // An image to represent the apple
    private Bitmap mBitmapApple;
}
```

The `Apple` class has a `Point` object that we will use to store the horizontal and vertical location of the apple. Note that this will be a position on our virtual grid, and not a specific pixel position.

There is a second `Point` variable called `mSpawnRange` as well that will eventually hold the maximum values for the possible horizontal and vertical positions at which we can randomly spawn the apple each time a new one is required.

There is also a simple `int` called `mSize`, which we will initialize in a moment, and it will hold the size in pixels of an apple. It will correspond to a single block on the grid.

Finally, we have a `Bitmap` called `mBitmapApple`, which will hold the graphic for the apple.

The Apple constructor

Add the constructor for the `Apple` class and then we will go through it:

```
/// Set up the apple in the constructor
Apple(Context context, Point sr, int s){

    // Make a note of the passed in spawn range
    mSpawnRange = sr;
    // Make a note of the size of an apple
    mSize = s;
    // Hide the apple off-screen until the game starts
    mLocation.x = -10;

    // Load the image to the bitmap
    mBitmapApple = BitmapFactory
            .decodeResource(context.getResources(),
            R.drawable.apple);

    // Resize the bitmap
    mBitmapApple = Bitmap
            .createScaledBitmap(mBitmapApple, s, s, false);
}
```

In the constructor code, we set the apple up ready to be spawned. First of all, note that we won't create a brand new apple (call `new Apple()`) every time we want to spawn an apple. We will simply spawn one at the start of the game and then move it around every time the snake eats it. He'll never know if you don't tell him.

The first line of code uses the passed-in `Point` reference to initialize `mSpawnRange`.

An interesting thing going on here that is related to references is that the code doesn't copy the values passed in; it copies the reference to the values. So, after the first line of code, mSpawnRange will refer to the exact same place in memory as the reference that was passed in. If either reference is used to alter the values, then they will both refer to these new values. Note that we didn't have to do it this way; we could have passed in two int values and then assigned them individually to mSpawnRange.x and mSpawnRange.y. There is a benefit to doing it this slightly more laborious way because the original reference and its values would have been encapsulated. I just thought it would be interesting to do it this way and show and point out this subtle but sometimes significant anomaly.

Next, mSize is initialized to the passed-in value of s.

Just as an interesting point of comparison to the previous tip, this is very different to the relationship between mSpawnRange and sr. The s parameter holds an actual int value, not a reference or any connection whatsoever to the data of the class that called the method.

Next, the horizontal location of the apple mLocation.x is set to -10 to hide it away from view until it is required by the game.

Finally, for the Apple constructor, two lines of code prepare the Bitmap ready for use. First, the Bitmap is loaded from the apple.png file and then it is neatly resized using createScaledBitmap to both the width and height of s.

Now code the spawn and getLocation methods and then we will talk about them:

```
// This is called every time an apple is eaten
void spawn(){
    // Choose two random values and place the apple
    Random random = new Random();
    mLocation.x = random.nextInt(mSpawnRange.x) + 1;
    mLocation.y = random.nextInt(mSpawnRange.y - 1) + 1;
}


// Let SnakeGame know where the apple is
// SnakeGame can share this with the snake
Point getLocation(){
    return mLocation;
}
```

The spawn method will be called each time the apple is placed somewhere new, both at the start of the game and each time it is eaten by the snake. All the method does is generate two random int values based on the values stored in mSpawnRange and assigns them to mLocation.x and mLocation.y. The apple is now in a new position ready to be navigated to by the player.

The getLocation is a simple getter method that returns a reference to mLocation. SnakeEngine will use this for collision detection.

Add the draw method to the Apple class as follows:

```
// Draw the apple
void draw(Canvas canvas, Paint paint){
   canvas.drawBitmap(mBitmapApple,
               location.x * mSize, location.y * mSize, paint);

}
```

When this method is called from SnakeEngine, the Canvas and Paint references will be passed in for the apple to draw itself. The advantages of doing it this way are not immediately obvious from the simple single line of code in the draw method. You might think it would have been slightly less work to just draw the apple in the SnakeGame class's draw method? However, when you see the extra complexity involved in the draw method in the Snake class, then you will better appreciate how encapsulating the responsibility to the classes to draw themselves makes SnakeEngine a much more manageable class.

Using the apple

The Apple class is done, and we can now put it to work.

Add the code to initialize the Apple object (mApple) in the constructor at the end as shown:

```
// Call the constructors of our two game objects
mApple = new Apple(context,
         new Point(NUM_BLOCKS_WIDE,
                     mNumBlocksHigh),
                  blockSize);
```

Notice that we pass in all the data required by the Apple constructor so it can set itself up.

We can now spawn an apple as shown next in the `newGame` method by calling the `spawn` method that we added when we coded the `Apple` class previously. Add the highlighted code to the `newGame` method:

```
// Called to start a new game
public void newGame() {

    // reset the snake


    // Get the apple ready for dinner
    mApple.spawn();

    // Reset the mScore
    mScore = 0;

    // Setup mNextFrameTime so an update can triggered
    mNextFrameTime = System.currentTimeMillis();
}
```

Next, we can draw the apple by calling its `draw` method from the `draw` method of `SnakeGame`, highlighted as follows:

```
// Draw the score
mCanvas.drawText("" + mScore, 20, 120, mPaint);

// Draw the apple and the snake
mApple.draw(mCanvas, mPaint);

// Draw some text while paused
```

As you can see, we pass in references to the `Canvas` and `Paint` objects. Here, we see how references are very useful because the `draw` method of the `Apple` class will be using the exact same `Canvas` and `Paint` as the `draw` method in the `SnakeGame` class because when you pass a reference, you give the receiving class direct access to the very same instances in memory.

Anything the `Apple` class does with `mCanvas` and `mPaint` is happening to the same `mCanvas` and `mPaint` in `SnakeGame`. So, when the `unlockCanvasAndPost` method is called (at the end of the `draw` method in `SnakeGame`), the apple drawn by the `Apple` class will be there. The `SnakeGame` class doesn't need to know how.

Running the game

Run the game and an apple will spawn. Unfortunately, without a snake to eat it, we have no way of doing anything else:

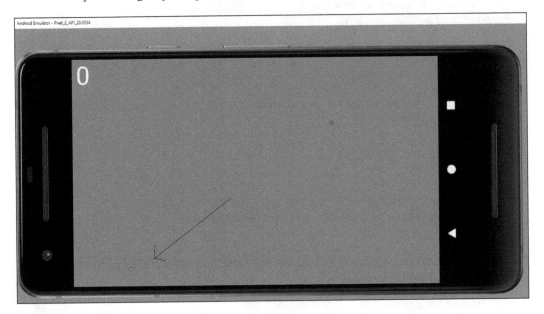

Summary

We have reused what we learned about threads, bitmaps, and live game loops, except this time, we have set up a system that will control the frame rate to just ten updates a second. When we code our snake in the next chapter, we will see how this creates an authentic retro movement.

Next, we will learn a new Java concept so that we can handle coding a snake in the next chapter.

29
Enumerations and Finishing the Snake Game

Welcome to the final chapter of the book and the last Java topic. We will first learn about Java enumerations and then we will put them straight to work in helping us to finish the Snake game.

In this chapter, we'll cover following topics:

- Learn about Java enumerations
- Add sound to the project
- Code the Snake class
- Finish the Snake game

 All the code and assets for this project are in the Chapter 28 folder of the download bundle. Note that for this project, the completed game, as it will be by completing the steps up to the end of this chapter, is in the Chapter 28 folder. There is no separate code bundle for this chapter.

First, enumerations.

Enumerations

An **enumeration** is a list of all the possible values in a logical collection. Java enum is a great way of, well, enumerating things. For example, if our app uses variables that can only be in a specific range of values, and if those values could logically form a collection or a set, then enumerations are probably appropriate to use. They will make your code clearer and less error-prone.

To declare an enum in Java, we use the enum keyword, followed by the name of the enumeration, followed by the values the enumeration can have, enclosed in a pair of curly braces { ... }.

As an example, examine this enumeration declaration. Note that it is a convention to declare the values from the enumeration all in uppercase:

```
private enum zombieTypes {
    REGULAR, RUNNER, CRAWLER, SPITTER, BLOATER, SNEAKER
};
```

Note at this point that we have not declared any instances of zombieTypes, just the type itself. If that sounds odd, think about it like this. We created the Apple class, but to use it, we had to declare an object/instance of the class.

At this point, we have created a new type called zombieTypes, but we have no instances of it. So, let's do that now:

```
zombieTypes therresa = zombieTypes.CRAWLER;
zombieTypes angela = zombieTypes.SPITTER
zombieTypes michelle = zombieTypes.SNEAKER

/*
    Zombies are fictional creatures and any resemblance
    to real people is entirely coincidental
*/
```

We can then use ZombieTypes in if statements as follows:

```
if(therresa == zombieTypes.CRAWLER){
    // Move slowly
}
```

Next is a sneak preview of the type of code we will soon be adding to the Snake class. We will want to keep track of which way the snake is heading, and so will declare this enumeration:

```
// For tracking movement Heading
private enum Heading {
    UP, RIGHT, DOWN, LEFT
}
```

Don't add any code to the Snake class just yet.

We can then declare an instance and initialize it as follows:

```
Heading heading = Heading.RIGHT;
```

We can change it when necessary with code like this:

```
heading = Heading.UP
```

We can even use the type as the condition of a switch statement (and we will) as follows:

```
switch (heading) {
        case UP:
                // Going up
                break;

        case RIGHT:
                // Going right
                break;

        case DOWN:
                // Going down
                break;

        case LEFT:
                // Going left
                break;
}
```

The Snake game is taking shape. We now have an apple that spawns ready to be eaten, although we have nothing to eat it yet. We have also seen the Java enum keyword and how it is useful for defining a range of values along with a new type. We have also strongly hinted that we will use an enum to keep track of which direction the snake is currently moving in.

Now we can code the Snake class and finish the Snake game and make it fully playable. We will put what we learned about enum to good use. Before we do, let's add the sound effects to the project.

Add the sound to the project

Before we get to the code, let's add the sound files to the project. You can find all the files in the assets folder inside the Chapter 28 folder. Copy the entire assets folder and then, using your operating system's file browser, go to the Snake/app/src/main folder of the project and paste the folder, along with all the files. The sound effects are now ready for use.

Coding the Snake class

Add the single import statement and the member variables to the Snake class. Be sure to study the code; it will give some insight and understanding to the rest of the Snake class:

```
import java.util.ArrayList;

class Snake {

    // The location in the grid of all the segments
    private ArrayList<Point> segmentLocations;

    // How big is each segment of the snake?
    private int mSegmentSize;

    // How big is the entire grid
    private Point mMoveRange;

    // Where is the center of the screen
    // horizontally in pixels?
    private int halfWayPoint;

    // For tracking movement Heading
    private enum Heading {
        UP, RIGHT, DOWN, LEFT
    }

    // Start by heading to the right
```

```
    private Heading heading = Heading.RIGHT;

    // A bitmap for each direction the head can face
    private Bitmap mBitmapHeadRight;
    private Bitmap mBitmapHeadLeft;
    private Bitmap mBitmapHeadUp;
    private Bitmap mBitmapHeadDown;

    // A bitmap for the body
    private Bitmap mBitmapBody;
}
```

The first line of code declares an `ArrayList`. It is called `segmentLocations` and holds `Point` instances. The `Point` object is perfect for holding grid locations, so you can probably guess that this `ArrayList` will hold the horizontal and vertical positions of all the segments that get added to the snake when the player eats an apple.

The `mSegmentSize` variable is of the `int` type and will keep a copy of the size of an individual segment of the snake. They are all the same size, so just the one variable is required.

The single `Point mMoveRange` will hold the furthest points horizontally and vertically that the snake head can be at. Anything more than this will mean instant death. We don't need a similar variable for the lowest positions because that is simple — zero, zero.

The `halfwayPoint` variable is explained in the comments. It is the physical pixel position, horizontally, of the center of the screen. We will see that despite using grid locations for most of these game calculations, this will be a useful variable.

Next up in the previous code, we have our first enumeration. The values are UP, RIGHT, DOWN, and LEFT. These will be perfect for clearly identifying and manipulating the way in which the snake is currently heading.

Right after the declaration of the `Heading` type, we declare an instance called `heading` and initialize it to `Heading.RIGHT`. When we code the rest of this class, you will see how this will set our snake off heading to the right.

The final declarations are five `Bitmap` objects, one for each direction that the snake head can face, and one for the body that was designed as a directionless circle shape for simplicity.

Coding the constructor

Now add the constructor method for the Snake class. There is lots going on here, so read all the comments and try to work it all out for yourself. Most of it will be straightforward after our discussion about the Matrix class in *Chapter 20, Drawing Graphics*. We will go into some details afterward:

```
Snake(Context context, Point mr, int ss) {

        // Initialize our ArrayList
        segmentLocations = new ArrayList<>();

        // Initialize the segment size and movement
        // range from the passed in parameters
        mSegmentSize = ss;
        mMoveRange = mr;

        // Create and scale the bitmaps
        mBitmapHeadRight = BitmapFactory
                .decodeResource(context.getResources(),
                        R.drawable.head);

        // Create 3 more versions of the
        // head for different headings
        mBitmapHeadLeft = BitmapFactory
                .decodeResource(context.getResources(),
                        R.drawable.head);

        mBitmapHeadUp = BitmapFactory
                .decodeResource(context.getResources(),
                        R.drawable.head);

        mBitmapHeadDown = BitmapFactory
                .decodeResource(context.getResources(),
                        R.drawable.head);

        // Modify the bitmaps to face the snake head
        // in the correct direction
        mBitmapHeadRight = Bitmap
                .createScaledBitmap(mBitmapHeadRight,
                        ss, ss, false);

        // A matrix for scaling
```

```
Matrix matrix = new Matrix();
matrix.preScale(-1, 1);

mBitmapHeadLeft = Bitmap
        .createBitmap(mBitmapHeadRight,
                0, 0, ss, ss, matrix, true);

// A matrix for rotating
matrix.preRotate(-90);
mBitmapHeadUp = Bitmap
        .createBitmap(mBitmapHeadRight,
                0, 0, ss, ss, matrix, true);

// Matrix operations are cumulative
// so rotate by 180 to face down
matrix.preRotate(180);
mBitmapHeadDown = Bitmap
        .createBitmap(mBitmapHeadRight,
                0, 0, ss, ss, matrix, true);

// Create and scale the body
mBitmapBody = BitmapFactory
        .decodeResource(context.getResources(),
                R.drawable.body);

mBitmapBody = Bitmap
        .createScaledBitmap(mBitmapBody,
                ss, ss, false);

// The halfway point across the screen in pixels
// Used to detect which side of screen was pressed
halfWayPoint = mr.x * ss / 2;
}
```

First of all, the `segmentLocations` variable is initialized with `new ArrayList<>()`. Then, `mSegmentSize` and `mMoveRange` are initialized by the values passed in as parameters (`mr` and `ss`). We will see how we calculate the values of those parameters when we create our `Snake` instance in `SnakeEngine` later.

Next, we create and scale the four bitmaps for the head of the snake. Initially, however, we create them all the same. Now we can use some of the matrix math magic we learned about in the *Rotating bitmaps* section in *Chapter 20, Drawing Graphics*.

To do so, we first create a new instance of `Matrix` called `matrix`. We initialize `matrix` by using the `prescale` method and pass in the values `-1` and `1`. This has the effect of leaving all the vertical values the same while making all the horizontal values their inverse. This creates a horizontally flipped image (head facing left). We can then use the matrix with the `createBitmap` method to change the `mBitmapHeadLeft` bitmap to look like it is heading left.

Now we use the `Matrix` class's `prerotate` method twice, once with a value of `-90`, and once with a value of `180`, and again pass `matrix` as a parameter into `createScaledBitmap` to get the `mBitmapHeadUp` and `mBitmapHeadDown` ready to go.

It would be perfectly possible to have just a single `Bitmap` for the head and rotate it based on the way the snake is heading as and when the snake changes direction during the game. With just 10 frames per second, the game would run fine. However, it is good practice to do relatively intensive calculations like these outside of the main game loop, so we did so just for good form.

Next, the `Bitmap` for the body is created and then scaled. No rotating or flipping is required.

The last line of code for the constructor calculates the midpoint horizontal pixel by multiplying `mr.x` by `ss` and dividing the answer by `2`.

Coding the reset method

We will call this method to shrink the snake back to nothing at the start of each game. Add the following code for the `reset` method:

```
// Get the snake ready for a new game
void reset(int w, int h) {

    // Reset the heading
    heading = Heading.RIGHT;

    // Delete the old contents of the ArrayList
    segmentLocations.clear();

    // Start with a single snake segment
    segmentLocations.add(new Point(w / 2, h / 2));
}
```

The `reset` method starts by setting the snakes `heading` variable back to the right (`Heading.RIGHT`).

Next, it clears all body segments from the `ArrayList` using the `clear` method.

Finally, it adds back into the `ArrayList` a new `Point` that will represent the snake's head when the next game starts.

Coding the move method

The `move` method has two main sections. First, the body is moved, and lastly the head. Code the `move` method and then we will examine it in detail:

```java
void move() {
    // Move the body
    // Start at the back and move it
    // to the position of the segment in front of it
    for (int i = segmentLocations.size() - 1;
            i > 0; i--) {

        // Make it the same value as the next segment
        // going forwards towards the head
        segmentLocations.get(i).x =
                segmentLocations.get(i - 1).x;

        segmentLocations.get(i).y =
                segmentLocations.get(i - 1).y;
    }

    // Move the head in the appropriate heading
    // Get the existing head position
    Point p = segmentLocations.get(0);

    // Move it appropriately
    switch (heading) {
        case UP:
                p.y--;
                break;

        case RIGHT:
                p.x++;
                break;

        case DOWN:
                p.y++;
```

```
                    break;

            case LEFT:
                    p.x--;
                    break;
        }


        // Insert the adjusted point back into position 0
        segmentLocations.set(0, p);


    }
```

The first part of the move method is a `for` loop that loops through all the body parts in the `ArrayList`:

```
    for (int i = segmentLocations.size() - 1;
            i > 0; i--) {
```

The reason we move the body parts first is that we need to move the entire snake, starting at the back. This is why the second parameter of the `for` loop condition is `segmentLocations.size()` and the third `i--`. The way it works is that we start at the last body segment and put it into the location of the second to last. Next, we take the second to last and move it into the position of the third to last. This continues until we get to the leading body position and we move it into the position currently occupied by the head. This is the code in the `for` loop that achieves this:

```
    // Make it the same value as the next segment
    // going forwards towards the head
    segmentLocations.get(i).x =
    segmentLocations.get(i - 1).x;

    segmentLocations.get(i).y =
    segmentLocations.get(i - 1).y;
```

This diagram should help visualize the process:

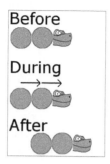

The technique works, regardless of the direction in which the snake is moving, but it doesn't explain how the head itself is moved. The head is moved outside the `for` loop.

Outside the `for` loop, we create a new `Point` called p and initialize it with `segmentLocations.get(0)`, which is the location of the head, prior to the move. We move the head by switching on the direction the snake is heading and moving the head accordingly.

If the snake is heading up, we move the vertical grid position up one place (`p.y--`), and if it is heading right, we move the horizontal coordinate right one place (`p.x++`). Examine the rest of the `switch` block to make sure you understand it.

[We could have avoided creating a new `Point` and used `segmentLocations.get(0)` in each case statement, but making a new `Point` made the code clearer.]

Remember that p is a reference to `segmentLocations.get(0)`, so we are done with moving the head.

Coding the detectDeath method

The `detectDeath` method checks to see whether the snake has just died, either by bumping into a wall or by attempting to eat itself:

```
boolean detectDeath() {
    // Has the snake died?
    boolean dead = false;

    // Hit any of the screen edges
```

```
if (segmentLocations.get(0).x == -1 ||
        segmentLocations.get(0).x > mMoveRange.x ||
        segmentLocations.get(0).y == -1 ||
        segmentLocations.get(0).y > mMoveRange.y) {

    dead = true;
}


// Eaten itself?
for (int i = segmentLocations.size() - 1; i > 0; i--) {
    // Have any of the sections collided with the head
    if (segmentLocations.get(0).x ==
            segmentLocations.get(i).x &&
            segmentLocations.get(0).y ==
            segmentLocations.get(i).y) {

        dead = true;

    }
}
return dead;
}
```

First, we declare a new `boolean` called `dead` and initialize it to `false`. Then we use a large `if` statement that checks whether any one of four possible conditions is `true` by separating each of the four conditions with the logical OR || operator. The four conditions represent disappearing off the screen to the left, right, top, and bottom (in that order).

Next, we loop through the `segmentLocations`, excluding the first position that has the position of the head. We check whether any of the positions are in the same position as the head. If any of them are, then the snake has just attempted to eat itself and is now dead.

The last line of code returns the value of `dead` to the `SnakeGame` class that will take the appropriate action depending upon whether the snake lives to face another `update` call or whether the game should be ended.

Coding the checkDinner method

The `checkDinner` method checks to see whether the snake head has collided with the apple. Look closely at the parameters, code the method, and then we will discuss it:

```
boolean checkDinner(Point l) {
    //if (snakeXs[0] == l.x && snakeYs[0] == l.y) {
    if (segmentLocations.get(0).x == l.x &&
```

```
            segmentLocations.get(0).y == l.y) {

        // Add a new Point to the list
        // located off-screen.
        // This is OK because on the next call to
        // move it will take the position of
        // the segment in front of it
        segmentLocations.add(new Point(-10, -10));
        return true;
    }
    return false;
}
```

The `checkDinner` method receives a `Point` as a parameter. All we need to do is check whether the `Point` parameter has the same coordinates as the snake head. If it does, then an apple has been eaten. We simply `return true` when an apple has been eaten and `false` when it has not. `SnakeGame` will handle what happens when an apple is eaten, and no action is required when an apple has not been eaten.

Coding the draw method

The `draw` method is reasonably long and complex. Nothing we can't handle, but it does demonstrate that if all this code were back in the `SnakeGame` class, then the `SnakeGame` class would not only get quite cluttered, but would also need access to quite a few of the member variables of this `Snake` class. Now imagine if you had multiple complex-to-draw objects and it is easy to imagine that `SnakeGame` would become something of a nightmare.

To begin the `draw` method, add a signature and `if` statement as shown in the following:

```
void draw(Canvas canvas, Paint paint) {
    // Don't run this code if ArrayList has nothing in it
    if (!segmentLocations.isEmpty()) {
        // All the code from this method goes here
    }
}
```

The `if` statement just makes sure the `ArrayList` isn't empty. All the rest of the code will go inside the `if` statement.

Add this code inside the `if` statement, inside the `draw` method:

```
// Draw the head
switch (heading) {
    case RIGHT:
            canvas.drawBitmap(mBitmapHeadRight,
                            segmentLocations.get(0).x
                        * mSegmentSize,
                            segmentLocations.get(0).y
                        * mSegmentSize, paint);

            break;

    case LEFT:
            canvas.drawBitmap(mBitmapHeadLeft,
                            segmentLocations.get(0).x
                        * mSegmentSize,
                            segmentLocations.get(0).y
                        * mSegmentSize, paint);

            break;

    case UP:
            canvas.drawBitmap(mBitmapHeadUp,
                            segmentLocations.get(0).x
                        * mSegmentSize,
                            segmentLocations.get(0).y
                        * mSegmentSize, paint);

            break;

    case DOWN:
            canvas.drawBitmap(mBitmapHeadDown,
                            segmentLocations.get(0).x
                        * mSegmentSize,
                            segmentLocations.get(0).y
                        * mSegmentSize, paint);

            break;
}
```

The `switch` block uses the `Heading` enumeration to check which way the snake is facing/heading, and the `case` statements handle the four possibilities by drawing the correct `Bitmap` based on which way the snake head needs to be drawn. Now we can draw the body segments.

Add this code in the `draw` method inside the `if` statement right after the code we just added:

```
// Draw the snake body one block at a time
for (int i = 1; i < segmentLocations.size(); i++) {
    canvas.drawBitmap(mBitmapBody,
                segmentLocations.get(i).x
                * mSegmentSize,
                segmentLocations.get(i).y
                * mSegmentSize, paint);
}
```

The `for` loop goes through all the segments in the `segmentLocations` array, excluding the head (because we have already drawn that). For each body part, it draws the `mBitmapBody` graphic at the location contained in the current `Point` object.

Coding the switchHeading method

The `switchHeading` method gets called from the `onTouchEvent` method and prompts the snake to change direction. Add the `switchHeading` method:

```
// Handle changing direction
void switchHeading(MotionEvent motionEvent) {

    // Is the tap on the right hand side?
    if (motionEvent.getX() >= halfWayPoint) {
        switch (heading) {
                // Rotate right
                case UP:
                        heading = Heading.RIGHT;
                        break;
                case RIGHT:
                        heading = Heading.DOWN;
                        break;
                case DOWN:
                        heading = Heading.LEFT;
                        break;
                case LEFT:
                        heading = Heading.UP;
                        break;

        }
    } else {
            // Rotate left
```

```
switch (heading) {
    case UP:
        heading = Heading.LEFT;
        break;
    case LEFT:
        heading = Heading.DOWN;
        break;
    case DOWN:
        heading = Heading.RIGHT;
        break;
    case RIGHT:
        heading = Heading.UP;
        break;
    }
  }
}
```

The `switchHeading` method receives a single parameter that is a `MotionEvent` instance. The method detects whether the touch occurred on the left or right of the screen by comparing the x coordinate of the touch (obtained by `motionEvent.getX()`) to our member variable, `halfwayPoint`.

Depending upon the side of the screen that was touched, one of two `switch` blocks is entered. The `case` statements in each of the switch blocks handle each of the four possible current headings. The `case` statements then change `heading`, either clockwise or counterclockwise by 90 degrees, to the next appropriate value for `heading`.

The `Snake` class is done, and we can, at last, bring it to life.

Using the snake class and finishing the game

We have already declared an instance of `Snake`, so initialize the snake immediately after initializing the apple in the `SnakeGame` constructor, as demonstrated by the following highlighted code. Look at the variables we pass into the constructor so that the constructor can set the snake up ready to slither:

```
// Call the constructors of our two game objects
mApple = new Apple(context,
        new Point(NUM_BLOCKS_WIDE,
        mNumBlocksHigh),
        blockSize);

mSnake = new Snake(context,
```

```
                    new Point(NUM_BLOCKS_WIDE,
                    mNumBlocksHigh),
                    blockSize);
```

Reset the snake in the `newGame` method by adding the highlighted code that calls the `Snake` class's `reset` method every time a new game is started:

```
// Called to start a new game
public void newGame() {

    // reset the snake
    mSnake.reset(NUM_BLOCKS_WIDE, mNumBlocksHigh);

    // Get the apple ready for dinner
    mApple.spawn();

    // Reset the mScore
    mScore = 0;

    // Setup mNextFrameTime so an update can trigger
    mNextFrameTime = System.currentTimeMillis();
}
```

Code the `update` method to first move the snake to its next position and then check for death each time the `update` method is executed. In addition, call the `checkDinner` method, passing in the position of the apple:

```
// Update all the game objects
public void update() {

    // Move the snake
    mSnake.move();

    // Did the head of the snake eat the apple?
    if(mSnake.checkDinner(mApple.getLocation())){
            // This reminds me of Edge of Tomorrow.
            // One day the apple will be ready!
            mApple.spawn();

            // Add to  mScore
            mScore = mScore + 1;

            // Play a sound
```

```
            mSP.play(mEat_ID, 1, 1, 0, 0, 1);
}


// Did the snake die?
if (mSnake.detectDeath()) {
        // Pause the game ready to start again
        mSP.play(mCrashID, 1, 1, 0, 0, 1);

        mPaused =true;
}

}
```

If `checkDinner` returns `true`, then we spawn another apple, add one to the score, and play the eating sound. If the `detectDeath` method returns `true`, then the code plays the crash sound and pauses the game (which the player can start again by tapping the screen).

We can draw the snake simply by calling its `draw` method, which handles everything itself. Add the highlighted code to the `SnakeGame` draw method:

```
// Draw the apple and the snake
mApple.draw(mCanvas, mPaint);
mSnake.draw(mCanvas, mPaint);

// Draw some text while paused
if(mPaused){
```

Add this single line of highlighted code to the `onTouchEvent` method to have the `Snake` class respond to screen taps:

```
@Override
public boolean onTouchEvent(MotionEvent motionEvent) {
    switch (motionEvent.getAction() & MotionEvent.ACTION_MASK) {

        case MotionEvent.ACTION_UP:
            if (mPaused) {
                    mPaused = false;
                    newGame();

                    // Don't want to process snake
                    // direction for this tap
                    return true;
            }

            // Let the Snake class handle the input
```

```
            mSnake.switchHeading(motionEvent);
            break;

        default:

            break;

    }
    return true;
}
```

That's it. The snake can now update itself, check for dinner and death, draw itself, and respond to the player's touches.

Running the completed game

Run the game. Tap the left-hand side to face 90 degrees left and the right-hand side to face 90 degrees right. See if you can beat my high score shown in the following screenshot:

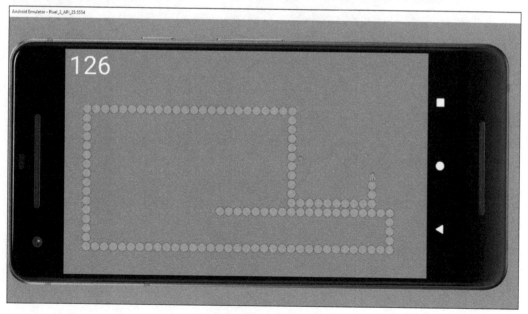

Still hungry- must eat!

And when you die, the game pauses to view the final catastrophe and a message about how to start again. This is shown in the following screenshot:

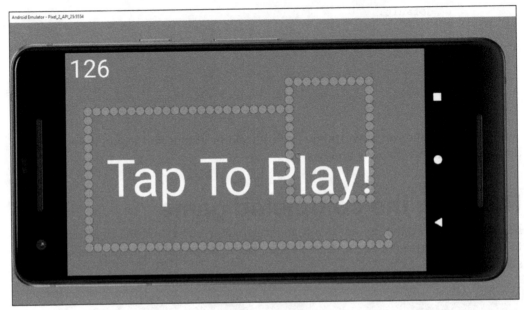

That didn't taste so good!

You have successfully completed the final project.

Summary

In this chapter, we got the chance to use much of what we have learned throughout the book as well as something new, enum.

Possibly the most important lesson from this chapter is how we saw that encapsulating and abstracting parts of our code to specific relevant classes helps to keep our code manageable.

Why not look at the final chapter to see what you might want to do next?

A Quick Chat Before You Go

30

We are just about done with our journey. This chapter is just a few ideas and pointers that you might like to look at before rushing off and making your own apps:

- Publishing
- Making your first app
- Carrying on learning
- Thanks

Publishing

You easily know enough to design your own app. You could even just make some modifications to one of the apps from the book.

I decided not to do a step-by-step guide to publishing on Google's Play store because the steps are not complicated. They are, however, quite in-depth and a little laborious. Most of the steps involve entering personal information and images about you and your app. Such a tutorial would read something like the following:

1. Fill this text box
2. Now fill that text box
3. Upload this image
4. And so on

Not much fun or use.

To get started, you just need to visit `https://play.google.com/apps/publish` and pay a modest fee (around $25) depending on your region's currency. This allows you to publish games for life.

> If you want a checklist for publishing, take a look at the following URL: `https://developer.android.com/distribute/best-practices/launch/launch-checklist.html`, but you will find the process intuitive (if very drawn out).

Making an app!

You could ignore everything else in this chapter if you just put this one thing into practice.

> Don't wait until you are an expert before you start making apps!

Start building your dream app, the one with all the features that's going to take Google Play by storm. A simple piece of advice, however, is this: do some planning first! Not too much, and then get started.

Have some smaller and more easily achievable projects on the sidelines; projects you will be able to show to friends and family and that explore areas of Android that are new to you. If you are confident about these apps, you could upload them to Google Play. If you are worried about how they might be received by reviewers, then make them free and put a note in the description about it being "just a prototype", or something similar.

If your experience is anything like mine, you will find that as you read, study, and build apps, you will discover that your dream app can be improved in many ways and you will probably be inspired to redesign it or even start again.

When you do this, I can guarantee that the next time you build it, you will do it in half the time and twice as good, at least!

Carrying on learning

If you feel like you have come a long way, you are right. There is always more to learn, however.

Carrying on reading

You will find that as you make your first app, you suddenly realize that there is a gap in your knowledge that needs to be filled to make some feature come to life. This is normal and guaranteed; don't let it put you off. Think of how to describe the problem and search for the solution on Google.

You might also find that specific classes in a project will grow beyond the practical and maintainable. This is a sign that there is a better way to structure things and there is probably a ready-made design pattern out there somewhere that will make your life easier.

To pre-empt this almost inevitability, why not study some patterns right away. One great source is *Head First: Java Design Patterns*, available from all good book stores.

GitHub

GitHub allows you to search and browse code that other people have written and see how they have solved problems. This is useful, because by seeing the file structure of classes, and then dipping into them, often shows how to plan your apps from the start and prevent you from starting off on the wrong path. You can even get a GitHub app that allows you to do this from the comfort of your phone or tablet. You can even configure Android Studio to save and share your projects to GitHub.

For example, search for `android fragment` on the homepage, www.github.com, and you will see more than 1,000 related projects that you can snoop through, as demonstrated in the following screenshot:

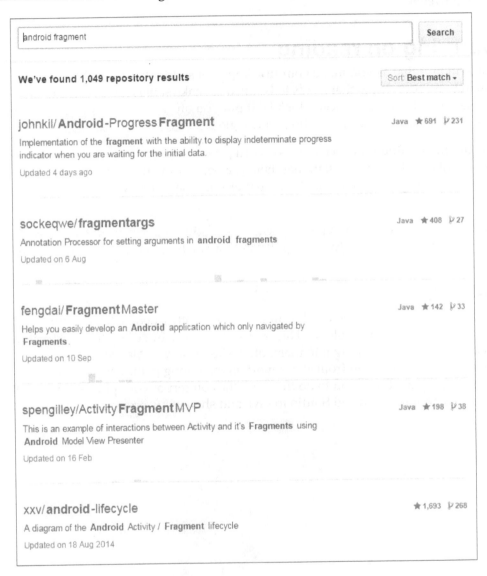

StackOverflow

If you get stuck, have a weird error, or an unexplained crash, often the best place to turn is Google. Do this and you will be surprised how often StackOverflow seems to be prominent in the search results, and for good reason.

StackOverflow allows users to post a description of their problem, along with sample code, so the community can respond with answers. In my experience, however, it is rarely necessary to post a question because there is almost always somebody who has had the exact same problem.

StackOverflow is especially good for bleeding-edge issues. If a new Android Studio version has a bug, or a new version of the Android API seems to not be doing what it should, then you can be almost certain that a few thousand other developers around the world are having the same problem as you. Then, some smart coder, often from the Android development team itself, will be there with an answer.

StackOverflow is also good for a bit of light reading. Go to the `www.stackoverflow.com` home page, type `Android` in the search box, and you will see a list of all the latest problems that the StackOverflow community are having:

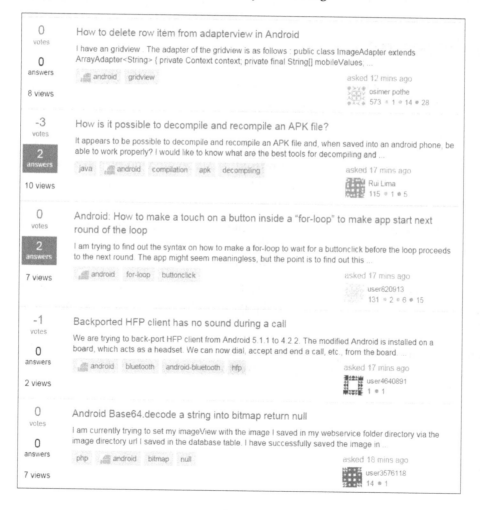

I am not suggesting that you dive in and start trying to answer them all just yet, but reading the problems and the suggestions will teach you a lot and you will probably find that more often than not, you have the solution, or at least an idea of the solution.

Android user forums

Also, it is well worth signing up to some Android forums and visiting occasionally to find out what the hot topics and trends are from a user's perspective. I don't list any here because a quick web search is all that is required.

If you're serious, then you can attend some Android conferences where you can rub shoulders with thousands of other developers and attend lectures. If this interests you, do a web search for Droidcon, Android Developer Days, or GDG DevFest.

Higher-level study

You can now read a wider selection of other Android books. I mentioned at the start of this book that there were very few, arguably no, books that taught Android programming to readers with no Java experience. That was the reason I wrote this book.

Now you have a good understanding of OOP and Java, as well as a brief introduction to app design and the Android API, you are well placed to read the Android "beginner" books for people who already know how to program in Java, just like you do now.

These books are packed full of good examples that you can build or just read about to reinforce what you have learned in this book, use your knowledge in different ways, and, of course, learn some completely new stuff too.

It might also be worth reading some pure Java books. It might be hard to believe, having just waded through around 750 pages, but there is a whole lot more to Java than there was time to cover here.

I could name a number of titles, but the books with the largest number of positive reviews on Amazon tend to be the ones worth exploring.

My other channels

Please keep in touch:

- www.gamecodeschool.com
- www.facebook.com/gamecodeschool
- www.twitter.com/gamecodeschool
- www.youtube.com/channel/UCY6pRQAXnwviO3dpmV258Ig/videos
- www.plus.google.com/114785498572480147747/posts
- www.linkedin.com/in/gamecodeschool

Goodbye and thank you

I had a lot of fun writing this book. I know that's a cliché, but it's also true. Most importantly though, I hope you managed to take something from it and use it as a stepping stone for your future in programming.

You are perhaps reading this for a bit of fun or the kudos of releasing an app, a stepping stone to a programming job, or maybe you actually do build that app to take Google Play by storm.

Whatever the case, a big thank you from me for buying this book and I wish you all the best in your future endeavors.

I think that everybody has an app inside of them and all you need do is work hard enough to get it out of you.

Other Books You May Enjoy

If you enjoyed this book, you may be interested in these other books by Packt:

Learning Java by Building Android Games - Second Edition

John Horton

ISBN: 978-1-78883-915-0

- Set up a game development environment in Android Studio
- Implement screen locking, screen rotation, pixel graphics, and play sound effects
- Respond to a player's touch, and program intelligent enemies who challenge the player in different ways
- Learn game development concepts, such as collision detection, animating sprite sheets, simple tracking and following, AI, parallax backgrounds, and particle explosions
- Animate objects at 60 frames per second (FPS) and manage multiple independent objects using Object-Oriented Programming (OOP)

Beginning C++ Game Programming

John Horton

ISBN: 978-1-78646-619-8

- Get to know C++ from scratch while simultaneously learning game building
- Learn the basics of C++, such as variables, loops, and functions to animate game objects, respond to collisions, keep score, play sound effects, and build your first playable game.
- Use more advanced C++ topics such as classes, inheritance, and references to spawn and control thousands of enemies, shoot with a rapid fire machine gun, and realize random scrolling game-worlds
- Stretch your C++ knowledge beyond the beginner level and use concepts such as pointers, references, and the Standard Template Library to add features like split-screen coop, immersive directional sound, and custom levels loaded from level-design files
- Get ready to go and build your own unique games!

Leave a review - let other readers know what you think

Please share your thoughts on this book with others by leaving a review on the site that you bought it from. If you purchased the book from Amazon, please leave us an honest review on this book's Amazon page. This is vital so that other potential readers can see and use your unbiased opinion to make purchasing decisions, we can understand what our customers think about our products, and our authors can see your feedback on the title that they have worked with Packt to create. It will only take a few minutes of your time, but is valuable to other potential customers, our authors, and Packt. Thank you!

Leave a review - let other readers know what you think

Index

A

access modifiers
  about 259
  method access modifiers 261, 262
  method access summary 263
  methods 261
accessors 266
Activity class 485
adapter 398
addition operator 193
advanced persistence
  about 433
  Java exceptions 434, 435
  JavaScript Object Notation (JSON) 434
Andriod Studio
  about 9
  setting up 10-16
  step 16, 17
Android
  about 2, 3, 8
  apps interaction 164, 165
  learning 3
  naming conventions and code style,
    reference 347
  version 557, 558
  version, detecting 558
  working 4
Android API 5
Android app
  about 17, 20-27, 164
  deploying 28, 29
  deploying, on Andriod emulator 30, 32
  executing, on Andriod emulator 30, 32
  executing, on real device 33
  step 27, 28

Android application PacKage (APK) 8
Android coordinate system
  about 493
  drawing 493, 494
  plotting 493, 494
Android design guidelines 579, 580
Android emulator
  active apps, viewing 98
  app drawer, accessing 97
  emulator control panel 94, 96
  exploring 93
  switching, between apps 98
  using, as real device 96
Android Intents
  about 419, 420
  activity, switching 420
  data, passing between activities 421, 422
Android lifecycle
  about 165
  demo app 170
  phases 166, 167
  phases, handling 167-170
Android project
  anatomy 70
Android resources 17
Android's Java code
  classes 19
  methods 19, 20
  package 18
  structure 18
Android specific UI guideline
  reference 150
Android SQLite API
  about 651
  database cursors 654, 655
  queries, building 652, 653, 654

queries, executing 652, 653, 654
SQLiteDatabase 652
SQLiteOpenHelper 652
Android Studio
overview 68, 69
Android Studio theme designer
using 156-159
Android time zone
reference 333
Android UI design
exploring 102, 103
Android UI elements
about 290
Anonymous class 303
Buttons, using 293-303
Inner class 303
references 290
TextView widgets, using 293-303
animation demo app 460
laying out 461-466
wiring up, in Java 470-480
XML animations, coding 466-470
animations
designing, in XML 456
duration, controlling 457
fading in 456
fading out 456
features 459
in Android 455
instantiating, with Java code 458, 459
interpolators 460
listeners 459
moving 456
properties, combining with Set 458
repeating 457, 458
rotate animations 457
scaling 457
stretching 457
anonymous class 303, 311-315
Apple class
coding 683, 684
game, executing 688
using 686, 687
Apple constructor 684, 686
application
Android user forums 714
creating 710

GitHub 711
higher-level study 714
learning 711
reading 711
StackOverflow 712, 714
application logic 578
Application Programming
        Interface (API) 1, 4
ARGB (Alpha, Red, Green and Blue) 330
ArrayList
about 389, 390
adding, to Note to Self project 401
for loop 391
polymorphic 391, 392
arrays
about 190, 379
example 381-383
multi-dimensional, example 385-388
nth dimension, entering 385
object 380, 381
out of bounds exception 389
polymorphic 392
assignment operator 193
attributes 135
auto-generated assets
exploring 633-636
auto-generated code
exploring 633-636

B

Basic Activity project
about 87, 88
activity_main.xml file 90, 91
content_main.xml file 93
exploring 89
MainActivity.java, extra methods 92, 93
MainActivity.java file 89
Bitmap
about 496
creating 494, 495
manipulating 495
Matrix class 496
Bitmap class
about 484, 485
drawing, with code 484

Bitmap manipulation demo app
  about 499
  graphic, adding 499-503
break keyword 215
buttons
  adding, by editing XML code 52, 53, 54
  adding, to layout file 46
  adding, via visual designer 46, 47
  attributes, editing 48-51
  call different methods, creating 57, 58
  positioning, in layout 55-57
  unique id attributes, assigning 54, 55
  using 293-303
  XML code, examining 51, 52

C

calling method 41
camel casing 186
Canvas class
  about 483-485
  Activity content, setting 487
  drawing, with code 484
  instances of classes, preparing 486
  objects, initializing 487
  using 486
Canvas demo app
  about 488
  coding 488, 489
  project, creating 488
Canvas Demo app
  Bitmap initialization, exploring 490
  Color.argb, explaining 491-493
  drawing, on screen 490, 491
CardView
  used, for building UI 143, 144
chaining 270
CheckBox widget 316, 317
class
  about 6, 244
  code 245
  implementing 245
  object, declaring 246-249
  object, initializing 246-249
  object, using 246-249
  using, as parameter in method
    signature 253, 254

class access modifiers
  about 259
  default 259
  public 259
class declaration 41
classes 19, 190
classes app 249-253
class use
  class access, in summary 259
  class access modifiers 259
  controlling, with access modifiers 259
code comments 183-185
Color class
  reference 331
color wheel
  reference 84
comparison operator 203
compiling 4
concatenation 199
configuration qualifiers
  about 590-592
  limitation 592
console 36
constant 270
ConstraintLayout
  layouts, converting 338
  view, resizing 121, 122
constructor 246, 267
continue keyword 216
control flow statements 213
controller 578
correctness 524
custom buttons
  adding, to screen 537, 538

D

Dalvik Executable (DEX) 4
Dalvik Virtual Machine (DVM) 4
data
  about 20
  Component Tree, used 131, 132
  handling, with arrays 378-380
  laying out, with TableLayout 130
  main menu, linking 133, 134
  persisting, with SharedPreferences 427, 428
  reloading, with SharedPreferences 428

storing, with variables 185, 186
table columns, organizing 132, 133
TableRow, adding to TableLayout 130
using, with variables 185, 186
database 648
Database 101 648
database class
coding 655-659
data types
reference 189
deadlock 524
decrement operator 195
demo app, Android lifecycle
coding 170-173
executing 173, 174
output, examining 174, 175
density-independent pixels (dp)
used, for sizing 136
de-serialization 434
development environment 9
device detection mini-app
about 582-585
executing 588-590
MainActivity class, coding 586, 587
dialog boxes, Note to self app
coding 361
DialogNewNote class, coding 361-365
DialogShowNote class, coding 365-368
DialogFragment class
chaining process, used for configuration
342, 343
coding 340-342
using 344-346
DialogFragment configuration
chaining, using 342, 343
dialog window
about 339, 340
Demo project, creating 340
DialogFragment class, coding 340
DialogFragment class, using 344-346
dots-per-inch (dpi) 82
do while loop 216
draw method
coding 517, 518
printDebuggingText method,
adding 518, 519
drivers 8

dynamic arrays
about 383
example 383, 384

E

EditText widget 308
Empty Activity project
about 70-73
exploring 73, 74
java folder 77, 78
manifests folder 74-77
res/drawable folder 80
res folder 79
res/layout folder 80
res/mipmap 81, 82
res/values 83
encapsulation
about 257, 258
class use, controlling with access
modifiers 259
mini-app 271-275
variable use, controlling with access
modifiers 260
enumeration 690, 691
exceptions 434
Exploring Layouts project
creating 103, 104
expressions
about 195
demo app 196-199
Extensible Markup Language (XML) 18

F

for loop 217
fragment app 595-601
Fragment classes
Age Database app, executing 663, 664
coding 636-640
coding, DataManager used 660, 662
empty files, creating for classes 636
using 643
Fragment id 615
Fragment layouts
coding 636
empty files, creating for layouts 637
holder, adding to layout 644

MainActivity.java, coding 644, 645
Navigation Drawer menu, editing 643
using 643
Fragment Pager /slider app
activity_main layout 620
building 615
fragment_layout 618
fragment slider app, executing 621
MainActivity class, coding 618-620
SimpleFragment class, coding 615-617
fragment reality check 602
fragments
about 592, 593
lifecycle 593
managing, with FragmentManager 594
fragments, lifecycle
onAttach method 593
onCreate method 593
onCreateView method 593
onDetach method 593
onStart method 593

G

game engine
coding 672
constructor, coding 674, 676
draw method, coding 679, 680
members, coding 672-674
newGame method, coding 676, 677
onTouchEvent, coding 681
pause and resume, coding 681, 682
run method, coding 677
update method, coding 679
updateRequired method, coding 678
game loop
about 513, 521-523
Activity lifecycle, used for
      initiating thread 530
Activity lifecycle, used for
      stoping thread 530
implementing, with thread 527
run method, coding 531, 532, 533
run method, implementing 528
Runnable, implementing 528
thread, coding 528
thread, starting 529, 530

thread, stoping 529, 530
garbage collector 291
getters 263
graphical mask 80
graphics
adding 683
Gravity
using 141, 142
greater than operator 204
greater than or equal to operator 205

H

Heap
about 290-292
advantage 292
HelloWorldActivity.java file
class 41
classes, importing 40
code folding, in Andriod Studio 40
examining 38, 39
Java code, summary 42
method, inside class 41, 42
package declaration 40

I

if keyword
else keyword 207-210
using 206, 207
image gallery/slider app
building 606, 607
executing 613, 614
layout, implementing 607, 608
MainActivity class, coding 611-613
PagerAdapter class, coding 608-611
ImageView class
about 485
drawing, with code 484
ImageView widget 309
increment operator 194
infinite loop 215
inheritance
about 275, 277
example 278-282
Inner class 303
instances 6, 76

integrated development
  environment (IDE) 9
interface 5
interpolators
  about 459, 460
  reference 460

J

Java
  about 2, 3
  code comments 183-185
  code, indenting 202, 203
  decisions, creating 202
  fundamentals 181, 182
  if keyword, using 206, 207
  jargon 182, 183
  learning 3
  object oriented 6, 7
  operators 203
  operators, used for testing variables 206
  switch cases 210
  Switch demo app 211, 212
  syntax 182, 183
  UI widgets, creating without XML 307, 308
  working 4
Java code
  comments 58
  message code, adding to
    onCreate method 60, 61
  output, examining 61, 62
  structure 177, 178
  used, for setting view 145
  used, for wiring up UI 112-114
  writing 59, 60
Java Collections 393, 394
Java Development Kit (JDK) 1, 9
Java methods
  about 224
  output, examining 64, 65
  writing 62-64
Java project
  exploring 38
JavaScript Object Notation (JSON) 419

K

key-value pairs 421
keywords 183

L

layers 578
layout files
  including, in another layout 152-55
layouts
  about 103
  content_delete.xml, designing 641
  content_insert.xml, designing 640
  content_results.xml, designing 642, 643
  content_search.xml, designing 642
  converting, to ConstraintLayout 338
  creating 118, 119
  designing 640
layout_weight property
  using 140, 141
less than operator 204
less than or equal to operator 205
LinearLayout
  adding 105, 106
  generated XML, examining 107, 108
  multi-line TextView, adding to UI 111, 112
  TextView, adding to UI 108-110
  used, for building menu 105
  workspace, preparing 106, 107
LiveDrawingActivity class
  coding 506-509
live drawing app
  executing 534, 552, 554
  LiveDrawingActivity 506
  LiveDrawingView 506
  Particle 506
  ParticleSystem 506
  viewing 506
Live Drawing project
  creating 505
LiveDrawingView 510
LiveDrawingView class
  coding 509-513
  draw method 519, 520

draw method, coding 517, 518
member variables, adding 513-515
SurfaceView class 519, 520
LiveDrawingView constructor
coding 516, 517
locking 524
logcat 36
logcat output
filtering 36-38
logical AND operator 205
logical NOT operator 204
logical OR operator 205
log output
examining 35, 36
loops
demo app 218-222
do while loop 216
for loop 217
while loop 213, 214

M

MainActivity class
coding 586, 587
screen orientation, unlocking 587
margin
using 139, 140
match
used, for determining size 137, 138
material design
about 101, 102, 155
guidelines, reference 155
reference 150
Matrix class
about 496
Bitmap, inverting to opposite
direction 497, 498
bitmap, rotating 498
Memo app
building 2
memory management
warning 241
messages
coding, to developer 59
coding, to user 59
method overloading
about 233-236

exploring 233-236
methods
about 19, 20
exploring, with demo apps 231
method structure
about 224, 225, 226
body 230
modifier 226
name of method 229
parameters 229, 230
return type 227, 228
model 578
model-view-controller pattern 578
multi-line comment 184
multiplication operator 194
mutators 266

N

name method 41
naming convention 186
NavigationView 624, 625
nesting 115-118
NOT equal operator 204
Note to self app
about 346, 395
code files, obtaining 347, 348
completed app 348-352
creating, for english speakers 445
creating, for gerrman speakers 445
creating, for spanish speakers 445
dialog boxes, coding 361
Dialog designs, implementing 356-361
executing 414-417
executing, in german language 450, 452
executing, in spanish language 450, 452
floating action button, coding 372-375
german language, adding 446, 447
MainActivity class, coding 431-433
naming conventions, using 346, 347
new dialogs, displaying 369-371
Note class, coding 353-355
project, building 352
settings page, adding 422
settings persist, creating 429
Settings screen layout, designing 423, 424
SettingsActivity class, coding 429-431

SettingsActivity, creating 422
spanish language, adding 446
string resources, adding 447-449
String resources, preparing 352, 353
String resources, using 346, 347
translations work, creating in
    Java code 452, 453
user data, backing up 435-442
user enabled, to switch settings
    screen 425, 426

O

object-oriented language 6
object-oriented programming (OOP)
    about 5, 7, 242, 275, 277
    encapsulation 242, 243
    inheritance 243, 244
    polymorphism 243
    using 244
objects
    about 6
    declaring 306, 307
    initializing 306, 307
    setting up, with constructors 266, 267
OnTouchEvent method
    coding 551, 552
    handling 549, 550
    HUD, finishing 552
operators
    addition operator 193
    assignment operator 193
    decrement operator 195
    division operator 194
    increment operator 194
    multiplication operator 194
    reference 195
    subtraction operator 193
    variable values, modifying with 192
operators, Java
    about 203
    comparison operator 203
    greater than operator 204
    greater than or equal to operator 205
    less than operator 204
    less than or equal to operator 205

logical AND operator 205
logical NOT operator 204
logical OR operator 205
NOT equal operator 204
overridden methods 176, 177

P

package 18
package declaration 40
padding
    using 139, 140
paging 605
Paint class 484, 485
particle system effect
    implementing 538, 539
    Particle class, coding 540, 541
    ParticleSystem class, coding 542-547
    particle systems, spawning in
        LiveDrawingView class 547, 548
polymorphism
    about 282, 283
    abstract classes 283, 284
    interfaces 285, 286
precise UI
    building, with ConstraintLayout 120
    CalenderView, adding 120
    Component Tree window, using 122, 123
    constraints manually, adding 124, 125
    text clickable, creating 129
    UI elements, adding 126, 128
    UI elements, constraining 126-128
primitive types
    about 187
    boolean type 188
    char type 188
    double type 188
    float type 188
    int type 188
    long type 188
private variables
    accessing, with getters 263-266
    accessing, with setters 263-266
project explorer 70
publishing
    guidelines 709

Q

qualifiers 82

R

radio button 310, 311
radio group 310, 311
random diversion 378
real world apps 580-582
real world methods
  about 231, 232
  variable scope, discovering 233
RecyclerAdapter
  about 397, 398
  adding, to Note to Self project 401
  class, coding 404-407
  getItemCount, coding 409
  ListItemHolder inner class, coding 410
  NoteAdapter constructor, coding 407
  onBindViewHolder method,
    coding 408, 409
  onCreateViewHolder method, coding 408
  using 398, 400
  widgets display, problem 398
  widgets display, solution 398
RecyclerAdapter classes
  used, for coding MainActivity 411
RecyclerView
  about 397, 398
  adding, to Note to Self project 401
  list item, creating 402, 403, 404
  setting up, with ArrayList of notes 400, 401
  setting up, with RecyclerAdapter 400, 401
  Show Note button, removing 401, 402
  using 398, 399, 400
  widgets display, problem 398
  widgets display, solution 398
RecyclerView classes
  addNote method, modifying 413
  code, adding to onCreate 411, 412
  showNote method, coding 413
  used, for coding MainActivity 411
reference types
  about 189
  arrays 190
  classes 190
  strings 189, 190

res/values, Empty Activity project
  about 83
  colors.xml file 83
  strings.xml file 84, 85
  styles.xml file 85, 86, 87
RGB color system
  reference 331

S

scalable pixels (sp)
  used, for sizing fonts 137
scopes 236, 237
ScrollView
  used, for building UI 143, 144
serialization 434
setters 263
signature method 41, 224
Simple Database app
  delete 628
  examining 625, 626
  insert 627
  results 630
  search 629
Simple Database project
  initiating 631, 632
snake class
  checkDinner method, coding 700, 701
  coding 692, 693
  constructor, coding 694, 695
  detectDeath method, coding 699, 700
  draw method, coding 701, 702, 703
  move method, coding 697, 698, 699
  reset method, coding 696
  switchHeading method, coding 703, 704
  using 704-707
snake game
  app full screen, creating 670
  app landscape, creating 670
  controlling 668, 669
  empty classes, adding 670
  executing 682, 683, 707, 708
  initiating 669
  SnakeActivity, coding 670, 672
  sound, adding 692
  sound effects, adding 672
Software Development Kit (SDK) 9

SoundPool class
about 558
initializing 559, 560
sound files, loading into memory 561
sound, playing 562
sound, stopping 563
Spinner 557
Spinner widget
about 563
sound demo, coding 569-574
sound demo, laying out 566-569
sound FX, creating 563-566
SQLite 648
SQLite example code
about 649
database structure, updating 651
data, inserting into database 650
data, retrieving from database 651
table, creating 650
SQL syntax primer 649
Stack 290-292
StackOverflow
URL 713
static methods
about 268-270
mini-app 271-275
string identifier 449
string resources 445
strings 189, 190
Structured Query Language (SQL) 648
sub class 278
sub-packages 18
subtraction operator 193, 194
super class 277
surface 484
SurfaceView 510
swipe menu 606
Switch widget 315, 316

T

table 648
tablet emulator
creating 159, 160, 162
TextClock widget 317
TextView widget
using 293-303

themes
design 155
threads
about 513, 523, 524
problems 524-527

U

UI, building
card content, creating 146, 148, 149, 150
CardViews, adding to layout 151, 152
dimensions, defining for CardViews 150
image resources, adding 145
view, setting with Java code 145
UI widgets
CheckBox widget 316, 317
creating, from Java without XML 307, 308
EditText widget 308
ImageView widget 309
radio button 310, 311
radio group 310, 311
Switch widget 315, 316
TextClock widget 317
User Interface (UI)
about 17, 18, 35
building, with CardView 143, 144
building, with ScrollView 143, 144
wiring up, with Java code 120

V

variable access modifiers
about 260
default 261
private 261
protected 260
public 260
variables
about 185, 236, 237
data, storing 185, 186
data, using 185, 186
declaration 191
default values 192
initialization 191, 192
primitive types 187, 188, 189
reference types 189
types 186, 187
using 190

values, modifying with operators 192
variable use
   controlling, with access modifiers 260
   variable access modifiers 260
   variable access summary 261
view 116, 578
view group 116

W

while loops
   about 213, 214
   break keyword 215
   continue keyword 216
widget exploration app
   anonymous class, using for Button 334
   CheckBoxes, coding 329
   coding 327, 328
   color, modifying 330, 331
   creating 317

executing 336, 337
   project, setting up 318-327
   RadioButtons, coding 332, 334
   reference, obtaining 328, 329
   size, modifying 331
   Switch, coding 335
   transparency, modifying 330
   UI, preparing 318-327
wrap
   used, for determining size 137, 138

X

XML layout
   buttons, adding 46
   examining 42, 44
   UI layout elements 44, 45
   UI text elements 45
XML layout code
   exploring 38

CPSIA information can be obtained
at www.ICGtesting.com
Printed in the USA
FFHW011430190819
54345642-60030FF

9 781789 538502